PRACTICAL INFORMATION

The French Government Touris (01) 491 76 22 and 610 Fifth Ave information and literature.

How to get there. – You car commercial and package tour flight by cross Channel ferry or Hovercra agent and remember, if you are go Whitsun, to book well in advance.

GW00708169

Papers and other documents. – A vali... British a Visitor's Passport) is all that is required; for the car you need a valid **driving licence**, **international driving permit, car registration book** and a **nationality plate** of the approved size. Insurance cover is compulsory and although the Green Card (an International Insurance Certificate) is no longer a legal requirement for France it is the most effective proof of insurance cover and is internationally recognised by the police and other authorities.

Caravan owners must, in addition, produce the caravan **logbook** and an inventory for customs clearance; Green Card endorsement for caravan and trailer. A **carnet** is required to import temporarily certain vehicles: pleasure craft over 5.5 m long and motor boats.

Motoring regulations. – Certain motoring organisations run accident insurance and breakdown service schemes for their members. Enquire before leaving. A **red warning triangle** or hazard warning lights are obligatory in case of a breakdown.

In France it is compulsory for the front passengers to wear **seat belts** if the car is equipped with them. Children under ten should be on the back seat.

The **speed limits**, although liable to modification, are motorways 130 kph - 80 mph; national trunk roads 110 kph - 68 mph; other roads 90 kph - 56 mph and in towns 60 kph - 37 mph. The regulations on speeding and drinking and driving are strictly interpreted – usually by an on the spot fine and/or confiscation of the vehicle. Remember to cede priority to vehicles joining from the right and there are tolls on the motorways.

Medical treatment. – For EEC countries it is necessary to have Form E 111 which testifies to your entitlement to medical benefits from the Department of Health and Social Security. With this you can obtain medical treatment in an emergency and, after the necessary steps, a refund of part of the costs of treatment from the local Social Security offices *(Caisse Primaire de Sécurité Sociale)*. It is, however, still advisable to take out comprehensive insurance cover.

Currency. – Regulations are liable to alteration: find out the latest allowances permitted when obtaining travellers' cheques and the permitted amount of foreign currency at one of the international travel agencies or banks before leaving. Your passport is necessary as identification when cashing cheques in banks. Commission charges vary with hotels charging more highly than banks especially when obliging on holidays or at weekends.

Duly arrived:

Consulates: British, 6 Rue La Fayette, Nantes. Tel 48 57 47.

Tourist Information Centres or *Syndicats d'Initiative* 🖪 are to be found in most large towns and many tourist resorts. They can supply large scale town plans, timetables and information on local entertainment facilities, sports and sightseeing.

Poste Restante. – Name, *Poste restante*, Poste Centrale, Department's postal number followed by the town's name, France. The Michelin Guide gives local postal code numbers.

Electric current. – Mostly 220-230 volts, in some places, however, it is still 110 volts. European circular two pin plugs are the rule – remember to take an adaptor.

Where to stay. – In the Michelin Guide France you will find a selection of hotels at various prices in all areas. It also lists local restaurants, again with prices.

Public holidays. – National museums and art galleries are closed on Tuesdays. The following are days when museums and other monuments may be closed or may vary their hours of admission:

New Year's Day	France's National Day **(14 July)**
Easter Sunday and Monday	Assumption **(15 August)**
May Day **(1 May)**	All Saints' Day **(1 November)**
Ascension Day	Remembrance Day **(11 November)**
Whit Sunday and Monday	Christmas Day.

In addition to the usual school holidays at Christmas, Easter and Summer there are week long breaks in February and early November.

Opening times and admission prices. – The **visiting times** indicate the hours of opening and closing and it is important to remember that many châteaux, museums, etc, refuse admittance from up to an hour before the actual closing time.

When **guided tours** are indicated, the departure time for the last tour of the morning or afternoon will once again be prior to the given closing time. Most tours are conducted by French speaking guides but in some cases the term guided tour may cover group visiting with recorded commentaries. Some of the larger and more frequented châteaux offer guided tours in other languages. Enquire at the ticket or book stalls. Other aids for the foreign tourist are notes, pamphlets or audio guides.

The **admission prices** indicated are for adults, however reductions for children, students and parties are common. In some cases admission is free on certain days, eg Wednesdays, Sundays or public holidays.

SEASONS

The Loire Valley and its splendid series of châteaux can be admired at any time of the year. However the tourist who wishes to enjoy the scenery as well as the architecture will try to avoid the crowds and extreme heat of July and August. In May and June the region is particularly attractive with the fresh greenery of the countryside and a profusion of wild flowers. September is also a good month with relatively fine weather.

The climate of the Loire Basin benefits from the proximity of the sea and the Atlantic winds penetrate freely, clearing the air in winter and providing a refreshing breeze in summer. In former times these winds, which blow with trade wind regularity, filled the sails of the boats plying the Loire and turned the sails of the numerous windmills perched on the hilltops. This mild climate has made the valley what it is – a region of vineyards, arable farms, nurseries and horticultural gardening.

Upstream from Orléans the maritime influences are greatly diminished and a semi continental climate is the rule with very harsh winters and heavy summers on the plateaux.

The Orléanais and Beauce are troubled by severely cold winds while the Blésois suffers occasional frosts – and even the Loire is sometimes full of drift ice.

In Touraine and Anjou the maritime climate is marked by hot summers tempered by sea breezes, mild autumns and benign winters, accounting for the Mediterranean type vegetation: palms, eucalyptus, magnolias, cedars, camellias, hydrangeas, medlars, monkey puzzle and fig trees. Spring is often damp but it is also warm and comes early, encouraging the early vegetables.

FISHING

The many rivers, streams and pools of the region teem with a wide variety of species. Blay, roach and dace are common throughout the region, with the Loire giving pike and even striped mullet, which in summer comes as far up river as Amboise. Catfish, tench and carp abound in the deeper pools of the Loire, Indre and Loir, while the Sologne pools are a haven for perch.

Trout fishing is best in the Creuse, Sauldre, the streams of Anjou and the tributaries of the Loir. The Berry, Briare and Orléans Canals are a source of eels and crayfish can be caught with special nets. For salmon and shad fishing flat bottomed boats are necessary while the commercial salmon fishers use nets, supported by poles, strung right across the river *(see p 105).*

It is essential to obtain a membership card bearing the necessary fishing tax stamps. The latter vary according to the category of the waterway, the type of fishing and the region. Apply to the Departmental Federations for angling clubs and associations in the following towns.

28 Chartres; 37 Tours; 41 Avaray near Mer; 45 La Ferté Saint Aubin; 49 Angers; 53 Laval and 72 Le Mans.

Tourist Information Centres and fishing tackle dealers may also be able to help with additional details.

Whatever type of fishing he chooses the angler must observe the federal and local regulations. For further particulars on such regulations, the close seasons and hours, the classification of waterways (first and second category and public or private), minimum size of fish, etc, apply to the same addresses given above.

SHOOTING

The diversity of the region offers a wealth of game and a choice of sport be it shooting, wildfowling or hunting with hounds.

The plains of the Beauce and meadowlands of Anjou and Touraine provide cover for partridges, pheasants, quails, thrushes, larks, hares and rabbits alike.

Deer and roe deer are confined to the wooded areas of the Baugeois, Château-la-Vallière, Loches and the Valençay district. Wild boar are to be found in the dense forests of Orléans and Amboise and around Chambord.

The islands and banks of the Loire abound with teal and mallard, while the Sologne, a shooters' paradise, provides a bag of wildfowl (ducks, teal and snipe), and other game including pheasants, wild boar and deer.

It is generally necessary to belong to a shooting association be it a private syndicate or a local society or club. However, certain organisations and/or individuals welcome occasional visitors and provide daily permits. *For further information apply to the following organisation: St-Hubert Club de France, 10 Rue de Lisbonne, 75 008 Paris or to the secretaries of the departmental shooting federations* (Federations de chasse départementales).

LONG DISTANCE FOOTPATHS

The region with its pleasant countryside and many fine forests is ideal walking country. There are many recommended signposted routes in addition to the offical Long Distance Footpaths known as *Sentiers de Grande Randonnée* in France. The following cross the region.

Footpath	Places along the route
GR 3	Beaugency, Chaumont-sur-Loire, Rilly-sur-Loire, Amboise, Montlouis-sur-Loire, Vouvray, Chinon.
GR 31	St-Thibault.
GR 32	Fay-aux-Loges.
GR 35	Cloyes, Vendôme, Montoire-sur-le-Loir, Vouvray, Château-du-Loir, Le Lude.
GR 36	Marigné-Laillé, Le Lude, Saumur, Montreuil-Bellay, Thouars.

THE CHÂTEAUX OF THE LOIRE

Between Sancerre and Nantes the banks of the Loire and the valleys of its tributaries offer an incomparable series of magnificent buildings rich alike in art and history and all in a harmonious setting.

The landscape. – The Loire landscape, with its simple, quiet lines, owes its charm to the subtle light that plays over it, displaying wide, pale blue skies, long stretches of often sluggish river, calm watercourses with soft reflections, sunny slopes with fertile vineyards, green valleys, smiling, flower decked villages and peaceful scenes. For these reasons it is also often referred to as the "Garden of France".

Castles and Châteaux. – The finest châteaux in the region were built in the Renaissance period (16C). Among these are Amboise, Azay-le-Rideau, Chambord, Chaumont, Châteaudun, Chenonceau, Ussé, Villandry, etc. Also worthy of mention are the castles of Angers, Chinon, Langeais, Loches and Sully, which were built in the Middle Ages, and the châteaux of Cheverny, Valençay and Serrant dating from the Classical period (17 and 18C).

Their history. – In the 15 and 16C the châteaux were the favourite residences of the Valois. From Charles VII to Henri III, the kings of France often stayed in them. As the court moved from one to another in obedience to the sovereign's whim, life in these places was extremely lively.

Some of these buildings were the scenes of tragic or moving happenings which had a great effect on the history of France, such as the crushing of the Amboise Conspiracy in 1560, the murder of the duc de Guise at Blois in 1588 and, above all, the "recognising" of Charles VII by Joan of Arc at Chinon in 1429. This last was an essential step in the marvellous progress which was crowned, in the Loire country, by the relief of Orléans.

(After photo: Bertault-Foussemagne, Éd. Arthaud)

The Loire at Candes

The towns and abbeys. – The beautiful countryside and the historic châteaux are not the only attractions of this region.

Towns have long existed at the main bridging points of the great river: Gien, Orléans, Beaugency, Blois, Tours, Saumur and Angers. They have suffered much, especially in war, as a result of their strategic value as bridgeheads.

Happily almost all the finest buildings were spared and several towns such as Châteaudun, Laval, Loches and Vendôme have conserved older quarters with many picturesque houses in the traditional local styles while other towns have programmes of restoration for such quarters as in Blois, Chinon, Le Mans and Tours.

The Middle Ages with the upsurge in religious faith saw the establishment and growth of powerful abbeys in the area. St-Benoît and Fontevraud still have today some magnificent examples of Romanesque architecture.

Witness also to the mysticism of the mediaeval period are the Abbey at Vendôme, Candes Church and the Cathedrals of Le Mans and Tours.

The wines of the Loire. – A visit to the Loire country will not only offer the tourist pure artistic joys and moving reminders of French history.

The slopes along the river and its tributaries produce excellent wines which will please gourmets: dry and aromatic Sancerre wines, fresh and fruity wines from the districts of Orléans and Blois, great vintages from Touraine – Vouvray, Montlouis, Azay-le-Rideau, Chinon, Bourgueil, St-Nicolas – sparkling wines from Saumur, the Loudun light reds and the sweet and heady wines of Anjou.

(After photo: Yvon)

Château de Chinon

INTRODUCTION TO THE LOIRE COUNTRY

The garden of France. – From whatever direction you approach the region be it across the immense plains of the Beauce, the harsher Berry countryside or the green *bocage*, wooded farmland, country of the Gâtine Mancelle, you will always be welcomed in the heart of the Loire country by the sight of vines, white houses and flowers.

For many foreigners this is perhaps one of the most typically French landscapes of them all with its peaceful, moderate and gentle countryside, a succession of blessed havens.

But make no mistake, the "Garden of France" is not a sort of Eden full of fruit and flowers. The historian Michelet once described it as a "homespun cloak with golden fringes", meaning that the valleys – the golden fringes – in all their wonderful fertility, bordered plateaux whose harshness was only tempered by occasional fine forests.

Geology. – Hemmed in by the ancient crystalline masses of the Morvan, Armorican Massif and Massif Central, the Loire region is actually part of the Paris Basin.

In the Secondary Era the area invaded by the sea was covered by a soft chalky deposit known as the **tuffeau** or tufa. This is now exposed along the valley sides of the Loir, Cher, Indre and Vienne. Also deposited were the limestones of the **gâtines** (sterile marshlands) often interrupted by tracts of sands and clays supporting forests and heathlands.

Once the sea had retreated, great freshwater lakes deposited more limestones, the surface of which is often covered with a topsoil of loess or silt. These areas are known as **champagnes** or *champeignes*.

During the Tertiary Era the folding of the Alpine mountain zone, created the Massif Central, and rivers descending from this new watershed were often laden with sandy clays which when deposited gave areas such as the Sologne and the Forest of Orléans.

Later subsidence in the west permitted the invasion by the **Faluns Sea** or Mer des Faluns as far as Blois, Thouars and Preuilly-sur-Claise. The heritage of this marine incursion, are a series of *falunières*, or shell marl beds to be found on the borders of the Ste-Maure Plateau, and the hills edging the Loire to the north.

Rivers originally flowing northwards were attracted in a westerly direction by the sea, thus explaining the great change of direction at Orléans.

The sea finally retreated for good leaving an undulating countryside with the river network the most important geographical feature. The alluvial silts or **varennes** deposited by the Loire and its numerous tributaries were to add an extremely fertile element to this already rich and varied geological pattern.

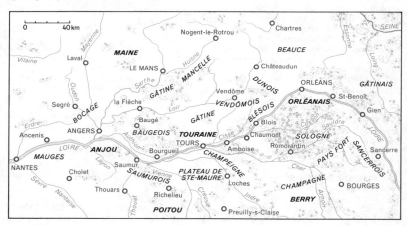

THE REGIONS

Physically very diverse the Loire region reaches from the Sancerre Hills in the east to the *bocage* landscapes of Maine and Anjou in the west. The northern parts of Berry, by virtue of its vineyards and châteaux, can be included in the Loire area.

The transitional districts of Pays Fort and Sancerrois with their clay soils are essentially a *bocage* landscape with many walnut trees. This was the countryside described by Alain Fournier in his novel, *Le Grand Meaulnes*.

Between the Cher and Arnon and the Indre is the area known as the **Champagne**. Essentially an area of limestone soils but often silty, it has tracts of *mardelles*.

Orléanais and Blésois. – Below Gien the valley opens out, the hills are lower and a refreshing breeze makes the leaves tremble on the long lines of poplars and willows. This is the gateway to the Orléanais which covers the Beauce, the Loir Valley (ie the Dunois and Vendômois), the Sologne and Blésois or Blois region.

Between Gien and Orléans the Loire meanders on the floor of a rich, wide valley.

In the vicinity of St-Benoît the valley, commonly known as the **Val**, is a series of meadows, beyond which horticulture predominates with the growing of seedlings and rosebushes on the alluvial deposits known locally as *layes*. Orchards and vineyards flourish on the south facing slopes.

From Orléans to Chaumont the Loire cuts into, on its northern bank, the **Beauce** limestone and further downstream into the flinty chalklands and tufa. On the southern side the river laps the alluvial sands brought down by its own waters, and which, besides growing asparagus and early vegetables, are also covered in dense brushwood, through this the kings of France once used to hunt. The great châteaux then begin: Blois, Chambord, Cheverny, Chaumont . . .

The **Beauce**, the granary of France, a treeless plain covered with a thin layer (2 m - 6 ft maximum) of fertile silt or loess, is extended to the area between the Loire and Loir *(p 96)* by the Petite Beauce. On the latter the *limon* gives way to clays: the Forest of Marchenoir. Villages, grouped round the pond and well, generally consist of a series of traditional closed courtyard type farms.

In the **Sologne** *(p 145)* and the **Forest of Orléans** *(p 126)* patches of poor crops alternate with the woodland.

Touraine. – The **Val**'s comfortable opulence delights the visitor already attracted by the luminous beauty of the light. The Loire, blue between golden sandbanks, flows slowly along its course hollowed out of the soft tufa chalk. Channels no longer occupied by the main river are divided into dead end reaches known as *boires* or occupied by tributary streams such as the Cher *(p 70)*, Indre *(p 86)*, Vienne *(p 76)* and Cisse *(p 58)*.

From Amboise to Tours the flinty chalk soils of the valley sides are clad with vineyards producing the well known Vouvray and Montlouis wines. **Troglodyte** houses have been carved out of the white tufa so that the passerby may well see plumes of smoke rising from amidst the vines.

The **Véron** *(p 76)*, lying between the Loire and the Vienne, is a patchwork of small fields and gardens rising above the riverside osier beds, willows and poplars. The landscape is dominated by the tall chimney of the Avoine-Chinon Nuclear Power Station *(p 76)*.

The plateaux of Touraine are not the harsh wastelands described by Michelet. The **Gâtine** of Touraine, between the Loir and Loire, was once a great forest: cut, cleared and improved the area is now agricultural land, although large tracts of heath and woodland still exist.

(After photo: Yvonne Sauvageot)

Vouvray — Troglodyte house

The sands and clays of the Touraine **Champeigne**, with its walnut studded fields, are covered with the Forests of Brouard and Loches and the Montrésor Gâtine. The plateaux of Montrichard and Ste-Maure *(p 136)* are similar in many ways to the Champeigne.

On the borders of Poitou the undulating landscapes of the **Richelais** and **Thouarsais** are dotted with red pantile roofed dwellings which are reminiscent of the south of France.

Anjou. – Anjou like the Touraine has little physical unity but is typified more easily by the gentleness of its countryside, so lovingly sung of by Du Bellay. The area includes the Maine-et-Loire Department and parts of the Mayenne and Sarthe in the north and Indre-et-Loire in the east.

The fertile **Bourgueil varenne**, or alluvial plain, extends along the north bank of the Loire. Spring vegetables flourish surrounded by the famous vineyards planted on the warm, dry gravels lying at the foot of the pine covered hills. Between the willow lined Authion and the Loire, green pasturelands, known locally as *prèe*, alternate with rich market gardens growing vegetables, flowers and fruit trees. Downstream from Angers are grown both vines, especially the famous vineyard coulée de Serrant, and hemp, in the vicinity of Béhuard.

The pleasant **Saumurois**, lying south of the Loire and extending from Fontevraud and Montsoreau to Doué-la-Fontaine and the Layon Valley *(p 92)* has three differing aspects: woods, plains and hillsides, the last often vine clad, produces the white wine to which the town of Saumur has given its name. The many caves in the steep, tufa valley sides of the Loire around Chênehutte-les-Tuffeaux, are now used for mushroom growing.

North of the river the sandy **Baugeois** *(p 51)* is an area of woods (oak, pine and chestnut) and arable land.

Downstream from Angers is the schist countryside of Black Anjou which contrasts so sharply with the limestones of White Anjou. The

(After photo: Yan)

Brissac — Wine harvest

countryside is greener heralding the *bocage* typical of the West and Armorican Massif. An area of wooded farmland or English hedgerow countryside it is characterised by a patchwork of small fields surrounded by hedge topped banks crisscrossed by deep lanes leading to small farmsteads. To the north is the Ségréen *bocage*, crossed by the Mayenne and Oudon while the **Mauges** *(p 114)* was the centre of Royalist insurrection, providing the perfect terrain for ambushing.

Around Angers, the capital of Anjou, nursery and market gardens abound specialising in flowers and seedlings.

Maine. – Only the southern part of this region is included in the guide.

The **Bas-Maine** otherwise known as Black Maine, watered by the Mayenne and Oudon is a region of sandstones, granites and schists, supporting a *bocage* type of vegetation. Geographically this area is part of the Breton Armorican Massif.

The **Haut-Maine**, covering the Sarthe and Huisne basins, is known as the White Maine because of its limestone soils.

THE ECONOMY

The bountiful Loire Valley assures the local population of an honest and comfortable livelihood. Although basically an agricultural region, recent years have seen the establishing of numerous industries.

Activities of the past. – Many of the traditional local activities have disappeared: namely the growing of madder; of saffron in the Gâtinais; of anise, coriander and liquorice in Bourgueil; and the silk industry based on the mulberries and silk worms introduced to Touraine by Louis XI. The once familiar fields of hemp around Bréhément and Béhuard, have dwindled in number as have the dependent ropeworkers. Only occasionally does anyone now gather wild chicory or the unpalatable choke pears which were used to make perry.

Cottage industries have disappeared with the last of the local craftsmen although Villaines is still a centre for wickerwork, but coopers, cartwrights and sabot makers are now few and far between. The flints of Meusnes and Villentrois are only used for the firearms industry.

Gone also are the blacksmiths' forges which were once so numerous on the forest outskirts. The coal of the Layon Basin is no longer worked and the silk manufacturers of Tours have capitulated to competition as have the manufacturers of *étamine*, the woollen fabric used to make ecclesiastical garments, in the Maine.

The drastic decline in river traffic on the Loire has resulted in the closure of the boatyards at Angers and the sail making factories at Ancenis. However, there is still a demand for slates from Trélazé and the tiles and bricks made from Sologne clay but, rather astonishingly, the very fine white tufa stone from Bourré and Pontlevoy, which distinguishes the houses of Touraine, is no longer worked.

AGRICULTURE

Vines (p 30), cereals and fodder crops are to be found nearly everywhere but it is the great variety of fruit and vegetables which most astonishes the visitor.

Fruit. – Ripening well in the local climate the succulent fruits of the region are renowned throughout France. Many have a noble pedigree: the *Reine-Claude* plums are named after Claude de France the wife of François I, the *Bon-chrétien* pears originated from a cutting planted by St. Francis of Paola in Louis XI's orchard at Plessis-lès-Tours. They were introduced into Anjou by **Jean Bourré**, Louis XI's Finance Minister. Rivalling the latter are the following varieties: *de Monsieur, William*, a speciality of Anjou, *Passe-Crassane* and *Beurré Hardy*.

Apples grow well throughout the region, the old variety *Crat vert* which is ripe only at springtime is still to be found in the vicinity of St-Martin-d'Auxigny; the *pomme de Madeleine* grows in the Val while the well known *Reinette* comes from Le Mans. The American Golden has in many cases superseded the local varieties.

In addition there are the strawberries of Saumur, the quince of Orléans, the clingstone apricots (or yellow fleshed peaches) of Touraine, blackcurrants, raspberries, redcurrants and gean or wild cherries which give the liqueur called *guignolet*, of Angers. Lemons, figs and pomegranates are also grown in the area.

Melons were introduced to the region by Charles VIII's Neapolitan gardener. Already in the 16C the variety and quality of the local fruit and vegetables was much praised by Ronsard among others.

The walnut and chestnut trees of the plateaux yield oil and the much prized wood and the edible chestnuts, often roasted during evening gatherings.

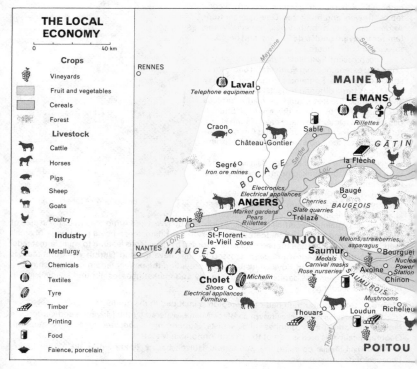

THE LOCAL ECONOMY

0   40 km

Crops
- Vineyards
- Fruit and vegetables
- Cereals
- Forest

Livestock
- Cattle
- Horses
- Pigs
- Sheep
- Goats
- Poultry

Industry
- Metallurgy
- Chemicals
- Textiles
- Tyre
- Timber
- Printing
- Food
- Faience, porcelain

RENNES

Laval — Telephone equipment

MAINE

LE MANS — Rillettes

Craon

Château-Gontier

Sablé

GÂTIN

Segré — Iron ore mines

BOCAGE

Sarthe

la Flèche

Electronics, Electrical appliances

ANGERS

Baugé

BAUGEOIS

Cherries

Market gardens, Pears, Rillettes

Slate quarries

Trélazé

Ancenis

St-Florent-le-Vieil — Shoes

ANJOU

Melons, strawberries, asparagus

NANTES   MAUGES

Saumur — Medals, Carnival masks, Rose nurseries

Bourgueil

Nuclear Power Station

Avoine

Chinon

SAUMUROIS

Cholet — Shoes, Electrical appliances, Furniture

Michelin

Mushrooms

Thouars

Loudun

Richelieu

POITOU

Early vegetables. – The main vegetable growing region is the Val de Loire and it has the supreme advantage in that its products, in general, are ready two weeks before those of the Paris region. Asparagus from Vineuil and Contres, potatoes from Saumur, French beans from Touraine and artichokes from Angers are despatched to Rungis, the main Paris market. Anjou is the leading producer of mushrooms, one of the region's more original crops. They are grown in the former tufa quarries situated near Montrichard, Montoire and Saumur.

The Orléans region grows great quantities of lettuce, cucumbers and tomatoes, all in massive greenhouses.

Flowers and nursery gardens. – Pots of geraniums or begonias, borders of nasturtiums and climbing wistaria with its pale mauve clusters adorn the houses of the region while the gardens are a profusion of camellias and hydrangeas. The region of Orléans-la-Source, Olivet and Doué-la-Fontaine is famous for its fields of flowers and rose nurseries. Tulips, gladioli and lilies are grown (for bulbs) near Soings in the Blésois.

Nursery gardens proliferate on the alluvial soils of the Loire, specialising in fruit trees, yew, cypress and cedar trees along with exotic shrubs. The lighter soils of Véron, Bourgueil and the Angers district are propitious to the growing of artichokes, onions and garlic for seed stock.

LIVESTOCK

Cattle, sheep and pigs. – In the fodder growing areas (champagnes and gâtines) young dairy stock are reared inside while elsewhere beef and dairy cattle feed on the pastures of the Maine and Anjou valleys and *bocages*. The most popular breeds are the Normandy *Maine-Anjou* and the *Pie noire*. Charolais cattle are fattened in the Mauges area. Milk production with the French Frisian *Pie noire* breed, is concentrated in the valleys of Touraine.

Sheep rearing, an activity on the decline, is limited to the limestone plateaux of the Beauce and Haut-Maine where the black faced *Bleu du Maine* prospers. Pigs are to be found everywhere but especially in Touraine, Maine and Anjou where the popular pork meat specialities of *rillettes* and *rillons* are current in Vouvray, Tours, Le Mans and Angers. The ever growing demand for the well known goats' cheeses has resulted in an increase in goat keeping.

Market days in the west country are highly colourful occasions: the liveliest are the pig markets at Ancenis and Craon and the great calf sales and goat markets at Château-Gontier and Cholet.

Horses. – The well known horse rearing activity was adversely affected by the spread of motorised vehicles throughout the countryside. However many a small town still has its racecourse and local riding clubs and schools keeping alive the local interest in horses and horseriding and its ancillary crafts.

INDUSTRY

Although the role of industry in the Val is far from predominant, a recent growth is noticeable in the main towns and in the development of ancillary industries based on the transformation of agricultural produce.

With the exception of Châteaudun and Vendôme, the main industrial centres are to be found along the Loire at Gien, Sully, St-Denis-de-l'Hôtel, Orléans, Beaugency, Mer, Blois, Amboise, Tours and Angers.

Michelin tyre factories have been installed at Orléans, Tours and Cholet.

Finally two nuclear power stations are in operation at Avoine-Chinon and St-Laurent-des-Eaux.

HISTORICAL NOTES

BC 59-51	Caesar conquers Gaul: four centuries of Roman occupation follow.
AD 313	Edict of Milan: Christians are granted freedom of worship.
4C	St. Martin, the greatest Bishop of the Gauls and onetime legionary in the Roman army founds the first monastery on Gallic soil at Ligugé in Poitou and Marmoutier near Tours in 372.
397	St. Martin died at Candes.
476	Decline of the Roman Empire because of the Barbarian invasions.
573	Gregory of Tours arrives from Clermont-Ferrand.
7C	Founding of the Benedictine Abbey of Fleury, later to be named St-Benoît.
late 8C	Alcuin of York formed a school for copyists at the behest of Charlemagne.
732	Charles Martel crushes the Saracens at Poitiers.
768-814	Charlemagne.
843-877	Charles the Bald.
9C	Norman invasions reach Angers, St. Benoît and Tours.

THE CAPETS (987-1328)

996-1031	Robert II.
1010	Foundation of the Benedictine abbey at Solesmes.
1060-1108	Philippe I.
1066	William the Conqueror lands in England
1104	First Council of Beaugency.
1137-1180	Louis VII.
1152	Second Council of Beaugency; Eleanor of Aquitaine marries Henry Plantagenet.
1154	Henry Plantagenet becomes King of England as Henry II.
1164-70	Thomas Becket in France during his exile *(Chinon, Le Mans, Tours)*.
1172	Thomas Becket murdered in Canterbury Cathedral.
1174	Founding of the Hospital of St John *(Angers)*.
1176	Foundation of the Carthusian charterhouse at Le Liget; nuns from Fontevraud settled at Amesbury in expiation for the murder of Becket.
1180-1223	Philippe-Auguste.
1189	Death of Henry II Plantagenet at Chinon. Capets versus Plantagenets with the principal antagonists being Philippe-Auguste and Richard Lionheart *(Chinon, Langeais, Loches)*.
1199	Richard Lionheart dies at Chinon and is buried at Fontevraud.
1204	John Lackland loses Anjou. Last of the Angevin kings he dies in 1216.
1215	Magna Carta.
1226-1270	St. Louis or Louis IX.
1285-1314	Philippe IV, the Fair.
1307	Philippe le Bel dissolves the Order of the Knights Templars *(Arville)*.

THE VALOIS (1328-1589)

1337-1453	Hundred Years War: 1346 Crécy; 1348 Black Death; 1356 Poitiers; 1415 Agincourt.
1380-1422	Charles VI.
1418	The Massacre at Azay-le-Rideau.
1420	Treaty of Troyes: Henry V of England is recognised King of France.
1421	Battle of Vieil-Baugé: the Angevins and Scots mercenaries defeat the English.
1422-1461	Charles VII.
1427	The Dauphin Charles installs his court at Chinon.
1429	Joan of Arc delivers Orléans; tried and burnt at the stake two years later *(Rouen)*.
1446	The Dauphin versus Agnès Sorel *(Loches)*.
1453	Battle of Castillon: final defeat of the English on French soil.
1455-1485	Wars of the Roses: Margaret of Anjou leader of Lancastrian cause *(Dampierre-sur-Loire)*.
1461-1483	Louis XI.
1476	Unrest among the powerful feudal lords; royal marriage at Montrichard.
1483-1498	Charles VIII.
1491	Marriage of Charles VIII and Anne of Brittany at Langeais.
1494-1559	The Campaigns in Italy.
1496	Early manifestations of Italian influence on local art *(Amboise)*.
1498-1515	Louis XII; he divorces and remarries Charles VIII's widow *(Chinon)*.
1515-1547	François I.
1519	French Renaissance: Chambord started; Leonardo da Vinci dies at Clos-Lucé.
1539	The Emperor Charles V visits Amboise and Chambord.
1547-1559	Henri II.
1559-1560	François II.
1560	Amboise Conspiracy; François II dies at Orléans.

1560-1574	Charles IX.
1562-1598	Wars of Religion.
1562	The Abbey of St-Benoît is pillaged by the Protestants; battles at Ponts-de-Cé, Beaugency and Sancerre.
1572	Massacre of St. Bartholomew in Paris.
1574-1589	Henri III.
1576	Founding of the Catholic League by Henri, duc de Guise to combat Calvinism.
1588	The murder of Henri, duc de Guise and the Cardinal of Lorraine *(Blois)*.

THE BOURBONS (1589-1792)

1589-1610	Henri IV.
1589	Vendôme retaken by Henri IV from the Catholic Leaguers.
1598	Edict of Nantes; marriage of César de Vendôme *(Angers)*.
1600	Henri IV marries Marie de' Medici.
1602	Maximilien de Béthune or Richelieu buys Sully.
1610-1643	Louis XIII.
1619	Marie de' Medici flees Blois.
1620	Building of the college by the Jesuits at La Flèche.
1626	Gaston d'Orléans, brother of Louis XIII receives the County of Blois.
1643-1715	Louis XIV.
1651	During the Fronde – civil war directed against Mazarin – Anne of Austria, Mazarin and the young Louis XIV seek refuge at Gien.
1669	Première of Molière's play *Monsieur de Pourceaugnac* at Chambord.
1685	Revocation of the Edict of Nantes.
1715-1774	Louis XV.
1719	Voltaire exiled at Sully.
1756	Foundation of the Royal College of Surgeons at Tours.
1770	The duc de Choiseul in exile at Chanteloup.

THE REVOLUTION AND FIRST EMPIRE (1789-1815)

1789	Taking of the Bastille
1793	Insurrection and ensuing strife between the Blues and the Whites *(Cholet, Laval, Les Mauges)*.
1795	Vendéen War; Proclamation of the Republic.
1803	Talleyrand purchased Valençay.
1804-1815	First Empire under Napoleon Bonaparte.
1808	Internment of Ferdinand VII, King of Spain, at Valençay.

THE RESTORATION AND SECOND REPUBLIC (1815-1852)

1815-1830	Restoration of the Bourbons: Louis XVIII, Charles X.
1830-1848	July Monarchy: Louis-Philippe.
1832	The first steamboat on the Loire.
1832-1848	Conquest of Algeria; 1848 internment of the Algerian leader *(Amboise)*.

THE SECOND EMPIRE (1852-1870)

1852-1870	Napoleon III as Emperor.
1870-1871	Franco-Prussian War.
1870	Proclamation of the Third Republic; following the encirclement of the Emperor and army at Sedan.
	Defence of Châteaudun; Tours was the headquarters of the Provisional Government.

THE THIRD REPUBLIC (1870-1940) TO 20C

1873	The Legitimist Pretender, comte de Chambord, wrecks his chances of success *(Chambord)*; Amédée Bollée completes his first car, *l'Obeissante (Le Mans)*.
1908	Wilbur Wright's early trials with his aeroplane.
1914-1918	First World War.
1919	Treaty of Versailles.
1923	The first Twenty-four hour race at Le Mans.
1939-1943	Second World War.
1940	Defence of Saumur; historic meeting at Montoire.
1945	Armistice of Reims.
1946	Fourth Republic.
1952	Inauguration of the *son et lumière* performances at Chambord.
1958	Fifth Republic.
1969	New university campus at Orléans-la-Source; Opening of the Avoine-Chinon Nuclear Power Station followed six years later by St-Laurent-des-Eaux.
1970	Founding of the University of Tours.
1974	The A 10 motorway links Tours and the capital.

THE LONG, RICH PAST OF THE LOIRE COUNTRY

Romans and Barbarians. – From the beginning of the conquest of Gaul by the Romans, the inhabitants of the Loire country showed their independent spirit. The "Carnutes", who lived between Chartres and Orléans, gave the first signal for resistance to Caesar's legions.

In the 3C, Christianity came in with St. Gatian and triumphed with St. Martin: at the end of the 4C the tomb of St. Martin at Tours became the national sanctuary of the Merovingians *(p 150)*. The Saint's name is commemorated annually on 11 November – St. Martin's Day.

For two centuries the Loire country suffered from invasions of Barbarians. Bishop St. Aignan stopped the Huns, who had come from the shores of the Caspian Sea, from entering Orléans. Two centuries later Charles Martel prevented the Saracens, who were moving north from the Iberian Peninsula, from crossing the Loire.

Fresh disaster followed one hundred years later: the Normans came up the river, killing, pillaging and desecrating from Nantes to St-Benoît-sur-Loire and looting the treasure of St. Martin. Robert le Fort, Count of Blois and Tours stopped their advance but their depredations continued till 911 following the agreement of St-Clair sur Epte, creating the Duchy of Normandy.

Lords and castles. – The weakness of the last Carolingian kings encouraged the independence of turbulent and ambitious feudal lords. The Orléans region remained essentially a Capetian domain, its capital one of the sovereign's preferred residences but Touraine, Blésois, Anjou and Maine became so many separate States where the king's authority was hardly recognised. This was the age of powerful barons, who raised armies and struck coinages of their own. Every strategic point from Orléans to Angers was crowned by the stronghold of some warring feudal lord.

The counts of Blois had formidable enemies in the counts of Anjou, the most famous of whom was **Foulques Nerra** *(p 43)*. Foulques was a formidable tactician, and as such he was the true precursor of Philippe-Auguste and Richard Lionheart. He slowly encircled his rival Eudes II's domain, the County of Blois, which was eventually to fall to his son, Geoffroi Martel.

The dynasty of the counts of Anjou reached its zenith with the Plantagenets *(p 44)*. In 1154 one of them became King Henry II of England. They now reigned over an Empire *(p 19)* which stretched from the north of England to the Pyrenees. Theirs was a formidable power facing the weaker Capet kings of France but the latter did not hesitate to resist their awesome neighbours. Fortunately for the Capets, quarrels between the Plantagenets helped them to success. In 1216 Philippe-Auguste confiscated all the provinces of John Lackland (the Bad King John of English schoolbooks), who had murdered his nephew, the Duke of Brittany. The Loire country became French again.

St. Louis entrusted the territory to his brother, Charles of Anjou. This prince and his successors left their provinces to conquer the Kingdom of Naples. But the memory of the last of the dukes of Anjou, Good King René, has lingered in the minds of the people *(p 44)*.

Joan of Arc. – The Hundred Years War (1337-1453) brought back the English, who became masters of half the country.

Then **Joan of Arc** appeared and persuaded Charles VII to give her a command *(p 73)*. With her little army she entered beleaguered Orléans, stormed the English strongholds and freed the city *(p 121)*. The fleeing enemy was beaten on the Loire, at Jargeau, and in the Beauce, at Patay. In spite of the betrayal of Compiègne and the stake at Rouen, the enemy's total defeat was now assured.

The decline. – The dark period of the Wars of Religion (1562-1609) brought devastation and massacre: this was the time of the Amboise Conspiracy *(p 41)* and the bloody Massacre of St. Bartholomew. Henri III connived at the assassination of the Guise brothers in the Château de Blois *(p 54)*. Churches and abbeys were sacked by the Huguenots.

The accession of Henry IV (1589), which restored peace, marked the end of the most brilliant period for the Loire Valley. At the end of the 18C political decline was followed by a certain loss of prosperity.

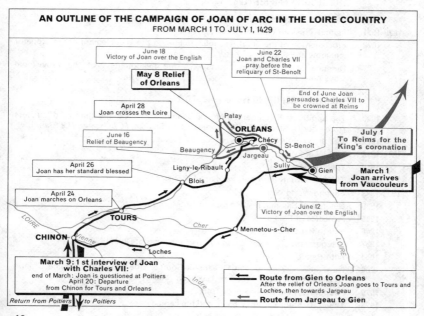

AN OUTLINE OF THE CAMPAIGN OF JOAN OF ARC IN THE LOIRE COUNTRY
FROM MARCH 1 TO JULY 1, 1429

June 18
Victory of Joan over the English

June 22
Joan and Charles VII
pray before the
reliquary of St-Benoît

**May 8 Relief
of Orleans**

End of June Joan
persuades Charles VII to
be crowned at Reims

April 28
Joan crosses the Loire

Patay

June 16
Relief of Beaugency

ORLÉANS

Chécy

**July 1
To Reims for the
King's coronation**

Beaugency

St-Benoît

April 26
Joan has her standard blessed

Ligny-le-Ribault

Jargeau

Sully

**March 1
Joan arrives
from Vaucouleurs**

Blois

Gien

April 24
Joan marches on Orleans

LOIRE

TOURS

June 12
Victory of Joan over the English

CHINON

Vienne

Cher

Mennetou-s-Cher

LOIRE

Loches

**March 9: 1st interview of Joan
with Charles VII:**
end of March: Joan is questioned at Poitiers
April 20: Departure
from Chinon for Tours and Orleans

Indre

⬅ **Route from Gien to Orleans**
After the relief of Orleans Joan goes to Tours and
Loches, then towards Jargeau

⬅ **Route from Jargeau to Gien**

Return from Poitiers ▼ *to Poitiers*

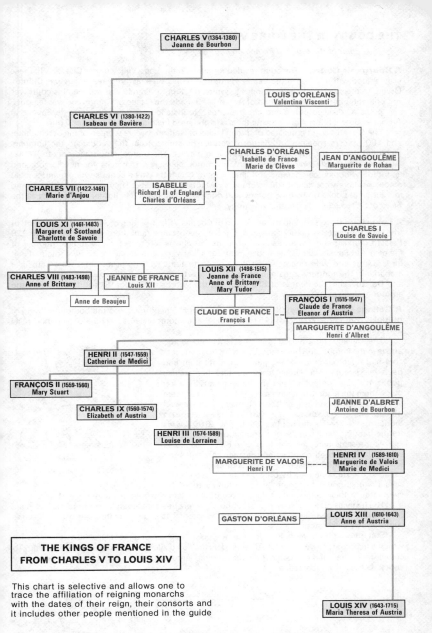

THE KINGS OF FRANCE FROM CHARLES V TO LOUIS XIV

This chart is selective and allows one to trace the affiliation of reigning monarchs with the dates of their reign, their consorts and it includes other people mentioned in the guide

Prior to the Revolution, the guild of mariners using the Loire and dating from the 14C was disbanded and gone was the animated commercial traffic on this great highway. Onetime exports included wine, wool from Berry, iron ores from the Massif Central, Forez coal, Beauce grain and fine materials from Tours while the upstream traffic consisted of cargoes of exotic goods from overseas.

For a time the importance of the towns declined. Orléans closed its sugar refineries and its stocking and vinegar factories. Amboise ceased to weave cloth. The silk factories of Tours were abandoned and the cotton mills of Saumur stood idle.

Troubled times. – During the French Revolution, Anjou was one of the chief battlegrounds of the Blues (Republicans) and the Whites (Royalists). Angers was taken and retaken by both parties; Saumur was captured by the Whites. Then Santerre arrived from Paris with a troop of Revolutionaries, but the pleasures of the "Garden of France" so cooled their ardour that they laid down their muskets and cast off their accoutrements.

In 1870 at the beginning of the Franco-Prussian War and following the surrender of the French army under the Emperor at Sedan, an improvised force, known as the *Armée de la Loire*, gathered to the north of the Loire. Despite two early victories at Orléans and Coulmiers, they were pushed back to Le Mans. The Provisional Government then left Tours to take refuge at Bordeaux.

During the First World War the Americans established their headquarters at Tours and the Loire was defended by American troops, the "Sammies".

On 10 June 1940, with the menace of the advancing German army, the Government left Paris for Tours and the Château de Cangé, southeast of Tours between St-Avertin and Larçay was to become the temporary Presidential residence. On the 13th the decision was taken to transfer the government once again to Bordeaux. This one week in June saw much destruction in the Loire country: bridges bombed and towns damaged. With September 1944 came the Liberation by the combined forces of the Americans and the French Resistance.

The region had suffered greatly but luckily it retained its essential charm.

THE COURT IN THE LOIRE VALLEY

(See chart of the Kings of France on page 17)

A Bourgeois Court. – The court resided regularly in the Loire Valley under Charles VII; these visits ended with the last of the Valois, Henri III. Charles VII's favourite residence was Chinon. Owing to the straitened circumstances to which the King of France was reduced his court was not brilliant; but the arrival of Joan of Arc in 1429 made the Castle of Chinon for ever famous.

Louis XI disliked pomp and circumstance. He installed his wife, Charlotte de Savoie, at Amboise, but he himself rarely came there. He preferred his manor at Plessis-lès-Tours.

The Queen's court consisted of fifteen ladies in waiting, twelve women of the bedchamber and 100 officers (persons in charge of various functions, from the saddler to the librarian, including the doctor, the chaplain and the lute player). The budget amounted only to 37 000 *livres*, of which 800 *livres* were spent on minor pleasures: materials for needlework and embroidery, books, parchments and illuminating. Charlotte was a serious woman and a great reader: her library contained 100 volumes, a vast total for that time. They were works of piety and morality and books on history, botany and domestic science. A few lighter works, such as the *Tales of Boccaccio*, relieved this solemnity.

A Luxurious Court. – With the accession of Charles VIII, "the King of Amboise", at the end of the 15C, the taste for luxury appeared. Furnishings became rich: there were in the castle 220 Persian, Turkish and Syrian carpets, 45 beds, 60 chests, 60 tables, an incredible number of Flemish and Parisian tapestries and sumptuous silverware. A magnificent aviary contained rare birds. Lions and wild boars, which were made to fight with huge mastiffs, were kept in a menagerie. The armoury contained a fine collection of armour, the battle axes of Clovis, St. Louis and Du Guesclin, the dagger of Charlemagne, the swords of Charles VII and Louis XI and the armour of Joan of Arc.

A Gallant Court. – Louis XII, who was miserly or at least frugal, was the bourgeois "King of of Blois". But under François I (1515-47) the French court became a school of elegance, taste and culture.

The Cavalier King added men of science, poets and artists to the knights and bourgeois by whom his predecessors had been surrounded. Women, who until then had been relegated to the Queen's service and treated like pupils in a girls' school, played an effective part; the King made them the leaders of a new society. He expected them to dress perfectly and he gave them clothes which showed off their beauty: he would spend 200 000 *livres* at a time on fabrics and finery. He did not hesitate to pay 26 000 *livres* for the hangings and carpets of a single room.

The salamander
Crest of François I

At the same time the King took care that these ladies were treated with all courtesy and respect. A gentleman who had permitted himself to speak slightingly of them escaped the supreme penalty only by flight – "So great", says a contemporary historian, "was the King's anger, he swore that whoever reflected on the honour of these ladies would be hanged."

The festivals given by François I at Amboise, where he spent his childhood and the first years of his reign, were of unprecedented brilliance. Weddings, baptisms and the visits of princes were sumptuously celebrated.

Sometimes they were held in the country, as in the case of a reconstruction of a siege, for which a temporary town was built, defended by the duc d'Alençon and captured by the King. To create the illusion of a real battle, bombards hurled large balls which knocked down those they struck. Quite a few were killed.

The porcupine
Crest of Louis XII

The ermine
Crest of Anne of Brittany
and Claude of France

The Franciscan girdle and ermine tufts
Crest of Anne of Brittany

The Last Valois. – Under Henri II and his sons, Blois remained the habitual seat of the court when it was not at the Louvre. It was Henri III who drew up the first code of etiquette and introduced the title "His Majesty", taken from the Roman Emperors.

The Queen Mother and the Queen had about 100 ladies in waiting. Catherine de' Medici also had her famous "Flying Squad" of pretty girls, who kept her informed and assisted her intrigues. About 100 pages, aged from fourteen to seventeen, acted as messengers.

The King's suite included 200 gentlemen in waiting and over 1 000 archers and Swiss guards. A multitude of servants were busy about the castle. Princes of the Blood and great lords also had their households. Thus, from the time of François I, about 15 000 people surrounded the king; when the court moved, 12 000 horses were needed.

Queens and Great Ladies. – The official position enjoyed by women at court around the king, often enabled them to play an important if not always a useful part in the political affairs of the country. It also enabled them to protect and develop the arts.

Agnès Sorel *(p 93)* adorned the court of Charles VII at Chinon and at Loches. She gave the King good advice and constantly reminded him of the urgent problems facing the country which had barely emerged from the Hundred Years War (1337-1453).

Louise de Savoie, the mother of François I, with her insatiable ambition lived only for the success and aggrandisement of her son, her "Caesar", who owed the throne of France to her intrigues.

On the other hand, the love life of François I had so many heroines that it would be impossible to enumerate them. One of his mistresses, the duchesse d'Étampes, holds a place apart. Until the King's death she ruled the court.

Diane de Poitiers (p 68) the celebrated mistress of Henri II, made important decisions of policy, negotiated with the Protestants, exchanged Spanish prisoners and distributed honours and magistracies.

The foreign beauty of Mary Stuart, the hapless wife of the little King François II, who died at seventeen after a few months' reign, threw a brief lustre over the court in the middle of the 16C.

A different type altogether was Marguerite de Valois, the famous Queen Margot, sister of François II, Charles IX – whose name is coupled with that of Marie Touchet (p 125) – and Henri III. Her escapades frequently alarmed her mother, Catherine de' Medici and her marriage to Henri of Navarre, the future King Henri IV, did little to tame her.

THE ANGEVIN EMPIRE

This term applies to the territories extending from the north of England to the Pyrenees that were the suzerainty of Henry II and his successors who were known as the Angevin kings. Sometimes the surname Plantagenet is used for members of the family descended from Geoffrey of Anjou and usually includes all kings from Henry II to Edward III. The Angevin kings were more French than English in speech, habits and customs and their connections with the Loire country, at the heart of this Empire, were numerous and varied.

Geoffrey Plantagenet (1113-51), Count of Anjou, was born in Le Mans. It was his nickname, Plantagenet (p 44) which was adopted for the royal house. His marriage in 1128 to Matilda, the granddaughter of William the Conqueror and widow of the German Emperor, established an alliance between Normandy and Anjou and Maine. It was Matilda who fought with her cousin Stephen for the English throne on Henry I's death in 1135. Geoffrey died at the age of thirty-nine and was buried in Le Mans Cathedral. His tombal plaque can be seen in the Tesse Museum (p 112).

The eldest son, Henry Plantagenet (1133-89) was quickly caught up in the dynastic struggles in both England and France. He was the creator of the great Angevin Empire. Henry acquired most of his continental lands before his accession to the English throne. Through his mother he inherited Normandy (1150), and Anjou, Maine and Touraine in 1151 and with his marriage the next year to Eleanor of Aquitaine he added Aquitaine, Gascony, Poitou and Auvergne. The King of France, Louis VII who had divorced Eleanor by the Second Council of Beaugency (p 52), was confronted with a vassal whose empire equalled his own. Two years later Henry became King of England, ruler of an Anglo-French empire which rivalled that of his inveterate enemy the Capet. A great sovereign, Henry fought to consolidate his territorial gains but his reign was disturbed and empire imperilled by his quarrelling and discontented sons and his own dispute with his Chancellor and later Archbishop of Canterbury, Thomas Becket, which ended with the latter's murder.

Henry II outlived three of the Plantagenet princes. The youngest William died in infancy while his heir, Henry (1155-83), a true knight found his amusement on the jousting fields. He died at Martel having sacked St. Amadour's shrine in Rocamadour. The third son Geoffrey (1156-86), a firm friend of Philippe-Auguste, was killed in a tournament in 1186. Henry had divided his empire among his remaining sons but this only led to quarrels and wars, often actively fostered by the French King. With Queen Eleanor imprisoned in England Henry II died a solitary death in Chinon, attended only by the faithful William Marshal.

Henry's heir, Richard Lionheart (1157-99) was a true Angevin, great warrior king, and Queen Eleanor's favourite. Soon after his accession he set out on the Third Crusade, accompanied by Philippe-Auguste. It was during this Crusade that Richard agreed to marry Berengaria of Navarre (p 113) despite his bethrothal twenty-one years previously to Alais the French King's sister. Captured and imprisoned on his return journey he learned of his brother's treachery and on release he hastily returned to France, via England, to do combat with his arch enemy. The rest of his ten year reign was spent defending his French empire. He died in 1199 as a result of a wound incurred at the siege of Châlus. He was buried at Fontevraud (p 81) where his mother had retired in her old age.

The last of Henry II's sons, John Lackland (1166-1216) was no warrior and much of his time was spent intriguing. Philippe-Auguste was quick to wrest Normandy, Anjou, Maine and Touraine from him and, with his French possessions greatly diminished, he faced revolts by the Barons in England who were demanding a charter of liberties. The Magna Carta was signed in 1215.

The second half of the 13C saw the continuation of the Capet and Plantagenet struggles with each trying to consolidate their position and justify their territorial claims. Treaties were rife but the confiscation of Guyenne in 1337 and Edward III's renewed claim to the French throne led to the outbreak of hostilities known as the Hundred Years War (1337-1453). Early victories at Crécy and Calais were followed by a period of truces and then campaigns in the south led by the Black Prince and John of Gaunt against the great French warrior Du Guesclin. Both royal houses were troubled by dynastic problems. In France there was the bitter civil war between the Burgundian and Armagnac factions, with the English ultimately allied to the former. Agincourt in 1415 was their victory.

When Paris was occupied in 1418 by the Burgundians, the uncrowned Dauphin (p 73) fled to Bourges and was known by his enemies as the King of Bourges. The Loire became the theatre of the war. It was then that Charles invoked anew the Auld Alliance (1295) seeking Scots help in the face of Henry V's attacks. The arrival of 6 000 Scottish soldiers in 1419 under John the Earl of Buchan, later made High Constable of France, Archibald Douglas and Sir John Stewart of Darnley, rewarded with Aubigny (p 48) fought at Baugé and Cravant. The situation was critical, with half the kingdom in the hands of the English.

Joan of Arc's intervention in 1429 with the relief of Orléans was the beginning of the end of this once great empire. In spite of the efforts of military commanders such as the veteran general John Talbot, Earl of Shrewsbury and the Duke of Bedford, the brother of Henry V, the English rule in France was to end with the Battle of Castillon in 1453 and loss of Calais five years later.

ART AND ARCHITECTURE

ECCLESIASTICAL ARCHITECTURE

To assist readers unfamiliar with the terminology employed in ecclesiastical architecture, we describe below the most commonly used terms.

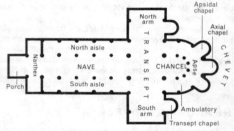

The ground plan. – Basically a church consists of a chancel, where the clergy worship and where the high altar and reliquaries are to be found, and a nave, for the faithful. Early churches, which were rectangular in shape and were known as "basilical" in their plan, consisted of these elements only. It was the Romanesque architects who created the more usual Catholic plan based on the Cross. At the entrance a narthex was built to receive those who had not been baptised and, later, pilgrims who came for special services. Aisles were added to enlarge the nave. In pilgrimage churches, the aisles were prolonged to circle the chancel in an ambulatory, thus allowing the faithful to process freely. Chapels were sometimes built on to the apse (radiating chapels) and the arms of the transept (transept chapels).

Romanesque (11-12C). – The year 1000 at the end of the troubled history of the early Middle Ages which had been marked by Norman invasions and conflicts between feudal lords, saw a renaissance in the art of building. Simultaneously the royal prerogative was asserted and there was an upsurge in religious faith expressed materially in monastic buildings.

Churches became larger and loftier – heavy stone vaulting, replacing wood, tended to crush the supporting walls where openings were reduced to a minimum and side aisles were built tall to buttress the nave *(see cross section)*. Vaulting was semicircular or **barrel** with transverse ribs in the early periods, later to become **groined**. Columns were gener-

Semicircular or barrel vaulting
1 vault - 2 transverse arch

Groined vaulting
1 main arch - 2 groin
3 transverse arch

ally cylindrical while arches were semicircular and decoration tended to represent floral or geometric motifs and fantastic figures. In England by contrast the equivalent Norman period produced long naves, flat east ends, towers and spires. The typical French sculptured doorway *(see illustration below)* was rare.

The Romanesque style had strong regional characteristics.

Orléanais. – The two most remarkable edifices are both Carolingian and monastic: the church at Germigny-des-Près and the Benedictine basilica at St-Benoît-sur-Loire *(p 133)*. The Cher Valley also has a rich heritage of Romanesque sanctuaries, namely at St-Aignan, Selles-sur-Cher and a more modest one at St-Loup.

Touraine. – Architecture in this region shows a strong Poitou influence with features such as column buttressed apsidal or radiating chapels; domes and doorways without tympana. The square or octagonal bell towers are crowned with spires and angle bell turrets *(see illustration below)*.

Anjou. – Here the main examples of this style are to be found in the vicinity of Baugé and Saumur. The church at Cunault shows a distinct Poitou influence with its five bays of broken barrel vaulted nave supported by groined vaulted side aisles, as does the abbey church at Fontevraud, the most northerly example of a dome covered church, more typical of the Aquitaine area.

Doorway
1 archivolt - 2 recessed orders or arches
3 tympanum - 4 splaying - 5 capitals

Bell towers
saddle-back roof
1 louvers

spire with
bell turrets

Romanesque to Gothic. – The **Plantagenet** or **Angevin** style got its name from Henry II Plantagenet *(p 44)*. This transitional style reached its zenith in the early 13C and was already superseded by the end of the same century. The most characteristic feature of the style was the Angevin vaulting. While in Gothic vaulting all the keys are at roughly the same level in the

St-Maurice Cathedral
Mid 12C

Angevin vaulting
Late 12C

St-Serge: chancel
Early 13C

Plantagenet equivalent with its more rounded or domical form, the keys of the diagonal (ogive) arches are at least 3 m - 10 ft above the keys of the transverse and stringer arches (eg St-Maurice Cathedral, Angers).

Towards the end of the 12C Angevin vaulting became finer with more numerous and gracious ribs springing from slender columns. The early 13C saw the beginning of lierne vaulting with elegant sculptures.

From the Loire Valley this style spread to the Vendée, Poitou, Saintonge and the Garonne.

Gothic (12-15C). –

The main features are the diagonal or ogive vaulting and systematic use of the pointed or lancet arch. A skeleton framework supported the main stress of the vaulting *(see cross section)*. The stress passed from relieving arches to the pillars – later to become mere extensions of the arches – which were in turn directly supported by external flying buttresses. Walls became thin and openings were glazed with expanses of glass. The style was lofty and luminous.

Quadripartite vaulting
1 diagonal - 2 transverse
3 stringer - 4 flying buttress
5 keystone

Lierne and tierceron vaulting
1 diagonal - 2 lierne
3 tierceron - 4 pendant
5 corbel

Quadripartite vaulting, with its essential elements the diagonal and transverse ribs, was common and later followed by **sexpartite** vaulting, when covering rectangular instead of square bays. This involved the addition of a transverse arch, crossing the vault at its apex. From the 15C onwards the search for more decorative effects led to the adding of subsidiary ribs – called **lierne and tierceron** (St-Serge, Angers) – and the creation of a ridge rib with carved bosses and pendants.

The great French **chevets** date from this period. Strictly speaking the chevet includes the apse, surrounding ambulatory and radiating chapels. This form of east end was typical and provided impressive ensembles with as many as thirteen chapels as at Le Mans or Orléans *(illustration)*.

Gothic chevet
1 axial or lady chapel - 2 double course
flying buttress - 3 north arm of transept
4 apse - 5 bell tower on the façade
6 spire over the transept crossing

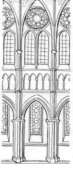

Lancet
(13C)

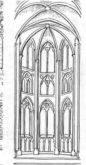

Gothic elevations
Radiant
(late 13C-14C)

Flamboyant
(15C)

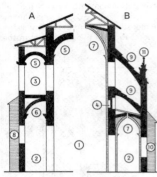

The three Gothic periods can be distinguished by decorative motifs: an initial or 13C phase was characterised by pointed arches and **lancet** windows with geometric *tracery; a second or **Radiant** (Rayonnant) of 13-14C, with circular patterned tracery and the third or **Flamboyant** style (15C) showing flame like designs. These correspond with the English early, middle and late Gothic styles.

The abbey church of Vendôme is a good example of French Gothic while the evolution of the Gothic style is well represented by St-Gatien Cathedral in Tours *(p 153)*. Both edifices have good Flamboyant west fronts.

Transverse section through nave

1 nave - 2 aisle - 3 gallery - 4 triforium
5 barrel vaulting - 6 half barrel vaulting
7 ogive vaulting - 8 buttress - 9 flying buttress
10 buttress - 11 pinnacle

(A) Romanesque (B) Gothic

Renaissance and Classical (16-18C). – Renaissance ecclesiastical buildings in the Loire, like the châteaux, show a strong Italian influence in their decoration *(see p 23)*. The pointed arch, typical of the Gothic period, is replaced by basket handled or semicircular arches and statue filled niches become a common feature. Although rare, the Renaissance edifices of the region are well worthy of a visit, in particular, the church at Montrésor *(illustration)* and the chapels at Ussé, Champigny-sur-Veude and La Bourgonnière.

Renaissance doorway
Montrésor Church
1 basket-handle arch

Classical dome
Dome surmounted
by a lantern
1 flame ornament

Classical ecclesiastical buildings (17-18C) tend to be more majestic with superimposed Greek orders, pedimented doorways and domes. Examples are the dome of N.-D. des Ardilliers, Saumur and the pediment of St-Vincent's in Blois.

Church Furnishings

Regrettably, much of the early church furniture – rood screens and beams, altarpieces, fonts, pulpits, pews, stalls and lecterns – especially the pieces in wood did not survive the various religious conflicts and the Revolution.

Rood beam or tref. – This supports the triumphal arch at the entrance to the chancel. The rood carries a Crucifix flanked by statues of the Virgin and St John and sometimes other personages from the Calvary.

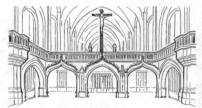

Rood screen. – This replaces the rood beam in larger churches, and may be used for preaching and reading of the Epistles and Gospel. From the 17 C onwards many disappeared as they tended to hide the altar.

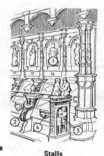

Stalls
1 high back
2 elbow rest
3 cheekpiece
4 misericord

Altar with retable or altarpiece
1 retable or altarpiece - 2 predella
3 crowning piece - 4 altar table - 5 altar front
Although they are becoming rare, certain
Baroque retables regroup several altars

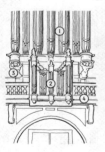

Organ
1 great organ case
2 little organ case
3 caryatids
4 loft

SECULAR ARCHITECTURE

Rich in history this area has left us incomparable pieces of secular architecture among which the châteaux – be they mediaeval fortress or elegant residence – are the most famous.

During the Carolingian and early Capetian dynasties weak kings and a disunited kingdom encouraged the independence of turbulent and ambitious feudal lords. Touraine, the district of Blois, Anjou and Maine became so many separate States with local lords who raised armies, struck coinages and created small fortified cities – often encircled with ramparts, separated from the towns proper – as at Amboise, Loches and Angers. These feudal fortresses and strongholds were built to withstand numerous sieges.

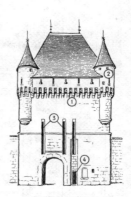

Strategically sited, all strongholds were heavily fortified: sombre castles were encircled with ramparts and vested with massive towers with wooden hoardings, quadrangular keeps (Langeais, Montrichard, Beaugency and Montbazon) and curtain or revetment walls (Loches and Chinon). Against such defences the besiegers used a variety of assault weapons or tactics: including sapping, catapults (arbalests, tower crossbows, espringels, mangonels and trebuchets), battering rams and assault towers.

Corner towers became round or semicircular, following the First Crusade, and their bases were thickened. The wood hoardings gave way to stone machicolations. However the advent of the age of cannon (mid 15C) transformed military architecture, towers became low, squat bastions and curtain walls were reinforced by round or square flanking towers.

Towers and curtain walls
1 hoardings - 2 crenellations - 3 merlon
4 arrow slit or lancet
5 curtain wall
6 bridge or drawbridge

Fortified gatehouse
1 machicolations
2 watch turrets
3 slots for the arms of the drawbridge
4 postern

Gothic. – The 15C saw a new generation of buildings following on the mediaeval fortress. Not entirely free of the constraints of the Middle Ages these massive but elegant buildings showed a greater search for comfort, light and decoration, eg Le Plessis-Bourré and Plessis-Macé *(illustrations p 127)*.

Many of the châteaux of the period were brick buildings with stone ornamentation (eg Le Moulin at Lassay). The manor Clos-Lucé at Amboise is another good example. Town houses were adorned with overhanging turret staircases and tall dormer windows, while houses of brick and timber work abounded.

Renaissance. – With the expulsion of the English (end of the Hundred Years War 1453) aided by Joan of Arc and the subsequent creation of a consolidated kingdom, military architecture as such was to become the exclusive domain of the king with a view to defending his frontiers. It was the Loire Valley that became the favourite abode of royalty and the court who abandoned the earlier royal residences of the Louvre, Bastille and Conciergerie in Paris. The king

Renaissance ornament

Frieze on the grand staircase at Azay-le-Rideau

1 shell - 2 vase - 3 foliage
4 dragon - 5 nude child
6 cherub - 7 cornucopia
8 satyr

became the promoter of all building: Louis XI built Langeais and Plessis-Lès-Tours; Charles VIII Amboise; Louis XIII a wing of Blois and François I another wing at Blois and Chambord.

This was the period of the itinerant court – and the attending French nobles, no longer feudal lords, and officers of State – also built elegant residences or town houses. Such was the case of the financiers Semblançay with a château of the same name, Robertet at the Hôtel d'Alluye in Blois and the Château du Bery, Bohier at Chenonceau and Berthelot at Azay-le-Rideau.

Prior to the Italian campaigns, Italian artists such as Francesco Laurana, Niccolo Spinelli and Jean Candida worked for both King René of Anjou and Louis XI doing sculpture and medallions. However it was with the return of Charles VIII from Naples in late 1495 accompanied by many craftsmen from Naples that the new Renaissance style began to flourish. The

Renaissance coffered ceiling
Grand staircase at Azay-le-Rideau
1 pendant - 2 coffer - 3 medallion

Renaissance orders
François I Wing, Blois

1 chimney - 2 attic - 3 dormer window - 4 balustrade - 5 single mullioned window - 6 double mullioned window - 7 cornice - 8 pilaster - 9 moulding

Italian influence favoured the imitation of Classical Antiquity. Semicircular or basket handled arches replaced pointed ones while ceilings with compartments or coffers replaced, for the most part, the ogival vaults and ornamentation was in the true Antique tradition.

Buildings such as Amboise, Chaumont, Chenonceau, Azay-le-Rideau, or Chambord retain a feudal aspect – curtain walls, rounded towers and moats – but the defensive devices were purely ornamental. Watchpaths tended to disappear although the machicolations were retained for their decorative effect. Façades were decorated with niches, medallions and large pilaster framed windows giving plenty of light. Steeply pitched and pointed roofs were adorned with highly decorated chimneystacks and tall pinnacled and pedimented dormer windows.

The château at Amboise, the Louis XII Wing at Blois and the north wing of Châteaudun all demonstrate early manifestations of the new Italian decorative style which triumphed on the inner façade of the François I Wing at Blois *(illustration adjoining)*.

Later as at Chambord and Le Lude, the decoration was adapted by local masters such as Pierre Trinqueau.

Architecturally the Italian influence is most noticeable in the outer façade of the François I Wing at Blois. With its rhythmic bay design, incorporating three tiers of open loggias, this front strongly resembles certain Italian palaces.

The famous staircases of the Loire châteaux were also modelled on Italian examples whether they were superimposed spiral ones as at Chambord and Blois or straight flights with coffered ceilings as at Chenonceau, Azay-le-Rideau *(illustration p 23)* and Poncé-sur-le-Loir.

Civic architecture also showed Renaissance influences as in the town halls of Beaugency, with its characteristic semicircular arches and superimposed orders, Orléans and Loches. Private mansions typical of the Renaissance are to be found at Orléans (Maisons de François I, de la Coquille and d'Alibert), Blois (Hôtel d'Alluye), Tours (Hôtels Gouin and Babou de la Bourdaisière) and Angers (Hôtel de Pincé).

Classical (17-18C). – The late 16C was a period of unrest with the Wars of Religion (1562-98) and many of the châteaux remained uninhabited. The accession of Henri IV in 1589 restored peace and marked the end of the most brilliant period for the Loire. The court returned to Paris and the nobility sought to live in the shadow of the Sun King (1643-1715). Versailles was the greatest factor in the decline of the châteaux. Architecture in the valley sank into decadence. Beautiful buildings were built by architects and sculptors and decorators were brought from Paris, eg J. Hardouin Mansart and Coysevox at Serrant and Pierre le Mercier at Richelieu.

In the 17C the style became more severe and there was a striving after majestic effects. The pompous manner of Louis XIV displaced the graceful fantasy of the Renaissance and feudal picturesqueness. Pediments, whether triangular or curvilinear, became the fashion, as did domes and the Greek orders, eg the Gaston d'Orléans Wing at Blois *(illustration adjoining)*. Towers were replaced by pavilions with great saloons and monumental chimneypieces adorned with caryatids. The exposed beams of the ceilings were elaborately painted. Steeply pitched or mansard roofs were common.

Magnificent châteaux were built as at Ménars and Montgeoffroy, others were remodelled but the 18C was the great age of town planning. The projects at Orléans, Tours and Saumur included long vistas aligning with magnificent bridges, the work of Perronet, Soyer and Cessart.

Classical façade (17C)
Gaston d'Orléans Wing, Blois

Gardens and Parks

The earliest gardens belonged to monasteries such as Bourgueil, Marmoutier and Cormery where there was usually within the precincts an orchard, vegetable garden, fishponds and medicinal or herb garden. In the Middle Ages walled gardens were the norm. Flower beds were introduced in the 15C to his Anjou manors by Good King René and to Plessis-lès-Tours by Louis XI. Fountains, arbours, aviaries and menageries figured prominently in early gardens.

During the Renaissance Charles VIII commissioned an Italian, Pacello de Mercogliano, to design the gardens at Amboise and Blois. Arabesques of boxwood edged masses of flowers, clipped yew trees and fountains were common themes in these geometric or knot gardens. Chenonceau and Villandry *(illustration p 162)* display good examples of this style.

At Richelieu (1631) the garden was an extension of the building as at Versailles, while 18C Craon has a formal French garden extended by a park in the 18C English landscape style.

STATELY HOMES, CHÂTEAUX AND ROYAL PALACES

	THE LOIRE REGION	ILE-DE-FRANCE	ENGLAND
	Angers, Chinon, Loches Luynes, Saumur	Bastille, Conciergerie, Louvre, Vincennes	Ightham Mote, Penshurst Place, The Tower, Palace of Westminster (1834*), Windsor
15C	Montreuil-Bellay, Montsoreau, Plessis-Bourré, Plessis-Macé, Talcy, Ussé		Hever, Greenwich, Oxburgh Hall, Richmond
16C	Azay-le-Rideau, Beauregard, Blois, Chambord, Champigny-sur-Veude, Chaumont (décor), Chenonceau, Gué-Péan, Talcy, Valençay, Villandry, Villesavin.	Chantilly (Petit Château), Ecouen, Fontainebleau, Louvre (Le Vieux Louvre), St-Germain-en-Laye (Château Vieux)	Bridewell Palace (1864*), Compton Wynyates, Hampton Court, Nonsuch Palace (1680*), St James's
17C	Blois (Gaston d'Orléans Wing), Brissac (main building), Richelieu (19C*), Serrant (chapel), Valençay (south wing)	Luxembourg, Marly-le-Roi, Maisons-Laffitte, St. Germain-en-Laye (Château Vieux rebuilt), Vaux-le-Vicomte, Versailles	Audley End, Bolsover Castle, Chastleton House, Hatfield House, Knole
18C	Chanteloup (1823*), Menars, Montgeoffroy Valençay (Tour Neuve)	Chantilly (stables), Compiègne (rebuilt), Petit Trianon	Blenheim Palace, Buckingham Palace, Castle Howard, Chatsworth, Chiswick House, Harewood, Kenwood House, Seaton Delaval, Syon House

*Demolished or destroyed by fire

The vanished châteaux of the Loire

Bury: *Superb residence, built by Florimund Robertet, which fell into ruins.*
Champigny-sur-Veude: *Rebuilt 1508-43; destroyed on Richelieu's orders; chapel remains.*
Chanteloup: *Early 18C château enlarged by Choiseul, destroyed in 1823; pagoda remains.*
Richelieu: *Built early 17C for Richelieu, demolished after the Revolution.*
Le Verger: *Built in 1482 for Pierre de Rohan, demolished in 1776 on the Cardinal's orders.*

TRADITIONAL RURAL ARCHITECTURE

The varying regional characteristics of rural architecture is determined in large part by the availability of local building materials. For the various geographical regions mentioned see the map on p 10.

On the plateaux and bocages. – The **Beauce**, a great grain growing plain, has large farms with steadings arranged around a courtyard. Access is through an imposing doorway and the buildings include barns, machinery and livestock sheds and the farmhouse overlooking a vegetable garden. The plaster coated houses are roofed with flat tiles.

A common feature in the **Dunois** and **Vendômois** houses is a chequerwork pattern created by the alternation of stone and flint.

The long, low cottages of the **Sologne** and forested **Berry** are roofed with either flat tiles or thatch. The oldest have a timber framework with cob – a clay, gravel and straw mixture – for the intervening walls. More recent constructions resort to the use of brick.

On the plateaux between the Rivers Cher, Indre and Vienne, rural dwellings are often surrounded by clumps of walnut and chestnut trees. Flat tiles predominate in the countryside with slates more common in the towns and villages. The farmhouse can usually be distinguished by the form of its roof – with four slopes.

Between the Sologne and the Loire it is fairly common to find red brick houses with white tufa stone dressings.

In **Anjou** it is possible to distinguish three distinct areas: the white limestone of White Anjou to the east, the schists of Black Anjou, and the *bocage* countryside, namely Mauges, Craonnais and Segréen. The local blue black slates are found everywhere except in the Mauges. In the Maine limestone is used in the White Maine or Sarthe Department and granite or schist in the Black Maine or Mayenne Valley.

In the Valley. – In the Loire and its tributaries the charming flower decked houses resemble in many ways the typical vine grower's house. This one storeyed cottage has few and small windows, a beehive shaped oven for bread making adjoining an outside wall, an exterior staircase, with a door underneath giving access to the cellar. The building generally groups under one roof the communal living quarters or room, implement shed and the stable. A wistaria or rambling rose usually adorn the walls.

(After photo: Arthaud)

Cottage in the Val

Also characteristic of the valleys are the troglodyte dwellings (p 11) carved out of the tufa stone with their chimneys sprouting out from the plateau surface. Often enhanced by pot plants or a climbing vine, these dwellings usually have a southern aspect and are sheltered from the prevailing winds. Cosy in winter they are appreciated for their coolness in summer.

MURAL PAINTINGS AND FRESCOES

In the Middle Ages the interiors of ecclesiastical buildings were decorated with paintings, motifs or edifying scenes. There developed in the Loire Valley and its tributaries a school of mural painting akin to the famous Poitou school. The remaining works of this school are well preserved due to the mild climate and relative lack of humidity.

The paintings of the Loire country are recognisable by the dull faint colours against light backgrounds. The style is livelier and less formalized than in Burgundy or the Massif Central while the composition is more sober than in Poitou. Two techniques were employed: **fresco work** (from the Italian word *fresco:* fresh) was done with watercolours on fresh plaster (with which the colours combined) thus eliminating any retouching and **mural painting**, less durable where the colours were applied to a dry surface.

Romanesque Period. – The art of fresco work with its Byzantine origins was adopted by the Benedictines of Monte Cassino in Italy, who in turn transmitted the art to the monks of Cluny in Burgundy. The latter, responsible for the safe conduct and welfare of pilgrims on their way to Santiago da Compostela, used this art form in their abbeys and priories, from whence it spread throughout the whole country.

The technique. – The fresco technique was the one most commonly used, although beards and eyes were often added when the plaster was dry which accounts for the usual lack of these features. The figures, drawn with a red ochre, were sometimes highlighted with touches of black, green and the sky blue so characteristic of the region.

The subject matter. – Often inspired by miniatures the subjects were meant to instruct the people in the truths of religion and also to instil a fear of sinning and of Hell. The most common theme for the oven vaulting is Christ the King enthroned, majestic and severe, the reverse of the façade often carries a Last Judgment, the walls show scenes from the New Testament, while the Saints and Apostles are often found on the pillars. Other frequently portrayed subjects are the Struggle of the Vices and Virtues and the Work of the Months.

The most interesting examples. – Good examples of fresco painting are found throughout the Loir Valley, at Areines, Souday, St-Jacques-des-Guérets, Lavardin and especially St-Gilles in Montoire. The Cher Valley also retains certain striking ensembles as at St-Loup and St-Aignan. The crypt in the church of Tavant, in the Vienne Valley, still boasts lively works of a very high quality.

In Anjou a certain Foulques is said to have supervised the decoration of the cloisters of the Abbey of St-Aubin in Angers. His realistic style although slightly stilted in the drawing, would seem to spring from the Poitou school. More characteristic of the Loire Valley are the Virgin and Christ the King from Pontigné in the Baugé region.

There are also interesting Romanesque and Gothic frescoes at Pritz near Laval in the Maine.

(After photo: Éd. Plon)

Areines Church — Saint's head

Gothic Period. – The frescoes of the 13C still resembled those of the Romanesque period and it is not till the 15C and the end of the Hundred Years War that we see the introduction of interesting compositions which remained till the mid 16C. These were more truly mural paintings than frescoes and new subjects were added to the traditional scenes: a gigantic St. Christopher often appeared at the entrance to a church while the legend of the Three Living and the Three Dead, or three proud huntsmen meeting three skeletons, symbolised the brevity and vanity of human life.

The most interesting examples. – Mural paintings are found at Alluyes and Villiers in the Loir Valley. Two compositions with strange iconography are to be seen in the neighbouring churches of Asnières-sur-Vègre and Auvers-le-Hamon. On the borders of the Sologne the church of Lassay has a picturesque St. Christopher.

In Anjou a good style of mural painting developed in the 15C as the lords of King René's court imitated their seigneur who decorated his manors with allegorical compositions which have unfortunately disappeared. It was thus that Bertrand de Beauvau had his chapel in Pimpéan decorated about 1460 with mural paintings of a noble elegance. In the early 16C a Nativity and Adoration of the Kings ornamented the Château de la Sorinière. The Benedictine church of Cunault has effigies of saints, among them being a superb figure of St. Christopher.

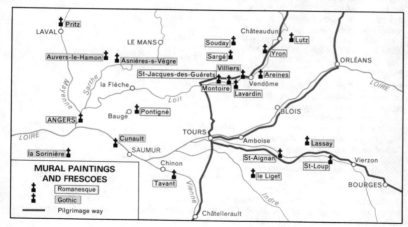

MURAL PAINTINGS AND FRESCOES
Romanesque
Gothic
Pilgrimage way

STAINED GLASS

A **stained glass window** is made up of a series of panels fixed with lead to an iron frame. The perpendicular divisions of a window are called lights. Metal oxides were added to the constituent materials of white glass to give a wide range of colours. Sheets of coloured glass were then split with a hot iron and trimmed with an iron tool or grozing iron. Diamond cutters were used in the 14C. Details were often drawn in with dark paint and fixed by firing. Often quite surprising effects and variations were obtained by varying the length of firing, the impurities in the oxides and defects in the glass. The earliest stained glass windows date from the 10C but there are now no existing examples.

13C stained glass window
Angers — Cathedral

16C stained glass window
Champigny-sur-Veude

12-13C. – Colours were brilliant and intense with blues and reds predominating, the glass and leads were thick, the subject matter was naïve and restricted to a series of superimposed medallions.

Grisaille windows were composed of clear though greenish glass with foliage designs on a cross hatched background giving a grey or grisaille effect.

14-15C. – The master glaziers discovered yellow, tones were lighter, leads finer and windows themselves were bigger. Figures were often surmounted by Gothic canopies.

16C. – Windows became delicately coloured pictures, often copying Renaissance canvases. Examples remain at Champigny-sur-Veude, Laval, Montrésor and Sully.

17-19C. – The traditional stained glass was often replaced by coloured glass paints or enamels and painted glass. Orléans Cathedral has both 17 and 19C glass (the life of Joan of Arc).

20C. – With the need to restore and replace old glass there has been a revival in this art form. Present day workshops produce to the designs of the painter glaziers, Max Ingrand, Alfred Manessier and Jean le Moal.

GEMMAIL

This modern art medium consists of assembling particles of coloured glass over an artificial light source. The inventors of this art form were the Frenchmen **Jean Crotti** (1878-1958) and the Malherbe-Navarre brothers. See the Gemmail Museum in Tours.

TAPESTRIES

Cloth hangings and embroidered panels (samplers) existed in the 8C but it was only in the 14C that tapestries proper were to become popular, being employed to exclude draughts and divide up cavernous halls. The master weavers worked from cartoons or preparatory sketches using wool woven with silk, gold or silver threads on horizontal looms (low warp or *basse-lisse*) or vertical looms (high warp or *haute-lisse*).

Religious subjects. – A luxury art tapestries represented an investment or made a handsome present. Commissions for châteaux or even specific rooms were later to find their way into churches. Perhaps the most famous 14C work is *The Angers Apocalypse* (Château d'Angers), a set of seven panels. *The Angels carrying the Instruments of the Passion* (Château d'Angers) is an early 16C work.

Mille-fleurs. – The *mille-fleurs* or thousand flowers tapestries evoke late mediaeval scenes – showing an idealized life of enticing gardens, tournaments and the hunt – against a green, blue or pink background strewn with flora and small animals. These are traditionally attributed to the Loire Valley workshops. Good examples exist at Saumur, Langeais and Angers.

Renaissance to 20C. – Paintings replace cartoons and finer weaving techniques and materials render greater detail possible. The number of colours multiply and panels are surrounded by borders.

In the 18C the art of portraiture is introduced into the tapestries.

The modern revival of this art is epitomised by the works of the famous French tapestry designer **Jean Lurçat** (1892-1966) whose great work, *Le Chant du Monde* is on exhibition in the St. John's Hospital at Angers. Three dimensional effects are part of the panoply of modern day weavers.

(After photo: Archives photographiques)

Mille-fleurs Tapestry Angers : Lady at the Organ

FAMOUS NAMES IN THE ARTS AND SCIENCES

Old France is found in the Loire country which created and cherished the ancient forms of the language. Here it is said that the best French is spoken. From time immemorial the Loire region has inspired the devotion of its native and adopted poets and novelists and as a result was the setting for many works. Many were to play an important role in the development of French literature.

Middle Ages. – Under St. Martin's influence and even later in the 6C Tours was to become a centre of great learning. Bishop **Gregory of Tours**, the chronicler, wrote the history of the Gaulish people *(Historia Francorum)* and **Alcuin of York** was invited by the Emperor Charlemagne to found a school of calligraphy. Masterpieces produced included Charlemagne's Gospel Book and the Bible of Charles the Bald.

One of the most popular works of the later Middle Ages was *The Romance of the Rose*, a poem of courtly love by **Guillaume de Lorris** (*c* 1200/10-1240). Left unfinished, the conclusion was written by **Jean de Meung** and the whole became a highly influential work in European literature. The poem was to greatly influence Geoffrey Chaucer who undertook the task of translating it into English.

Charles d'Orléans (1391-1465), a prince of royal blood and father of Louis XII, was one of the greatest of the courtly poets. Captured at Agincourt in 1415 he spent twenty-five years in exile in England where he also acquired a name for his verses in English. On his release, he returned to Blois, where he was patron of the lyric poet **François Villon** (1431-63) who was twice banished from Paris. Of his stays in the Loire one was as a prisoner in the Bishop of Orléans's cells at Meung-sur-Loire.

Renaissance and Humanism. – In the course of the Hundred Years War the centre of French culture moved with the court from Paris to Touraine and new universities were founded at Orléans (1305) and Angers (1364). These became centres of learning attracting scholars from far afield, including Erasmus and Calvin, William Elphinstone who was to found Aberdeen University and William Barclay the jurist who held the Chair of Law and died in Angers.

The humanist **Etienne Dolet** (1509-46) from Orléans was burnt at the stake for his atheistic doctrines and François I's valet **Clément Marot** (1496-1544), who attained the appointment of Court Poet, was suspected of heresy and exiled on several occasions.

Born near Chinon **Rabelais** (1494-1553) the archetype humanist writer and a physician is known for his satirical masterpiece, *Gargantua* and *Pantagruel* in which he portrays the preoccupations of the time. His native country is the setting for parts of the story *(p 75)*.

(After engraving: photo Éd. Horizons de France)

Rabelais

La Pléiade. – In the 16C this group of seven writers aimed to develop and elevate the French language, in part by imitating Classical verse. Although the undoubted leader was **Pierre de Ronsard** from Vendôme it was **Joachim Du Bellay** who in 1549 wrote their manifesto, *The Defence and Illustration of the French Language*. The others were **Jean-Antoine de Baïf** from La Flèche, **Rémi Belleau** from Nogent, Jean Dorat, Etienne Jodelle and Pontus de Tyard. All held at some time the appointment of Court Poet and their odes and sonnets celebrated their native countryside.

Classicism and the Age of Enlightenment. – With the end of the Wars of Religion and the return of the court to the Ile-de-France the subject matter tended to become more philosophical. **Honorat de Bueil**, marquis de Racan manifested a great love of nature while **Théophraste Renaudot**, a native of Loudon is known as the "Father of French journalism".

It was the Protestant Academy at Saumur which approved the earliest works of the philosopher and mathematician, **René Descartes**. The founding in 1686 at Angers of the Academy of Fine Arts was to make this a truly active cultural centre. Chambord was the venue for the premières of two of Molière's plays.

In the following century **Néricault-Destouches**, a playwright from Tours was to follow in Molière's footsteps with his moralising comedies of character. Illustrious visitors to the region included Voltaire at Sully, Rousseau at Chenonceau and Beaumarchais, author of *The Barber of Seville*, sojourned at Vouvray from where he could readily visit the banished duc de Choiseul at Chanteloup.

The Romantics. – After the Empire it was no longer the great royal palaces but the smaller châteaux which were the centres of the literary world. The pamphleteer **Paul-Louis Courier** (1772-1825) and the popular song writer **Béranger** (1780-1857) during the second Bourbon restoration were both sceptical and anti monarchist, as well as politically liberal. **Alfred de Vigny** (1797-1863) a native of Loches and one of the foremost French Romantic writers told in his historical novel *Cinq-Mars* the tale of an idyllic Touraine.

However the great man of letters of the 19C was **Honoré de Balzac** (1799-1850), a native of Tours educated at Vendôme. He made his beloved countryside the setting for some of his novels in his great fresco of French society *The Human Comedy*. His retreat was the small Château de Saché.

The 20C. – The Orléans poet, **Charles Péguy** (1873-1914) wrote of Joan of Arc and the Beauce and Chartres in particular. Novelist and author **Marcel Proust** also made the Beauce the setting for his monumental work in several parts *A la recherche du temps perdu (Remembrance of Things Past)*. **Max Jacob** (1876-1944), the poet and contemporary of Picasso retired to the calm and seclusion of the abbey at St-Benoît-sur-Loire.

Alain Fournier is famous for his novel *Le Grand Meaulnes (The Wanderer)* set in the Sologne. The Academician **Maurice Genevoix** (b 1890) described his native country through the eyes of his famous poacher, Raboliot. **Georges Bernanos** (1888-1948), an original Catholic writer is interred not far from Pellevoisin.

The humorist **Georges Courteline** (1858-1929) came from the Touraine which was the retreat of many writers of international reputation: Maurice Maeterlinck, Nobel Prize winner in 1911, at Coudray-Montpensier, Anatole France, Nobel Prize winner in 1921, at La Béchellerie and Henri Bergson, Nobel Prize winner in 1927, at La Gaudinière.

Although born in Paris, **René Benjamin** (1885-1948) adopted the Touraine where he wrote his prodigious *History of the Life of Balzac* and novels describing life in the area. Angers was the home of the Academician **René Bazin** (1853-1932), a novelist who was greatly attached to the simple virtues of provincial life and nature. His great nephew **Hervé Bazin** (b 1911), a rebel and Bohemian, was known for his virulent attacks against the traditional values of family, Church and motherhood, inspired it was said by his experiences in his native town of Angers.

Laval was the birthplace of **Alfred Jarry** (1873-1907), the author of *Ubu Roi*, considered to be the first work of the Theatre of the Absurd.

The Fine Arts. – The presence of many royal palaces and stately châteaux attracted the very best of European craftsmen during two centuries. Only a few of the many who contributed to the fine arts can be mentioned here.

Jean Fouquet, Official Portraitist and Miniaturist to Charles VII and Louis XI, was the major French painter of the Renaissance. The altarpiece, *The Pietà of Nouans* is one of his better known works. Both the **Master of Moulins** and **Jean Bourdichon** left a small number of works. The musician Clement Janequin (1480-1565) adopted Anjou as his native countryside and was for a long time head of the Choir School at Angers Cathedral.

Jean and **François Clouet** although of Flemish extraction were both Court Painters to the Valois dynasty. Their fine portrait drawings of notables of the period, including one of Mary Stuart, are of great historic interest.

Following the Renaissance there are two well known names with Loire connections – the engraver and sculptor **David d'Angers** (1788-1856), famous for his hundreds of portrait medallions of major figures of the time, and **Henri Rousseau**, called Le Douanier (1844-1910), another native of Angers and precursor of the Naïve school.

The famous American sculptor **Alexander Calder** (1898-1976), inventor of mobiles and stabiles, lived near Saché.

Science. – This is one of the traditional homes of medical progress. It was here during the Renaissance that the notable surgeon **Amboise Paré** (1517-90) laid the foundations of the science of modern surgery and among other achievements perfected the technique of ligaturing arteries. The Royal College of Surgeons was founded in Tours in 1756 and is now the Faculty of Medicine and Pharmacy.

It was also in Tours that **Bretonneau** (1778-1862) carried out his research on infectious diseases. His work was to be carried on by his pupils, **Trousseau** and **Velpeau**.

The inventor and physician **Denis Papin** (1647-1714) was born near Blois. Papin had already made his name with his work on the air vacuum and his invention of the steam digester or pressure cooker, before he was forced into exile by the Revocation of the Edict of Nantes in 1685. He spent many years in Marbourg and Cassel and then London where he died.

The physicist **Jacques-A. C. Charles** (1746-1823), inventor of Charles's Law, from Beaugency, built the first hydrogen balloon. The Mongolfier brothers, who were at the same time experimenting with hot air balloons assisted at the maiden flight of Charles's balloon in 1783 in Paris. In 1804 he married Julie who was the Elvire of the Romantic poet Lamartine's first collection *Méditations Poétiques*.

BOOKS TO READ

The Loire by Vivian Rowe *(Eyre Methuen – 1975)*

Loire Valley by J. J. and J. Walling *(Harrap – 1974)*

The Châteaux of France by Hubert Fenwick *(Hale – 1975)*

The Loire by S. Jennett *(Batsford – 1975)*

Valley of the Loire by G. Pillement translated by A. Rosin *(Johnson – 1965)*

Eleanor of Aquitaine and the Four Kings by Amy Kelly *(Harvard University Press – 1950)*

The Devil's Crown, A History of Henry II and his sons by Richard Barber *(British Broadcasting Corporation)*

Access in the Loire (Holiday guide for the disabled). Obtainable from Mr. G. R. Couch, 68B Castlebar Road, Ealing, London W5 200

Editions of works mentioned below can be obtained through public libraries.

Loire and its Châteaux by Pepin *(Thames & Hudson – 1971)*

The Châteaux of France by Ralph Dutton *(Batsford – 1957)*

The Châteaux of the Loire by Ian Dunlop *(Hamish Hamilton – 1969)*

Châteaux of the Loire by Jacques Levron *(Nicholas Kaye)*

The Loire Valley by Henry Myhill *(Faber & Faber – 1978)*

Châteaux of the Loire I Love *(Tudor Publishing Company, New York – 1971)*

The following novels have settings in the area.

Honoré de Balzac: Eugénie Grandet, Le Curé de Tours, La Femme de Trente Ans, L'Illustre Gaudissart, Le Lys dans la Vallée.

René Benjamin: La Vie Tourangelle

Alain-Fournier (Henri Alban Fournier): Le Grand Meaulnes

Maurice Genevoix: Raboliot.

Emile Zola: Earth

Marcel Proust: A la recherche du temps perdu, Jean Santeuil

Charles Péguy: Jeanne d'Arc

François Rabelais: Gargantua and Pantagruel comprising Pantagruel, Gargantua, Tiers Livre, Quart Livre

FOOD AND WINE

THE GOD OF WINE

"September soup". – The wines of France, and the Loire region in particular, have been held in great repute from time immemorial – Alcuin of York was to sing their praises, Rabelais declared that "the good September soup" was the greatest treasure of the Loire country and the *Dive Bouteille* or Sacred Bottle was the quest of his *Quart Livre*.

All wines marketed commercially come into three categories namely *Appellation Contrôlée* (AC), *Vins Délimités de Qualité Supérieure* (VDQS) and *vins de consommation*. The **Val de Loire** is one of the AC regions, a label which guarantees the geographical origin and method of manufacture. Within each region there are a variety of wines named after smaller areas, villages, parishes, châteaux, etc. *Coteaux* means vineyards.

The main varieties of vine *(cépage)* used are the *Cabernet Franc, Chasselas, Sauvignon, Chenin, Breton* and *Pineau (Pinot) de la Loire*. The term *pineau* is not to be confused with the French army slang word, *pinard*, meaning wine ration.

Local wines. – The best known white wines are Vouvray and Montlouis from the *Pineau de la Loire* stock.

Vines qualified as *breton* are a Cabernet Franc grape which originally came from the Bordelais and are now used in the region to produce red wines such as Bourgueil and Chinon. Other red Anjou wines are the Rouge de Cabernet and Saumur-Champigny with a raspberry flavour. The Cabernet de Saumur is a dry rosé. Another red comes from the Loudun slopes using the *breton* vines.

The Sancerre wines with their gunflint flavour are reputed issue of the *Sauvignon* plant. From a wealth of local wines others worthy of a mention are the *gris meuniers* from the Orléanais and the *gascon*, which are pale and have a low alcoholic content.

The Coteaux du Loir produce both a dry white wine and a bitter tasting red which improves with the keeping. From the Sologne, the Romorantin wine is light and pleasant. The wine of the Loire Valley has a delicate bouquet, tastes of the grape and is not very intoxicating.

For the vintage years see the current Michelin Guide France (Food and Wine).

The **cellars** are often former quarries, opening into the white chalk of the hillsides. The entrances are at road level, allowing ease of access for vehicles. The galleries may extend for several hundreds of metres, opening out at times to form halls which are used for the meetings and celebrations of local societies.

Wine growers' brotherhoods are similar in origin to the mediaeval guilds. Examples are the *Sacavins* (Angers), *Entonneurs rabelaisiens* (Chinon – first Saturday in June, last Sunday in September and on the Feast of St. Vincent, the patron saint's day) la Chantepleure (Vouvray), la Coterie des Closiers (Montlouis). These local governing bodies preserve the tradition of fine drinking and joyously initiate new members, *chevaliers*, to the brotherhood.

Opportunities are numerous for visiting vineyards – some even have signposted routes such as the *"route du Vouvray" (p 102)* – and inspecting cellars, tasting rooms and installations.

In the Temple of Bacchus. – Here you are, facing, as a guest, the barrels of the last vintage, firmly fixed on their stands; it is *vin ordinaire* (common wine) that runs into the silver cup as the plug is withdrawn. You admire the ruby by daylight; then the wine grower fills each glass. The glass has no foot; you will not be tempted to set it down before it is empty. *Nunc est bibendum.* This wine must not be swallowed at a draught; you must test the bouquet first, and then give a knowing glance to your host before drinking it in little sips. When you come to the end, no words of praise are necessary: just click your tongue.

From a large pocket in his grey apron the wine grower will take a huge key. A lock grates and the cellar, the sanctuary of the "Sacred Bottle", is open. The red, yellow, blue and white caps peep from pigeonholes sunk in the rock all around: Vouvray, heady Montlouis with its flintlock flavour, aromatic Sancerre, Chinon with its taste of violets, Bourgueil reminiscent of raspberries, and their brothers of Anjou, sparkling Saumur, wines drawn from Serrant and the Layon. Finally, in a place to themselves, the vintages of 1943, 1945, 1947, 1949, 1953, 1955, 1959, 1969, 1970 and 1971 – the glory of the Loire, the pride of the wine grower, so much nectar to be tasted reverently.

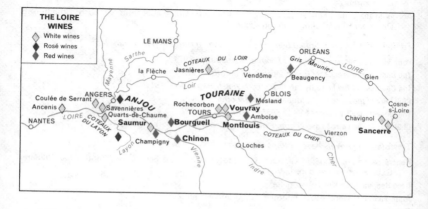

A few local proverbs

Thunder in April
Augurs a good harvest

Touraine and Anjou, the lands of
Good fruit, great minds and good wines

Shooting stars in September
Barrels overflowing in November

After the soup a draught of wine
Keeps you healthy and fine

REGIONAL SPECIALITIES

Here are some of the specialities with a selection of local wines *(see notes below)*.

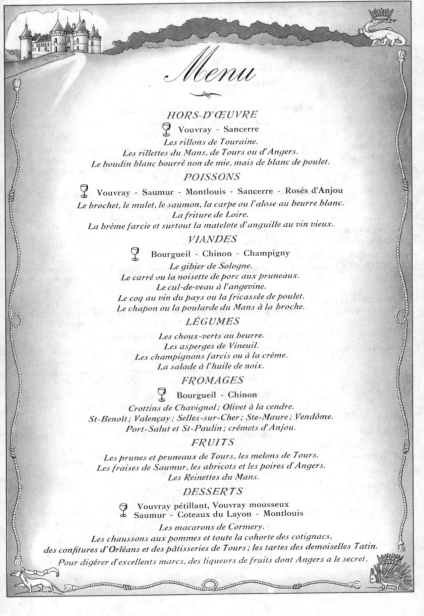

Menu

HORS-D'ŒUVRE

Vouvray - Sancerre

Les rillons de Touraine.
Les rillettes du Mans, de Tours ou d'Angers.
Le boudin blanc bourré non de mie, mais de blanc de poulet.

POISSONS

Vouvray - Saumur - Montlouis - Sancerre - Rosés d'Anjou

Le brochet, le mulet, le saumon, la carpe ou l'alose au beurre blanc.
La friture de Loire.
La brème farcie et surtout la matelote d'anguille au vin vieux.

VIANDES

Bourgueil - Chinon - Champigny

Le gibier de Sologne.
Le carré ou la noisette de porc aux pruneaux.
Le cul-de-veau à l'angevine.
Le coq au vin du pays ou la fricassée de poulet.
Le chapon ou la poularde du Mans à la broche.

LÉGUMES

Les choux-verts au beurre.
Les asperges de Vineuil.
Les champignons farcis ou à la crème.
La salade à l'huile de noix.

FROMAGES

Bourgueil - Chinon

Crottins de Chavignol ; Olivet à la cendre.
St-Benoît ; Valençay ; Selles-sur-Cher ; Ste-Maure ; Vendôme.
Port-Salut et St-Paulin ; crémets d'Anjou.

FRUITS

Les prunes et pruneaux de Tours, les melons de Tours.
Les fraises de Saumur, les abricots et les poires d'Angers.
Les Reinettes du Mans.

DESSERTS

Vouvray pétillant, Vouvray mousseux
Saumur - Coteaux du Layon - Montlouis

Les macarons de Cormery.
Les chaussons aux pommes et toute la cohorte des cotignacs,
des confitures d'Orléans et des pâtisseries de Tours ; les tartes des demoiselles Tatin.
Pour digérer d'excellents marcs, des liqueurs de fruits dont Angers a le secret.

Hors-d'œuvre: various types of potted pork; pork (blood) sausage stuffed with chicken meat.

Fish: pike, grey mullet, salmon, carp or shad with butter sauce (butter shallots and vinegar); small fried fish from the Loire; stuffed bream and eels simmered in matured wine with mushrooms, small onions and prunes (in Anjou).

Main course: game from Sologne; pork with prunes; veal in a cream sauce made with white wine and brandy; casserole of chicken in a red wine sauce or in a white wine and cream sauce with onions and mushrooms; spit roasted capon or large hen.

Vegetables: green cabbage with butter; Vineuil asparagus; mushrooms stuffed or with a cream sauce; lettuce with walnut oil.

Cheese: St-Benoît, Vendôme, Port-Salut and St-Paulin are made from cow's milk; Chavignol, Valençay, Selles-sur-Cher, Ste-Maure and crémets are made from goat's milk. The latter are small fresh goat's cream cheese; Olivet is factory made with a coating of charcoal.

Fruit: plums and prunes from Tours; melons from Tours; Saumur strawberries; apricots and pears from Angers; Reinette apples from Le Mans.

Dessert: macaroons from Cormery; apple pastries; quince and apple jelly; preserves from Orléans and Tour pastries; caramelised apple turnovers.

Liqueurs: to help the digestion there are excellent marcs and fruit liqueurs, notably those from Angers.

Marcs: pure white spirit obtained from pressed grapes.

PRINCIPAL FESTIVALS

In addition to the principal events listed below the region plays host to a variety of fairs: Anjou Wines – Angers; Four Day and Onion Fairs – Le Mans and Garlic Fair – Tours. There are numerous pilgrimages (Cléry–St-André, Gardes, La Chapelle-du-Chêne) including the unusual pilgrimage – rally to St. Christopher *(p 136)*.

CALENDAR OF EVENTS

DATE AND PLACE		PAGE	EVENT
Easter Sunday	Solesmes	144	**Easter ceremony**
Easter (Holy Saturday at 10pm)	St-Benoît-sur-Loire	133	**Great Easter ceremony**
April	Le Mans	108	**24 Hour Race:** annual motor cycle race on the Bugatti Circuit
7 and 8 May	Orléans	121	**Festival of Joan of Arc:** floodlighting of the cathedral on the 7th; religious service in the cathedral, procession, military parade on the 8th.
Whitsunday	Châteauneuf-sur-Loire	66	**Rhododendron Carnival**
Mid June	Le Mans	108	**24 Hour Race:** annual automobile race on the Circuit des 24 heures.
Fridays and Saturdays from mid June to end of July	Sully-sur-Loire	147	**Music Festival**
2nd fortnight in June and 1st fortnight in July	Anjou	43	**Anjou Festival:** throughout the Maine-et-Loire Department: drama, music, dancing and art exhibitions.
Last weekend in June and 1st weekend in July	Grange de Meslay	156	**Touraine Music Festival** with the participation of musicians of international repute
14 July	Doué-la-Fontaine	79	**International Rose Show**
Last weekend in July	La Ménitré		**Headdress Parade:** with the participation of local folklore groups. A hundred young girls in local costumes and headdresses. Further information Tel Angers 88 69 93
End of July	Saumur	140	**Military Tattoo:** including motor vehicles and horses with displays by the *Cadre Noir*
Saturdays: July and August	Cheverny	72	**Concert of Horn Music**
15 August	Molineuf	58	**Bric-à-brac Fair:** antiques and other collector's items
24 December	Solesmes	144	**Midnight Mass**
24 December	St-Benoît-sur-Loire	133	**Midnight Mass**
24 December	Fay-aux-Loges	126	**Midnight Mass:** preceded by organ recital in the church
24 December	Anjou		**The Naulets Mass:** held each year in a different small country church. Angevin folklore groups sing carols in the local dialect. Further information Tel Angers 88 69 93

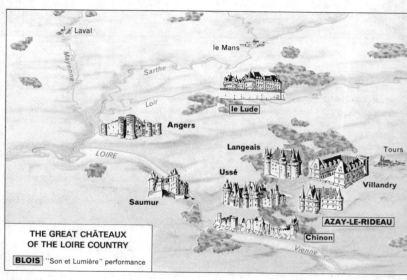

Laval

Mayenne

Sarthe

le Mans

Loir

le Lude

LOIRE

Angers

Langeais

Tours

Ussé

Villandry

Saumur

AZAY-LE-RIDEAU

Chinon

Vienne

THE GREAT CHÂTEAUX
OF THE LOIRE COUNTRY

BLOIS "Son et Lumière" performance

SON ET LUMIÈRE PERFORMANCES

This type of performance was inaugurated at Chambord in 1952 by Mr. M. P. Robert-Houdin. The history of the châteaux and their owners is presented in an original manner with the shows lasting from 20 minutes to 2 hours.

Amboise: Soirées à la Cour du Roy François Ier (Evenings at the Court of François I). – *Performances at 10pm on the 2, 4, 5, 9, 11, 12, 16, 18, 19, 23, 25 and 26 July and the 1 and 2 August; Price: 25 F.*

Azay-le-Rideau: Image de la Touraine, Symbole de la France** (Touraine, the symbol of France). – *Performances at 10pm 1 to 20 April, 26 and 27 April, 1, 2, 3, 4, 10 and 11 May and from 25 August to 28 September and 4 and 5 October; 10.30pm on 17, 18, 24, 25 and 26 May and from 1 June to 24 August; additional performances at 11.15pm from 28 June to 24 August; Price: 6F. Recorded commentaries in English.*

Beaugency: La cité des sires de Beaugency (The city of the Lords of Beaugency). – *Whit Saturday to 1 September at 9.45pm (9.30pm from 15 August to 1 September); Price: 5F.*

Blois: Les esprits aiment la nuit* (Spirits prefer the night). – *Performances at 9.15pm in French and 10pm in English on the 28, 29 and 30 March, 4, 5, 6, 7, 11, 12, 13, 18, 19, 20, 25, 26 and 27 April, and from 25 August to 21 September; 10pm in French and 10.45pm in English from 1 to 14 May and 1 to 24 August; 10.30pm in French and 11.15pm in English from 15 May to 31 July. There are no performances on the 5 and 19 July, 5 August and 6 September and on Thursdays except in July and August; Price: 8F.*

Chambord: Le combat du jour et de la nuit** (The Conflict between Night and Day). – *Performance at 10pm on 5, 6 and 7 April; 10.15pm from 1 to 14 May; 10.30pm from 15 to 31 May; 11pm 1 June to 31 July; 10.30pm from 1 to 15 August; 10pm from 16 to 31 August; and 9.30pm from 1 to 30 September; Price: 12F.*
Visit the château by night from 8pm onwards or two hours before the performance.

Chenonceau: Promenade-Spectacle nocturne (Spectacle in the illuminated gardens). – *Performance at 10pm on 23, 24, 25 and 26 May and from 14 June to 20 September; Price: 14F.*

Chinon: Jeanne de France (Joan of Arc). – *Performance at 10.45pm from 15 June to 14 July; 10.30pm from 15 July to 15 August and 10pm from 16 August to 14 September. There are no performances on Mondays and Tuesdays; Price: 10F.*

Le Lude: Les glorieuses et fastueuses soirées au bord du Loir*** (Sumptuous nights on the banks of the Loir). – *From 12 June to 6 September on Thursdays, Fridays and Saturdays with additional performances on the 13 July and 10 and 17 August. Performances at 10.30pm in June and July; 10pm in August and September.*
There are fireworks displays on Friday evenings: 3F supplement. Prices range from 10 to 35F.

St-Aignan-sur-Cher: *A new show with the participation of over a thousand people. – Performances on Fridays and Saturdays at 10pm from 1 to 31 August and in addition on the 14 July; Price: 25F.*

Valençay: Prison dorée ou les princes d'Espagne en exil (A gilded prison for the exiled Spanish princes). – *On Saturdays and evenings preceding fêtes (ie 13 July and 14 August) at 9.45pm; time: 2 hours; Price: 23F.*

It is advisable to confirm the above information by making further enquiries at the following Tourist Information Centres: Blois (Tel 74 06 49), Tours (Tel 05 58 08) and Le Lude (Tel 94 62 20). Places can also be reserved for evening bus tours to certain châteaux namely Amboise, Azay-le-Rideau, Le Lude and St-Aignan-sur-Cher. Apply to the Tourist Centre in Tours.

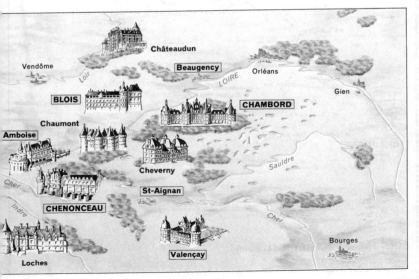

TOURING PROGRAMMES

ANJOU

Round tour from Angers via Le Mans (391 km)
Round tour from Angers via Thouars (317 km)

0   10   20 km

★★LE MANS

Huisne

Sarthe

Parigné-l'Evêque

24   D 79   Fillé   63   D 304

Asnières-s-Vègre ★   la Suze-s-Sarthe

Grez-en-Bouère   48   D 41   *Sarthe Valley*   p 139

D 28   43   Solesmes   Bercé Forest ★

Château-Gontier   Sablé-s-Sarthe   D 15   p 53

Malicorne-s-Sarthe   D 30   MAYET

l' Escoublère   23   Aubigné-Racan

2   D 78   Gallerande ★

N 162   la Flèche   D 13   26   23

Mayenne Valley   Bazouges-s-le Loir   *Loir Valley ★★*

p 115   N 23   le Lude   Loir

44   Durtal   p 98

D 191   Loir   31

le Plessis-Bourré ★   D 18

6   D 141

14   Feneu   Baugé   *Chandelais Forest ★*

ANGERS ★★★   Chartrené   Bocé

N 162   Montgeoffroy ★   p 51

★ Serrant   D 111   59   D 60

p 104   Trélazé   Beaufort-en-Vallée

15   D 952

12   Béhuard ★   St-Maur Abbey

8   Rochefort-s-Loire   D 55   66   *Loire Valley ★★★*

Angevin Corniche   D 761   90   D 952   p 104

Chalonnes-s-Loire   9   Brissac   Chemellier   2.5   Boumois ★

Beaulieu-s-Layon   ★★ Cunault   17

D 125   Thouarcé   13   Dampierre-s-Loire

66   D 83   ★★ Saumur   p 103

Layon Valley   Doué-la-Fontaine   24   D 960   Parnay   25

p 92   D 178   St-Cyr-en-Bourg   **MONTSOREAU ★**

Asnières Abbey   D 761

Passavant-s-Layon   D 69   Montreuil-Bellay ★

D 159   Bouillé-Loretz   D 938   23

26   Thouet

THOUARS

⬭	Overnight stop
⚔	Castle or château
†	Religious building
⋰	Interesting ruins
▲	Miscellaneous sights
◣ p 159	Route described on p 159

LOIRE

Vienne

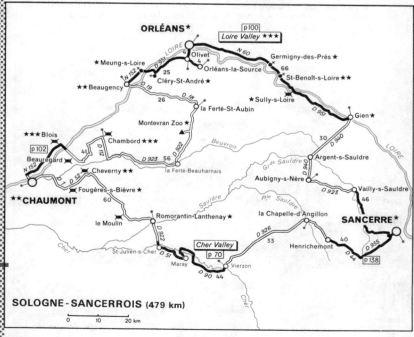

ORLÉANS ★   p 100

LOIRE   *Loire Valley ★★★*

★ Meung-s-Loire   Olivet   N 60   Germigny-des-Prés ★

N 152   D 951   25   Orléans-la-Source   66

Cléry-St-André ★   St-Benoît-s-Loire ★★

★★ Beaugency   D 19   26   D 18   ★ Sully-s-Loire

la Ferté-St-Aubin   D 951   Gien ★

Montevran Zoo ★

★★★ Blois   Chambord ★★★   30   D 940

p 102   41   D 112   D 923   56   D 922   Argent-s-Sauldre

Beauregard   la Ferté-Beauharnais   Gde Sauldre   LOIRE

N 152   Cheverny ★★   Aubigny-s-Nère   D 940

D 7   Fougères-s-Bièvre ★   Vailly-s-Sauldre

★★ CHAUMONT   60   D 923   46

le Moulin   Romorantin-Lanthenay ★   la Chapelle-d'Angillon   **SANCERRE ★**

Pte Sauldre

Cher   D 922   *Cher Valley*   D 926   33   Henrichemont   40   D 955

St-Julien-s-Cher   D 51   p 70   44   D 44   p 138

Maray   Vierzon

D 90   44   Cher

SOLOGNE - SANCERROIS (479 km)

0   10   20 km

34

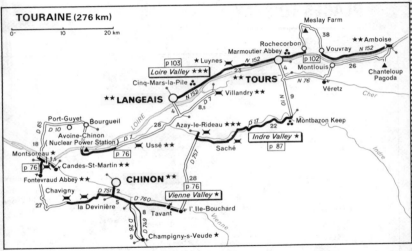

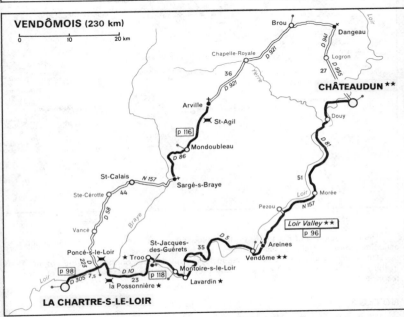

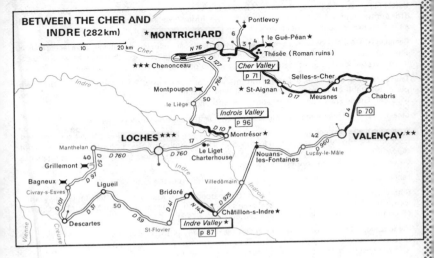

With this guide

*use the **Michelin Maps** at a scale of 1:200000.*
For coverage of this region see page three.

PLACES TO STAY

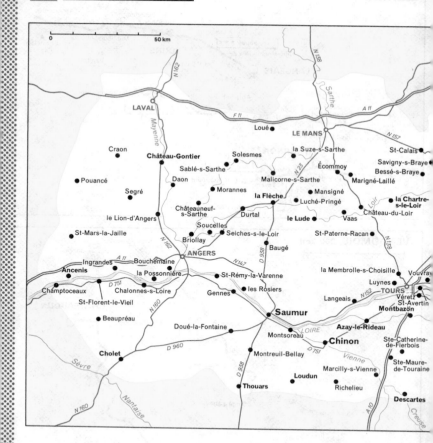

The map above and the tables on the following pages give information concerning the accommodation and leisure facilities offered by a series of towns.

The towns, whose names are shown in sepia capital letters on the maps are not included in the tables, as it is taken for granted that they have all the necessary facilities of a tourist resort.

NOTES

Hotels (H). – A selection of the town's hotels is given in the current Michelin Red Guide **France**. This annual guide gives a choice of pleasant or secluded hotels with a list of their facilities as well as the periods when seasonal hotels are open.

Camping (C). – This covers sites included in the current Michelin Guide **Camping Caravaning France**. The sites selected are classified and the individual headings cover such topics as: shops, bars, laundries, games rooms, miniature golf, swimming pools and children's amusements.

Tourist centre (T). – Local Tourist Information Centres or *Syndicats d'Initiative* supply town plans, timetables and information on local entertainment facilities, sports and sightseeing. The Michelin Guide **France** gives their addresses and telephone numbers.

Cinema (▥). – This indicates a cinema which has at least one show per week.

Swimming pool or bathing place. – The symbol ⌁ denotes a heated swimming pool; ⌁ an unheated pool and ≋ supervised bathing in fresh water. The Michelin maps at 1:200 000 *(see the layout diagram on p 3 for coverage of the region)* indicate swimming pools, beaches and bathing places on rivers, lakes or other stretches of water.

Festivals. – The most important local festivals are shown in the table on p 32.

Golf. – The following towns have a golf course open to visitors. See the Michelin Guide France for further details. Angers (9 holes), La Ferté–St-Aubin (18), Laval (9), Le Mans (18), Orléans (Fay-aux-Loges 9), Sully-sur-Loire (18) and Tours (18).

Horseracing. – In addition to the riding centres indicated in the tables there is horseracing in the following towns: Aubigny-sur-Nère, Chinon, Craon, Durtal, Ecommoy, Gennes, Le Lion d'Angers, Romorantin-Lanthenay, Saumur, Segré and Thouars.

The companion guides in English in this series on France are

   Brittany, Dordogne, French Riviera,
   Normandy, Provence, Paris.

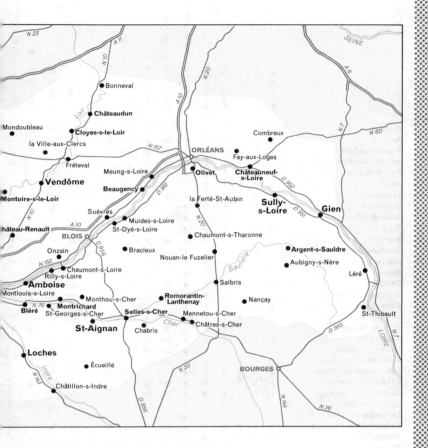

Choosing your hotel or restaurant

The tables overleaf give at a glance the facilities offered by various towns in the region. For more details, however, consult the Michelin Guide **France** which offers a wide range of information including a selection of hotels and restaurants. The listings include establishments of all classes ranging from the luxury hotel to other recommended accommodation at moderate prices. The entries also include the recreational facilities offered by each hotel, eg swimming pools, tennis courts, beach, gardens, etc.

Also included are a selection of restaurants worthy of your attention be it for a carefully prepared meal at moderate prices or with a high standard of cooking indicated by stars. The description of the latter generally indicates some of the culinary specialities and the local wines with which to accompany them.

Camping in the region

The number of camping and caravanning sites in the Loire Valley has been considerably increased to accommodate the ever growing number of enthusiasts.

Possession of a camping licence or international camping carnet is not compulsory for camping in France, but some site owners sometimes require one of these documents to be produced before granting admission.

For further details, campers are advised to refer to the annual Michelin Guide **Camping Caravaning France**, which offers a selection of the best equipped and most agreeably situated camping sites.

Planning your route

The Michelin **Maps** at a scale of 1:200 000 (1 cm:2 km) cover the whole of France. Route planning becomes easy as they differentiate between motorways, major roads (red), secondary (yellow) and other roads.

Towns listed in the hotel and restaurant guide are underlined in red and places with a town plan in the same guide are also indicated.

Other useful information includes high gradients or dangerous stretches of road, car ferries, load and height limits for bridges.

Touristic details cover such themes as: golf courses, stadiums and sports grounds, racecourses, beaches, bathing places and swimming pools, long distance footpaths, panoramas, scenic routes, State forests and interesting sights.

Those maps in this series covering the region are shown on page 3.

These publications, the traveller's friends, are all revised regularly and are an essential complement to the Green Guides.

Place	Hotels (H)	Camping (C)	Tourist centre (T)	Doctor	Chemist	River/lake (●)	Park/gardens	Cinema	Swimming/bathing	Sailing	Water skiing	Footpaths	Tennis	Horse riding (●)	Bicycles (B)
Amboise	H	C	T	✓	✓	●	✓	✓	✓	–	–	✓	✓	●	B
Ancenis	H	–	T	✓	✓	●	✓	✓	✓	✓	–	✓	✓	●	B
Argent-sur-Sauldre	H	C	T	✓	✓	●	✓	✓	✓	✓	✓	✓	–	–	B
Aubigny-sur-Nère	H	C	T	✓	✓	●	✓	✓	✓	–	–	–	✓	–	B
Azay-le-Rideau	H	C	T	✓	✓	●	✓	✓	✓	–	–	–	✓	–	B
Baugé	H	C	T	✓	✓	–	✓	✓	✓	–	–	–	✓	●	B
Beaugency	H	C	T	✓	✓	●	✓	✓	✓	–	–	✓	✓	–	B
Beaupréau	H	–	–	✓	✓	●	–	–	✓	–	–	–	✓	–	–
Bessé-sur-Braye	–	C	T	✓	✓	●	–	✓	–	–	–	✓	✓	–	–
Bléré	H	C	T	✓	✓	●	–	✓	✓	✓	✓	–	✓	–	–
Bonneval	H	–	T	✓	✓	●	✓	✓	✓	–	–	–	✓	–	–
Bouchemaine	–	C	T	✓	✓	●	–	–	✓	–	–	✓	✓	–	–
Bracieux	H	C	–	✓	✓	●	–	–	✓	–	–	–	✓	–	B
Briollay	–	C	–	✓	–	●	–	–	–	–	–	–	–	–	–
Chabris	H	–	T	✓	✓	●	–	–	✓	–	–	✓	✓	–	–
Chalonnes-sur-Loire	H	C	T	✓	✓	●	✓	✓	✓	–	–	✓	✓	–	–
Champtoceaux	H	–	T	✓	✓	●	✓	–	–	–	✓	✓	✓	●	–
La Chartre-sur-le-Loir	H	C	T	✓	✓	●	✓	✓	✓	–	–	✓	✓	–	B
Château-du-Loir	H	C	T	✓	✓	●	✓	✓	✓	–	–	✓	✓	–	B
Châteaudun	H	C	T	✓	✓	●	✓	✓	✓	–	–	✓	✓	–	–
Château-Gontier	H	C	T	✓	✓	●	✓	✓	✓	–	✓	–	✓	–	–
Châteauneuf-sur-Loire	H	–	T	✓	✓	●	✓	✓	–	–	–	–	✓	–	–
Châteauneuf-sur-Sarthe	H	–	T	✓	✓	●	✓	–	✓	–	–	✓	✓	–	B
Château-Renault	H	C	T	✓	✓	●	✓	✓	✓	–	–	✓	✓	●	–
Châtillon-sur-Indre	H	C	T	✓	✓	●	✓	✓	–	–	–	–	✓	–	–
Châtres-sur-Cher	–	C	T	✓	–	●	–	–	–	–	–	–	✓	–	–
Chaumont-sur-Loire	H	–	T	✓	✓	●	–	–	✓	–	–	–	✓	–	–
Chaumont-sur-Tharonne	H	–	T	✓	–	●	✓	–	✓	–	–	✓	✓	–	–
Chinon	H	C	T	✓	✓	●	✓	✓	✓	–	–	✓	✓	●	B
Cholet	H	–	T	✓	✓	●	✓	✓	✓	✓	✓	✓	✓	●	–
Cloyes-sur-le-Loir	H	C	T	✓	✓	●	✓	✓	–	–	–	–	✓	●	B
Combreux	H	–	–	–	–	●	–	–	✓	–	–	–	–	–	–
Craon	H	–	T	✓	✓	●	✓	–	✓	–	–	–	✓	–	–
Daon	H	C	T	✓	–	●	–	–	–	–	✓	–	–	–	–
Descartes	–	C	T	✓	✓	●	✓	✓	✓	–	–	–	✓	–	–
Doué-la-Fontaine	H	C	T	✓	✓	–	✓	✓	✓	–	–	–	✓	–	–
Durtal	–	C	T	✓	✓	●	✓	✓	✓	–	–	✓	✓	–	–
Ecommoy	H	C	T	✓	✓	–	✓	✓	✓	–	–	✓	✓	–	–
Ecueillé	H	–	T	✓	✓	●	–	✓	–	–	–	–	✓	●	–
Fay-aux-Loges	H	–	–	✓	✓	●	–	–	✓	–	–	✓	–	●	–
La Ferté-St-Aubin	H	–	T	✓	✓	●	✓	✓	✓	–	–	✓	✓	●	–
La Flèche	H	C	T	✓	✓	●	✓	✓	✓	–	–	–	✓	●	–
Fréteval	–	C	–	✓	–	●	–	–	–	–	–	–	–	–	–
Gennes	H	C	T	✓	✓	●	✓	–	✓	–	–	✓	✓	–	B
Gien	H	C	T	✓	✓	●	✓	✓	✓	–	✓	✓	✓	●	–
Ingrandes	H	C	T	✓	✓	●	✓	✓	✓	–	✓	✓	✓	–	B
Langeais	H	C	T	✓	✓	●	–	✓	✓	✓	✓	–	✓	–	–
Léré	–	C	–	✓	✓	●	–	–	✓	–	–	–	✓	–	–
Le Lion d'Angers	H	C	T	✓	✓	●	✓	–	✓	–	–	–	✓	–	B
Loches	H	C	T	✓	✓	●	✓	✓	✓	–	–	✓	✓	●	B
Loudun	H	–	T	✓	✓	–	✓	✓	✓	–	–	✓	✓	–	–
Loué	H	C	T	✓	✓	●	✓	–	✓	–	–	✓	✓	–	–
Luché-Pringé	H	C	T	✓	✓	●	–	–	✓	–	–	–	✓	–	B
Le Lude	H	C	T	✓	✓	●	✓	✓	✓	–	–	✓	✓	–	–
Luynes	H	–	T	✓	✓	●	–	–	✓	–	✓	–	✓	–	–
Malicorne-sur-Sarthe	H	C	T	✓	✓	●	–	–	✓	–	–	–	✓	–	–
Mansigné	H	C	T	✓	✓	●	–	–	✓	✓	–	–	✓	–	–
Marcilly-sur-Vienne	–	C	T	✓	–	●	–	–	–	–	–	–	–	●	B
Marigné-Laillé	–	C	T	✓	–	●	–	–	–	–	–	✓	–	–	–
La Membrolle-sur-Choisille	–	C	–	✓	–	●	–	–	–	–	–	–	✓	–	–
Mennetou-sur-Cher	H	C	T	✓	✓	●	–	–	✓	–	–	–	✓	–	–
Meung-sur-Loire	–	C	T	✓	✓	●	✓	✓	✓	–	–	✓	✓	–	–
Mondoubleau	H	C	T	✓	✓	●	–	–	✓	–	–	–	✓	–	–
Montbazon	H	–	T	✓	✓	●	✓	✓	✓	–	–	–	✓	–	–
Monthou-sur-Cher	H	–	T	–	–	●	–	–	–	–	–	–	✓	●	–
Montlouis-sur-Loire	–	C	T	✓	✓	●	–	✓	✓	–	–	–	✓	●	–

38

	Hotels = H	Camping site = C	Tourist centre = T	Doctor	Chemist	River, lake or stretch of water = ●	Park or public gardens	Cinema	Swimming pool or bathing place	Sailing	Water skiing	Footpaths	Tennis	Horse riding	Bicycles for hire = B
Montoire-sur-le-Loir	H	C	T	•	•	●	•	•	•	–	–	•	•	–	B
Montreuil-Bellay	H	C	T	•	•	●	•	–	•	–	–	•	•	•	–
Montrichard	H	C	T	•	•	●	•	•	•	–	–	•	•	–	B
Montsoreau	H	C	T	•	–	●	•	–	–	–	•	–	–	–	–
Morannes	–	C	T	•	•	●	•	–	•	–	–	–	–	–	B
Muides-sur-Loire	H	C	T	•	•	●	•	•	–	–	–	–	–	–	–
Nançay	H	C	–	–	–	●	–	–	–	–	–	–	–	–	B
Nouan-le-Fuzelier	H	C	T	•	•	●	–	–	•	–	–	•	•	–	B
Olivet	H	C	T	•	•	●	•	–	•	–	–	•	•	–	–
Onzain	H	–	T	•	•	●	•	–	•	–	–	–	•	–	–
La Possonnière	–	C	T	•	•	●	–	–	–	–	•	•	•	–	–
Pouancé	H	C	T	•	•	●	•	–	•	•	–	•	•	–	–
Richelieu	H	–	T	•	•	●	•	•	•	–	–	–	•	–	B
Rilly-sur-Loire	H	–	–	–	–	●	–	–	–	–	–	–	–	–	–
Romorantin-Lanthenay	H	C	T	•	•	●	•	•	•	–	–	•	•	•	–
Les Rosiers	H	C	T	•	•	●	•	–	•	–	–	–	–	–	–
Sablé-sur-Sarthe	H	–	T	•	•	●	•	•	•	•	–	–	•	•	–
St-Aignan	H	C	T	•	•	●	•	•	•	•	–	–	•	–	B
St-Avertin	H	C	T	•	•	●	•	–	•	–	–	–	•	–	B
St-Calais	H	C	T	•	•	●	–	–	•	•	–	–	•	–	–
St-Dyé-sur-Loire	H	C	T	–	–	●	•	•	•	–	–	•	–	–	–
St-Florent-le-Vieil	H	C	T	•	•	●	•	•	•	–	–	•	–	–	–
St-Georges-sur-Cher	–	C	T	•	•	●	–	–	•	–	–	–	–	–	B
St-Mars-la-Jaille	–	C	–	•	•	●	•	–	•	–	–	–	•	–	–
St-Paterne-Racan	–	C	T	•	•	–	•	–	•	–	–	–	–	–	–
St-Rémy-la-Varenne	–	C	–	–	–	●	–	–	–	–	–	–	–	–	–
St-Thibault	H	C	T	•	•	–	–	–	•	•	•	•	•	–	–
Ste-Catherine-de-Fierbois	–	C	T	•	•	●	–	–	•	–	–	–	•	–	–
Ste-Maure-de-Touraine	H	–	T	•	•	●	•	•	•	–	–	•	•	–	B
Salbris	H	C	T	•	•	●	•	•	•	•	–	•	•	•	B
Saumur	H	C	T	•	•	●	•	•	•	•	•	•	•	•	B
Savigny-sur-Braye	–	C	–	•	•	●	–	–	•	–	–	–	•	–	–
Segré	H	–	T	•	•	●	•	•	•	•	•	–	•	•	B
Seiches-sur-le-Loir	H	–	T	•	•	●	•	–	•	–	–	•	•	–	–
Selles-sur-Cher	H	C	T	•	•	●	–	–	•	–	–	•	•	–	–
Solesmes	H	–	T	•	–	●	–	–	–	–	–	–	•	–	–
Soucelles	–	C	–	–	–	●	–	–	–	–	–	–	–	–	–
Suèvres	–	C	–	–	–	●	–	–	–	–	–	–	–	–	–
Sully-sur-Loire	H	C	T	•	•	●	•	•	•	–	–	•	•	•	–
La Suze-sur-Sarthe	–	C	–	•	•	●	•	–	•	–	–	•	•	–	–
Thouars	H	C	T	•	•	●	•	•	•	–	–	•	•	•	B
Vaas	–	C	–	•	•	–	–	–	•	–	–	•	–	–	–
Vendôme	H	C	T	•	•	●	•	•	•	–	–	•	•	•	B
Véretz	H	–	–	•	•	●	–	–	–	–	–	–	–	–	–
La Ville-aux-Clercs	H	–	–	•	•	●	–	–	•	–	–	•	•	–	–
Vouvray	–	–	T	•	•	●	–	–	•	–	–	•	•	–	–

CONVENTIONAL SIGNS

Sights

*** Worth a journey
** Worth a detour
* Interesting

Italic type indicates natural sights
The names of towns and sights described in the guide appear in black on the maps.

Town plans		Maps		Town plans
	Sightseeing route	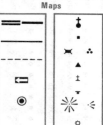	Church, chapel	
	Variant		Monument, statue	
	Walk		Castle, ruins	
	Start of the sightseeing tour		Miscellaneous sights	
	Staging point		Cross or calvary	
A Z B	Letters pinpointing a sight on a town plan		Viewing table	
			Panorama, view	
			Factory or power station	

Roads

	Motorway		Footpath	
	Major through road		Distance in kilometres	
	Road		Pass, col	
	Tree lined street		Street passing through arch, tunnel, gateway	
	Dual carriageway		Load limit on bridge	
	Pedestrian street		Level crossing ; road bridge over railway ; rail bridge over road	
	Road in uncertain condition		Railway line and station	
	No through road, restricted passage		Best parking place when sightseeing	
	Stepped street			
	Road under construction			

Miscellaneous

	Reference number common to town plans and Michelin maps	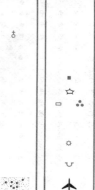	Covered market, cemetery	
	Catholic Church, Chapel		Outdoor, indoor swimming pool	
	Protestant Church		Stadium	
	Public buildings with main entrance		Golf course, racecourse	
	Coach station		Cross, fountain	
	Main post office (with poste restante)		Monument, statue	
	Tourist Information Centre		Fort, ramparts	
	Hospital		Castle, ruins	
	Barracks		Water tower	
	Public, private gardens		Tower, gasometer	
	Woods		Factory or power station	
			Quarry	
			Airport	

C	Chamber of Commerce	P	Prefecture	*D*	Local department road
G	Police station (Gendarmerie)	POL.	Police	*R F*	Forest road, track
H	Town Hall (Hôtel de Ville)	T	Theatre	*GR*	Long distance footpath
J	Law courts (Palais de justice)	U	University	*Ussé*	Reference point
M	Museum	Thiers (R.)	Shopping street	*Pop* 14280	Population
		A 1	Motorway	*Rtn*	Return, round trip
		N 57	National or trunk road		

The maps and plans are
orientated with north at the top.

TOWNS, SIGHTS AND TOURIST REGIONS

AMBOISE ★★

Michelin map 📕 16 – *Local map p 102* – Pop 11 116 – *Facilities p 38*

Amboise appears at its most picturesque when seen from the north bank of the Loire or from the bridge. The château, high above the town, has been greatly reduced in the course of the centuries but still stands proudly, its history rich in dramatic events.

HISTORICAL NOTES

The spur on which the château stands has been fortified since the Gallo-Roman era. A bridge was thrown across the river in the earliest times and the military importance of Amboise then increased *(1)*.

For part of the 11C there were two fortresses on the promontory and one in the town, all three keeping up perpetual warfare. The counts of Amboise gained the upper hand and the domain belonged to the family until it was confiscated by Charles VII.

King Charles VIII and the Renaissance (end of the 15C). – Louis XI gave Amboise as a residence to his Queen, Charlotte de Savoie. It was here that the Dauphin, the future Charles VIII, was born and spent his childhood. He was only thirteen when he ascended the throne, and his elder sister, Anne de Beaujeu, kept him in tutelage. Nine years later, in 1492, he ordered work on Amboise to begin. Little by little one of the biggest and finest royal residences, both a palace and a fortress, rose from the ground.

Charles VIII had a taste for luxury and on his return from Italy in 1495, he brought many treasures back to Amboise: furniture, pictures, fabrics and various utensils. He had also recruited a team of men of science, architects, sculptors, decorators, gardeners and tailors. Directly he returned the King ordered the master gardener Pacello to lay out an ornamental garden on the terrace at Amboise.

Charles VIII died at Amboise in 1498 after a blow on the head sustained when passing through a low doorway on his way to see a game of fives being played in the moat of the castle.

The date – 1496 – marks the beginning of Italian influence on French art. At Amboise itself, where work had begun four years earlier, its effect was only barely perceptible, but it was accentuated under Louis XII and it was at its height in the reign of François I (1515-47).

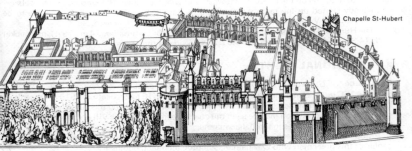
Chapelle St-Hubert

Amboise — Château in the 16C
Only those parts of the château drawn in black are now standing

The whirl of gaiety under François I (beginning of the 16C). – François d'Angoulême, the future François I, was only six when he arrived at Amboise with his mother, Louise de Savoie, and his sister Margaret, who was to be the famous and learned Margaret, Queen of Navarre. At the castle, where they now resided and in which he was to live for the first three years of his reign, the young François was given a complete intellectual, sporting and military education. This was the most brilliant period in the life of Amboise. Court life was organised and regulated. Magnificent festivals, comprising balls, tournaments, masquerades and wild beast fights, followed one another in constant succession. François I finished the wing of the castle that had been begun by Louis XII. An enthusiast for the arts, he brought the great **Leonardo da Vinci** to Amboise, where the artist spent the last years of his life and was buried.

The Amboise Conspiracy (1560). – This abortive plot was led by a Protestant gentleman, **La Renaudie**, who formed a group of Reformers in Brittany who planned to go to Blois in twos and threes. Meeting there, they were to ask the young King, François II's permission to practise their religion, and also try, no doubt, to lay hands on the Guises, who were deadly enemies of the Huguenots.

But the plot was betrayed. The court immediately left Blois, which could not be defended, and took refuge at Amboise. There the plotters were killed or arrested as they arrived. La Renaudie perished. The suppression of the revolt was pitiless.

---

(1) In the Middle Ages there were only seven bridges between Gien and Angers. Troops then moved very slowly and the possession or loss of a bridge had a great influence on operations. Towns at bridgeheads drew great profit from the passage of merchandise.

AMBOISE★★

Last phase (from the 16C to the present day). – After these terrible events the kings abandoned the castle. Louis XIII went there only to hunt in the forest.

Amboise passed with Blois into the hands of Gaston d'Orléans, the brother of Louis XIII. After the death of Gaston, Amboise returned to the Crown and served as a State prison.

In 1631, during one of the many rebellions, the castle was taken by the royal troops and the outer fortifications were razed to the ground.

Louis XV made a present of Amboise to his Minister, the duc de Choiseul *(see opposite)*. At the Revolution it was confiscated and later Napoleon awarded it to Roger Ducos, a former member of the Directory. As there were no subsidies to keep it up, the Senate had a large part of the castle demolished. The remains were damaged by bombing in 1940.

Now part of the Fondation St-Louis set up by the comte de Paris, Pretender to the French throne, to preserve the château as part of the French national heritage.

■ THE CHÂTEAU★★ *time: ¾ hour*

Guided tours 9am to noon and 2 to 7pm (5.30pm from 1 November to 15 March); 8F. Son et Lumière performances are given in summer, see p 33.

Terrace. – You enter the castle by a ramp which opens on to the terrace overlooking magnificent countryside. In the time of Charles VIII the terrace was entirely surrounded by buildings. Festivals were held in this enclosed courtyard: tapestries adorned the walls, a sky blue awning gave protection from the weather.

Chapel of St-Hubert. – This, the jewel of Amboise, is curiously set astride the ramparts and was originally the Queen's oratory. With pleasing proportions and finely sculpted decoration it is crowned by a delicate spire. The lintel is even more famous: on the left St, Christopher carries the Infant Christ while on the right St. Hubert, the patron saint of hunting, looks at a cross which has appeared between the antlers of a stag. It is the work of Flemish masters employed by the French court.

The internal decoration in the Flamboyant style is very rich. The stained glass windows which were destroyed in 1940 have since been replaced by a modern master, Max Ingrand, representing various scenes from the life of St. Louis. Human bones, including those of Leonardo da Vinci, have been transferred to the north transept.

King's Apartments (Logis du Roi). – Several rooms are graced with fine furniture, mostly Gothic, and tapestries, among which is a beautiful Oudenaarde *verdure*. The elegant Hall of States was the home for nearly five years of the Algerian leader, Abd el-Kader.

Minimes Tower (Tour des Minimes ou des Cavaliers). – This round tower, 21 m - 69 ft in diameter, is famous for its ramp – up which horsemen can ride – which rises spirally round a core 9 m - 30 ft wide. From the top, one overlooks the northern face of the castle with its Plotters' Balcony and there is a fine extensive view of the Loire and its valley.

When **Charles V** was received at Amboise by François I, night had fallen. Guards holding torches stood in line on the ramp, which was hung with tapestries. The Emperor, on horseback, had already started up the ramp when a tapestry caught fire. If certain chroniclers are to be believed, Charles V was nearly suffocated in the confusion that followed.

The Hurtault Tower resembles the Tour des Minimes but is broader (24 m - 79 ft), has thicker walls (4.30 m - 14 ft) and overlooks the southern side of the castle.

■ ADDITIONAL SIGHTS

Clos-Lucé★. – *Guided tours 9am to noon and 2 to 7pm; closed 2-31 January; 10F.*
This 15C red brick manor house was the home from 1516 to his death in 1519 of **Leonardo da Vinci**, who had been invited to France by François I. Entirely restored it is furnished in the 15C style. The chapel, on which may be seen the coats of arms of Charles VIII and his wife, Anne of Brittany, contains frescoes in the Italian manner.

Models (1952) of machines made by Leonardo are displayed in the basement showing the genius of this great man who was painter, sculptor, architect, engineer . . .

In the courtyard the small gallery, with wooden arches, dates from the time of Louis XI (15C). From the recently planted Renaissance style garden on the northern terrace there is a fine view.

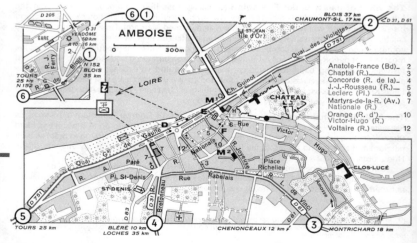

Anatole-France (Bd)_	2
Chaptal (R.)_	3
Concorde (R. de la)_	4
J.-J.-Rousseau (R.)_	5
Leclerc (Pl.)	6
Martyrs-de-la-R. (Av.)	7
Nationale (R.)	
Orange (R. d')	10
Victor-Hugo (R.)	
Voltaire (R.) _	12

St-Denis. – Mainly 12C church. The northern elevation is astonishing for the height of the nave, supported by flying buttresses and adjoined by the squat bell tower. Inside the Angevin vaulting and Romanesque capitals in the nave are worthy of attention. In the south aisle are a 16C Entombment, to the right in a niche a recumbent Mary Magdalene and in the north aisle the Drowned Woman, no doubt the work of the Italian artist Il Primaticcio, whose young wife was drowned in the Loire.

Fontaine d'Amboise (D). – This modern fountain (1918) is the work of the painter Max Ernst.

Museum (Musée de l'hôtel de ville – M¹). – *Open 9am to noon and 2 to 6pm; closed at weekends and on public holidays.*

This early 16C mansion was formerly the town hall. It contains a collection of royal signatures, a 14C Virgin and 19C paintings.

Postal Museum (Musée de la Poste – M². – *Open 1 April to 30 September from 9.30am to noon and 2 to 6.30pm; the rest of the year 10am to noon and 2 to 5pm; closed Tuesdays and on certain public holidays; 6F.*

Installed in the Hôtel Joyeuse, an early 16C mansion, the museum has important collections on postmasters, messengers and their dispatches; uniforms, **badges**, a few coaches and motor vehicles. The two ground floor rooms depict the service in the early years when horses were used while the history of the letter post is traced on the first floor, and the maritime service on the second.

St-Florentin (E). The church itself dates from the 15C while the crown of the bell tower was altered during the Renaissance.

Tour de l'Horloge (F). – Built by Charles VIII this clock tower is set above one of the town gates.

EXCURSION

Chanteloup Pagoda (Pagode de Chanteloup). – *3 km - 2 miles, leave Amboise by ④, the D 31, then take the avenue on the right, signposted, to the Pagoda. Open 1 April to 14 November, except on Monday mornings, from 8am to 6pm; the rest of the year, except Mondays, 9am to 5pm; 4F.*

This folly, a pagoda, is all that remains of a splendid 18C château built by the **duc de Choiseul**, Minister to Louis XV, in imitation of Versailles. The buildings fell into disuse and were demolished by property dealers in 1823.

When Choiseul was exiled to his estates, at the instigation of Mme du Barry, he made Chanteloup an intellectual and artistic centre. In gratitude for the loyalty of his friends he commissioned the architect, Le Camus, to build the pagoda (1775-78), following the Chinoiserie craze which was prevalent at the time. The pagoda is 44 m - 144 ft high and has seven decreasing tiers. From the top *(149 steps)* there is a fine **panorama** of the Loire Valley as far as Tours and the Forest of Amboise.

(After photo: Yvonne Sauvageot)

The Chanteloup Pagoda

ANGERS ★★★

Michelin map 🔢 20 – *Local maps pp 103, 104 and 115* – Pop 142 966

The former capital of Anjou stands on the banks of the Maine, formed by the confluence of the Mayenne and the Sarthe, 8 km - 5 miles before joining the Loire. For many centuries the population numbered 30 000.

A flourishing trade is based on Anjou wines, liqueurs, fruit and vegetables, cereals, flowers, medicinal plants and other horticultural products. The annual Anjou Wine Fair *(second fortnight in January)* attracts members of the Scavins wine brotherhood which was founded in 1905. A second solemn session is held in June for the International Air Rally of the Wines and Châteaux of Anjou. There is an active electronics industry and umbrellas and parasols continue to be one of Angers' traditional products.

The **Anjou Festival** *(p 32)*, with its many varied events (drama, music, dance, poetry, art, etc), takes place throughout the Maine et Loire department and draws large crowds.

HISTORICAL NOTES

In the 1C BC Angers was peopled by hunters and fishermen. Their chief was Domnacus, who took to the forests and never submitted to the Romans when they conquered the city.

The Normans at Angers (9C). – Repeatedly under attack from the Normans the town was taken in 867 and occupied for six years. To drive them out, Charles the Bald and the King of Brittany revived the stratagem by which Cyrus took Babylon 1 500 years before. They dug a canal above Angers into which they meant to divert the waters of the Maine. Appalled at the prospect of seeing their boats grounded, the Normans hastened to abandon the town.

First House of Anjou (10–13C). – Under the first counts, Anjou lived through a particularly brilliant period. It was with **Foulques Nerra** (987-1040), who succeeded at seventeen, that the real Angevin power was created which at its height rivalled even the Capets, the ruling house of France. Ambitious and unscrupulous, criminally violent, greedy and grasping, he had fits of Christian humility and repentance when he would shower gifts and endowments on churches and monasteries or take the pilgrim's staff and set out for Jerusalem. A great builder, he erected twenty keeps and numerous ecclesiastical buildings in Anjou and Touraine (Chaumont, Langeais, Durtal . . .).

Second House and the Plantagenets. – It was Foulques V who married his son Geoffrey to Matilda *(1)* the granddaughter of William the Conqueror. The young husband habitually wore a sprig of broom *(genêt)* in his cap, hence the name Plantagenet which was given to him and clung to his descendants.

The son of Geoffrey and Matilda, **Henri Plantagenet** married Eleanor of Aquitaine the divorced wife of the King of France, Louis VII, in 1152. To his domains which included Anjou, Maine, Touraine and Normandy, he then added Poitou, Perigord, Limousin, Angoumois, Saintonge, Gascony and suzerainty over Auvergne and the counties of Toulouse. Two years after his marriage he became King of England under the name of **Henry II** and his power formidable.

The Capet monarchy cut a poor figure beside its former vassal. What saved it in the coming struggle was the separatist spirit in the provinces annexed by the Plantagenets. Henry's reign was troubled by personal quarrels, firstly with Thomas Becket, Archbishop of Canterbury, previously his trusted Chancellor *(see windows in cathedral)* and secondly with his sons, Richard Lionheart and John Lackland, for the division of his empire. Of his reign, Henry spent a nominal fourteen years in Britain and he was to die, lonely and abandoned, at Chinon. In the end, Henri II, Richard Lionheart and John Lackland were all faced in turn by Philippe-Auguste, one of the greatest kings of France. Anjou was added to the royal domains in 1204 but England and France continued to struggle for supremacy up to the end of the Hundred Years War (1337-1453).

Third House of Anjou. – Established as a county in 1246 by St. Louis who gave it to his younger brother Charles it was raised to the status of a duchy in 1360 by Jean le Bon in favour of his son Louis. Thus from the 13C to the 15C the direct Capet princes and then the Valois held the coronet of Anjou.

At either end of this line of succession emerged two highly colourful figures, Charles I and King René. The former on an appeal from the Pope conquered Sicily and the Kingdom of Naples and dreamed of adding the Holy Land, Egypt and Constantinople to his conquests. However the Sicilian Vespers (1282) – with the massacre of 6 000 Frenchmen – brought him rudely back to reality.

Good King René the last of the dukes – one of the most cultivated minds of his time – was also Count of Provence and titular King of Sicily. René was married twice, first when he was twelve to Isabelle de Lorraine and the second time to a young bride of twenty one, Jeanne de Laval – the popular Queen Jeanne. At the end of his reign Anjou was annexed by his nephew Louis XI and he himself left Angers for his lands in the south, notably Aix-en-Provence, where he ended his days at the age of seventy-two in 1480.

It was during this period that the University of Angers was founded and it became a centre for students from many nations. The Scottish jurist William Barclay held the Chair of Law and died in Angers.

From Henri IV to our times. – It was at the Castle of Angers that Henri IV, in 1598, ended the League troubles by betrothing his son César *(p 159)* to Françoise de Lorraine, the daughter of the duc de Mercœur, leader of the opposing Catholic faction, the Leaguers. The bride and groom were six and four years old respectively. A week later the Edict of Nantes was signed ending the Wars of Religion.

From the beginning of the Revolution of 1789 Angers was strongly in favour of reform. The cathedral was sacked and turned into a Temple of Reason. The uprising in Vendée *(p 114)* began in 1793 and the town of Angers was hotly disputed by both Republicans and Royalists.

■ **MAIN SIGHTS** *time: 4 hours*

Château★★★ (AZ). – *Open 1 April to 30 September 9am to noon and 2 to 7pm; 1 October to 31 March 10am to noon and 2 to 5pm; closed 1 January, 1 May, 1 November, and 25 December; 7F; Sundays and public holidays: 3.50F; Guided tours in July and August at 11am and 3.30pm.*

The castle of Foulques was rebuilt by St. Louis between 1228 and 1238 and is a fine specimen of feudal architecture *(p 23)*. Closely packed slates are interrupted at intervals by courses of white stone. The moats are now laid out as gardens. The seventeen round towers, strung out over 1 km - $\frac{1}{2}$ mile, are 40 to 50 m - 131 to 164 ft high. Formerly one or two storeys taller they were crowned with pepperpot roofs and machicolations. The towers were lowered to the level of the curtain walls under Henri III during the Wars of Religion. The original order had been to dismantle the fortress, but the governor in charge of the operation delayed matters and by the King's death most of the building was still intact.

The buildings inside the ramparts are 15C. The chapel and royal apartments, Logis Royal, were built by Yolande d'Aragon while the gatehouse and northern range were the work of her son, the Good King René. The Governor's Lodging, Logis du Gouverneur, was altered in the 18C. Galleries were added in the 20C to house the *Apocalypse Tapestry.*

The château is renowned for its unique collection of tapestries which allows the visitor to follow the evolution of this art from the 14C to 17C.

Apocalypse Tapestry★★★. – This, the most famous piece, is the oldest and largest that has come down to us. 168 m - 551 ft long and 5 m - 16 ft 5 in high the tapestry originally composed seven sections of equal size, each including a scene with a large figure and fourteen small pictures. Woven in Paris by Nicolas Bataille for Duke Louis I of Anjou between 1375 and 1380 after miniatures by Jean de Bondolf known as Hennequin of Bruges. It was bequeathed to the cathedral by Good King René and was afterwards thrown away and eventually sold by the Administration in 1843 as a piece of no value. The Bishop of Angers, by a lucky chance, bought it for 300 francs and had it restored.

---

(1) Matilda (1102-1164) was the daughter of Henry I by his first wife. She was married in childhood to the Emperor Henry V, and was herself still childless when her husband died in 1125. As both her brothers were now dead she returned to England and was recognised as her father's successor. The Great Council of England was reluctant to acknowledge a woman sovereign, and on Henry I's death both England and Normandy accepted his nephew Stephen as king. Matilda and her second husband attempted to win Normandy and, in 1141, after a revolt in the west of England and the capture of Stephen at Lincoln, Matilda was proclaimed Queen and crowned in London. After a defeat she was compelled to release Stephen, and in 1148 retired to Normandy, of which her husband had now gained possession.

The seventy pictures which remain are admirably displayed in a gallery built for the purpose. Nearly 107 m - 350 ft long the room is wide enough to allow one to stand back and admire the masterpiece as a whole. Two fragments are in the Burrell Collection.

Tapestries in the Logis Royal. – The **Passion Tapestry*** is a series of four late 15C Flemish works which are wonderfully rich in colour. The hanging showing the Angels carrying the Instruments of the Passion, in spite of its religious theme, belongs to the group of *mille-fleurs* tapestries. Note the 16C Lady at the Organ and the fragment showing Penthesilea, the Queen of the Amazons, one of the Nine Heroines, women with chivalrous virtues.

Tapestries in the Logis du Gouverneur. – The most interesting pieces are those showing the lives of Saints Maurille and Saturnin and the Oudenaarde *verdures*.

From the castle take the Promenade du Bout du Monde, skirt the Place du Château turn left into Rue Toussaint to reach Place Freppel.

(After photo: Arthaud, Grenoble)

Angers — Tapestry of the Instruments of the Passion

St. Maurice Cathedral** (Cathédrale St-Maurice – AZ). – This is a fine 12 and 13C building. The Calvary standing to the left of the façade is by David d'Angers.

Façade. – It is surmounted by three towers, the central tower having been added in the 16C. The doorway was damaged by the Protestants and the Revolutionaries, and in the 18C by the canons, who removed the central pier and the lintel to make way for processions. Notice the fine statues on the splaying. The tympanum portrays Christ the King surrounded by the symbols of the Four Evangelists.

Above at the third storey level are eight niches containing roughly carved bearded figures in 16C military uniforms, St. Maurice and his companions.

Interior. – The single nave is roofed with one of the earliest examples of Gothic vaulting which originated in Anjou in the mid 12C. This transitional style known as Angevin or Plantagenet vaulting *(see illustrations p 21)* has the characteristic feature that the keystones of the diagonal (ogive) arches are at least 3 m - 10 ft above the keys of the transverse and stringer arches giving a more rounded or domical form. In Gothic vaulting all the keys are at roughly the same level. The vaulting of St-Maurice covers the widest nave built at that time measuring 16.38 m - 64 ft across, whereas the usual width was from 9 to 12 m - 30 to 40 ft. The walls are covered with tapestries, mostly from Aubusson.

St-Maurice's **stained glass windows**** allow one to follow the evolution of the art of the master glaziers *(p 27)* from the 12C to the present day.

The capitals in the nave and the brackets supporting the gallery with its wrought iron balustrade are remarkably carved. The gallery is supported by a relieving arch at each bay.

1 – St. Catherine of Alexandria (12C.)
2 – Dormition and Assumption of the Virgin (12C).
3 – The martyrdom of St. Vincent of Spain (12C).
4 – Finely carved wooden pulpit (19C).

The Angevin vaulting in the transept is of a later period than that in the nave. The ribs are more numerous, lighter and more graceful. The evolution of this style was to continue in this direction.

5 – Transept rose windows (15C): to the left Christ showing his wounds and to the right Christ in Majesty.
6 – North transept side windows: St. Rémi and Mary Magdalene.

The chancel, finished in the late 13C, has the same Angevin vaulting as the transept. The 13C stained glass has particularly vivid blues and reds.

7 – The 18C altar is covered by a gilt wood canopy (baldachin) supported by six red marble columns.
8 – Statue of St. Cecilia in marble is by David d'Angers.

In Rome the sculptor fell in love with a young girl, Cecilia Odescalchi, who became a religious and it was in her memory that he created this work.

9 – Chancel windows (16C): to the left St. Christopher and to the right St. Peter.
10 – Carved stalls (18C).

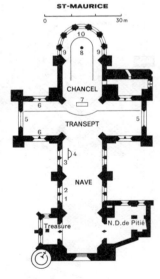

ST-MAURICE

0   30 m

CHANCEL
TRANSEPT
NAVE
Treasure
N.D. de Pitié

Note to the right the window representing the life of Thomas Becket. The modern windows of the chapel Notre-Dame-de-Pitié and the south aisle bear witness to a revival of this art which had been in decline since the 16C.

Treasure*. – *Open 1 May to 30 September 9am to noon and 2 to 5pm; out of season 10am to noon and 2 to 4pm; closed on Tuesdays, Sunday mornings and public holidays; 5F.*

Among the most interesting items are a Roman bath which served as a baptismal font for the dukes of Anjou; a red porphyry urn gifted by King René; the reliquary shrine of Bishop Ulger which was damaged during the Revolution; four silver statue reliquaries; a 17C reliquary cross made out of rock crystal; a magnificent 12C ivory horn; gold and silver gilt plate.

Maison d'Adam* (BZ A). – This picturesque 16C half timber house, overlooking the Place Ste-Croix, is adorned with amusing little carved figures.

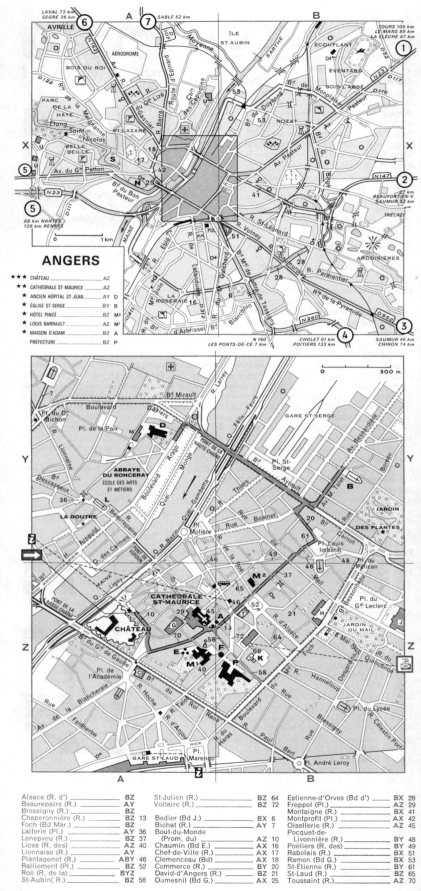

ANGERS

★★★	CHÂTEAU	AZ
★★	CATHÉDRALE ST-MAURICE	AZ
★	ANCIEN HÔPITAL ST-JEAN	AY D
★	ÉGLISE ST-SERGE	BY B
★	HÔTEL PINCÉ	BZ M²
★	LOGIS BARRAULT	AZ M¹
★	MAISON D'ADAM	BZ A
	PRÉFECTURE	BZ P

St-Serge★ (BY B). – *Closed on Sunday afternoons and on public holidays.* The church belonged till 1802 to the former Benedictine Abbey of St-Serge founded in 654 by Clovis II. The **chancel★★** is known for its elegant lierne vaulting rising from slender columns. This is a perfect example of Angevin vaulting *(p 21)*.

There are late 12C or early 13C grisaille windows in the chancel. Both the nave and its stained glass are 15C.

Take the Boulevard Ayrault to cross the river by the bridge, Pont de la Haute-Chaine to reach the Former Hospital of St. John.

Former Hospital of St. John★ (Ancien Hôpital St-Jean – AY D). – *Open 10am to noon and 2 to 6pm; closed on Mondays and public holidays; 2F.*

The very fine large hall for patients is roofed with Angevin vaulting *(p 21)*. It houses the remarkable series of ten contemporary tapestries, **Le Chant du Monde★★** *(The Song of the World)* by the painter and designer **Jean Lurçat** (1892-1966) who had been inspired by the Angers *Apocalypse.* With a total length of 80 m - 260 ft, they are striking for their intensity of colour and purity of line.

The works of Lurçat reflect his view of the world: The Great Threat, The Man of Hiroshima, The Great Charnel House, The End of Everything, Man in Glory in Peace, Water and Fire, Champagne, Conquest of Space, Poetry and Sacred Ornaments. Woven from 1957 to 1966 the last piece was finished after Lurçat's death. The final work was intended to cover seven more hangings.

A door at the far end of the ward *(ask the caretaker to open it)* leads to the cloisters and chapel. Also visible in the adjoining courtyard are the former storehouses: the lower half is a wine cellar with a spring (small Anjou Wine Museum and old wine presses); the upper part, originally the food storehouse, now serves as conference and meeting rooms *(not open to the public)*.

■ ADDITIONAL SIGHTS

Logis Barrault★ (Fine Arts Museum – AZ M¹). – *Open 10am to noon and 2 to 6pm; closed on Mondays and on public holidays; 1F.*

The Logis Barrault, a 15C building, bears the name of a Mayor of Angers. It contains the complete works of the sculptor David d'Angers (1788-1856), busts by J.-B. Lemoyne and Houdon and a good collection of primitives and paintings of the 17C and the French school of the 18C (Watteau, Boucher, Chardin, Lancret, Fragonard, Greuze . . .).

Picturesque ruins of the **Church of Toussaint** (AZ E) nearby, can be seen from the Rue Toussaint.

Tour St-Aubin (BZ F). – *Not open to the public.* This is the massive 12C bell tower of the former Abbey of St-Aubin.

Préfecture (BZ P). – *Not open to the public.* The offices are in the 17C buildings of the Abbey of St-Aubin, founded in 534 by the monks of St-Germain-des Prés on the order of King Childebert. Richly sculptured **Romanesque arcades★★** were uncovered in 1836. One arcade has 13C paintings depicting the Adoration of the Magi, and the Massacre of the Innocents.

Collegiate Church of St. Martin (Collégiale St-Martin – BZ K). – *Closed on Sundays.*

The present building stands in the chancel of a former church which at one time extended to the Rue St-Martin. Interest is focused on the Carolingian parts: sections of the walls, the round, banded – alternating brick and stone – arches of the chancel, roughly hewn interlacing and fleurs-de-lis in the right arm of the transept, behind the organ.

In the chapel to the right is a fine 14C smiling Virgin.

Hôtel Pincé (BZ M²). – *Open 10am to noon and 2 to 6pm; closed on Mondays and on public holidays; 1F.*

A graceful Renaissance mansion built for a Mayor of Angers and bequeathed to the town in 1861 contains the **Turpin de Crissé Museum** based on the painter's own fine collection. This included beautiful Greek and Etruscan vases, European and Japanese engravings, Chinese and Japanese objets d'art.

Old houses. – In the vicinity of the Hôtel Pincé: nos 5 and 7 Rue de l'Oisellerie (16C); no 21 Rue St-Laud (15C); nos 19 and 24 Rue des Poëliers (16C); no 31 Rue David-d'Angers (18C); nos 6 and 7 Rue Pocquet-de-Livonnière (16 and 18C).

La Trinité (AY L). – A 12C building with a 16C bell tower. There is a 15C polychrome *Pietà* in the crypt. *Open on Sundays and public holidays from 8.30am to noon, at other times apply to the caretaker.*

Ronceray Abbey (Abbaye du Ronceray – AY). – School of Arts and Crafts. *Not open to the public.* This was a convent for the daughters of the nobility founded in 940 and later a Benedictine abbey. Its name is derived from the finding of a small statue of the Virgin in a bramble thicket on this spot. The buildings date from the 17C.

La Doutre. – The old quarter on the north bank of the Maine has several timber framed houses: two, now restored, are in the Place de la Laiterie; five more border the Rue Beaurepaire, which skirts La Trinité Church. The most remarkable one is no 67, the House of the Apothecary (1582), which has statues of Science and Magnificence on the first floor and Friendship and Generosity on the second.

Former Abbey of St. Nicholas (Ancienne Abbaye St-Nicolas – AX N). – Now occupied by the Order of Sisters of the Good Shepherd, the monastery was entirely rebuilt in the 18C. From the front it looks far out over the surrounding countryside.

Gardens (Jardin des Plantes – BY). – Attractive gardens with a fine lake.

La Garenne Park (AX S). – *To the west. Take the Rue-Chef-de-Ville from the Place Monprofit. Open 16 March to 1 October from 7.30am to 7.30 or 8.30pm, the rest of the year from 8am to 6 or 7pm.*

This park overlooks the pretty Brionneau Valley and the St-Nicholas Lake.

EXCURSIONS

Les Ponts-de-Cé. – Pop 9 924. *7 km - 4 miles by* ④, *the N 160.* A straggling town, the main street crosses a canal and several arms of the Loire, affording some fine views from the bridges. The history of this small town includes many bloody episodes. Firstly under Charles IX 800 men at arms were thrown into the Loire and again in 1562 when the château was taken from the Huguenots, any surviving defenders were treated to a similar fate. In 1793 numerous Vendéens were shot on the island that surrounds the château.

Trélazé. – Pop 11 326. *8 km - 5 miles to the east.* Michelin map 🖸🖸 11. This town is known for its slate production, which dates back to the 12C. Originally extracted by open cast methods, the mines are now often as deep as 500 m - 1 640 ft. The shaping of the slates is done on the surface. Over 1 400 are employed with 400 working underground. The annual production amounts to 50 000 tons or 100 million slates; representing 60 per cent of the total French production.

ASNIÈRES-SUR-VÈGRE ★

Michelin map 🖸🖸 northwest of 2 – *Local map p 139* – Pop 406

Asnières lies in an attractive setting, on the floor of the Vègre Valley. Coming from Poillé by the D 190 there is an attractive view over the old houses with their high pitched roofs, the church and the residence called the Cour d'Asnières.

Bridge. – This mediaeval hump backed structure provides a charming **view★** of the river with long grasses swaying smoothly in the current, of the old mill still in working order, in its setting of fine trees and of the elegant manor with its turret and dormer windows on the right bank. Close to the mill stands a château known as the Moulin Vieux dating from the 17 and 18C.

Church. – This church with a Romanesque bell tower has Gothic **wall paintings★** 13C in the nave and 15C in the chancel. The most famous, on the inside wall of the main façade, shows Hell. On the left Christ is preparing to release the souls trapped in Limbo, attacking with a lance the three headed dog, Cerberus; in the centre Leviathan is swallowing up the Damned.

The walls of the nave and chancel evoke the New Testament cycle. The scenes on the north wall of the nave represent the Adoration of the Magi, Jesus' Presentation in the Temple and the Flight into Egypt.

Note in the chancel a Baptism of Christ, a Flagellation and a Crucifixion.

Cour d'Asnières. – Standing a little to the south of the church is a large but elongated Gothic building, with attractively paired windows. It was here that the canons of Le Mans, the one time lords of Asnières, exercised their seigneurial rights, hence the name *cour* meaning court.

EXCURSION

Château de Verdelles★. – *2.5 km - 1½ miles by the D 190 in the direction of Poillé. Temporarily closed to the public.*

This late 15C château has remained unaltered since its construction by Colas Le Clerc, Lord of Juigné. The building, transitional between the feudal castle and stately home, incorporates four greatly different towers grouped closely together round the central part of the château with its moulded windows.

The great spiral staircase is adjoined by an attractive suspended turret. The base console takes the form of a palm tree. The main doorway, surmounted by a crocketed gable, gives direct access to the great hall with its Renaissance fireplace.

AUBIGNY-SUR-NÈRE

Michelin map 🖸🖸 11 – Pop 5 545 – *Facilities p 38* – *See town plan in the current Michelin Guide France*

Aubigny's houses, with old and steeply pitched tiled roofs, line vast squares and irregular streets. The main street, Rue du Prieuré, links the château to the church quarter.

The Stuart City. – In 1423 Charles VII gave Aubigny to a Scotsman, John Stuart, his ally against the English, who was succeeded by Bernard Stuart. The latter was responsible for a reconciliation between Louis XI and his cousin, the future Louis XII. Next came Robert Stuart, known as the Marshal of Aubigny, who fought in Italy under François I.

Gentlemen and craftsmen from Scotland settled here. They established glassmaking and weaving using the white wool from the Sologne. Before the 19C the importance of cloth manufacture was so great that the town was known as Aubigny-les-Cardeux or the Carders' Aubigny. Rue des Foulons recalls the days when these craftsmen dressed the cloth by fulling it in the waters of the Nère.

As in the past, Aubigny is still a busy and active town with its fairs, its electric motor and lingerie factories and its sports ground.

■ **MAIN SIGHTS** *time: ½ hour*

Old houses★. – A number of early 16C half timber houses have survived. The oaks used in their construction were gifted by Robert Stuart from the nearby Forest of Ivoy.

The most interesting, **Maison du Bailli★**, in Rue de l'Église, is also known as Charles VII's house because of a now vanished medallion. Pass also François I's house at the corner of Rue de l'Église and Rue du Bourg-Coutant and in the latter the Maison St-Jean. The only 15C house to have survived the fire of 1512 stands in Rue du Pont-aux-Foulons.

St-Martin. – At the entrance to the chancel two 17C polychrome statues represent a charming Virgin and Child and a dramatic Christ Reviled, while in the chancel itself a 16C stained glass window depicts the life of St. Martin. There are fine 17C stone statues of the Evangelists. The fourth chapel on the left has a good collection of pastoral staffs; the third chapel to the right an admirable 17C wood *Pietà*.

■ ADDITIONAL SIGHTS

Château des Stuart. – The entrance gatehouse dating from the time of Robert Stuart is flanked by pleasing brick bartizans. The keystone of the vault is emblazoned with the Stuart coat of arms.

Gardens (Grands jardins). – Once belonging to the castle, these gardens laid out in the 17C are adorned with clipped hedges, arbours and fine trees.

Ramparts. – The three remaining round towers overlook the Mail which parallels the Nère with its various footbridges. There are views of the half timber houses and the small gardens.

EXCURSION

Château de la Verrerie. – *11 km - 7 miles to the southeast by the D 89. Guided tours 15 February to 15 November from 10am to noon and 2 to 7pm; closed on Tuesdays; 9F.*
John Stuart built this large isolated château in the 15C, near the Forest of Ivoy, in a lakeside setting, surrounded by oaks. From the southern bank of the lake, formed by the Nère, there is a good view of the castle, its towers, the Renaissance gallery pierced by mullioned windows and the chapel with a pointed spire. 16C frescoes have been uncovered inside the chapel.

AZAY-LE-RIDEAU ★★

Michelin map **64** 14 – *Local maps pp 76, 87 and 103* – Pop 2 749 – *Facilities p 38*

A tree clad setting on the banks of the Indre provides the backdrop for the Château d'Azay one of the gems of the Renaissance. Akin to Chenonceau, but less grandiose, its lines and dimensions suit the site so perfectly that it gives an unforgettable impression of elegance and harmony.

HISTORICAL NOTES

Azay-le-Brûlé (15C). – Strategically sited at a bridging point on the Indre on the main road from Tours to Chinon, Azay was fortified early.
The most tragic incident in its history was the massacre of 1418. When Charles VII was Dauphin he was insulted by the Burgundian guard as he passed through Azay. Instant reprisals followed. The town was seized and burnt and the Captain and his 350 soldiers were executed. Azay was called Azay-le-Brûlé (Azay the Burnt) until the 16C.

A financier's creation (16C). – When it rose from its ruins Azay became the property of **Gilles Berthelot**, one of the great financiers of the time. He had the present delightful mansion built between 1518 and 1529. His wife, Philippe Lesbahy, directed the work, as Catherine Briçonnet had directed that of Chenonceau.
But under the monarchy, fortune's wheel turned quickly for financiers. The rich Semblançay ended his career on the gibbet at Montfaucon. Berthelot saw the fatal noose draw near, took fright, fled and later died in exile. François I confiscated Azay and gave it to the Captain of his Guard, who was succeeded by several other proprietors. In 1905 the State bought the château.

■ THE CHÂTEAU★★★ time: ¾ hour

Château and park open 1 April to 30 September, 9am to noon and 2 to 6pm; 1 October to 31 March 10am to noon and 2 to 4.45pm; closed 1 January, 1 May, 1 November and 25 December; 8F; 4F on Sundays and public holidays.
Tickets are issued at the gate of the main courtyard. Guided tours for the château, visitors are free to walk in the gardens.
Son et Lumière★★ *performance see p 33.*

Though Gothic in outline, Azay is modern in its bright appearance and its living accommodation. The mediaeval defences are purely symbolic and testify only to the high rank of the owners. The massive towers of other days have given way to harmless turrets with graceful forms. Dormer windows spring from the corbelled watchpath, the machicolations lend themselves to ornament and the moats are mere placid reflecting pools. Partly built over the Indre, the château consists of two main wings at right angles. The decoration shows the influence of the buildings erected by François I at Blois: pilasters flank the windows, mouldings separate the storeys but here there is a strict symmetry throughout the design of the building.
The most remarkable part of the mansion is the great gable with double openings containing the grand staircase. At Blois the staircase is still spiral and projects from the façade; at Azay as at Chenonceau which was built a few years earlier, it is internal and the flights are straight.
The interior of the château has been arranged as a Renaissance museum with fine furniture and tapestries.

■ ADDITIONAL SIGHT

St-Symphorien. – This curious 11C church, altered in the 12 and 16C, has a double gabled **façade★**. Embedded to the right are remains of the 5 and 6C building: two rows of statuettes and a strange lozenge shaped brickwork.

EXCURSIONS

Château de l'Islette. – *2.5 km - 1½ miles to the west by the D 57.*

Built from 1526 to 1531, slightly after Azay-le-Rideau, the château was greatly influenced by its august neighbour.

The south front is plain with decoration limited to the mouldings, separating the different storeys and mullioned windows on the top floor. The roofs are surrounded by a parapet walk complete with machicolation and battlements. The two massive towers flanking this range are crowned by bell shaped roofs.

Château de Saché. – *6.5 km - 4 miles following the D 751 southwards to the Indre. Beyond the bridge turn left on to the D 17. Open 9am to noon and 2 to 7pm (5.30pm from 1 October to 14 March); closed on Wednesdays out of season and in December and January; time: 1 hour; 5F.*

Built in the 16C but altered later, it was here that **Balzac** wrote some of his novels: *Le Père Goriot, The Quest of the Absolute, The Lily of the Valley.* His bedroom remains as it was in his lifetime and other rooms have been arranged as a Balzac museum: portraits, manuscripts, first editions and other souvenirs of the 1850 period. The dining and sitting rooms still contain their original furniture and decorations.

More recently the village of Saché was the French home of the sculptor **Alexander Calder** (1898-1976), originator of mobiles and stabiles. Several outdoor works can be seen at Le Carroi to the north of the village.

(After photo: Sylvain Knecht)

Château de Saché

Villaines-les-Rochers. – Pop 808. *6.5 km - 4 miles to the south by the D 751 and the D 17 to the left after the bridge over the Indre, and finally the D 57 to the right.*

Wickerwork has always been the mainstay of the village of Villaines-les-Rochers. The green rushes and black and yellow osiers are cut in winter and steeped in water until May when they are taken out, stripped and woven.

Apply to the Société Coopérative agricole de Vannerie, in the centre of the village, to see the basketmakers at work and the permanent exhibition. Open 9am (10am on Sundays and holidays) to noon and 2 to 7pm; afternoons only from 1 November to 31 March; same hours during the week for workshops.

BAUGÉ

Michelin map **64** 2, 12 – Pop 3 944 – *Facilities p 38*

Baugé, a peaceful town with noble dwellings, formerly in the heart of the Anjou forests the favourite hunting ground of the dukes of Anjou, is the capital and market town of the surrounding region, a countryside of heaths, forests and vast clearings.

The True Cross of Anjou. – Brought from the Holy Land by Jean d'Alluye, the one time overlord of Baugé, this relic of the True Cross was given to the Abbey of La Boissière. It was transferred for safe keeping in 1790 to a hospice in Baugé where it now remains *(see opposite).* Initially known as the Cross of Anjou this double armed cross was adopted by the House of Lorraine, and finally became the emblem of the Free French Forces in 1940.

■ **SIGHTS** *time: ¾ hour*

Château. – *Open 1 June to 15 September from 11am to noon and 3 to 6pm; 3F.*

This much restored 15C building now serves as town hall, tourist information office and museum (arms, faience and numismatic collections).

In the 15C Baugé was one of the favourite residences of Yolande d'Aragon and of her son the Good King René. It was the King himself who supervised in 1455 the building of the turrets, dormer windows, the oratory and the intriguing bartizan on the rear façade, where the master masons are portrayed. An ogee arched doorway gives access to the **spiral staircase** which terminates with a magnificent palm tree vault, decorated with the Anjou-Sicily coat of arms.

Hôpital St-Joseph. – *Open 10am (10.30am on Sundays) to noon and 3 to 5.30pm (4.30pm from 1 October to 31 May); closed on Thursday mornings; apply to the office during the week, and to the first floor of the hospice on Sundays.*

Founded in 1643 the hospice is run by the St-Joseph Order of Hospitallers.

Berthelot (R.M.)	2	Le-Gouz-de-la-B. (Av.)	7
Clemenceau (R. G.)		Lofficial (R.)	8
David (R. A.)	3	Melun (R. Anne-de)	9
Foch (Bd Mar.)	4	Renan (R. Ernest)	10
Gaulle (Av. Gal de)	5	Victor-Hugo (R.)	12
Girouardière (R. de la)	6	Voltaire (R.)	13

The **dispensary*** with its fine parquet flooring and wall panelling has a colourful collection of faience pots from Lyon and Narbonne with Italian or Hispano-Moresque decoration.

The chapel, separated from the ward by a corridor, has a large altarpiece with a gilded wooden tabernacle, dating from the 17C.

Les Filles du Cœur de Marie Chapel (B). – *Open Mondays to Saturdays 11am to noon and 2.30 to 5pm (4pm from 1 October to 31 March); Sundays from 3 to 4pm; ring the doorbell at 8 Rue de la Girouardière.*

Formerly part of an 18C hospice the chapel is now the sanctuary for the famous **Cross of Anjou** *(see opposite).* Supposedly part of the True Cross, brought from the Holy Land in 1241, it was ornamented in the 14C with gold crucifixes on both sides and precious stones.

Hôtels. – Noble mansion houses with tall doorways line the peaceful streets of old Baugé: Rues Voltaire, David, de la Girouardière and Place Jules-Ferry.

EXCURSIONS

The Baugeois. – *Round tour of 38 km - 24 miles – about 1 hour – Local map below.* Leave Baugé towards the east by the D 141 which follows the Couasnon Valley before entering forested countryside.

Dolmen de la Pierre Couverte. – About 3 km - 2 miles from Baugé branch off to the left taking the signposted path leading to the dolmen standing in a forest clearing *(½ hour on foot Rtn).*

By car again, take the D 141 in the direction of Pontigné, which affords fine views to the right of the Couasnon Valley and the forested massif of Chandelais.

Pontigné. – Pop 299. The church is crowned by an unusual twisting spiral bell tower. Inside Angevin vaulting covers the nave while the Romanesque capitals of the transept sport monstrous heads and waterleaf motifs. In the apsidals 13-14C mural paintings depict Christ the King and the Resurrection of Lazarus on one side and the Virgin in Majesty and St. Luke on the other.

Chandelais Forest* (Forêt de Chandelais). – This is a magnificent State owned property, covering 800

hectares - 2 000 acres. The splendid full grown oaks and beech trees are replanted every 210 years.

Follow the forest road to the central crossroads before turning right in the direction of Bocé. Then take the D 938 to the left towards Cuon.

Cuon. – Pop 486. Behind the church with the curious conical spire is a charming 15C manor house.

From Cuon take the road to Chartrené. The wooded park on the left marks the site of the Château de la Grafinière.

Château de la Grafinière. – A restored but still imposing 15C building. The main avenue leads to a monument to Christ the King, standing in the park.

Beyond Chartrené turn left to the D 60. After 4.5 km - 3 miles follow the D 211 to your right, crossing heaths and woodlands, to reach Fontaine-Guérin.

Fontaine-Guérin. – Pop 587. The belfry of the much altered Romanesque church is crowned by a twisting spire. Inside the 15C roof is decorated with 126 colourful painted panels.

Follow the Couasnon Valley, taking the D 144 in the direction of Le Vieil-Baugé and passing within sight of the ruins of the Château de la Tour de Pin.

Le Vieil-Baugé. – Pop 1 097. Site of a battle in 1421 when the English were defeated by an Angevin army supported by Scottish mercenaries lead by John, the Earl of Buchan, who was later rewarded with the baton of High Constable of France. Dominating the valley from its hilltop position the town is renowned for the curiously twisting and leaning spire of its church. The choir is 13C with Angevin vaulting while the façade adorned with pilasters and the south transept arm with its coffered ceiling are both Renaissance, by Jean de Lespine.

La Boissière. – *22 km - 14 miles to the east via the D 766 and the D 767. Description p 108.* The chapel was originally built to house the True Cross of Anjou *(see opposite).*

Jarzé; Montplacé. – *Round tour of 20 km - 12 miles – about ½ hour.* Leave Baugé to the northwest by the D 766.

Jarzé. – Pop 1 331. In the one time domain of Jean Bourré *(p 127),* Jarzé's former collegiate church is in the Flamboyant style. The stalls in the chancel have amusingly historiated cheekpieces, while the seigneurial chapel to the right is covered with lierne and tierceron vaulting. The 15C statuette in a recess on the last pillar before the chancel probably represents the son of Jean Bourré holding a pear, recalling that his father introduced the good Christian pear into Anjou *(p 12).*

4 km - 2½ miles from Jarzé on the road to La Flèche, the D 82, turn right.

Notre-Dame de Montplacé Chapel. – Standing in a beautiful setting, this chapel has a remarkable doorway. Intricately sculpted details show the Instruments of the Passion on the door panels, cherubs supporting a coat of arms, crowned by a 17C Virgin – the whole adorned with fruit, garlands, etc. Fine view of Jarzé and its surrounding countryside.

Once a walled and fortified town, Beaugency remains a picture of the Middle Ages in its green and pleasant riverside setting.

It is the venue for annual drama and music festivals *(p 32)*.

The Two Councils of Beaugency (12C). – It is curious that both should have had to deal with difficulties in the royal families. The First Council (1104) excommunicated **Philippe I** who had repudiated the Queen and abducted and married Bertrade, the wife of the Count of Anjou. After his reconciliation with the Church, Philippe was buried at the Abbey of St-Benoît *(p 133)*.

The Second Council (1152) annulled the marriage of **Louis VII** with **Eleanor of Aquitaine**. The King accused the Queen of misconduct; the Queen alleged her own consanguinity with her husband to a degree forbidden by the Church. This was one of the great events of the Middle Ages; later, the Queen was to marry again with Henry Plantagenet, the future King Henry II of England. Eleanor's dowry, almost all of southwestern France, then passed under English rule.

A disputed town. – Beaugency commanded the only bridge that crossed the Loire between Blois and Orléans before modern times. For this reason the town was often attacked *(see note 1 p 41)*. During the Hundred Years War (1337-1453) it fell into English hands four times: in 1356, 1412, 1421 and 1428. It was delivered by Joan of Arc in 1429.

The town was then caught up in the turmoil of the Wars of Religion (1562-98). Leaguers and Protestants held it by turns. At the time of the fire started by the Huguenots in 1567, the abbey was burnt down, the roof of Notre-Dame collapsed and so did that of the keep.

■ **MAIN SIGHTS** time: 1½ hours

Start from the **Place St-Firmin** or the **Place Dunois** which together form a picturesque area. At night this quarter is lit by old street lamps that give it a particular charm.

Tour St-Firmin. – This tower is all that remains of a 16C church destroyed during the Revolution. A street used to pass under the tower. To the right is the former hospice, Villa Notre-Dame. Open the door a little way to get a glimpse of the charming courtyard.

Keep★ (Donjon). – This is a fine example of 11C military architecture. At the time, keeps were rectangular and supported by buttresses, becoming circular later. This one is impressively massive. The five storeys of the interior are in ruins.

Château. – *Guided tours from 9 to 11.30am and 2 to 6pm (4pm from 1 October to 15 March); closed on Tuesdays out of season; 4F.* Son et Lumière *performance see p 33*.

BEAUGENCY

Abbaye (R. de l')	2
Cordonnerie (R.)	4
Dr Hyvernaud (Pl.)	5
Dunois (Pl.)	6
Maille-d'Or (R.)	7
Martroi (Pl. du)	
Pont (R. du)	
Prateau (R. du)	9
Sirène (R. de la)	10

Built in the 15C by Dunois, Joan of Arc's companion, the château now contains a **regional museum** with collections of costumes, headdresses, waistcoats and furniture of the Orléans district. Other sections deal with souvenirs of local celebrities, the Loire bridges, local wines, childhood and toys (antique dolls).

Notre-Dame. – This was built in the 12C as the church to the former abbey and it was here that the Councils deliberated. To replace the Romanesque vaulting destroyed by fire, false Gothic vaulting of wood was painted to look like stone. However, placed too low, it has spoilt the building's proportions.

Go beneath an archway between the château and the church. Bear right into the Rue du Pont and right again to reach the Quai de l'Abbaye.

You will pass in front of the 18C **Abbey of Notre-Dame** (B), which used to be served by Augustinian Canons and is now partly turned into a hotel. You will then come to the **Tour du Diable** (D), which was part of the fortifications protecting the bridgehead. In the Middle Ages the Loire washed around the foot of the tower.

■ **ADDITIONAL SIGHTS**

Hôtel de Ville (H). – *Apply to the caretaker, from 9am to noon and 2 to 6pm; closed on Mondays; 1.50F.* This pretty but restored Renaissance building looks out over the square that was once the Dunois tennis court. In the council chamber are eight embroidered **hangings★** dating from the 17C and originally from the Abbey of Notre-Dame.

Tour de l'Horloge (E). – The tower was a gateway in the 12C city wall.

Maison des Templiers (F). – Interesting Romanesque windows.

Petit Mail. – Dominating the Loire the Little Mall planted with large trees affords a beautiful view over the valley.

Porte Tavers (K). – Formerly part of the old city wall.

BELLEGARDE

Michelin map 🔢 1 – Pop 1 479

Lying in the midst of a fertile countryside of grain fields, market gardens and rose nurseries, Bellegarde groups its houses round a vast square. Formerly known as Choisy-aux-Loges it was renamed in 1645 when it was bought by the Duke of Bellegarde.

Château. – This 14C keep quartered with bartizans is still surrounded by a moat. The brick pavilions with stone dressings, beyond the moat, were intended to lodge staff and guests. The pavilion to the right of the gate, now the town hall, has a fine room with Regency panelling *(to visit apply to the town hall, Tel 95 10 03)*.

The stables are decorated with three horses' heads on the pediment by Coysevox.
Turn left to reach the Place du Marché and the church.

Church. – This Romanesque building has a delightfully harmonious façade. The decoration of the central doorway is interesting: torsaded and ringed engaged piers support sculptured capitals depicting fantastic animals and foliage. In the wide nave there is a collection of 17C **paintings:** Annibale Carracci's *St. Sebastian;* Lebrun's *Descent from the Cross;* Mignard's *St. John the Baptist* with the infant Louis XIV as St. John.

EXCURSION

Boiscommun. – Pop 679. *7.5 km - 5 miles to the northwest by the D 44.*

Of the castle only two towers and other ruins remain and these can be seen from the path which now follows the line of the former moat.

The **church** with its Romanesque doorway has a Gothic nave with a majestic elevation. It is relatively easy to discern the different periods of construction by looking at the changes in the capitals, the form of the high windows and openings of the triforium. At the end of the aisle, above the sacristy door, is a 12C stained glass window showing the Virgin and Child. On leaving, glance at the organ loft, ornamented with eight painted figures (16C) in costumes of the period.

BERCÉ Forest ★

Michelin map 🔢 4

The Bercé Forest is all that remains of the once immense natural Forest of Le Mans which formerly extended from the Sarthe to the Loir. The 5 442 hectares - 21 sq miles cover a plateau incised by small valleys. This state owned forest comprises pines to the west, the remainder being a mixture of oak and beech trees. It is exploited for quality oak which yields a pale yellow wood with a fine grain much in demand for veneering and for export.

ROUND TOUR IN THE BERCÉ FOREST
53 km - 33 miles – about 1½ hours

Forest recreational areas include parking facilities, picnic places and shelters.

St-Vincent-du-Lorouër. – The priory church has a pretty Renaissance façade carved out of tufa stone.

The D 96 between St-Vincent and Pruillé-l'Eguillé, affords good views over the forest.

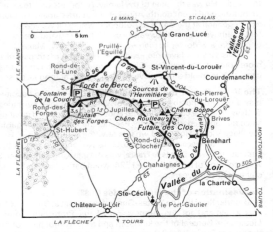

Fontaine de la Coudre. – *Car park.* This is the source of the Dinan, a tributary of the Loir. It is to be found amidst the tall oaks of the stand known as the Futaie des Forges.

Sources de l'Hermitière. – *Car park.* Resurgent springs in wooded glade.

Futaie des Clos★. – This, the finest stand in the forest, contains great soaring oaks, many of which are at least 340 years old.

Go on foot to see these patriarchs of the forest; both oaks: chêne Boppe, now only a stump protected by a roof, was felled by lightning in 1939 at the venerable age of 262; nearby is chêne Roulleau, 43 m - 141 ft tall and a mere 340 years old.

Château de Bénéhart. – A fine rusticated doorway pierces an elegant façade. Two round towers flank the staircase turret and the dormer windows are crowned by sculpted pediments.

The Veuve Valley (Vallée de la Veuve). – Between Bénéhart and St-Vincent, poplars and willows mark out the river's course. On the vineyard covered slopes (cellars are dug out of the tufa stone) stand several charming 16C manor houses, note in particular Follet, not far from St-Pierre, with its corner turrets and sculpted dormer windows.

ÉTANGSORT VALLEY★ (Vallée de l'Étangsort)
3.5 km - 2 miles from Brives to Courdemanche via the D 64 – Local map above

Especially attractive in its upper reaches this green valley has its slopes strewn in places with vast blocks of sandstone. Poplars and willows mark the river course and meadows are partitioned by hedges. Half way up terraced farmsteads are surrounded by a patchwork of enclosed fields while woodland crowns the valley sides. Here and there are attractively flower decked villages.

Courdemanche. – Pop 674. The church, with a harmonious Renaissance doorway, has a stained glass window representing the Crucifixion in the north aisle. The crypt is covered with a 17C coffered ceiling and has a 17C Last Supper on wood.

BERCÉ Forest★

LE GRAND-LUCÉ
5 km - 3 miles from St-Vincent-du-Lorouër via the D 304 – Pop 1 890 – Local map p 53

This is a pleasantly situated market town.

Church. – Inside the columns rise to the vaulting ribs uninterrupted by capitals. This is a characteristic feature of the Flamboyant style *(p 22)*. A 16C Crucifix is placed on the high altar.

Château. *– Apply to the caretaker's house to visit the park and exterior of the château*. This elegant, pedimented building now houses a medical centre. An oval courtyard overlooks the landscaped park with its noble perspectives.

The times indicated in this guide
when given with the distance allow one to enjoy the scenery
when given for sightseeing are intended to give an idea of
the possible brevity or length of a visit.

BLOIS ★★★
Michelin map **64** 7 – *Local map p102* – Pop 51 950

Blois is the business centre of a farming district, the chief products of which are wheat, wine, strawberries, bulbs and vegetables. Foremost among the last is asparagus, which was first planted about 1870 on the south bank of the Loire, at Vineuil and Saint-Claude, and has since spread towards Contres and the Sologne wherever the soil is light and fertile. The industry round Blois is mainly concerned with the manufacture of chocolate.

The pride of Blois is the château which illustrates the art and history of the whole district.

HISTORICAL NOTES

A charmer: Louis d'Orléans (1372-1407). – Blois is one of the bridgeheads which played such an important part in the Middle Ages. In the early times a powerful county was established over the town and district of Blois. In 1391 the county was bought by Louis, Duke of Orléans, the brother of Charles VI. During the latter's periodic fits of madness, Louis was involved in the power struggle with the dukes of Burgundy, and in 1407 he was assassinated in Paris by order of the Duke of Burgundy, John the Fearless. Louis's widow, Valentina Visconti, retired to Blois and carved on its walls the disillusioned motto: *Plus ne m'est rien, rien ne m'est plus* (Nothing means anything to me any more). She died, inconsolable, the following year.

A poet: Charles d'Orléans (1391-1465). – Charles, the eldest son of Louis d'Orléans, inherited the castle. He was the poet of the family. At the age of fifteen he married the daughter of Charles VI, but she died in childbirth. At twenty he married again. He went to fight the English and proved a poor general at the Battle of Agincourt where he was taken prisoner, but his poetic gift helped him to survive twenty-five years of captivity in England. He returned to France in 1440, and being once more a widower he married, at the age of fifty, Marie de Clèves, who was then fourteen.

Blois was his favourite residence. He demolished part of the grim old fortress and built a more comfortable mansion. Charles formed a little court of artists and men of letters. Great joy came to him in old age: at seventy-one he had at long last a son and heir, the future Louis XII.

The Versailles of the Renaissance (16C). – Having become a royal residence, Blois was to play a part comparable with that of Versailles in later centuries. **Louis XII** and his wife, **Anne of Brittany**, liked the castle. The King added a wing and had great terraces and gardens, which have since disappeared, designed by Pacello, the Italian master gardener of Amboise. These covered the Place Victor-Hugo and what is now the station quarter.

In 1515 **François I** succeeded Louis XII, and it is to him that we owe the finest part of the château. His wife, **Claude de France**, was the late King's daughter. She was brought up at Blois and was very fond of it. She died in 1524, when barely twenty-five, after having given the King seven children in eight years.

Assassination of the duc de Guise (1588). – The historical interest of the château reached its peak under **Henri III**. The States-General twice met at Blois. The first time was in 1576, when there was a demand for the suppression of the Protestant Church. In 1588 **Henri de Guise**, the Lieutenant-General of the kingdom and all powerful head of the League in Paris, supported by the King of Spain, forced Henri III to call a second meeting of the States-General, which was then the equivalent of Parliament. Five hundred deputies, nearly all supporters of Guise, attended. Guise expected them to depose the King. The latter, feeling himself to be on the brink of the abyss, could think of no other means than murder to get rid of his rival. The killing took place in the château itself, on the second floor. Eight months later Henri III himself succumbed to the dagger of Jacques Clément.

In 1617 **Marie de' Medici** was banished to Blois by her son, Louis XIII. After two years of gilded captivity the Queen Mother escaped. Although she was stout, she was lowered by night on a rope ladder into the moat. After this exploit there was a reconciliation between mother and son.

A conspirator: Gaston d'Orléans (1608-60). – In 1626 Louis XIII, to get rid of his brother, Gaston d'Orléans, granted him the county of Blois. He tried to keep that perpetual conspirator at a distance by persuading him to rebuild the château with his financial aid. Gaston d'Orléans asked the great architect François Mansart (1598-1666 – generally considered to be the originator of the great "mansard" or curb roof) to draw up plans for a huge building to take the place of its predecessor.

Work went on busily at Blois for three years. Then the future Louis XIV was born and the prospect of ascending the throne grew dim for Gaston. Richelieu thought it unnecessary to humour him any longer: he cut off subsidies and the building slowed down. For the last years of his life the conspirator, now tamed, used the François I Wing. He embellished the gardens, made a collection of rare plants and died an exemplary death surrounded by his little court.

■ THE CHÂTEAU ★★★ *time: 1½ hours*

Guided tours 9am to noon and 2 to 6.30pm (5.30pm from 1 February to 15 March; 5pm from 1 October to 31 January); closed 1 January and 25 December; audiovisual presentation; 8F includes the St-Saturnin Cemetery.
Son et Lumière★ *performance see p 33.*

Enter the Place du Château by the ramp and, starting from the Place Victor-Hugo, go round the building to the left. Park your car in the Place du Château.

(After photo: Cie Aérienne Française)

Château de Blois

Feudal period :
1 Salle des États (13C) ; 2 Tour du Foix (13C)
Gothic-Renaissance transitional period :
3 Charles d'Orléans Gallery (late 15-early 16C) ;
4 St-Calais Chapel (1498-1503) ; 5 Louis XII Wing (1498-1503)
Renaissance period :
6 François I Wing : Façade des Loges (1515-1524)
Classical period :
7 Gaston d'Orléans Wing (1635-1638)

Place du Château Façade. – This consists of two very different parts: on the extreme right the Chamber of States (1) is a relic of the former feudal castle; in the centre and on the left is the pretty building of brick and stone erected by Louis XII (5). The latter building shows no symmetry and openings were still placed according to the amiable whims of the Middle Ages.

Two windows on the first floor have balconies. The one on the left opened from Louis XII's bedroom. His Minister, Cardinal d'Amboise, lived in the nearby house, which was destroyed in June 1940 and has since been rebuilt with only moderate success. When the King and the Cardinal took the air on their balconies they could chat together. The great Flamboyant gateway is surmounted by an alcove containing a modern copy of an equestrian statue of Louis XII. The windows' consoles are adorned with spirited carvings. The coarse humour of the period is sometimes displayed with great candour (first and fourth windows to the left of the gateway).

To the right of the façade a short flight of steps leads to an attractive chamber with ogive vaulting.

The inner courtyard. – Cross the courtyard to reach the delightful terrace (good **view** of St-Nicolas Church and the Loire) on which stands the **Tour du Foix** (2) which formed part of the mediaeval wall.

Return to the courtyard which is lined with buildings from every period – Gothic, Renaissance and Classical – which, together, make up the château, one of the great sights of the Loire valley.

St-Calais Chapel (4). – Of the King's private chapel which was rebuilt by Louis XII, only the chancel remains. Mansart demolished the nave when he built the Gaston d'Orléans Wing. The modern stained glass windows are by Max Ingrand.

Charles d'Orléans Gallery (3). – Although called Charles d'Orléans it is probable that this gallery dates from the Louis XII period. Till the alterations in the 19C this gallery was twice its present length and connected the two wings at either end of the courtyard. Note the unusual basket-handle arches.

Louis XII Wing (5). – The corridor or gallery serving the various rooms in the wing marks a step forward in the search for more comfort and convenience. Originally rooms opened on to one another. At each end of the wing a spiral staircase gave access to the different floors. The decoration is richer and Italianate panels of arabesques adorn the pillars.

François I Wing (6). – The building extends between the 17C Gaston d'Orléans Wing and the 13C feudal hall, Salle des États (1). Only twelve years passed between the completion of the Louis XII Wing and the commencement of the François I Wing, but the progress made was important. It meant the triumph of the Italian decorative style.

French caprice, however, persisted in the general plan. The windows were made to correspond with the internal arrangement of the rooms, without regard for symmetry; they were sometimes close together, sometimes far apart; their mullions were sometimes double, sometimes single; and pilasters sometimes flanked the window openings, sometimes occupied the middle of the bay.

Château de Blois — François I staircase

A magnificent **staircase** was added to the façade and it was to be the first of a series. Since Mansart demolished part of the wing to make room for the Gaston d'Orléans building, this staircase is no longer in the centre of the façade. It climbs spirally in an octagonal well, three faces of which are embedded in the wall. This masterpiece of architecture and sculpture was evidently designed for great receptions. The well is open between the buttresses and forms a series of balconies from which members of the court could watch the arrival of important people. The guards who saluted the guests stood on these balconies.

The decoration is varied and elaborate. The royal insignia are used together with all the customary themes of the Renaissance (p 23).

Gaston d'Orléans Wing (7). – This range by François Mansart in the Classical style, is in sharp contrast to the rest of the building. Seen from the inner courtyard the comparison with the other façades is unfavourable. To judge Mansart's work fairly it must be seen from outside the château and imagined in the context of the original design. The proposed building would have occupied not only the site of the château but also the square and it would have been linked with the forest by a series of terraces occupying the present station quarter.

Royal Apartments in the François I Wing. – You climb the François I staircase to reach the first floor where the guide shows various rooms in detail, some containing splendid fireplaces. The rooms unfortunately are not all furnished. The interior decoration was restored by Duban (19C) and the effect is now almost too gorgeous. In bygone times smoke from the great fireplaces, candles and torches quickly toned down the décor.

First floor. – The most interesting room is that of Catherine de' Medici. It still has its 237 carved wood panels concealing secret cupboards which may have been used to hide poisons, jewels or State papers or may have been made in accordance with the practice of having wall cupboards in Italian style rooms. They were opened by pressing a pedal concealed in the skirting board.

Second floor. – This is the scene of the murder of the duc de Guise. The rooms have been altered and the King's study is now included in the Gaston d'Orléans Wing. It is therefore, rather difficult to follow the phases of the assassination on the spot.

After the murder Henri III went down to his mother, Catherine de' Medici, and told her joyfully: "I no longer have a colleague, the King of Paris is dead!" "God grant", replied Catherine, "that you have not become the King of Nothing at All!" Untroubled by his conscience, the King went to hear Mass in the St-Calais Chapel.

The next day the Duke's brother, Cardinal de Lorraine, who had been thrown into gaol directly after the murder, was assassinated. His body was left with that of Guise in the Cabinet neuf, before being burnt and the ashes thrown into the Loire.

Salle des États (1). – This is the oldest part of the château and served as the council hall or great hall – the equivalent of Westminster Hall – to the counts of Blois. The States-General of 1576 and 1588 were held here.

The apartments in the Louis XII Wing. – A fine arts museum is installed on the first floor. It consists of seven rooms and two galleries and contains furniture, paintings and other objets d'art dating from the 16C to the present day. Note also the fragments of frescoes which have been uncovered on some of the walls. The religious art museum on the ground floor is temporarily awaiting transfer

■ WALK ROUND THE CHATEAU★★ time: ½ hour

To get a better idea of the site of the château and to appreciate to the full its outer façades, walk round the outside following the itinerary given. Start from the Place du Château.

Place du Château. – Originally the feudal forecourt it was enclosed by the wall. At the far end of the square stood the Church of St-Sauveur which was destroyed in the 19C.

It was here in 1429 while on her way to Orléans (p 16) that Joan of Arc had her standard blessed by the Archbishop of Reims. Wishing to do battle with troops in a state of grace, Joan dismissed the loose women who followed the soldiers everywhere and made her troops take Communion.

Take the staircase which goes down to the left of the château and turn right into the Rue St-Lubin (note the old houses – nos 36 and 38) then turn right again into the Rue des Fossés-du-Château. Take the stairway on the left up to the counterscarp (contrescarpe).

Gaston d'Orléans Wing. – Good views of this wing on its own can be had from the moat and the counterscarp (contrescarpe). Its Classical style now avoids direct comparison with the gay and lively Renaissance façades and its spacious dignity is better appreciated.

Before returning to the Place Victor-Hugo you should go up to the small terrace garden.

From the terrace there is an excellent **view★** of the upper town grouped round the cathedral and of the François I Wing or Façade des Loges in the near foreground.

The François I Wing or the Façade des Loges (6). – The original wing overlooked the courtyard and had no outlook on the town side as it was backed against the feudal wall. It was François I who decided to extend on the town side of the wall, supporting the construction on a stone foundation. The result was the typically Italian loggia front known as the Façade des Loges.

It is the arrangement of two storeys of loges surmounted by a gallery which gives this wing an aspect so different from the other parts of the château. It strongly resembles certain Italian palaces. But here again the asymmetry of the windows – corresponding exclusively to an internal arrangement of rooms – watch towers, balconies and pilasters is typically French. There is an impressive line of gargoyles at roof level.

Also visible from the terrace is the **Pavillon d'Anne de Bretagne** (B) to the left of the square. This building originally stood isolated in the gardens of the château and it was to a small oratory abutting this pavilion that Louis XII and his Queen, Anne of Brittany, came to pray for a son.

The **Church of St-Vincent** (D) bordering the square was built during the 17C in the Classical or Jesuit style.

Go down to the square, Place Victor-Hugo, and complete the tour of the exterior by taking the Rue de la Voûte-du-Château (the Robert-Houdin Museum, see p 58, is on the left) to reach the Place du Château.

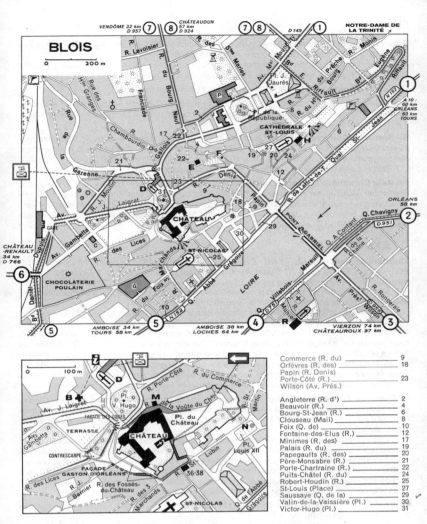

■ ADDITIONAL SIGHTS

St-Nicolas★. – This church is the most interesting one in Blois. It was formerly part of the Benedictine Abbey of St-Laumer. Its Classical style buildings, now transformed into a hospital, stand between the church and the Loire. The chancel, transept and the adjoining bay of the nave date from the late Romanesque period. The rest of the nave is Gothic. There are lovely historiated capitals in the chancel and on the left is a 15C altarpiece.

Hôtel d'Alluye★ (E). – A fine private mansion built in 1508 for Florimond Robertet, the Treasurer of Charles VIII, Louis XII and François I. The façade is of stone and brick. There is a beautiful courtyard with an Italianate gallery and medallions of the twelve Caesars.

There is also a remarkable stone spiral staircase with palm tree vaulting.

Denis Papin Statue (F). – After Louis XII, Blois's most famous citizen was Denis Papin (1647-1714). This physicist invented the steam digester, the forerunner of today's pressure cooker. Forced into exile by the Revocation of the Edict of Nantes, he was to publish his memorandum, "How to soften bones and cook meat quickly and cheaply", in England. He also spent some time in Germany under the patronage of the Margrave of Hesse experimenting with steam and discovering "a new way of raising water by the use of fire". His work was to lead to the development of the steam engine. On the death of his patron he returned to England where he was to die in poverty.

Episcopal Palace(Ancien Évêché – H). – This was built at the beginning of the 18C by the elder Gabriel, the father of the architect of the Place de la Concorde in Paris. It now serves as town hall.

There is a good **view★** from near the statue of Joan of Arc in the adjoining garden.

St-Louis Cathedral. – The nave and chancel, which were destroyed by a whirlwind, were rebuilt in the Gothic style in the 17C. This was done at the suggestion of Colbert, who married a lady of Blois in this church. The 10 and 11C crypt is interesting.

Old Quarter. – Stretching from the cathedral down to the Loire this picturesque quarter has some interesting houses: nos 5 and 7 Rue du Puits-Châtel, no 5 Rue Fontaine-des-Élus and no 10 Rue des Papegaults.

Notre-Dame-de-la Trinité. – The basilica, designed by the architect Paul Rouvière, was built between 1937 and 1944. Inside there is fine stained glass and a Stations of the Cross sculpted out of cement by Lambert-Rucki. The 60 m - 200 ft high campanile affords an extensive view of the surrounding countryside (240 steps; admission free). The carillon which consists of forty-eight bells, with the largest weighing over 5.3 tonnes - 5 tons, is one of the best in Europe. *Concerts in summer: first Sunday of the month noon to 1pm; third Sunday of the month 4 - 4.30pm.*

Robert-Houdin Museum (M). – *Open from 30 March to 30 June, Sundays and holidays 2 to 6pm; 1 July to 31 August 10am to noon and 2 to 6pm; 5F.*

Four rooms evoke the memory of the famous magician, Jean-Eugène Robert-Houdin (1805-71) who was a native of Blois. The great escapist Harry Houdini was to adopt his name.

Louis XII Fountain (N). – This is an attractive Flamboyant fountain.

Pont-Gabriel. – Built between 1717 and 1724 by the elder Gabriel it replaced an earlier bridge, bordered by houses and mills, which was swept away by the Loire. A hump backed construction, it affords a good **view** of the town.

St-Saturnin Cemetery (R). – *Open 15 March to 31 October, except on Mondays and Tuesdays, from 10am to 12.30pm and 2.30 to 5.30pm; the rest of the year on Wednesdays, Saturdays and Sundays 10am to noon and 2 to 5pm; combined ticket with château.*

This is a rare example of a galleried cemetery. Lapidary museum.

Poulain Chocolate Factory (Chocolaterie Poulain). – *Guided tours: 16 May to 30 June and in September Mondays to Thursdays at 8.45 and 10.15am and 2 and 4pm, Fridays at 8.45 and 10.15am only; in July and August Mondays to Thursdays at 8.45 and 10.15am, Fridays 8.45am; closed on public holidays; 2F. Apply in advance to Chocolat Poulain, service "visites", 6 Avenue Gambetta, Tel 78 39 21 extension 339.*

EXCURSIONS

Château de Beauregard. – *9 km - 6 miles by ③ and the D 956 to Cellettes or from the D 765. Guided tours 29 March to 30 September from 9.30am to noon and 2 to 6.30pm (5pm in the off season): closed on Wednesdays out of season and from 8 January to 9 February; 8F.*

The château, built in 1550, has preserved its Renaissance aspect despite alterations in the 17 and 19C. This was another of François I's smaller hunting lodges.

The Château is renowned for its remarkable **Portrait Gallery★** with its series of 363 portraits of notable people, and its floor of Delft tiles depicting an army on the march – a record of arms and uniforms at the time of Louis XIII. The wainscoting and timber ceiling are decorated with paintings by the Blois decorator Jean Mosnier who also worked at Cheverny. The **Cabinet des Grelots** is a charming little closet with carved and gilded oak panelling and a fine 16C **coffered ceiling** using decorative techniques by Francisque Scibec one of the Italian artists who worked at Fontainebleau and Anet. Hexagonal caissons decorated with embossed and painted leather surround the central motif portraying the original owner Jean du Thier's coat of arms.

Château de Troussay. – *15 km - 9 miles by ③, the D 956, then left after Cormeray. Guided tours from the Easter holidays to 11 November (Sundays and public holidays only during term time); 10.30am to 12.30pm and 2.30 to 6.30pm (7pm in summer, 2 to 5pm from September to November); time: 25 mins; 7F.*

This small château was refurnished in the late 19C by the historian Louis de la Saussaye with furnishings and items from other now vanished historic buildings of the region. In particular the wood carvings and stone sculpture including the Louis XII porcupine and the fine chapel **door★** with linenfold panels from Florimond Robertet's former Château de Bury. Note the Louis XII floor tiles on the ground floor. The outbuildings contain a collection of agricultural implements and tools and domestic objects, all typical of the Sologne region.

Mulsans. – *Pop 306. 14 km - 9 miles to the north by ⑧, the D 924, before turning right to Villerbon and then taking the D 50.*

The church has a fine 12C Romanesque **bell tower**, decorated with arcading and twin round arched openings typical of the Flamboyant style. A **Renaissance gallery** with twisted and carved colonnettes shelters the entrance porch and partly encircles the church.

Molineuf; Cisse Valley. – *Round tour of 32 km - 20 miles – about ¾ hour. Leave Blois by ⑥, the D 766, which crosses the beautiful Blois Forest.*

Molineuf. – Pop 552. This village lies in the Cisse Valley on the outskirts of the Blois Forest.

Follow the D 766 to Orchaise where you turn right on to the D 135A. Return to Molineuf by the D 135 following the Cisse (fine glimpses of the river) amidst vineyards and crops. Cross the D 766 and take the D 155 for a short distance before forking off to the left to Bury.

Bury. – The hamlet of Bury retains some old houses and the remains of a fortified gateway. From the crossroads a path leads up to the ruined château *(not open to the public)* which was once the superb residence of Florimond Robertet *(p 163)*.

Coulanges. – Pop 279. In the church is a curious 16C prayer stool with carved panels and choir stalls which originally came from the now ruined Guiche Abbey.

La BOURGONNIÈRE Chapel ★

Michelin map 🔟 18 – *9 km - 6 miles southeast of Ancenis – Local map p 104*

This delightful Renaissance chapel stands in the grounds of the 19C Château de la Bourgonnière. Amidst the farm buildings are a battlemented keep and other remnants of the original 15C castle.

St-Sauveur Chapel★. – *The D 751 passes nearby; to visit apply at the farm buildings to the left of the château. Open 1 April to 1 November 10am to noon and 2 to 6pm; mornings only out of season; Sundays and holidays afternoons only; closed 10 to 15 August; time: 30 mins; 4F.*

Towered, turreted and buttressed the chapel built between 1508 and 1523 is decorated with shells, the initials LC and the Greek letter tau (τ) – all attributes of the Antonines, mediaeval Order of Hospitallers who nursed those with St. Anthony's Fire, or ergotism.

The doorway is surmounted by an ornately decorated lintel while the door panels are carved with taus *(see above)*.

The nave's beautiful star vaulting has coats of arms and pendants. The oratory to the right has a rare seigneurial pew embellished with 16C Italianate grotesques. The centre retable is surmounted by a remarkable statue of Our Lady, attributed to Michel Colombe between St. Sebastian and St. Anthony the Hermit. The **altarpiece★** on the left, highly ornamented with foliated scrolls and cherubs is probably the work of a Tuscan or Northern Italian artist.

BOURGUEIL

Michelin map 64 13 – *Local map p 103* – Pop 3 620

Bourgueil is well situated in a fertile region where the hillsides are covered with vines. Ronsard often stayed there and it was there that he met the "Marie" of his love songs. Nowadays the little town's renown derives from the full bodied red wines produced by the Breton vines found only in that area: the vines are of the *Cabernet* variety and were brought from the Bordelais in the 17C by a Breton abbot who was Richelieu's secretary.

The only traces of its once powerful **abbey** are a few Gothic and Classical style buildings *(to visit apply to the caretaker between 2 and 6pm)*. The interesting parish **church** *(closed on Sunday afternoons and holidays)* has a late 12C chancel which is a fine example of the Angevin style. The nave has been extensively restored.

EXCURSIONS

Restigné. – Pop 1 198. *5 km - 3 miles to the east by the D 35.*

The church in this wine growers' village, which lies a little way off the main road, has an interesting lozenge patterned façade and a south doorway whose lintel is carved with fantastic beasts and a representation of Daniel in the Lions' Den. Inside, the Angevin chancel has a square east end and resembles that of Bourgueil with lofty vaulting and sculptured keystones. The 15C vaulting above the 11C nave is of wood.

Les Réaux, Chouzé-sur-Loire. – *8 km – 5 miles to the south by the D 749 and then at Port-Boulet the N 152 to the right.*

Les Réaux. – *Not open to the public.* Built in the 15C it belonged to a certain Tallemant des Réaux whose *Historiettes* described early 17C society. There now remains a fine brick and stone gatehouse, flanked by round towers, a keep and an 18C pavilion.

Return to the N 152 and continue to Chouzé.

Chouzé-sur-Loire. – Pop 2 147. This village was once an active port. It was in the charming 15C **manor house** (in a street near the main square), with its turrets and sculpted dormer windows, that Marie d'Harcourt, the wife of Dunois, the Bastard of Orléans, died on 1 September 1464.

BRISSAC, Château de ★

Michelin map 64 11 – *Local map p 103*

"A new château not completed in an old castle only half destroyed", the words of the present twelfth Duke of Brissac. The result, a mixture of styles but nevertheless an imposing building, standing in its own fine park.

The history of France is reflected in the history of this historic mansion and the famous military family of Cossé-Brissac, the owners since 1502. The first Duke won fame when he captured Le Havre from the English in 1563. The second Duke was the Governor of Paris, who in the name of the Holy League opened the city gates to Henri IV after his conversion and it was he who in 1606 started the construction of the present day château in the ruins of the 15C castle. Work ceased on the Duke's death in 1621, and much damage was incurred during the Revolution. The ninth Duke built a new but smaller château in the park, which was later to be destroyed. The mid 19C saw the beginning of a long period of restoration and today this historic mansion is still occupied by descendants of the same family.

Guided tours 9.30 to 11.30am and 2.15 to 5.45pm (4.15pm from 15 October to 15 March); closed on Tuesdays from 15 September to 1 July; time: ¾ hour; 10F.

The main or east front has a central building flanked by two round battlemented towers, remnants of the original 15C castle. Baroque in inspiration, the numerous storeys are ornamented with pilasters, broken pediments, quoins, cartouches and a mass of sculptured detail making for an arresting ensemble all the more so for the whiteness of the tufa stone.

The immensity of the apartments is worthy of a duke and designed to receive an itinerant court. The richly furnished rooms have intricately painted and gilded ceilings and are hung with magnificent tapestries. The portrait gallery has a series of pre-Revolution Presidents of the Audit Office while the library contains many books of historical value.

To the north of Brissac on the Angers road, stands a restored windmill *(illustration p 11)*.

CANDES-ST-MARTIN ★★

Michelin map 64 west of 13 – *Local maps pp 76 and 103* – Pop 269

The old village of Candes *(illustration p 9)*, which used to be fortified, stands at the confluence of the Loire and the Vienne. It has a fine church, built on the spot where the legendary St. Martin died in 397 *(p 150)*.

Church★★. – *Time: ½ hour.* The building was erected in the 12 and 13C and provided with defences in the 15C. The roadside façade is remarkable for its combination of military architecture and rich decoration.

The vault of the porch is supported by a central pillar on to which the ribs fall in a cluster. The doorway, inside the porch, is flanked by interesting statues.

Inside the nave is buttressed by aisles of the same height which are in their turn supported outside by simple buttresses. The Angevin vaulting rests on soaring piers, and the whole gives an impression of lightness. The older chancel is out of line with the nave.

By taking a byroad to the right of the church you can reach in a ¼ hour a nearby hillside, which affords a good **view** of the confluence of the two rivers.

EXCURSION

St-Germain-sur-Vienne. – Pop 324. *2.5 km - 2 miles by the D 751 in the direction of Chinon.* The Romanesque church belonging to this minute village which lies crowded up against the rock face has a doorway adorned with Carolingian sculptures: interlacing and chevron motifs. The chancel and half the nave are covered with beautiful vaulting in the Angevin style.

Chambord with its 440 rooms is the largest of the Loire country châteaux. Its scale foreshadows Versailles. Its sudden apparition at the end of an avenue and the sight of its white mass gradually widening and becoming clearer in detail, make a deep impression, even more striking at sunset. To this must be added the fine structural unity of the building, the rich decoration it owes to the Renaissance, which was then at its height, and finally two wonderful features: the grand staircase and the terrace.

HISTORICAL NOTES

A grandiose creation of François I (16C). – The counts of Blois, who were great hunters, built a fortified castle in this lonely corner of the game filled Forest of Boulogne, four leagues from their capital. This building was demolished by François I in 1519 when he came to build the present château. This construction he pursued with passionate enthusiasm.

Even when the Treasury was empty and the King had no money to pay the ransoms of his two sons held by Spain, when he was forced to raid the treasuries of his churches or to melt down his subjects' silver, work at Chambord went on steadily. François I in his zeal wished to divert the Loire and bring it to the foot of the château, but the architects recoiled before such a task, and a smaller river, the Cosson, was diverted instead.

Royal visits. – In 1539 the King was able to receive **Charles V** at Chambord. A group of young women in Greek costume went to meet the Emperor and strewed flowers at his feet. The visitor, charmed by this reception and amazed by the mansion, said to his host: "Chambord is a summary of human industry."

Henri II continued the building. It was at Chambord, in 1552, that the treaty with three German princes was ratified, bringing the three bishoprics of Metz, Toul and Verdun to the Crown. François II and Charles IX often came to hunt in the forest. Henri III and Henri IV hardly appeared at Chambord, but Louis XIII renewed the link.

The sport of kings. – Set in a forested area renowned for its good hunting, the first building on the site was no more than a hunting lodge. The domain was rich in game and lent itself to hawking. At one time there were more than three hundred falcons. The royal packs received every attention and for breeding purposes, the best dogs were brought from the four corners of Europe to improve the strain.

Hunting was the favourite mediaeval sport and princes were brought up to it from their very earliest days. Many women were also accomplished at the sport such as Diane de Poitiers. Louis XII took 5 m - 16 ft ditches in his stride. Despite his delicate constitution Charles IX used to hunt for as long as ten hours at a stretch, tiring in the process five horses and often spitting blood such were his exertions. He was invariably ill after each hunt and realized the exploit of stalking a stag without tiring the hounds.

La Grande Mademoiselle (17C). – Chambord was part of the county of Blois which Louis XIII granted to his brother, Gaston d'Orléans *(p 54)*. One can be both a conspirator and a good father: Gaston's daughter, "La Grande Mademoiselle", relates that her favourite game was to make her father go up and down one of the double spiral staircases while she passed him in the opposite direction, without ever meeting him. Later, it was at Chambord that she declared her love to Lauzun. She led him to a looking glass, breathed on it and traced the name of the irresistible charmer with her finger.

Louis XIV and Molière. – Chambord returned to the Crown under Louis XIV. The King stayed there nine times. It was there that Molière created *Monsieur de Pourceaugnac*, which he wrote in a few days in the château, and *Le Bourgeois Gentilhomme*.

At the first performance of *Pourceaugnac* the King never smiled. Lully, the author of the music, who played the part of an apothecary, had an inspiration: he jumped from the stage on to the harpsichord and fell through it. The King laughed and the play was saved.

Le Bourgeois Gentilhomme caused Molière renewed anguish. The King was icy at the first performance. The courtiers who were made fun of in the play were ready to be sarcastic. But after the second performance the King expressed his pleasure and the whole court changed their criticisms into compliments.

Maréchal de Saxe (18C). – Louis XV put the château at the disposal of his father in law, Stanislas Leczinski, the deposed King of Poland. Then he presented the domain, with 40 000 *livres* revenue, to the Maréchal de Saxe as a reward for his victory at Fontenoy. Was this a coincidence or a piece of mischief by the son in law? Maurice de Saxe was the natural son of Augustus of Poland, the lucky rival of Stanislas and the man who drove him from the throne.

The luxury loving, proud and violent Marshal filled the château with life and excitement. To satisfy his taste for arms he found quarters there for two regiments of cavalry composed of Tartars, Wallachians and even Negroes, whom he brought from Martinique. These strange troops rode fiery horses from the Ukraine which were allowed to run wild in the park and trained to assemble at the sound of a trumpet. The Marshal imposed iron discipline. For the least fault he hanged the culprits from the branches of an old elm.

More by terror than by courtship Maurice de Saxe won the favours of a well known actress, Mme Favart, and compelled her to remain at Chambord. He re-erected Molière's stage for her amusement. Monsieur Favart played the triple role of director, author and consenting husband.

The Marshal died at fifty-four, killed, some said, in a duel by the prince de Conti whose wife he had seduced. Others, more prosaically, ascribed his death to a neglected chill. Vainglorious even in death, Maurice de Saxe had given orders that the six cannon he had placed in the main courtyard of the château should be fired every quarter of an hour for sixteen days as a sign of mourning.

From the Revolution to the Restoration. – After the Marshal's death the château was neglected and gradually fell into disrepair. The Revolution destroyed what furniture was left.

In 1809 Napoleon gave Chambord as an entailed estate to his faithful Marshal Berthier, prince de Wagram. Brethier sold the timber and left the estate unoccupied. After his death the Princess was authorised to sell it. It was bought by public subscription in 1821 for the duc de Bordeaux.

■ **THE CHÂTEAU**★★★ *time: 1½ hours*

Open 1 April to 30 September 9 to 11.45am and 2 to 6.30pm; 10 to 11.45am and 2 to 4pm the rest of the year. Closed Tuesdays and 1 January, 1 May, 1 November, 25 December; 9F; Sundays and holidays: 4.50F.

*Son et Lumière** performance see p 33.*

The park. – The Chambord estate, the home since 1948 of the National Hunting Reserve, is immense. It covers 5 500 hectares - 13 600 acres of which 4 500 hectares - 11 120 acres are forested. The longest wall in France – 32 km - 20 miles – surrounds the park and has six gateways leading respectively into the same number of fine avenues.

Visitors are allowed into an area to the west of the estate, the rest being a protected zone. For those who wish to observe the game (deer, roe, wild boar . . .) feeding at dawn and dusk there are several observation points.

The Cosson, which was diverted for the purpose of feeding the moats, flows through the park. However Stanislas Leczinski was later to do away with the moats, thus losing the enhancing effect of the water.

The buildings. – The plan of Chambord is feudal: a central **keep** with four towers and a wall. But the Renaissance architecture evokes no warlike memories. This was a royal palace of pleasure.

The centrepiece of the imposing north-west front is the massive keep.

Visitors enter by the Porte-Royale.

The main courtyard. – From here there is a view of the keep which is joined to the corner towers by means of arcades surmounted by two storeys. In the original design the arcades stood on their own forming a terrace, a device which emphasised the massiveness of the keep.

The staircase. – The famous staircase is in the middle of the guardroom. At first it stood alone and rose straight to the roof; its effect was tremendous. But serious drawbacks – violent draughts and difficulty of access – compelled François I to have floors built connecting the staircase with the various storeys.

This unusual staircase consists of two spirals which are superimposed but do not meet. The central nucleus is pierced in such a way that one can see from one spiral to the other. The decoration in the Italian style, though not as good as that of Blois, is fine.

Above the terrace there is only one spiral. It winds within a magnificent lantern 32 m - 105 ft high.

The apartments. – For a long time the château was almost bare of furniture and interest was focused on the rich decorative sculpture as in the coffered ceilings of the halls at each level. Note throughout the crest of François I, the Salamander and the King's crowned initial, the Franciscan Girdle and ermine tufts.

Rooms on the ground and first floors have been refurbished to bring alive the memory of many of the personalities who came to Chambord.

The Salle des Soleils or Sun Room is so named after the sunbursts decorating the shutters. The painting by Baron François Gérard shows the Recognition of the Duke of Anjou as King of Spain while the Brussels tapestry portrays the Call of Abraham. The François I Hunting Room is hung with a series of 16C tapestries evoking the Hunts of François I after cartoons by Laurent Guyot.

The first floor apartments originally arranged during Louis XIV's reign are hung with tapestries and paintings, notably a portrait of Henri III by Clouet and another of Anne of Austria by Mignard. In François I's Bedchamber note the 16C gold embroidered velvet bedspread. One of these window panes supposedly carried a melancholy couplet summing up the knightly King's long experience of love: *Souvent femme varie, bien fol est qui s'y fie* (Every woman is fickle, he who trusts one is a fool).

François I's Cabinet was used as an oratory by Catherine Opalinska the wife of Stanislas Leczinski. After the Queen's Suite there is in the François I Tower, the Royal Bedchamber, which is now as it was during Stanislas Leczinski's time. In the King's Guards' Room is the huge porcelain stove, a souvenir of Maurice de Saxe. The Dauphin's Suite contains many mementoes of the comte de Chambord: paintings, the state bed presented by his followers, statues of Henri IV and the duc de Bordeaux, the first and last comte de Chambord, as children; and the collection of miniature artillery used by the young Prince. The cannon fired shot that could pierce a wall. Also on view is his manifesto of 5 July 1871 when he declared "Henri V will not abandon the white flag of Henri IV".

The second floor is devoted to the hunt: arms, trophies and other related items. One room has a series of animal paintings by 17C Flemish painters such as Snyders, Fyt and Boël. The adjoining room, in the Henri V Tower, is hung with tapestries relating the History of Meleager, who in Greek mythology was the leader of the Calydonian Boar Hunt.

The terrace. – Directly inspired by Italy, this presents a unique spectacle. The lantern, the gables, the dormer windows, 800 capitals, 365 chimneys, spires and bell turrets stand together. All are carved with the sculptor's chisel.

It was here that the court spent most of its time watching the start and return of the hunts, military reviews and manœuvres, tournaments and festivals. The thousand nooks and crannies of the terraces invited confidences, intrigues and assignments which played a great part in the life of that brilliant society.

CHAMPIGNY-SUR-VEUDE ★

Michelin map 🗋 10 – 6 km - 4 miles north of Richelieu – *Local map p 76* – Pop 845

Champigny lies in the green Valley of the Veude and still has some 16C houses. The most interesting sight, however, is the chapel, with its fine Renaissance windows, of the now vanished château.

Sainte-Chapelle★. – *Guided tours from 1 April to 30 September 9am to noon and 2 to 6pm; time: ¾ hour; 7F.*

The chapel, which is a remarkable example of Renaissance art at its height, was part of a castle built from 1508 to 1543 by Louis I and Louis II de Bourbon-Montpensier. The castle itself was later demolished on the orders of Cardinal Richelieu who felt that its magnificence outshone his nearby Château de Richelieu. Only outhouses remain but even these give some idea of the size and splendour of the château that was pulled down. The Sainte-Chapelle was saved by the intervention of Pope Urban VIII.

Louis I of Bourbon, who had accompanied Charles VIII to Naples, wanted the chapel to be in the transitional Gothic-Renaissance style.

The entrance portico, which was built later, is decidedly Italian in character: the detailed sculptured ornament is based on the insignia of Louis II of Bourbon and includes crowned and plain Ls, lances, pilgrims' staffs, flowers, fruit, etc. The porch has a coffered ceiling.

A fine wooden door dating from the 16C, carved with panels depicting the Cardinal Virtues, leads to the nave which has ogive vaulting with liernes and tiercerons. There also the visitor will see at prayer the figure of Henri de Bourbon, last Duke of Montpensier, carved by Simon Guillain at the beginning of the 17C.

Stained glass windows★★. – Installed in the middle of the 16C, these windows are the chapel's most precious jewel. The windows all together form a remarkable example of Renaissance glasswork *(see illustration p 27).*

The subjects portrayed are: at the bottom – thirty-four portraits of the Bourbon-Montpensier House from the time of St. Louis; above, the principal events in the life of St. Louis; at the top – scenes from the Passion. The window in the centre of the chevet shows a moving representation of the Crucifixion. The vividness and delicate combination of colours throughout should be noticed, particularly the purplish blues with their bronze highlights which are beyond compare.

La CHAPELLE-D'ANGILLON

Michelin map 🗋 11 – Pop 727

Lying in a hollow, La Chapelle-d'Angillon stands on the banks of the Petite Sauldre. It was here, on 5 October 1886, that the author of *Le Grand Meaulnes*, Alain-Fournier (Henri Alban Fournier) was born. This is the Ferté-d'Angillon of the novel and Fournier's house is on the left hand side of the road leading to Gien, 100 m - 109 yd from the crossroads.

Château de Béthune. – *Open 1 April to 31 October from 9am to noon and 2 to 7pm; 5F.*

This restored fortress has an 11C keep and later 15, 16 and 17C buildings. At one time it belonged to Sully who was owner of the nearby domain of Henrichemont.

St-Jacques. – The great Flamboyant window in the façade is surmounted by an ogee arch. A 16C stained glass window portrays the Crucifixion with angels collecting the blood of Christ. Note Fournier's name on the First World War memorial: his parents are buried in the adjoining churchyard.

EXCURSION

Loroy. – *7 km - 4 miles. Take the D 940 to the south and after 6 km - 4 miles the first road to the right. Visitors are allowed to walk round the abbey.*

This former Cistercian abbey, isolated in the heart of wooded countryside on the outskirts of the **St-Palais Forest**, was founded in 1125. The remains of the 13C church include the triumphal arch of the chancel and a chapel with fine capitals; this is the resting place of two archbishops, both members of the Sully family. The 17C monastic buildings surround cloisters of the same period.

CHÂTEAUDUN ★★

Michelin map 🗋 17 – *Local map p 97* – Pop 16 113 – *Facilities p 38*

Picturesquely perched on a promontory, rising up out of the Beauce Plain, Châteaudun and its castle command the meandering Loir. This, the market town for the Beauce and Le Perche, both rich agricultural regions, witnesses a thriving exchange of trade. An important centre for the grain trade, the vast Place du 18-October is the venue for bustling, colourful markets and fairs.

In the past the poppies of the Beauce furnished a poppy seed oil and the wool from the surrounding flocks was the staple of a textile industry evoked by certain street names such as Rue des Filoirs and des Fouleries.

The town suffered a series of conflagrations: burnt down in 1723 it was rebuilt in part to the plan of Jules Hardouin, only to be severely damaged in 1870 during a Prussian attack and again in 1940.

One of the most popular horse shows takes place in mid August on the former racecourse.

HISTORICAL NOTES

The town was the domain of the counts of Blois from the 10C onwards and it was the last of this line who in 1391 sold it to Louis d'Orléans *(p 54)*, father of the poet Charles d'Orléans. The latter gave the countship to his halfbrother, Dunois, the Bastard of Orléans and it was his successors, the Orléans-Longueville family that owned Châteaudun till the end of the 17C.

Dunois, the Bastard of Orléans. – The handsome Dunois *(c. 1403-68)*, faithful companion to the Maid, Joan of Arc, was the natural son of Louis d'Orléans. He fought the English from the age of fifteen and was to play a decisive role in the final French victory in the Hundred Years War. He is buried in the basilica at Cléry St-André *(p 77).*

■ THE CHÂTEAU★★
time: 1 hour

Guided tours from Palm Sunday to 30 September 9.30 to 11.45am and 2 to 6pm; 1 October to Palm Sunday 10 to 11.45am and 2 to 4.45pm; closed on Tuesdays, 1 January, 1 May, 1 November, 25 December; 6F.

The château rising vertically above the river, is impressive for its massive strength. There is a good view of the château from near the bridge on the right bank. Dating in part from the 12 and 16C the château was restored between 1930 and 1951 with great taste and care. The rooms are graced with fine furniture and rich tapestries.

From outside it has the austerity of a fortress while the buildings round the main courtyard resemble a stately mansion.

Keep. – *Not open to the public.* Dating from the 12C this is one of the first round keeps, one of the most imposing and the best preserved. Access is from inside the upper chapel. The three floors are linked by a spiral staircase built into the thickness of the wall, which also gives access to two watchpaths which circle the keep at the lower two levels. The upper chamber is covered by a magnificent 15C timberwork roof consisting of three levels of radiating beams each with a different off-centre point of convergence.

Sainte-Chapelle. – Built in the 15C for Dunois, this elegant construction is flanked by a square belfry and two oratories. The upper chapel with its fine wooden ceiling was intended for the servants. The well lit lower chapel has attractive ogive vaulting while the south oratory is adorned by a colourful late 15C mural painting depicting the Last Judgement. The series of fifteen charming **statues**★★ on imposts round the walls are excellent examples of the variety and scope of the local Loire workshops towards the end of the 15C. Twelve of them, placed there during Dunois's lifetime, are lifesize, polychrome statues representing different saints: St. Elizabeth, St. Mary of Egypt with her long tresses, St. Radegund the Queen with her sceptre, St. Apollinia with her instrument of torture, St. Barbara and her tower where she was held captive, St. Geneviève with her book, St. Catherine of Alexandria with her martyr's crown and the wheel, the instrument of her martyrdom, Mary Magdalene, the two St. Johns, the Baptist and Evangelist the patron saints of Dunois, St. Martha with the dragon, a majestic Virgin and Child,

(After photo: Revue géographique et industrielle de France)

Châteaudun from the river Loir

patroness of Marie d'Harcourt, Dunois's wife. Three smaller statues – St. Francis, St. Agnes and Dunois himself – were added later by Dunois's son François d'Orléans-Longueville and his daughter in law Agnès de Savoie.

Dunois Wing. – Started in 1460, it is in the true Gothic tradition, but it shows a greater concern for comfort and convenience typical of buildings of the period following the upheavals of the Hundred years War. The staircase built by Dunois's son François in the Gothic style is transitional between the usual mediaeval spiral staircase in a turret and the renowned Renaissance staircases. Three storeys high the courtyard façade is pierced by twin openings with Flamboyant tracery and decoration. The crocketed gables frame fleurs-de-lis.

The living quarters on the ground and first floors are served by two staircases. The rooms have attractive wooden ceilings with several massive main beams supporting other smaller rafters, great fireplaces and they are hung with fine tapestries. You also visit the room where the Revolutionary Tribunal met in 1793. The watchpath leads to the guardroom.

The two floors underground house the cellars, kitchens and dungeons.

Longueville Wing. – Built by members of the Orléans-Longueville branch of the family from 1511 to 1532 on foundations dating from the previous century, it was, however, left unfinished. On the courtyard façade the Italianate cornice supports a Flamboyant balustrade. The central column of the Renaissance staircase to the right, is decorated with panels of Renaissance motifs which are framed by Gothic mouldings.

This wing has three rooms to each floor. The ground floor includes the guardroom and the great Renaissance gallery, again hung with tapestries. Note the magnificent ceiling with moulded beams. The monumental chimneypieces are either Gothic or Renaissance.

There are again two underground floors for the kitchens and other servants quarters.

■ ADDITIONAL SIGHTS

Old town* (Vieille ville). – *Itinerary shown on the accompanying plan.* Starting from the Promenade St-Lubin, continue along Rue du Château, lined by overhanging houses, to a charming small square. One of the two old houses here is early 16C with sculpted pilasters, beams and medallions, while the second has historiated corner beams.

The Rue de la Cuirasserie, with an admirable hôtel with 16C corner turret, opens on to the Square de la Madeleine where to the right the building has a fine projecting frontispiece.

La Madeleine. – Adjoining the ramparts this church has some Romanesque remains, notably a 12C crypt and a curious doorway decorated with human figures and fantastic animals.

The former Augustinian abbey, in a Classical style, now houses the Law Courts.

Continue down Rue des Huileries to Rue de la Porte-d'Abas where on the left, near the ruins of a Roman gateway, stands the 16C Porters' Lodge (La Loge aux Portiers), ornamented with a statue of the Virgin.

Return to the Rue St-Lubin, picturesque with its central stream, and take the alley to the left where at no 13 there is a Renaissance doorway. Further on one passes the 15C doorway of the former Chapel of St-Lubin before reaching the Place du Château.

St-Valérien (D). – Distinguished by its tall belfry crowned by a crocketed spire, the church has a fine south doorway. Note on the right the Renaissance chapel. Alternatively slender and massive piers support the nave's vaulting, while the Renaissance chapel has a coffered ceiling.

Notre-Dame-du-Champdé (E). – All that remains of this cemetery chapel is a Flamboyant façade with finely worked ornamentation. A delicate balustrade is supported by sculpted consoles.

Promenade du Mail. – This tree shaded avenue dominating the Loir affords an extensive view which reaches to the Perche hillsides.

Museum (M). – *Open 1 March to 30 September, 9.30 to 11.30am and 2 to 6.30pm; the rest of the year 10 to 11.30am and 2 to 5pm; closed on Mondays; 4F.*

This local museum has a particularly interesting collection of birds and their nests on the first floor, in addition to a prehistoric section, mediaeval sculptures and Egyptian ceramics.

St-Jean-de-la-Chaîne (K). – In the suburb of St-Jean on the north bank of the Loir, stands this church which is reached by an early 16C ogee arched gateway. Built on the site of a Gallo-Roman temple the actual church is Romanesque with a massive tower dating from 1506. The nave and aisles were covered with pointed Gothic vaulting in the 15C.

EXCURSIONS

Lutz-en-Dunois. – Pop 386. *7 km - 4 miles by ②, the D 955, then turn left after the aerodrome.* Lutz has a charming Romanesque church with a low bell tower crowned by a saddleback roof. Inside there are notable 12 and 13C **mural paintings**: Apostles and the Bishop Saints on the oven vault; Christ's entry into Jerusalem, the Resurrection and Descent into Limbo on the nave walls.

Loigny-la-Bataille; Patay. – *Round tour of 76 km - 47 miles – about 2½ hours. Leave Châteaudun by ②, the D 927. At La Maladrerie turn right on to the D 39.*

Loigny-la-Bataille. – Pop 238. This village was the site of a battle during the Franco-Prussian War when the Zouave regiment (volunteers from the west of France and Belgium who had rallied to Pope Pius IX's call to defend the Vatican) distinguished itself in action, covering the retreat of the provisional French forces known as the *Armée de la Loire (p 17).* A chapel serves as a charnel house and contains the tombs of the French generals Sonis and Charette and a museum in the presbytery exhibits souvenirs of the battle *(9am to 5pm daily except Sunday mornings).*

Continue to Patay in the south via Terminiers.

Patay. – Pop 2 048. Here Joan of Arc defeated the fleeing English army in June 1429.

Return to Châteaudun via the D 136 and D 955.

Michelin map **63** 10 – *Local map p 115* – Pop 8 645 – *Facilities p 38*

This attractive old town in the very heart of Chouan country *(p 89)* was founded in the 11C by Foulques Nerra. The old town with its narrow, winding streets is grouped round the town hall (**H**) and Church of St-Jean. The hospital, convents and religious communities are all on the east bank. The Royalist leader Mercier, son of an innkeeper was born in Rue Trouvée. The confidant of Cadoudal he was killed in 1801 at the Battle of Loudéac, aged twenty-six.

The spacious quays recall the former glory of Château-Gontier as a busy port on the canalised Mayenne. Today the calf sales are the most important in France and Europe and on Thursday, market day, nearly 5 000 head of cattle are sold.

■ MAIN SIGHTS

time: ½ hour

St-Jean. – This Roman-esque building in flint and red sandstone, badly damaged in 1940, has since been restored to its original style.

Bare and austere in-side, the dome on pen-dentives over the transept crossing ends in colon-nettes. Modern stained glass adorns the windows. The restoration work in the transept led to the discovery of 12C frescoes – in the north arm: The Creation (of birds, beasts, Adam and Eve); the Tree of Good and Evil; the Temptation and Downfall of Eve. The Three Kings are portrayed in the St-Benoît Chapel. In the south arm: Noah's Ark, the End of the Flood with the appearance of the Dove.

The fine crypt divided into three aisles by massive columns has groined vaulting. The sacristy has St-Justus's arm reliquary which dates from 1470.

To the north of the church are the 17C buildings of the former priory.

Behind the chevet, terraces laid out on the former ramparts afford fine **views** of the Mayenne.

Bourg-Roussel (R.)	2	Gaulle (Quai de)	7	Pasteur (Quai)	14
Bourré (R. Jean)	3	Joffre (Av. Mal)	8	Quinefault (Pl.)	15
Cahour (R. Abel)	4	Leclerc (R. de la Don.)	9	République (Pl.)	16
Foch (Av. Mal)	5	Lemonnier (R. Gal)	10	Thiers (R.)	17
Gambetta (R.)	6	Olivet (R. d')	13	Trouvée (R.)	18

■ ADDITIONAL SIGHTS

Promenade du Bout-du-Monde. – These gardens, affording glimpses of the river, were laid out on the site of the former priory grounds.

Museum (**M**). – *Open 10am to noon and 2 to 7pm; closed on Tuesdays and in January.*
In addition to Graeco-Roman antiquities there are some good paintings and sculptures. Note the drawing by Le Brun, *The Battle between Constantine and Maxentius;* canvases by the 17C Dutch school; an important 16C Italian work, *Cleopatra;* an admirable **statue of St. Martha** by late 15C French school and a 14C marble Virgin.

La Trinité (**D**). – This 17C church was formerly the Ursulines' chapel. The pilastered façade is adorned by a statue of St. Ursula. It was in this chapel that Lucrèce Mercier came to pray after the execution of her fiancé the royalist leader, Cadoudal. She was later to take her vows with the Ursulines.

Notre-Dame-du-Genneteil (**E**). – This former church built of schist in the Romanesque style was once the college chapel.

Michelin map **64** northwest of 14 – Pop 1 592

This calm, small town ideal for tourists seeking a quiet haven is situated in a wooded region interspersed with many stretches of water.

Louise de la Baume le Blanc or better known as duchesse de La Vallière spent her childhood at La Vallière Manor, near the village of Reugny to the northeast of Tours.

Lady in waiting to Charles I of England's widow, Henrietta Maria, the gentle, gracious Louise captured the heart of the Sun King, Louis XIV, at Fontainebleau in 1662. She remained the royal mistress for five years before giving way to the haughty Mme de Montespan. Following her fall from favour she retired to the Carmelite Convent in Rue St-Jacques in Paris where she eventually took her vows. For the thirty-six years of her stay her piety, modesty and tolerance never failed her.

Étang du Val Joyeux. – *Access on foot starting from the church, or by car taking the D 749.* This vast stretch of water *(bathing and sailing facilities)*, formed by the River Fare, lies in an attractive wooded setting. The nearby hill is crowned by a church

Château-la-Vallière Forest. – This vast forest of pines and oaks, interspersed with stretches of heath is ideal for hunting.

EXCURSIONS

Château de Vaujours. – *3.5 km - 2 miles by the D 959 the Tours road, and afterwards the D 34 to the right.*

The romantic ruins of this château are preceded by a fortified barbican and a rampart wall marked out at intervals by round towers. Only one of the once battlemented towers stands in its entirety. The courtyard is bordered by the remains of the chapel and main building dating from the 15C. Louise de La Vallière, also retained the title of duchesse de Vaujours, but only visited the château once in 1669.

Marcilly-sur-Maulne. – Pop 275. *7 km - 4 miles to the west.* This village has several Renaissance dwellings. The **château** *(not open to the public)* was rebuilt at the end of the 16C by the Fouquet de Croissy family. It is an excellent example of the Classical style with its central and two corner pavilions complete with tall chimneys and French style roofs.

CHÂTEAUNEUF-SUR-LOIRE

Michelin map **64** 10 – *Local map p 101* – Pop 5 658 – *Facilities p 38*

Louis VI the Fat, Blanche of Castile and St. Louis stayed in the castle which has given its name to this town. Charles IV the Fair died there. The structure was rebuilt in the 17C by La Vrillière, the Grand Master of Ceremonies. Only the domed rotunda, which is used as the town hall, the outbuildings and the pavilions in the forecourt remain. The park is at its best at the end of May or the beginning of June, when the giant **rhododendrons** are in flower.

Loire Maritime Museum (Musée de la Marine de Loire). – *Open 24 May to 14 September from 10am to noon and 2 to 6pm; 29 March to 24 May and 14 September to 12 October at weekends and on public holidays only from 2 to 6pm; closed on Tuesdays and 12 October to Easter; 3F.*

Bear right, round the town hall and go down a few steps to enter the basement where the museum has been installed. Engravings showing the former river traffic, navigational instruments, models and photographs of the different craft, recall former days.

Church. – This 12 and 13C church contains a fine 17C marble mausoleum to La Vrillière.

CHÂTEAU-RENAULT

Michelin map **64** southwest of 6 – Pop 6 048 – *Facilities p 38*

Founded in the 11C by Renault, son of Geoffroi de Château-Gontier, the town stands on a promontory at the confluence of the Gault and the Brenne. The main street curves as it descends to the level of the two rivers.

The chemical and electronics industries have been added to the traditional activity of leather working.

Château. – Pass through the 14C gateway to reach the lime planted terraces which afford a fine view over the town. The upper part of the 12C **keep** has been dismantled. The château belonged to the owners of the château in Châteaudun, followed by two illustrious sailors: the marquis de Château-Renault who served under Louis XIV and the comte d'Estaing who was beheaded in 1793.

The former kitchens house a small exhibition of leatherwork *(open 15 May to 15 September on Wednesdays and weekends from 4 to 9pm).*

CHÂTILLON-SUR-INDRE ★

Michelin map **68** 6 – Pop 3 650 – *Facilities p 38*

Châtillon, a small town curiously clustered on to a mound dominating the Indre, is a jumble of tortuous streets, alleys and stairways bordered by ancient houses with old roofs. The town's activity is mainly based on agriculture, and market days are lively occasions.

Notre-Dame. – Although the transept and chancel without its original vaulting date from the 11C, the church is essentially a Romanesque building dating from 1112. The façade finished in 1180 is pierced by a **doorway** with remarkable historiated capitals: fantastic animals (Harpies and Sphinx); the symbolic dove feeding on the fruit of the vine; men struggling with monsters (vices); Adam and Eve expelled from the Garden of Eden; the miser's torment and a buffoon leading donkeys in a dance. The south gable is ornamented with a bas-relief depicting Christ the King surrounded by seraphim.

Inside admire the **capitals**. Those of the nave are ornamented with plant motifs and masks while those in the transept are historiated: Daniel in the Lions' Den; the monkey trainer; and scenes from the Life of St. Austrégisile, the church's patron saint.

Place du Marché. – This square affords a view over the meadow covered Indre Valley.

Château. – The round **keep** *(to visit apply to the caretaker, at no 2 on the square below; 2F),* still surrounded in parts by its revetment wall *(p 23),* dates from the early 13C. From the summit there is a pleasant panorama of the town and Indre Valley.

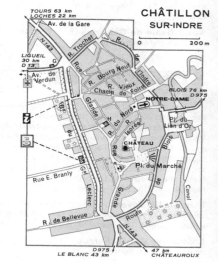

CHÂTILLON SUR-INDRE

Michelin map 🔢 16, 17 – *Local map p 102* – Pop 793 – *Facilities p 38*

Chaumont has a site overlooking the Loire similar to that of Amboise. There is an admirable view of the valley from its terrace. Surrounded by a beautiful park the building's feudal grimness is softened by Renaissance influences. The luxurious stables are a reminder of coaching days.

Catherine de' Medici at Chaumont (16C). – The former fortress of Chaumont was demolished twice; it was rebuilt between 1465 and 1510 by Pierre d'Amboise, by the eldest of his seventeen children, Charles I d'Amboise, and by his grandson, Charles II. The latter, thanks to his uncle, Cardinal Georges d'Amboise, who was in great favour with King Louis XII, became Grand Master of the King's Household, Marshal, Admiral of France and Lieutenant-General in Italy.

In 1560 Catherine de' Medici, the widow of Henri II, acquired the castle only as a means of revenge against Diane de Poitiers, the mistress of the late King *(p 68)*. The Queen compelled her rival to give up her favourite residence of Chenonceau in exchange for Chaumont. Diane de Poitiers, however, did not remain at Chaumont but retired to Anet where she lived until her death in 1566.

The stay of Catherine de' Medici at Chaumont and the existence there of a room connected by a staircase with the top of a tower have given rise to conjecture. The room was said to be the study for **Ruggieri**, the Queen's Astrologer, and the tower the observatory from which Catherine and her master plotter consulted the stars. It is said to be at Chaumont that Catherine read in the future the grim fate awaiting her three sons, François II, Charles IX, and Henri III (all of whom died violent deaths) and the accession of the Bourbons with Henri IV of Navarre.

Mass produced medallions. – In the 18C one of the proprietors of the castle, Le Ray, Governor of the Invalides, hired for 1 200 *livres* a year, plus lodging and heating, the services of the famous Italian artist **Nini**, a glass engraver and potter. Nini fitted out a workshop in the stables and an oven in a dovecote. With a hollow mould he reproduced many copies of medallions of more than a hundred famous people of the time. Le Ray made a large profit from this new industrial method of portraiture.

Madame de Staël (beginning of the 19C). – Exiled from Paris by Napoleon, she spent some time at Chaumont. When her guests praised the landscape of the Loire, she replied sadly: "Yes' it's an admirable scene, but how much I prefer my gutter in the Rue du Bac."

■ **THE CHÂTEAU** ★★ *time: 1 hour*

Open 1 April to 30 September from 9 to 11.45am and 2 to 6.30pm; 1 October to 31 March from 10 to 11.45am and 2 to 4pm; château only; 6F; 3F on Sundays and public holidays; closed on Tuesdays, 1 January, 1 May, 1 November and 25 December.

The park. – An uphill walk taking about ten minutes along a shady avenue giving glimpses of the Loire leads to the castle. This is a pleasant walk and will give an idea of the fine park with its centuries old cedars.

The building. – The outer west façade, which is the oldest, is severely military. Most of the windows that can be seen now did not exist originally. The two other façades, though they still have a feudal look, show the influence of the Renaissance.

At ground floor level there is a frieze bearing the interlaced Cs of Charles d'Amboise and his wife, Catherine, alternating with the emblem of the castle: a volcano or *chaud mont* (Chaumont). The emblem of Diane de Poitiers is carved in front of each machicolation: it consists either of two intertwined Ds or of the hunting horn, bow and quiver of Diana the Huntress.

Beyond the drawbridge the entrance gate is adorned with the arms of France, together with the initials of Louis XII and Anne of

(After photo: Yvon)

Château de Chaumont

Brittany. The hat of Cardinal d'Amboise is carved on the tower on the left, and the arms of Charles d'Amboise, Admiral and Marshal of France, on the right hand tower. These emblems are protected by small structures in a mixed Gothic and Italian Renaissance style.

On entering the courtyard go first to the terrace. It was built in the 18C on the site of the north wing, which had been demolished by an owner who liked the view. A magnificent Loire landscape can be seen from it.

The apartments. – On view among others are the rooms of the two rivals Catherine de' Medici and Diane de Poitiers, and Ruggieri's study. They contain fine tapestries, good furniture and a collection of Nini's medallions.

The stables. – They are about 50 m - 55 yd from the château. Their size and appointments give an idea of the part played by horses in the lives of princely families.

EXCURSION

Les Montils. – Pop 808. *9.5 km - 6 miles to the east of Chaumont via the D 751 and then the D 7. In the valley of the Beuvron this village has buildings which date from the 12C. Note in the main street the door to the left of the church.*

A tour of the principal Châteaux of the Loire is not complete without a visit to Chenonceau *(1)*. Generous planning and a well proportioned distribution of water and greenery have increased the beauty of a naturally fine setting. The buildings are elegantly decorated. Inside, magnificent furnishings gladden the eye of art lovers.

HISTORICAL NOTES

"The Château of Six Women". – The present château was built between 1513 and 1521 by **Thomas Bohier**, Collector of Taxes under Charles VIII, Louis XII and François I. The acquisition of Chenonceau by Bohier reads like a novel by Balzac.

The estate was the property of the Marques family, whose extravagance caused their ruin. The land was sold bit by bit. Bohier, who had his eye on Chenonceau, bought each of these lots. The owners, feeling the spider's web being spun round the château, tried desperately to avoid the inevitable. After twenty years of struggle, in 1512, they had to admit defeat. Bohier bought the château for 12 500 *livres* and had it all pulled down except the keep. The very next year the delightful mansion the tourist can see today began to rise on the Cher.

From that time onward there was an original feature in the history of Chenonceau. It could be called "The Château of Six Women" because of the leading part its hostesses played there for 400 years.

Katherine Briçonnet, the Builder (beginning of 16C). – Bohier married Katherine Briçonnet, a woman from Touraine who belonged to a family of great financiers. As Bohier was kept busy by his duties and often had to be with the armies in the area of Milan he could not supervise the works at Chenonceau, thus Katherine was the moving spirit.

One feels the feminine influence in the site chosen for the

(After photo: Yvon)

Château de Chenonceau

castle and its arrangement with an eye to comfort and convenience. For instance, for the first time, the rooms are placed on either side of a central vestibule, which makes service easier. Another novelty at Chenonceau was the straight flighted staircase, more practical and better suited for receptions than a spiral staircase.

Bohier died in 1524 and Katherine two years later. François I then had his Treasurer's accounts examined. He was found to owe large sums to the Treasury. To pay his debt his son gave up Chenonceau to the King.

Diane de Poitiers "the Ever-Beautiful". – In 1547, when Henri II ascended the throne, he gave Chenonceau to his mistress, Diane de Poitiers. She was twenty years older than he, but her beauty and charm were famous and in no way lessened by the years. "I saw her", wrote a contemporary, "at the age of seventy (in fact, she died at sixty-seven) "as beautiful to look upon and as attractive as at thirty. Above all, she had a wonderfully white skin and did not paint it. But they say she took some sort of broth and various drugs every morning. I don't know what they were."

Diane was the widow of Louis de Brézé. She had a splendid tomb built for him in Rouen Cathedral and she always wore mourning: black and white. Her influence over Henri II was such that he also wore mourning.

Diane ordered a fine garden and had a bridge built between the château and the bank of the Cher. She drew ample funds from the tax of twenty *livres* on every church bell levied by her lover, about which Rabelais said: "The King has hung all the bells in the kingdom round the neck of his mare."

The death of Henri II, killed by Montgomery's lance thrust in a tournament in 1559, brought his favourite face to face with Catherine de' Medici, who had become Regent. The Queen, who was patient and retiring, had accepted the situation in her husband's lifetime; now she meant to enjoy her revenge. Diane was greatly attached to Chenonceau and Catherine knew she would touch a tender spot by forcing her to yield it to her in exchange for Chaumont. With bitter despair the favourite left the banks of the Cher, made a short visit to Chaumont and retired to the Château d'Anet, where she died seven years later.

Catherine de' Medici, the Magnificent. – With her love of the arts Catherine de' Medici also had a love of magnificence, and she satisfied both at Chenonceau. She had a park laid out, built a two storey gallery on the bridge and added large outbuildings.

Grand festivals were frequent and the people marvelled at them. One was given for the arrival of François II and Mary Stuart; another for Charles IX was even more brilliant. Young women disguised as mermaids welcomed the visitors from the moats along the avenue leading to the château. Their singing was matched by that of the nymphs emerging from the thickets. But the appearance of satyrs scattered the graceful chorus. Nothing was lacking from these festivities. There were banquets, dances, masquerades, fireworks and a naval battle on the Cher.

Henri III presided over a sylvan festival that cost 100 000 *livres* and made a sensation. "The most beautiful and virtuous ladies of the court", we are told, "appeared half naked, with their hair loose, like brides, and with the Queen's daughters, waited on the guests."

Louise of Lorraine, the Inconsolable (end of 16C). – Catherine bequeathed Chenonceau to her daughter in law, Louise of Lorraine, wife of Henri III. After the King's assassination by Jacques Clément, Louise retired to the château, put on white mourning according to royal custom and

---

(1) The town of Chenonceaux has an x, not the château.

wore it to the end of her life; hence the name "White Queen" or "White Lady" that was given to her. Her bedroom, her bed, her carpets and chairs were covered with black velvet, and the curtains were of black damask; crowns of thorns and Franciscan girdles were painted in white on black ceilings. For eleven years, faithful to the memory of her husband, Louise divided her time between prayer, needlework and reading.

Madame Dupin, Lover of Letters (18C). – After Louise of Lorraine, Chenonceau fell into disuse until Dupin, the Farmer-General, became its owner.

Mme Dupin kept a salon which all the celebrities of the period attended. **Jean-Jacques Rousseau** was tutor to her son. It was for the benefit of this boy that he composed his treatise on education, *Émile*. In his *Confessions* he speaks warmly of that happy time. "We enjoyed ourselves much in that beautiful place, and we lived very well. I grew fat as a monk."

Mme Dupin grew old at Chenonceau, much beloved by the villagers, so that the château came through the Revolution undamaged. She was buried in the park, according to her wish.

Madame Pelouze, Lover of Antiquity (19C). – In 1864 Mme Pelouze bought Chenonceau and made it her life's work to restore the château. She refurbished it, recreating the interiors of Bohier's time. Catherine de' Medici had altered the main façade by doubling the windows and placing caryatids between them. The new openings were now walled up and the caryatids were moved into the park. A building which had been added between the chapel and the library was removed.

The château is now the property of the Menier family.

■ THE CHÂTEAU★★★

Open 16 March to 30 September from 9am to 7pm; 1 to 31 October from 9am to 6pm; 1 to 30 November from 9am to 5pm; 1 December to 31 January from 9am to noon and 2 to 4pm; 1 February to 15 March from 9am to 5pm; 10F; tickets from the caretaker; crèche for children in summer. Combined ticket for the château and museum; 8F.

During the tourist season an electric train (1F) links the entrance gate to the main courtyard of the château. In summer, when the water level permits, there are boat trips on the Cher.

Son et Lumière★ *performances are given in summer – see p 33.*

Arrival. – You will reach the château along a magnificent avenue of plane trees. The tourist who likes to indulge his fancy can try to imagine the entry of Charles IX, among mermaids, nymphs and satyrs. Standing back on the left, at the end of a path, you will see, on the right, the outbuildings erected to the plans of Philibert Delorme.

After crossing a drawbridge you reach a terrace surrounded by moats. To the left is Diane de Poitiers's Italian garden; to the right, that of Catherine de' Medici, bounded by the great trees in the park. On the terrace stands the keep of the original château remodelled by Bohier. Here you will read the initials "T.B.K." (Thomas Bohier and Katherine). You will find them again on the château, with the motto: *S'il vient a point, me souviendra.* The meaning of this motto is rather obscure. It may be: "If the building is finished it will preserve the memory of the man who built it."

CHENONCEAUX, N 76

CHENONCEAU
0   100 m

WAXWORKS MUSEUM

Diane de Poitiers' Garden

Keep

CHÂTEAU

Catherine de Medici's Garden

CHER

The château. – The château consists of a rectangular mansion with turrets at the corners. It stands on two piers of the former mill, resting on the bed of the Cher. The library and the chapel project on the left. Catherine de' Medici's two storeyed gallery stands on the bridge over the river. This building by Philibert Delorme has a classical simplicity contrasting with the rich, gay appearance given to the older portion by the sculptures on the balustrades, roof and dormer windows.

Ground floor. – The former guardroom is paved with majolica tiles and adorned with 16C Flemish tapestries; in the chapel is a delicate 16C Virgin and Child carved in Carrara marble; the fireplace in Diane de Poitiers's bedroom was designed by Jean Goujon; pictures hang in Catherine de' Medici's Green Cabinet as well as an Oudenaarde tapestry. The great gallery overlooking the Cher is 60 m – 197 ft long and has black and white chequered paving; incorporated in its ceiling is the ceiling of Louise of Lorraine's bedroom. In François I's bedroom hang paintings by Van Loo *(Three Graces)*, Il Primaticcio *(Diane de Poitiers as the Huntress Diana)*, and in a salon with a magnificent French style ceiling, works by Rubens *(Jesus and St. John)*, Mignard, Nattier *(Mme Dupin)* and a portrait of Louis XIV. Note the hall with its diagonal ribbed vault.

The kitchens. – There is an attractive dresser and a series of brass containers.

First floor. – One reaches it by a straight staircase, which at the time it was built was an innovation in France.

From the vestibule, with its Oudenaarde tapestries depicting hunting scenes and Carrara marble statues of Roman emperors brought by Catherine de' Medici from Florence, walk through to Gabrielle d'Estrée's bedroom, the Royal, or Five Queens' Bedroom, the bedroom of Catherine de' Medici and finally to that of César de Vendôme. All the rooms are furnished and adorned with fine Gobelins tapestries.

A small convent for Capuchin nuns was installed in the attics, complete with a drawbridge which was raised at night to separate the nuns from the castle's other occupants.

Waxworks Museum. – *Same visiting times as the château; 4F.* In the Dômes building, so named because of the configuration of the roof, are fifteen scenes evoking life in the château and the personalities connected with it.

The park. – Views of the château can be enjoyed from the banks of the Cher and the gardens.

Michelin map 🟦 15 to 19

From Vierzon to Tours, the Cher has created a rich expansive valley. Set along its banks are attractive small towns and châteaux, including the jewel of Chenonceau.

The Cher, a lazy flowing river with a slight gradient, meanders in the serene light, amidst meadows planted with poplars and hillside vineyards. Between Vierzon and St-Aignan the river laps against the sands of the Sologne on the north bank and the Valençay clays on the south. Further on towards Montrichard the river cuts into the hillsides of white tufa chalk, which are pierced by troglodyte dwellings and former quarries, now transformed into wine cellars or caves for mushroom growing. The river flows on to water the fertile alluvial plains *(varennes)* beside the Loire, where former courses of the Cher form reaches known as *boires*.

An open valley, the Cher provides a good route for river, rail and road communications, a fact that was appreciated even in Roman times. Since 1841, the now abandoned Berry Canal which starts at Bourges, has paralleled the river down to Noyers. Unusual narrow boats called *berrichons* used to ply on limited sections of the canal. Between Noyers and Tours navigation on the canalised Cher has likewise ceased leaving majestic canal reaches between the successive locks.

A pleasant climate, fertile river deposits and well exposed slopes ensure a comfortable living for the inhabitants: asparagus growing on the borders of the Sologne, vineyards on the limestone hillsides with fruit and vegetables in the sheltered areas. Chabris, Selles, and St-Aignan are famous for their delicious goats' milk cheeses.

From Vierzon to St-Aignan *– 72 km - 45 miles – about 4 hours – Local map below*

Leave Vierzon (description in the Michelin Green Guide Dordogne) by the N 20 in the direction of Châteauroux: 3 km - 1 mile later at St-Hilaire-de-Court take the D 90 to the right.

The road follows the crests of the Cher hills and provides fine views of Vierzon. Take the D 19 down into the valley and cross the river and Berry Canal at Thénioux before turning left into the N 76 which runs alongside the canal to Mennetou-sur-Cher.

Mennetou-sur-Cher. – Pop 984. *Facilities p 38.* This mediaeval town is encircled by 13C **ramparts** which retain three of the original five towers and three town gates.

The Grande-Rue, steep and winding, displays a variety of **old dwellings** including 13C Gothic houses with twinned windows, 15C half timbered and corbelled houses and 16C hôtels with pilasters.

The **church**, formerly part of the priory, has a 13C tower and a square chancel in the Angevin style *(p 21)*. The nave is 15C while most of the furnishings are 17C: *Pietà* (chapel left of nave); statues; the Prior's pulpit in the chancel; and a painting, *Birth of the Virgin*, by the school of Le Nain. Note the 13C baptismal basin.

From Mennetou return to the south bank by the D 37 crossing the village of **Maray**, renowned for its fair on the second Saturday in September, before turning right into the D 51. This winding road provides fine glimpses of the valley and Mennetou, while crossing a countryside of richly cultivated fields, vineyards, and oak, chestnut and walnut trees. Dotted at intervals are small châteaux and large farms, roofed with flat tiles and sometimes surrounded by moats.

St-Loup. – Pop 196. Situated on a hillside overlooking the valley, this village has a church *(apply to Mme Pernin for the key)* in the transitional Romanesque-Gothic style, with 13C mural paintings representing Christ in Majesty, Virgin of the seven Sorrows and the Crucifixion, all with the typical pale blue background. Note the beautifully carved early 16C **Prior's pulpit***.

Villefranche-sur-Cher. – Pop 1 751. *1 km - ½ mile beyond the D 51.* The church in the transitional Romanesque-Gothic style has remarkable capitals in the transept crossing and elegant Gothic vaulting in the choir.

Chabris. – Pop 2 495. *Facilities p 38.* Renowned for its wines and goats' milk cheese, Chabris is of Roman origin. The much altered **church** dedicated to St. Phalier is the scene of an annual pilgrimage *(first Sunday in September)*. Note in the north transept the stone decoration on the 11C and 13C walls: interlacing, fabulous animals and an Annunciation. The 11C crypt *(to visit apply at the presbytery)* contains the sarcophagus of the Saint.

Valençay**. – *14 km - 9 miles from Chabris by the D 4. Description p 158.*

Cross to the north bank and turn left on to the D 54 traversing vineyard country before returning to the south bank to reach Selles-sur-Cher.

Selles-sur-Cher. – *Description p 143.*

The D 17 leads to Meusnes.

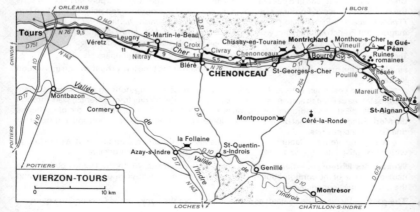

70

Meusnes. – Pop 937. Formerly a centre of world importance for the production of gunflints, Meusnes has retained the memory with a **gunflint museum** in the Mairie *(guided tours on weekdays from 9am to 1pm and 3.30 to 7pm; 2F)*. The exploitation of this stone with its rare qualities and the history of the industry are the main themes.

The church in a pure Romanesque style contains several fine 16C statues of Christ, St. Roch and St. Anne, the Virgin and a *Pietà*.

The D 17 approaches the Cher: fine view of St-Aignan *(p 133)* rising in tiers up the hillside.

Alternative route by the north bank. – *Extra 6 km - 4 miles. At Meusnes take the road to Châtillon-sur-Cher.*

Châtillon-sur-Cher. – Pop 1 349. Standing back from the N 76 in a green setting on the edge of the plateau, Châtillon has a 12-16C church *(to visit apply to M. Bouquet, Rue de L'Église)*. Inside are Romanesque baptismal fonts and on the left wall of the chancel a **panel**★ representing St. Catherine by the school of Leonardo da Vinci . Note the Saint's expression and her hands they are characteristic of the Master's style.

Rejoin the N 76.

Noyers-sur-Cher. – Pop 2 309. The 13C church with Angevin vaulting has a fine 16C statue of St. Sylvain.

1 km - ½ mile beyond Noyers, notice to the right the Chapel of St-Lazare with its bell gable which was formerly part of a leper or lazar house.

From St-Aignan to Tours – *71 km - 44 miles – about 3½ hours – Local map below*

Leave St-Aignan *(p 133)* by the D 17 which follows the Cher. Vineyards clothe the hillsides around Mareuil. At Pouillé turn right to cross the Cher by a narrow bridge. At Thésée take the N 76.

Thésée. – Pop 1 099. 1 km - ½ mile to the northwest are the remains of Roman Tasciaca, once a staging post and storehouse on the road between Bourges and Tours.

Excavations on the opposite bank of the Cher have revealed craftsmen's villages: several potters' kilns and pottery objects. *Exhibition in the Mairie 1 July to 31 August from 2.30 to 6.30pm; closed on Tuesdays; 3F.*

Shortly afterwards the cliff face is pierced by troglodyte dwellings.

Monthou-sur-Cher. – *Facilities p 38.* The Romanesque church has a fine semicircular arched doorway and the 11C apse displays diamond and rose shaped stonework patterns.

Château-du-Gué-Péan★. – *2 km - 1 mile beyond Monthou. Description p 85.*

Beyond Vineuil cross the river by the D 158 to reach the D 17, affording a good view of the sheer faces of the former white tufa chalk quarries of **Bourré** which are now transformed into wine cellars or caves for mushroom growing.

Montrichard★. – *Description p 120.*

After Montrichard the N 76 follows the foot of the wooded hillside before skirting the park of Chissay.

Chissay-en-Touraine. – Pop 850. The 15-16C Château de Chissay, standing in a wooded site, is flanked by round towers one of which has machicolations.

Take a left turn into the D 27 to cross to St-Georges.

St-Georges-sur-Cher. – Pop 1 803. *Facilities p 39.* This is a former port and wine producing centre.

The Romanesque **church** *(to visit apply at the presbytery)* with a square tower has interesting capitals in the chancel. There is a 17C St. Georges in the south transept and the St-Vincent Chapel has masonic batons and mariners' ex-votos.

Return again to the N 76 which passes through Chenonceaux.

Château de Chenonceau★★★. – *Description p 68.*

Between Chenonceaux and Civray a wine making plant and cooperative cellar incite the tourist to stop. After la Croix the N 76 crosses to the south bank of the Cher.

Bléré. – Pop 4 113. *Facilities p 38.* Bléré, a market town and small but growing industrial centre, possesses some fine old houses in the main square. The **church** was constructed by linking Romanesque chapels with 15C vaulting. The eastern nave is dominated by an octagonal tower and ends in a rounded apse; the central nave is Flamboyant; the southern nave is Romanesque. A Renaissance chapel, with baptismal fonts, has been added to the northern nave.

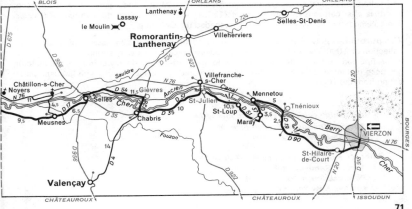

CHER Valley

Leaving Bléré by the east, the D 40, you will see in an old cemetery which has been converted into a square, a strange **funerary chapel** built in 1526 for Guillaume de Saigne, a former Treasurer of the French Royal Artillery under François I. The beautifully detailed carved decoration is Italianate.

The N 76 on leaving Bléré follows the Cher Valley before climbing to a wooded and vine covered plateau, from where there are fine glimpses of the valley.

Take the D 83, which twists down through vineyards to reach St-Martin-le-Beau.

St-Martin-le-Beau. – Pop 1 410. The church has a finely sculpted Romanesque doorway.

Return to the N 76 by Nitray.

Château de Leugny. – *Guided tours in July and August from 2 to 6pm; 5F.* This elegant building was the work of the architect Portier for his own use. It is furnished with Louis XVI style furniture.

On approaching Véretz there are fine views of the surrounding countryside.

Véretz. – Pop 1 336. *Facilities p 39*. The **church**, partly dug out of the living rock, possesses a curious seigneurial chapel which forms a gallery and communicates with the terraces of the château, where the main entrance to the church is situated. Arranged in the early 16C for Jean de la Brosse the Lord of Véretz and First Gentleman of the

(After photo: Arthaud, Grenoble)

Véretz Church
Mural painting

Bedchamber to François I, the chapel is decorated with mural paintings. Some of the more remarkable have been attributed to the school of Leonardo da Vinci, however others maintain that they are more probably the work of the artists of Fontainebleau.

Follow the N 76 to Tours (p 150).

CHEVERNY, Château de ★★

Michelin map **64** 17 – *Local map p 102*

Tourists who visit the imposingly white and symmetrical Château de Cheverny after those of Blois and Chambord will find the contrast striking. Blois bears the traces of four centuries of architecture; Cheverny was built without interruption entirely in the Classical style. Blois and Chambord are royal palaces; Cheverny is a stately home. The two great castles, now virtually empty of furniture, have lost their warmth and life; Cheverny has kept its handsome 17C furniture and sumptuous decoration.

Completed in 1634 by Hurault de Cheverny, the château's present owner is still a member of the same family. As at Chenonceau and Azay-le-Rideau, it was the lady of the house who directed the building.

(After photo: F. de Bertier)

Château de Cheverny

The apartments. – *Guided tours from 9am to noon and 2.15 to 5pm or 6.45pm during the tourist season; time ½ hour; 8F. Guided tours in English in summer.*

In the Grand Salon on the ground floor are several paintings: Jeanne d'Aragon from the school of Raphael; on the chimneypiece a portrait by Mignard of Marie-Johanne de Saumery, Countess of Cheverny. In the Petit Salon there are five Flemish tapestries after Teniers.

A majestic stone **grand staircase**, with straight flights, delicately adorned with sculptures representing fruit, flowers, weapons and artistic symbols, leads to the apartments.

Note, in the King's Bedroom and the guardroom, the rich painted **decoration** of the panelling and ceiling beams by the Blois painter Jean Mosnier (1600-56), and a series of five magnificent **tapestries** after cartoons by Simon Vouet (1590-1649) representing the *Labours of Ulysses*. These came from the Paris factory which preceded the Gobelins.

The outbuildings and the park. – In an outbuilding is the **Trophy Room**, which contains a collection of 2 000 deer antlers. The nearby **kennels** house a pack sixty strong.

A fine park surrounds the château. The formal garden immediately in front of the building has been replanted. On leaving, you will see the graceful village church, with its rustic porch dating from the 16C.

The companion guides in English in this series on France are
Brittany, Dordogne, French Riviera,
Normandy, Provence, Paris.

*Other **Michelin Green Guides** available in English*
Austria, Germany, Italy,
Portugal, Spain, Switzerland,
London, New York City.

Michelin map 🗺️ 9 – *Local maps pp 76 and 103* – *Pop 8 303* – *Facilities p 38*

The town of Chinon evokes the Middle Ages in its military aspect by the castle and in its city life by the old quarter. Literary associations as well as beautiful views and setting add to its artistic and historical interest. That great man of Chinon, Rabelais (1494-1553), was born at La Devinière *(p 75)* and spent his childhood at Chinon, which he left only to complete his studies first at Angers and then at Montpellier.

HISTORICAL NOTES

An Anglo-French Fortress (Middle Ages). – The Chinon Plateau overlooking the Vienne ends in a spur that almost reaches the river. This spur was fortified by the Romans and for ten centuries had a confused and tragic history.

Three masters of the art of fortification left their mark on the present castle: two of the Plantagenet Kings of England, Henry II and Richard Lionheart, and one King of France, Philippe-Auguste. It was in 1205 after an eight months' siege that the latter captured the fortress from the English.

The Court of the "King of Bourges" (beginning of the 15C). – At the accession of **Charles VII**, France was in an almost desperate situation. Henry VI, King of England, was also "King of Paris". Charles VII was only "King of Bourges" when, in 1427, he brought his little court to Chinon. The following year he called a meeting of the States-General of the central and southern provinces which had remained faithful to him. They voted him 400 000 *livres* to organise the defence of Orléans, then besieged by the English *(p 121)*.

Joan of Arc at Chinon (1429). – Escorted by six men at arms, Joan travelled from Lorraine to Chinon without encountering any of the armed bands which were ravaging the country. The people took this for a clear sign of divine protection. Waiting to be received by Charles VII, Joan spent two days at an inn in the lower town, fasting and praying.

When the peasant girl of eighteen was admitted to the palace, an attempt was made to put her out of countenance. The great hall was lit by fifty torches; 300 gentlemen in rich apparel were assembled there. The King hid among the crowd. A courtier wore his robes.

Joan advanced shyly, immediately recognized the King and went straight to him. "Gentle Dauphin", she said – for Charles, not having been crowned, was only the Dauphin to her – "my name is Jehanne la Pucelle [Joan the Maid]. The King of Heaven sends word by me that you will be anointed and crowned in the city of Reims, and you will be the Lieutenant of the King of Heaven, who is the King of France."

Charles was obsessed with doubts; he wondered whether Charles VI was really his father. His mother was Isabella of Bavaria, whose conduct was scandalous. When the Maid said to him: "I tell you in the name of Our Lord Christ that you are the heir of France and the true son of the King", he was reassured and almost believed in the heroine's mission.

His advisers were more stubborn. The poor girl was made to appear before the court at Poitiers. A bench of doctors and matrons was to decide whether she was bewitched or inspired. For three weeks she was cross examined. Her naïve replies, her swift repartee, her piety and confidence in her heavenly mission convinced the most sceptical. She was recognised as the "Messenger of God".

The Maid returned to Chinon, where she was equipped and given armed men. She left on 20 April 1429 to accomplish her miraculous and tragic destiny (see map p 16, "An Outline of the Campaign of Joan of Arc in the Loire Country").

The Divorce of Louis XII (end of 15C). – Chinon remained the seat of the court until 1450, when it was abandoned. The château, however, recovered a momentary glory in 1498, when King Louis XII received the Papal Legate, Cesare Borgia, there. Borgia brought him the Bull pronouncing his divorce.

Louis XII parted from Jeanne de France, the daughter of Louis XI, without regret. He had been only fourteen when the King compelled him to marry her. Her hunched back, diseased hip and simian appearance explained her husband's lack of ardour during their twenty-three years of married life. When Charles VIII died, Louis XII, according to the King's will, was to marry his widow, Anne of Brittany. He was much attracted to her, and this new marriage kept Brittany for the Crown. Thus the King had a double reason for celebrating the arrival of the liberating Bull with magnificent fêtes.

Decline. – The great Cardinal Richelieu took a fancy to Chinon and obtained possession of it, although not without difficulty. The château belonged to his family until the Revolution. It was badly kept and the fortifications and buildings began to crumble. Its decay became more marked under Napoleon I. Chinon then became the property of the Indre-et-Loire department, which carried out repairs and consolidated the ruins.

■ **MAIN SIGHTS** *time: 2 hours*

Bridge. – The bridge over the Vienne River, with some piers dating from the 12C, spans an island, where in 1321 all the Jews of Chinon were burned alive. Take a right turn on the **Quai Danton** and enjoy the **view**★★ of Chinon and its château. The quays of the right bank were once the site of the old fortified walls, the river being used as the moat.

Cross the Vienne and turn left into the Quai Charles VII and leave the car in the car park, on foot take the alley, which branches off to the right of the square, and leads to Rue Voltaire.

Old Chinon★★ **(Vieux Chinon).** – Characteristic of the 14-16C are the **streets**★ Rue Haute St-Maurice and Rue Voltaire bordered by old houses with wooden gables, corner turrets and mullioned windows and intersected by alleys which afford unusual views of the castle. There is a 15C gate at no 81 near the entrance to the Hôtel Bodard de la Jacopière; opposite, no 82, a 16C hôtel, has a beautiful interior courtyard; at no 73, the Palais du Bailliage, now the Gargantua Hôtel, has on its south front a fine staircase turret which can be seen from the Rue Jacques-Cœur.

Beyond the Place St-Maurice at no 44 is the House of the States-General, where Richard Lionheart wounded at the siege of Châlus, in the Limousin, died in 1199.

CHINON★★

The most picturesque corner is the **Grand Carroi★★** (*Carroi*=crossroads), the centre of activity in the Middle Ages. It forms a picturesque scene with its 11C brick decorated timber-work houses, overhanging upper storeys and a variety of 15C gables and turrets. One gets the impression that little has changed since Joan of Arc arrived at the inn in the Grand Carroi and used the edge of the well, at the corner of Rue Voltaire, to dismount.

House of the States-General (Maison des États-Généraux – M²). – *Open 1 June to 31 August from 10am to noon and 3 to 7pm; 1 September to 31 May from 10am to noon and 2 to 5pm; closed in January and on Tuesdays; 3F.*

This attractive house with a corner turret is associated not only with the death of Richard Lion-heart but also the meetings of the States-General called by Charles VII in 1427 and 1428. There are beautiful rooms: the main hall on the first floor has a full portrait of Rabelais by Delacroix; and the second floor, where the roof is in the form of a ship's hull, contains the collections of a local historical society. There are also Joan of Arc's relics (1431) and St. Mexme's cope brought back from the Holy Land during one of the Crusades as well as Gothic chests and several wooden statues of the Virgin.

Go to the Place de l'Hôtel de Ville and take to the left, behind the statue of Rabelais, the stairway that meets up with the Rue du Puy-des-Bancs, which leads you to the château.

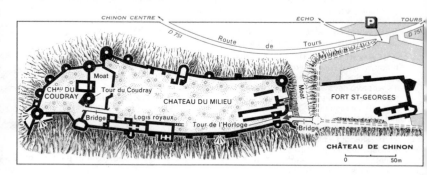

CHÂTEAU DE CHINON

Château★★. – *Open 9am to noon and 2 to 7pm (5.30pm from 1 October to 14 March); closed on Wednesdays out of season and during December and January; time: ¾ hour; 5F. Son et Lumière performance see p 33.*

This well fortified castle – 400 m by 70 m - 1 312 ft by 230 ft – is made up of three distinct fortresses separated by deep moats *(illustration p 9)*. To the east Fort St-Georges, in the centre, the Château du Milieu and to the west, the Château du Coudray.

Fort St-Georges. – Now dismantled it was a later addition built by the Plantagenet Henry II. The Vienne and some ravines protected the castle from the south, west and north, but the east was open to attacks from the plateau. Fort St-Georges reinforced the defences at this point. The fort was named after its chapel, dedicated to the patron saint of England. Henry II died here and his body was afterwards taken to Fontevraud. Henry's son Richard also died in Chinon *(see above)*.

Château du Milieu. – The moat between Fort St-Georges and the Château du Milieu or Middle Castle was originally spanned by a wooden bridge ending in a drawbridge. A stone bridge has taken its place.

Enter the bailey by the Clock Tower or Tour de l'Horloge. The gatehouse tower itself is curiously narrow: 5 m - 16 ft wide and 35 m - 115 ft high. Seen in profile from the town it looks like a column. A bell known as the Marie Javelle, hung in a lantern turret abutting the platform, rings every hour. The south curtain wall affords picturesque **views★★** of old Chinon, the Vienne and its valley.

The royal apartments or **Logis Royaux**, abut the outer wall. Joan of Arc was received *(p 73)* in the great hall, which was on the first floor of this building. Now only the first few steps and an

(After photo: Arthaud, Grenoble)

The Clock Tower

end gable with its fireplace remain. The ground floor rooms exhibit tapestries, paintings, Gallo-Roman sculptures and a statue of Joan of Arc by Dubois.

Château du Coudray. – This contains the keep or Tour du Coudray, built by Philippe-Auguste. Joan of Arc occupied the first floor during her stay in Chinon. The Templars were imprisoned here in 1308 and are believed to have been responsible for the wall graffiti to be seen on the second floor.

This part of the fortress has two other rather fine towers on the curtain wall.

Leave by the main entrance and make for the Route de Tours. Take the narrow road to the left leading to "the echo" (300 m - 328 yd Rtn).

The Echo★. – Stand near the post that marks the site of this phenomenon, turn towards the ramparts and speak or sing. You will be surprised by the clarity of the echo. You will also get a good view of the north perimeter wall.

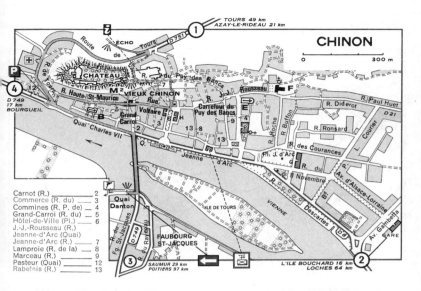

■ ADDITIONAL SIGHTS

Rue J.-J. Rousseau★. – This is a continuation of the Rue Voltaire. To the right, in the Rue de la Lamproie, no 15 was Rabelais's house. The Puy-des-Bancs crossroads is picturesque.

St-Maurice (B). – 12-16C. The nave and chancel are in a very pure Angevin style.

St-Étienne (E). – Rebuilt in ten months by Philippe de Commines (1480) whose coat of arms is on the façade.

St-Mexme (F). – A former basilica of the 10C now in disrepair.

From the corner of St-Mexme, the steep rise of the Pitoche, bordered by troglodyte houses, takes you to the **Chapel of Ste-Radegonde** (6-12C) cut into the rock.

EXCURSIONS

Château du Rivau; Champigny-sur-Veude★. – *Round trip of 34 km - 21 miles by ③ and the D 749 and turn left at Le Coudray.*

Château du Rivau. – *Guided tours 15 March to 31 October from 10am to noon and 2 to 7pm; time: ¾ hour; 10F.*
Built in the 13C Le Rivau was fortified in the 15C by Pierre de Beauvau, Chamberlain to Charles VII. It was here that Joan of Arc obtained horses for her troops before the siege of Orléans. Le Rivau also figures in Rabelais's work: after the Picrocholean War, Gargantua gave the château to one of his knights. The drawbridge, overlooked by the keep, leads to the court of honour, which is surrounded by mediaeval buildings and the Renaissance main building. During the tour, notice the 13 and 15C white tufa paving; the Gothic and Renaissance furniture. Throughout the château are various paintings by the contemporary artist Pierre-Laurent Brenot. Note in particular the canvas entitled *Le Cyclope* which portrays a Lady with a unicorn and figures the Château du Rivau in the distant background.

Champigny-sur-Veude★. – *Description p 62.*

Return to Chinon by the D 26 which follows the west bank of the river.

Rabelais's country★. – *Round trip of 26 km - 16 miles by ③ and the D 749.* The road runs beneath a continuous arch of enormous plane trees as far as St-Lazare where you turn right into the D 751, once a Roman road. 3 km - 2 miles further on turn left into the D 759 and right on to the D 24 which is continued by the D 117. This affords fine glimpses of a pleasant, undulating countryside interspersed with poplar and walnut trees and dominated by the Château du Coudray-Montpensier.

La Devinière. – *Open 9am to noon and 2 to 7pm (5.30pm from 1 October to 14 March); closed on Wednesdays out of season and in January and December; 4F.*
This manor was where **François Rabelais** (1494-1553), the author of the great satirical work *Gargantua* and *Pantagruel*, spent his childhood. Son of a local lawyer, Rabelais, the writer and scholar was also a Franciscan priest and eminent physician. Published in parts, his great work presents the preoccupations of the day through the lively exploits of the two main characters. His native region is the scene of the Picrocholean War and therefore associations with Rabelais or his works abound in the area.
The museum has documents relating to the life and works of Rabelais.

Continue along the D 117 on the way to **Lerné**, passing the ruins of the Château de Maulévrier. According to Rabelais it was from this village that the bakers of a special bread used to set out to sell their wares in Chinon. It was an incident between these bakers and some shepherds from nearby Seuilly, that sparked off the Picrocholean War described in *Gargantua*.

Château de Chavigny. – *Not open to the public.* Of the château erected by Le Muet in 1636 there remain some rather magnificent outbuildings and a dovecote, doorway, pavilion and chapel. The dry moats give some indication of the former plan of the building. A bridge leads to the Louis XIII style doorway which is flanked by the guardroom and surmounted by a curvilinear pediment.

Take the D 117 then the D 224 to reach Seuilly.

Seuilly. – *Pop 431.* The young Rabelais was educated at the Benedictine abbey which once stood in Seuilly. He was later to satirise the Benedictines through the character of Frère Jean.

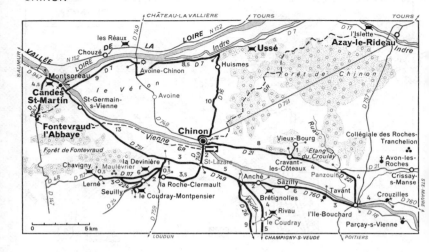

Château du Coudray-Montpensier. – *Not open to the public.* Built in 1481 by Louis I de Bourbon-Montpensier, and owned at one time by the writer Maurice Maeterlinck, the château now houses a medical and educational centre. The estate is privately owned.

La Roche-Clermault. – In Rabelais's tale, this château, owned by Grandgousier, was actively disputed by both sides.

Vienne Valley*. – *Round trip of 44 km - 27 miles; about 1½ hours.* Visitors particularly interested in early ecclesiastical architecture may make detours to Vieux-Bourg-de-Cravant and Crouzilles. *Leave Chinon to the east by the Rue J.-J.-Rousseau and the D 21.*

The road follows the chalky slope, passing some fine houses, until Cravant-les-Côteaux, an important wine growing centre.

Vieux-Bourg-de-Cravant. – *1 km - ½ mile from Cravant-les-Côteaux.* The nave of the church *(admission: 3F)* is a good example of the Carolingian style. Note the three windows in the south wall, and the door which was originally protected by a canopy whose rectangular Merovingian style pillars, adorned with interlacing, are now inside near the chancel. The chancel *(lit by projectors)* and south chapel added in the 15C have broken barrel vaulting.

Follow the D 21 to Panzoult and then take the D 221.

L'Ile-Bouchard. – *Description p 85.*

Crouzilles. – Pop 471. *4 km - 3 miles from L'Ile-Bouchard by the D 760.* The Poitou style Romanesque church with Angevin vaulting has four statue columns supporting the ogive vaulting of the chancel. The south transept contains the "beau Dieu de Crouzilles".

On returning to L'Ile-Bouchard cross the Vienne and take the D 760 which follows the wide river valley. The alluvial areas are either lush meadowlands or planted with cereals or vegetables while orchards and vineyards cover the valley sides.

Tavant. – *Description p 86.*

The route goes through **Sazilly** with its charming Romanesque church half hidden by cypresses, before passing the **Château de Brétignolles**, a Louis XII style building. Shortly afterwards one comes to Anché.

Anché. – Pop 363. The 13 and 15C church has to the right of the nave with its Angevin vaulting, a 13C bas-relief representing an abbot.

The D 760 rejoins the D 749 which eventually veers towards Chinon through an archway of plane trees.

Le Véron; Candes-St-Martin**; Fontevraud Abbey**. – *Round trip of 54 km - 34 miles by ①, D 751 then the D 16 to the left.*

The area between the Loire and the Vienne is composed of light alluvial soils or alluvial sediments deposited by the two rivers. This countryside is known as the **Véron**. Highly fertile the crops grown here include cereals, vines and fruit trees (plums for the famous prunes of Tours). It was in this area that Rabelais set his Abbey of Thélème.

Huismes. – Pop 1 031. Standing on the edge of the Forest of Chinon the village has a Romanesque church.

Avoine-Chinon Nuclear Power Station. – *A belvedere is equipped with plans and models which enable one to understand the working of the reactor.* Built in 1963 this was the first nuclear power reactor in France to generate electricity. This dual purpose plan combines plutonium and power production, with the emphasis on the latter. Chinon 1, the prototype, was shut down in 1973 but not destroyed and its great dome, with a diameter of 55 m - 180 ft, is the most striking feature. The present production units, known as Chinon 2 and 3, have a maximum output of 700 000 kW (compare Dungeness A with an output of 424 000 kW) and an average annual production of 3 500 million kWh.

Follow the Loire along the D 7, crossing the river to reach Candes and then turn right.

Candes-St-Martin**. – *Description p 59.*

Montsoreau*. – *Description p 121.*

Fontevraud Abbey**. – *Description p 81.*

Return to Candes and follow the D 751 to Chinon which affords fine views of the Vienne.

Chinon to Richelieu by steam train – *See Richelieu p 129.*

Michelin map 🆔 8 – *Local maps pp 102 and 145* – Pop 2 027

The only interesting feature of Cléry, but an exceptional one, is its basilica in which Louis XI is buried.

The present church had its origin in a humble chapel to which, in 1280, some ploughmen carried a statue of the Virgin found in a thicket. The cult of this statue spread through the district, and the chapel, being too small to accommodate the pilgrims *(1)*, was transformed into a church served by a college of canons. This was destroyed in 1428 by the English commander Salisbury, on his march to Orléans.

Charles VII and Dunois supplied the first funds for rebuilding, but the great benefactor of Cléry was **Louis XI**. When still Dauphin, during the siege of Dieppe, he made a vow: if he were victorious, he would give his weight in silver to Notre-Dame de Cléry. His prayer was answered and he kept his vow.

When he became King Louis XI dedicated himself to the Virgin and his attachment to Cléry was strengthened thereby. He was buried there by his wish. The building was completed by his son, Charles VIII.

■ THE BASILICA★ *time: ½ hour*

To visit the vault of Louis XI and St. James's Chapel, apply at the presbytery 1 Rue du Cloitre, behind the chevet of the church or at the sacristy.

The house in which Louis XI stayed during his visits to Cléry is on the right of the church, opposite the entrance. It is now a school.

Notre-Dame de Cléry is a 15C building with the exception of its square tower abutting the north side of the church, which is 14C and alone escaped destruction by the English. *Enter through the door into the transept.*

The interior of the church is both plain and graceful: there are no capitals on the pillars and no triforium. Today its grace appears rather cold. The church should be imagined in the warm light of its former stained glass windows and hung with tapestries.

The Tomb of Louis XI. – The tomb stands on the north side of the nave and is aligned with the Virgin's altar, so that it lies at an oblique angle to the axis of the church.

The King's marble statue is the work of an Orléans sculptor, Bourdin (1622). It took the place of the original bronze statue melted down by the Huguenots.

Louis XI's Vault. – Louis XI's bones and those of his wife, Charlotte de Savoie, are still in the vault which opens on to the nave near the tomb. The two skulls, sawn open for embalming, are in a glass case. Note the *litre (2)* which runs round the vaulting.

Tanguy de Châtel, who was killed during a siege while saving the life of Louis XI, is buried under a flagstone alongside the royal vault. Further to the right another stone covers the urn containing the heart of Charles VIII. The inscription on this urn is repeated on the nearest pillar.

Chapelle St-Jacques★. – *South aisle.* This was built by Gilles de Pontbriand, Dean of the church, and his brother to serve as their tomb. The Renaissance decoration is very rich. The vaulting is decorated with girdles, pilgrims' staffs and pilgrims' purses, for Cléry is on the pilgrimage route to St. James's shrine in Santiago de Compostela, Spain. The walls are studded with ermines' tails and bridges (the arms of the Pontbriands). There are three fine statues of which two are of wood: St. James in a pilgrim's cloak is 16C, St. Sebastian is 17C, and the Virgin with the very delicate features is 16C and of stone.

Chapelle de Dunois. – *South aisle.* Dunois and his family lie here *(p 62)*. The church at Cléry was finished when this chapel was added (1464) so that the construction of the vaulting was complicated by the presence of a buttress.

Stalls. – These were presented by Henri II. Their seats are carved with various human masks and the initials of the donor and his mistress, Diane de Poitiers (see cheekpieces of second row on the right).

Chancel. – On the modern high altar is a statue in wood of Notre-Dame de Cléry. She is covered by a cloak, and only the heads of the Virgin and the Child Jesus appear. In the central window a fine piece of 16C stained glass represents Henri III founding the Order of the Holy Spirit. All the other windows were destroyed by the Huguenots or in the Revolution.

Sacristy door. – In the second ambulatory bay on the right is the beautiful door to the sacristy, in pure Flamboyant style. Above it a small opening leads to an oratory from which Louis XI could follow the services without being seen.

COURTANVAUX, Château de

Michelin map 🆔 5 – 2 km - 1 mile to the northwest of Bessé-sur-Braye

Guided tours from 1 July to 31 August at 10 and 11am, 2, 3, 4, 5 and 6pm; 15 April to 30 June and September on Sundays and public holidays only at the aforementioned times; 3F.

Set in a shaded vale this Gothic building was the seat of a marquisate held successively by Louis XIV's Secretary of State for War, Michel Le Tellier, Marquis de Louvois and Pierre de Montesquiou, Marshal of France, the real D'Artagnan who was in fact cousin to Dumas's hero.

On the downfall of the Empire in 1815, the château was to emerge from 150 years of abandonment when the King of Rome's (Napoleon Bonaparte's son by Marie-Louise) governess came to live here. She was a Montesquiou hence the petname "Maman Quiou".

An avenue shaded by plane trees leads to the Renaissance gatehouse. The buildings have typical 15 and 16C features: tall roofs, mullioned windows and pointed pediments. The inner courtyard forms a terrace which is itself dominated by two terraces, all of which give a good idea of the château's site.

The main building called the "grand château", has on the first floor a suite of four rooms (47 m - 154 ft long) which were redecorated in 1882.

(1) The pilgrimage is still popular. It takes place on 8 September and the following Sunday.
(2) A litre is a black painted band, bearing the arms of a lord, which runs round a church or a chapel. The higher the rank of the nobleman, the higher it is placed.

CRAON

Michelin map 63 9 – Pop 4 763 – *Facilities p 38*

Astride the Oudon, this calm Angevin town lies in the heart of the *bocage* country. Arable farming and stock raising are the main activities of the region.

Craon is well known for its race meetings *(first and second Saturdays in September and third Saturday plus the following two days)*. From the esplanade behind the church there is a pleasant view of Craon. This was the birthplace of the philosopher writer, Volney, who enjoyed great fame in his lifetime.

Château. – *Park and gardens open 9am to noon and 2 to 7pm; enter from the Laval road: 1.50F.*
This elegant château built in the local white tufa from 1760 to 1770 is fronted by formal French gardens and surrounded by an English type park crossed by the winding Oudon. The garden front, regular and rusticated, is topped by a curvilinear pediment. The windows are adorned by Louis XVI style festoons. The courtyard front is in a more severe Neo-Classical style.

EXCURSIONS

Château de Mortiercrolles. – *11 km - 7 miles to the southeast by the D 25 and then a road to the left. Guided tours 1 July to 31 August from 2.30 to 6.30pm; closed on Tuesdays; time: ½ hour; 6F.*
This elegant château *(restoration in progress)* was built in the late 15C by Pierre de Rohan. A wide moat encircles the long wall with corner towers which is guarded by a remarkable gatehouse★ with alternating courses of brick and stonework, and fine machicolations in white tufa. In the courtyard to the right the façade of the main apartments is ornamented by superb dormer windows with frontons. At the rear of the courtyard the chapel of brick with stone courses was reroofed in 1969: the side door and piscina are decorated with attractive shell shapes.

La Frénouse. – *14 km - 9 miles to the northeast of Craon by the N 171 and D 126.* An avenue bordered by giant statues leads to La Frénouse, a former farm now restored and the unusual museum of sculpture.

Robert Tatin Museum. – *Open 10am to noon and 2 to 7pm (5pm from 2 October to 31 March); 5F.*
This somewhat surprising open-air museum consists of a sculptured ensemble surrounding a basin. The work of a single man, Robert Tatin, the totem pole like structures show a decidedly Latin American influence.

CUNAULT ★★

Michelin map 64 12 – 12 km - 8 miles to the northwest of Saumur – *Local map p 103*

The church at Cunault is a fine building erected from the 11C to the 13C. It was part of a rich Benedictine priory dependent on the Abbey of Tournus in Burgundy. In 1715 there were only five monks within the old walls and the monastery was closed.

Church★★. – *Time: ½ hour.* The nave forms a long building with a magnificent Romanesque belfry, ending in an 11C spire rising from the north aisle. The west front is fortified. Its doorway includes a fine 13C group depicting an Adoration of the Virgin who holds the Infant Christ in her arms.

On entering the visitor is struck by the pure lines of the nave's elevation and the whiteness of the stone. The main arcade of the nave rises majestically to the vaulting, which is supported by the tall aisles. Three bays have Angevin vaulting *(p 21)*; the other five are roofed with broken barrel vaulting. The north aisle contains a dome under the belfry. This was the transept crossing of the original church.

The chancel is raised and a false transept divides it from the nave.

The sculptures at Cunault are well known: 223 capitals (worth examining with fieldglasses), keystones to the vaulting, friezes and arcades have been carved with the chisel.

Decoration. – There are traces at Cunault of the painted decoration which, in the Middle Ages, emphasised the main architectural lines of the churches. Here and there, some lord's *litre (p 77)* may still be seen on the walls and pillars. Inside the façade, on the walls of the aisles and the pillars of the nave, fragments of paintings remain, one of which is 15C and depicts St. Christopher carrying the Infant Jesus.

Furnishings. – Go round the chancel, starting from the left. You will see an expressive 16C *Pietà*; a 16C oak vestment wardrobe; a painted wooden shrine dating from the 13C (wooden shrines are very rare – almost all the shrines that have come down to us are in metal) and, in the chapel off the false transept, on the right, a St. Catherine carved in wood of the 15C. In the south aisle, a recess contains a much damaged 14C reclining figure.

A pretty 16C house opposite the church was the Prior's residence.

(After photo: Arthaud)

Cunault Church
Saint Catherine

DAMPIERRE-SUR-LOIRE

Michelin map 64 12 – *Local map p 103* – Pop 453

Dampierre lies between the Loire and the valley side, riddled with caves and disused quarries, from which stone was once exported as far afield as England. Vine growing and mushroom growing are the main activities of this riverside town. Troglodyte houses stand side by side with charming white tufa Renaissance dwellings. On the valley slopes the vineyards produce a full bodied white wine, dry or medium dry, a *rosé* from the Cabernet grape, known as the *Cabernet de Saumur* and the *Champigny* red wine.

Church. – This simple building has a small Renaissance doorway. On the north wall of the nave is a very realistic 17C painting evoking the Last Sacraments, in a chapel to the right of the chancel is a 17C statue of St. Tanche holding his severed head in his hands. Note also a moving 17C statue of the Virgin and Child.

Margaret of Anjou's Manor. – In Rue Morains on the outskirts of Dampierre in the direction of Souzay stands a manor house with corner turrets overlooking the Loire. It was here that Margaret of Anjou, Queen Consort of Henry VI of England, died on 25 August 1482. Daughter of Good King René I of Anjou, Margaret played a leading role in the defence of the Lancastrian cause during the Wars of the Roses (1455-85). She waged a ceaseless fight to defend her son, Prince Edward's right to inherit the throne, but on his death at the Battle of Tewkesbury in 1471, and her husband's murder in The Tower soon afterwards, Margaret herself was put in custody. When ransomed by Louis XI in 1475 she returned here to her native country to spend the last years of her life.

DESCARTES

Michelin map 🔢 5 – Pop 4 481 – *Facilities p 38*

It was in Descartes, formerly known as La Haye, that **René Descartes** (1590-1650), the famous French philosopher, physicist and mathematician was baptised (his place of birth was in fact a nearby field), although the family home was in the neighbouring town of Châtellerault. At the age of eight he was sent to the Jesuit College of Henri IV in La Flèche where he received a semi military education, before joining the army under the Prince of Nassau. While pursuing his military career, he travelled widely in Europe, devoting most of his time to study, and the pursuit of his life's mission as it was revealed to him on 10 November 1619. In 1629 he went again to Holland where he stayed for twenty years, studying at various universities and writing and publishing some of his most famous works. In 1649 he accepted an invitation to the Swedish royal court, where he died on 11 February 1650.

This was also the home of the novelist **René Boylesve** (1867-1926) who described his native town in a novel entitled *L'Enfant à la Balustrade.*

EXCURSIONS

Balesmes. – *2 km - 1 mile to the northwest by the D 750.* Standing in the main street is the Romanesque church, which has, however, been restored. This white stone edifice has an attractive belfry over the transept crossing and oven vaulted apsidal chapels decorated with sculptured modillions.
The small round arched windows contain stained glass by Max Ingrand *(p 27).* The north and central apsidal chapels have fragments of frescoes.

Les Ormes. – *7 km - 4 miles to the west on the N 10.* Standing with its back to the Vienne, the château was in 1729 the seat of the Voyer d'Argenson family. *Not open to the public.*
Altered many times, the main front is in the 18C style. The central building, an early 20C reconstruction, is linked to two 18C pavilions by means of single storey arcades with roof top terraces. Two wings, at right angles to the main front, face one another across the grass covered courtyard. The park has some majestic **plane trees.** The former stables, known as **La Bergerie,** present a severe but striking façade on the other side of the N 10.

Ferrière-Larçon. – *16 km - 10 miles to the east by the D 100.*
Château du Châtellier. – *Not open to the public.* Standing on a rocky outcrop, commanding the Brignon Valley, this château dates from the 12, 13, 15 and 16C. To the east of its rampart is an imposing but most unusual round keep with a spur. Two bridges, undoubtedly drawbridges in former times, give access to the courtyard. The main building is flanked by an hexagonal tower.

Ferrière-Larçon. – Pop 418. The picturesque tile roofs of this village climb haphazardly up the valley slopes.

The **church** is an interesting mixture of styles with a Romanesque façade, nave and transept crossing tower and a Gothic chancel. The tower is particularly elegant and well proportioned. The narrow nave opens on to a wide chancel with lofty vaulting, recalling the Angevin style *(p 21).* The 13C capitals portraying oak leaf and water lily motifs or crockets assume astonishing proportions. The baptismal font is 12C.

DOUÉ-LA-FONTAINE

Michelin map 🔢 8 – *Local maps pp 92 and 103* – Pop 6 501 – *Facilities p 38*

The town has preserved a certain number of old houses with turrets and external staircases as well as several troglodyte dwellings. Doué, with its long history, is built over a network of underground quarries and galleries excavated out of the limestone rock. The town's main activities are rose growing and market gardening.

Arena. – *Open 1 April to 30 September from 8am to noon and 2 to 7pm; the rest of the year 9am to noon and 2 to 6pm; closed on Tuesday mornings out of season; 3F.*
Situated in the **Douces** quarter of the town, the so called arena, was in reality a quarry which was transformed in the 15C when rows of seats were cut out of the solid rock. The quarry is now used for theatrical and musical performances as well as flower shows *(rose shows in mid July).* The vast caves, under the seating, were for a long time inhabited and kitchens and other rooms are still visible. Vendéen prisoners were confined there.

St-Denis Collegiate Church. – *Exterior only.* Formerly run by a chapter of canons from the Benedictine priory at Cunault, the church is no more than a very romantic ruin in the Angevin style, transitional between the Romanesque and Gothic. Several of the capitals are historiated or portray fantastic animals.

Fountain. – In the lower part of the town is the source of the natural spring, which was tapped in the 18C and originally gave Doué-la-Fontaine its name.

The Zoo. – *Open 15 April to 15 September from 8am to 7.30pm; zoo: 15F; children: 7F; reserve: 12F; children: 6F.*
On the outskirts of Doué on the Cholet road, the zoo occupies a former quarry. In another nearby quarry is a **reserve** with a collection of carrion birds including vultures, marabou storks and other predatory species.

Michelin map **64** 2 – *Local map p 98* – Pop 16 352 – *Facilities p 38*

This charming Angevin town, pleasantly situated on the banks of the Loir, makes for an excellent place to break a journey. La Flèche is renowned for its *Prytanée*, a military college which has trained generations of officers.

Market town for the varied fruit produce from the Maine, La Flèche has recently experienced an industrial expansion with the building of several large factories, including the printing works of the paperback publishers *Livre de Poche*.

It was from the quays of La Flèche in the 17C that boats departed for Montreal, a suburb of which is still known as Laflèche.

Henri IV, the Gay Old Spark. – Having passed through various hands including the Plantagenets, La Flèche has finally given as part of a dowry to Charles de Bourbon-Vendôme, the grandfather of Henri IV of Navarre, of "Paris is well worth a Mass" fame. It was here that the young Prince Henri happily spent his childhood.

Cradle for officers. – In May 1607 **Henri IV** signed an edict confirming his previous gift to the Jesuits of his château to create a college. At its height the college had 1 500 pupils and counted among the more famous, Descartes. Following the Jesuits expulsion from France in 1762, the college became a military school before being made in 1808 a *Prytanée militaire (see below)*.

■ **MAIN SIGHTS** *time: 1 hour*

Prytanée militaire★. – *Guided tours from 9 to 11am and 2 to 5pm; time: 1 hour; entrance 150 m - 150 yd to the left of the main doorway.*

The *Prytanée* is essentially a school for the sons of officers and in certain cases of civil servants, leading to the school leaving certificate, the *baccalaureat*. In addition preparatory classes are provided for the entrance examinations to the prestigious *grandes écoles*, especially the service academies. All pupils wear a navy blue uniform.

Built between 1620 and 1653 by the Jesuits round a series of courtyards, the college is bordered on the far side by a French style park. The Sébastopol courtyard is overlooked by the sober exterior, dominated by two towers of the **St-Louis Chapel**. The chapel is typical of the layout adopted by the Society of Jesus: a single nave with Doric pilasters, lined by chapels; large galleries and the whole well lit. Gothic style vaulting testifies to its continued survival in the 17C.

In a niche in the north arm of the transept is a lead gilt urn in the shape of a

LA FLÈCHE

0 — 400 m

Boierie (R. de la)	2
Carnot (R.)	3
Collège (R. du)	4
Dauversière (R. de la)	5
Foch (Promenade Mal)	6
Gallieni (R. du Mal)	8
Grande Rue	
Grollier (R.)	9
Henri-IV (Pl.)	10
Marché-au-Blé (Pl. du)	12
Montréal (Bd de)	13
Rhin-et-Danube (Av.)	14
Thury-Harcourt (Av.)	15

heart, containing the ashes of the hearts of Henri IV and Marie de' Medici. The majestic altarpiece is the setting for an Annunciation by Restout. The delicately carved west end gallery is surmounted by an equally intricately carved organ (1637).

The garden end of the main or Austerlitz courtyard includes the Louis XVI Hôtel dating from 1784 which serves as the commanding officer's lodging.

The wing opposite consists of two galleries: the ground floor is an arcade while the upper floor is now the library. This entrance wing is pierced, on the street side, by a Baroque doorway surmounted by the statue of Henri IV.

Also open to the public are the Great Hall and Generals Hall and the Museum of Souvenirs.

Notre-Dame-des-Vertus. – This is a charming Romanesque chapel with a semicircular arched doorway and oven vaulted apses. *(To visit apply to the Maison d'Enfants, next door.)*

The nave vaulting is decorated with medallions containing plant motifs and landscapes. The Renaissance **woodwork★** originally from the chapel of the Château du Verger *(p 99)* will fascinate, particularly the "Muslim warrior" on the back of the main door. The nave carvings include medallions and religious attributes: the Last Supper near the pulpit.

■ **ADDITIONAL SIGHTS**

Château des Carmes and gardens (B). – The postern flanked by turrets, overlooking the Loir, is all that remains of the 15-17C château belonging to the Carmelites. Hemmed in by more recent buildings the cloisters are now laid out as a garden.

The former Carmelite gardens are now a public garden with fine lime, elm and plane trees and crossed by arms of the river.

The Carmes bridge affords a fine view of the river, château and garden.

St-Thomas (D). – The nave and aisles of this church have been altered. Note in the south aisle a late 16C painting on wood of the Holy Family showing Italian influence.

EXCURSIONS

La Tertre Rouge (Zoo)★. – *5 km - 3 miles. Leave La Flèche by ② and take the D 104 to the right. Follow the road for 1 km - ½ mile after the third level crossing.*
Open 10am to 7pm; 10am to 5pm out of season; 16F; children: 7F.
In a forest setting, the zoo has over 600 animals including 250 different species; mammals, birds, reptiles, etc. The **museum of natural science**, exhibits more than 600 examples of the local fauna in their natural environment.

St-Germain-du-Val. – *Round trip of 12 km - 8 miles. Leave La Flèche by ⑤ and turn right at Verron.*
It was in Verron at the manor la Cour des Pins, that the humanist **Lazare de Baïf** (1496-1547) was born. He was Ronsard's first patron. The road following the hillside which is covered with vines and fig trees, affords some attractive views.
St-Germain was one of Henri IV's favourite places and the birthplace of the opera and ballet composer, Leo Delibes whose works include the opéra comique, *Lakmé* and the ballets *Coppelia* and *Sylvia*.
The nearby Manor of Yvandeau, was where the Scottish philosopher and historian David Hume resided while writing his *Treatise of Human Nature*.
Return to La Flèche by the D 160 and the N 23.

When visiting London use the Green Guide "London"

Detailed descriptions of places of interest
Useful local information
A section on the historic square mile of the City of London with a detailed fold out plan
The lesser known London boroughs – their people, places and sights
Plans of selected areas and important buildings.

FONTEVRAUD-L'ABBAYE ★★

Michelin map **64** – southwest of 13 – *Local maps pp 76 and 103* – Pop 1 868

The town is famous for Fontevraud Abbey, one of the great curiosities of Anjou. It has a magnificent church containing the tombs of the Plantagenets, fine monastic buildings and the only Romanesque kitchen left in France.

HISTORICAL NOTES

Foundation (1099). – The Order at Fontevraud was founded by **Robert d'Arbrissel**, a preacher famous throughout Brittany and Anjou, who had previously spent some time as a hermit in the Mayenne Forest. The abbey was unique as a religious establishment in that it grouped five different monasteries: Ste-Marie housed the nuns, St-Lazare the lepers, St-Benoît the sick, La Madeleine the fallen women, and St-Jean de l'Habit, outside the main walls, the monks. Each unit had its own church, cloister, refectory, dormitory and kitchen.

At the head of this community Robert d'Arbrissel placed a woman who took the rank of Abbess and was later designated as the "Head and General of the Order". The Order had dependent houses in England and Spain. The one at Amesbury was founded by Henry II in repentance for the murder of Thomas Becket.

An aristocratic Order. – The success of the new Order was immediate and it quickly took on an aristocratic character; the abbesses, who were members of noble families, procured rich gifts and powerful protection for the abbey. It became the refuge for repudiated queens and daughters of royal or exalted families who took leave of the world voluntarily or under compulsion. There were thirty-six abbesses, many of royal blood including five from the House of Bourbon, between 1115 and 1789.

The Westminster of the Plantagenets. – As a family the **Plantagenets** or counts of Anjou poured wealth and blessings on the abbey and it was in the crypt *(now closed)* that Henry II, his Queen, Eleanor of Aquitaine and their son Richard Lionheart found their resting place.

(After photo: Archives Photographiques)

Fontevraud Abbey — Kitchen

Later transfers to the crypt, included the hearts of John Lackland and of his son Henry III, the rebuilder of Westminster Abbey which in the 13C became the traditional sanctuary of English sovereigns.

The Violation of the Abbey. – The Huguenots desecrated the abbey in 1562 and the Revolutionaries pillaged and completely destroyed the monks' monastery in 1793. In 1804 Napoleon converted the remaining buildings into a national prison which was only closed in 1963.

The Fine Arts Department is now engaged in restoring the buildings and opening them to the public.

■ **THE ABBEY**★★*time: 45 mins*

Guided tours: from 1 April to 30 September 9 to 11.45am and 2 to 6.30pm (10 to 11.45am and 2 to 4pm the rest of the year); closed on Tuesdays, 1 January, 1 May, 1 November and 25 December; 7F; 3.50F on Sundays and public holidays.

Abbey Church★★. – *Only on the lecture tours is one able to see the chevet of the abbey church.* The Church of Ste-Marie was consecrated in 1119 by Pope Calixtus II and although considerably restored in the 19C it remains a handsome Romanesque building. The original domes were destroyed at the time when the abbey served as a prison.

The majesty of the building is apparent immediately on entering. The imposing single nave with fine capitals is roofed by four domes on pendentives resting on tall square pillars. This is the most northerly of the curious domed churches of which other examples may be seen at Cahors, Périgueux, Angoulême, etc.

In the transept are the recumbent figures of four Plantagenets, the 12 and 13C tombs having disappeared. They belong to Henry II, his wife Eleanor of Aquitaine who died at Fontevraud in 1204, their son Richard Lionheart and lastly Isabelle of Angoulême, second wife of their other son, England's King John Lackland.

The tombs were defaced during the Revolution and were later moved to different places. The British Government has several times asked for their surrender in order to transfer them to Westminster or Windsor, where other sovereigns of England are buried. But France argued that the Plantagenets were also counts of Anjou and had themselves chosen their place of burial so the figures lie once more in the church.

The transept, chancel and ambulatory, all older than the nave, and built to the Benedictine plan, are full of light, provided by ten large windows.

Ste-Marie Cloisters. – The cloisters in the nuns' convent, or the Great Cloisters, have Renaissance vaulting except on the south side, which is still Gothic inspired. Go through a richly sculptured doorway in the east gallery to enter the **chapter house** which is decorated with 16C mural paintings, much restored, representing the abbesses.

St-Benoît Cloisters. – Also restored in parts the cloisters used to lead to the infirmary.

Refectory. – This large hall with its Romanesque walls is roofed with Gothic vaulting which replaced a timber ceiling in 1515.

Kitchen★★. – This highly unusual building, which was once known as the Évraud Tower, is an octagonal tower 27 m - 89 ft high, roofed with overlapping stones and originally flanked by eight apsidal chapels. In many respects it resembles the kitchen at Glastonbury.

What strikes the visitor is the skill with which the mediaeval builders solved domestic problems. Technical skill is backed by artistic feeling. The draught for the chimneys and the removal of smoke are ensured by ingenious arrangements. Five wood burning fireplaces and twenty chimneys are grouped together without any suggestion, outside or in, of the dreary surroundings in which communal meals are usually prepared.

It will be noted how gracefully the architect has passed from the octagonal plan to square and then back to the octagon. These variations enabled him to place his twenty chimney flues judiciously. A basket funnel, pierced for ventilation, covers the upper part. Alterations have spoilt neither the building's elegance nor its originality.

■ **ADDITIONAL SIGHTS**

St-Michel★. – *Recorded music and lighting; 1F.* A low lean-to gallery was built against the walls of this parish church in the 18C, giving it an unexpected character. Although the church was enlarged and remodelled in the 13 and 15C, an inner arcade with small columns and typical Plantagenet style vaulting remain of the original Romanesque building.

The church contains numerous **works of art★** which formerly belonged to the monastery. The high altar, which is made of wood and is finely carved and gilded, was made at the behest of the Abbess, Louise de Bourbon, in 1621. In a north side chapel is a 15C wooden Crucifix simultaneously tormented and at peace, and an impressive 16C Crowning with Thorns by the pupils of Caravaggio. In a Crucifixion painted on wood in an archaic style by Étienne Dumonstier, the artist sought to portray the pitiful waste of the struggles between Catholics and Protestants by depicting the protagonists at the foot of the Cross. One can make out Catherine de' Medici as Mary Magdalene, Henri II as the soldier piercing the heart of Christ, and their three sons, François II, Charles IX and Henri III. Mary Stuart is the Holy Woman with a crown.

Ste-Catherine. – This 13C chapel, surmounted by a lantern to the dead, stands in what was originally the churchyard.

FOUGÈRES-SUR-BIÈVRE, Château de ★

Michelin map **64** 17 – 8 km - 5 miles northwest of Contres – *Local map p 102*

The external appearance of the château, which is purely feudal, is in striking contrast to the majestic Renaissance of Chambord and strictly Classical Cheverny.

Open 1 April to 30 September from 9 to 11.45am and 2 to 6.30pm; the rest of the year from 10 to 11.45am and 2 to 4pm; closed on Tuesdays, 1 January, 1 May, 1 November and 25 December; time: 45 mins; 5F, 2.50F on Sundays and public holidays.

The building was begun in 1470. Already, twenty years before, Charles d'Orléans had pulled down the old fortified castle at Blois and built a more cheerful residence in its place. The builder of Fougères, Louis XI's Chancellor, did not follow the new fashion. He built a true stronghold round the square 11C keep. Completed later by the son in law, the castle incorporates a fine low arched gallery.

To visualise the castle in its original form you must imagine the moats, the drawbridge, the arrow slits which gave way to windows in the 16C, and the battlements of the keep which were removed when the roof was built over it.

GENNES

Michelin map **64** 11, 12 – *Local map p 103* – Pop 1 668

Gennes is pleasantly situated near the Loire, in a hilly countryside scattered with megalithic monuments.

St-Eusèbe. – Clinging to the valley side a 12C tower *(open Easter to 1 November on Sundays from 2 to 4pm; 1F)* and transept are all that are left standing of this church.

A memorial to the cadets of Saumur's military academy, who fell while defending the Loire in June 1940, has been erected in the close. From this point there is an extensive view of Gennes, the Avoine-Chinon Nuclear Power Station and as far as Longé and Beaufort.

EXCURSIONS

Cunault★★. – *2.5 km - 1½ miles to the southeast by the D 751. Description p 78.*

Les Rosiers. – Pop 1 824. *Facilities p 39. 1 km - ½ mile to the north.* A suspension bridge leads to this town on the north bank of the Loire. The parish church has a Renaissance **belfry** which is thought to be the work of the Angevin architect, Jean de l'Espine. The staircase turret adjoining the belfry has sculptured pediments above the last two windows.

The statue on the mall *(mail)* represents Jeanne de Laval who was the wife of Du Guesclin and then the Good King René of Anjou *(p 44).*

St-Georges-des-Sept-Voies. – Pop 626. *6.5 km - 4 miles to the west by the D 751, turn left at Le Sale-Village.* This charming priory is set amidst splendid cedar and elm trees. The 12-13C church *(open on Sundays only 1 July to 15 September, at other times apply for key to M. Forget, Place de l'église)* has an attractive, square, Romanesque tower built of granite. Inside is a polychrome, wooden altar of the 17C.

St-Maur-de-Glanfeuil Abbey. – *7 km - 4 miles to the northwest by the D 132.* Facing the Loire this ruined Benedictine abbey is named after St. Benedict's follower, St. Maurus who came from Italy to preach the Gospel and according to tradition founded a monastery in 542, on the site of the Roman villa of Glanfeuil.

Enter the courtyard which is bordered by two remaining 17C cloister galleries. The **chapel**, built in 1953 on the site of the former abbey church, is a plain building enhanced by the remarkable stained glass windows. The splintered glass technique used here gives bright, lively colours.

At a short distance is the Romanesque chapel, which was erected on the ruins of St. Maurus's oratory. It was here that the Saint's sarcophagus was found. There are traces of 15C wall paintings.

Château de Montsabert. – *13 km - 8 miles by the D 751 and a road leading to the right just after Coutures.* The château *(not open to the public)*, a simple 14C manor house once the property of the Laval family, was fortified by the High Constable of France, Du Guesclin. The outbuildings are 17C while the chapel is a century later. The visitor can see the round towers and square machicolated keep.

If you wish to explore the neighbouring areas
buy the following Michelin Green Guides
Normandy, Brittany and Dordogne

GERMIGNY-DES-PRÉS ★

Michelin map **64** 10 – 4 km - 3 miles to the southeast of Châteauneuf-sur-Loire – *Local map p 101* – Pop 371

The passing tourist will not regret a visit to one of France's earliest churches. In a Byzantine setting he will see a mosaic, unique in France, dating from the time of Charlemagne.

About AD 800 Theodulf, Bishop of Orléans and Abbot of nearby St-Benoit-sur-Loire and friend and counsellor of Charlemagne, founded Germigny. As Theodulf did not find the quiet he needed for his work among the abbey students, he built a "villa" or country house with adjoining oratory in the form of a Greek cross at Germigny.

The "villa" and oratory were burnt down in the 9C, no doubt by the Normans. The villa disappeared.

The church was repaired in the 15C, but one of the four apses was turned into a nave. Then, in the course of centuries, the building fell into disrepair.

Apart from the main apse and its mosaic, the tourist will find a reconstructed building (restored from 1839 to 1876). It looks much as it did in the 15C.

The Church★. – *It is best to visit the church with the parish priest. Ring the bell to the right of the entrance. Time: ½ hour.*

To the left, in the close in front of the church, the crown of the lantern of the dead from the former cemetery (16C) has been set up. The flame of remembrance burned in these little structures in the Middle Ages.

To picture the church as it was in the time of Charlemagne the tourist must, in his mind's eye, do away with the nave and substitute an apse identical with the other three. He must also imagine the vaulting and domes of the building decorated with coloured mosaics, the walls covered with ornamentation carved in a stucco facing, and the floor paved with inlaid marble and porphyry.

Some 6 and 7C Armenian churches have the same vaulting system, except that here the main dome has been replaced by a lantern tower.

Your attention will first be drawn to the lantern tower and its curious lighting effect. The small openings through which the light penetrates are fitted with panes of alabaster which filter the light and preserve the half tones. This successful process is again Byzantine in origin.

About 1840 archaeologists noticed small boys playing with little glass cubes found in the church. They discovered that these fragments came from a **mosaic★★** fixed to the roof of the east apse – the only original portion – and covered with thick plaster. It was stripped, recognised as dating from the time of Charlemagne and restored to its original state. It is a Byzantine mosaic of the 9C from the school of Ravenna.

The 130 000 small cubes that form it are of various colours: gold, silver, blue, green and red. The subject is the Ark of the Covenant, which housed the two tablets of the Law given to Moses by God, and it is surmounted by the two traditional cherubim. Two archangels, whose figures follow the shape of the vaulting, are showing the Ark. Between them the hand of God reaches down from the sky.

In the ambulatory, there is a primitive altar and a 12C piscina. In the nave, at the far end, is the baptismal font showing 11C forms of sculpture.

GIEN ★

Michelin map **65** 2 – *Local map p 101* – Pop 15 250 – *Facilities p 38*

Gien, a small town with many flowers, is well known for its faience. It was bombed several times between 1940 and 1944, and it suffered cruelly, but its recovery was rapid. Respect for the traditional forms of regional architecture and a careful use of local materials have given the reconstructed quarters an original and attractive appearance.

The faience factory, which was founded in 1821, lies to the west of the town and today covers an area of some 6 ha - 15 acres.

Gien is a very old bridgehead and like all places of this kind it has suffered many vicissitudes. **Anne de Beaujeu**, comtesse de Gien, particularly set her seal on it in the 15C. She was the eldest daughter of Louis XI, and her father said of her: "She is the least silly woman in France; I do not know of a wise one." Anne de Beaujeu gave Gien its castle, its present bridge, convents and churches. She enlarged and perfected its fortifications.

Another historical memory is that of the Fronde (the name given to a civil war in France which lasted from 1648 to 1652, and to its sequel, the war with Spain in 1653-59). Anne of Austria, Mazarin and the young Louis XIV, being forced to flee from Paris, took refuge at Gien. Turenne enabled them to return by defeating Condé and the Frondeurs at the Battle of Bléneau (1652).

■ **SIGHTS** *time: 1¼ hours*

From the old hump backed bridge there is a fine **view★** of the castle, the rebuilt houses on the banks and the Loire.

Château. – Rebuilt in 1484, the building has sober lines. Its only decoration consists of geometric figures in black bricks on the red brick walls and a few touches of white stone.

International Hunting Museum★ (Musée International de la Chasse). – *Open Palm Sunday to 31 October from 9 to 11.45am and 2.15 to 6.30pm (5.30pm the rest of the year); 8F.*

This museum, installed in the restored rooms of the castle, is attractively arranged. Its collection of weapons and souvenirs, tapestries, prints and pictures trace the history of the chase through the centuries. The **Great Hall★★** has a fine old timberwork ceiling and contains a remarkable collection of paintings by Desportes. There is also an exhibit on falconry.

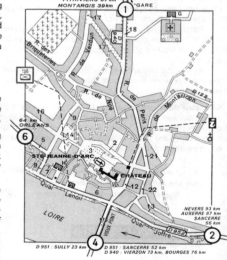

GIEN		Château (Pl. du)	3
		Clemenceau (R. G.)	5
0	300 m	Hôtel-de-Ville (R. de l')	7
		Jeanne-d'Arc (R.)	9
		Leclerc (Av. Gén.)	12
Gambetta (R.)	6	Louis-Blanc (R.)	13
Thiers (R.)	21	Marienne (R. Adj.)	14
Victor-Hugo (R.)	22	Paul-Bert (R.)	16
		Prés.-Wilson (Av. du)	17
Beaujeu (R. A.-de)	2	République (Av. de la)	18

Ste-Jeanne-d'Arc★. – The tower of this church dedicated to Joan of Arc is all that remains from the time of Anne de Beaujeu. The rest of the building, dating from the 19C, was destroyed in 1940 and rebuilt in 1954 in pink brick with black designs.

(After photo: Syndicat d'Initiative)

Gien

This is a successful example of post-war ecclesiastical architecture. Slim, round pillars, with terracotta capitals, divide the nave from the aisles. The pale light diffused by the stained glass windows enhances admirably the colour of the brickwork with its quiet but elegant decorative effects. Note the Stations of the Cross in Gien faience.

A door in the south aisle opens into a small room communicating with an octagonal baptistery. The purely designed red copper baptismal font stands on a brick pedestal which is the centrepiece of a mosaic.

EXCURSION

Beaulieu. – Pop 1 539. *23 km - 13 miles to the southeast by* ④*, the D 951.* This village on the south bank has a church with a Romanesque nave and Gothic transept and chancel. An 18C reredos backs the high altar.

GUÉ-PÉAN, Château du *
Michelin map 🔢 17 – 13 km - 8 miles east of Montrichard – *Local map p 70*

Make your way from Monthou-sur-Cher to this most attractive château, which was built at the end of the Renaissance, and appears as a blue and white building at the head of a peaceful valley. Oak trees cover the hillside slopes and the only sounds to be heard are those of the countryside.

Guided tours from 1 March to 15 November from 9am to 7.30pm; the rest of the year from 9.30am to 5.30pm (9am to 6.30pm on Sundays and public holidays); time: ½ hour; 10F.

The château is built round a square inner courtyard and is really a country house, although there are still some traces of fortifications in the plan, notably the four angle towers. The tallest tower has a bell shaped roof and machicolations decorated with a hollowed out scallop shell pattern; the right hand tower has been converted into a chapel.

The main ranges of the building are given a flow of line by their arcades and the graceful pilaster flanked windows. Roofs in the French manner, high pitched, elegant and remarkable in their variety crown the whole.

The tour includes a visit to the main tower guardroom and watchpath and several saloons furnished with chests, travelling boxes and chairs of the Louis XV and Louis XVI periods and adorned with tapestries and pictures by master painters (Guido Reni, the schools of Gérard, Fragonard, David, etc). The great saloon has a monumental fireplace designed by Germain Pilon; the library includes a rich collection of autographs and mementoes (manuscripts, portraits, etc).

A riding club occupies the outbuildings.

L'ILE-BOUCHARD
Michelin map 🔢 4 – *Local map p 76* – Pop 1 762

Formerly one of the Vienne ports, the ancient settlement of L'Ile-Bouchard spreads out on both banks amidst gardens and orchards. Its name is derived from the midstream island where a certain Bouchard is said to have built a fortress in the 9C, which was destroyed in the 17C. The estate was bought by Cardinal Richelieu and belonged to his descendants until 1789.

St-Léonard Priory. – The ruins of this priory lie to the south of the town on the lower slopes of the valley side. Having crossed the railway line take to the left, the Ruelle de la Vallée aux Nains. *To visit apply to the Syndicat d'Initiative or M. Corbineau, Rue de la Liberté.*

The 11C Romanesque apse in white tufa, an ambulatory and radiating chapels are all that remain standing of the priory church. The arcades are unusual having been added a century later to strengthen the construction.

The fascinating series of historiated **capitals*** represent from left to right:

First pillar: Annunciation and Visitation, Nativity, Adoration of the Shepherds and the Magi.

Second pillar: Circumcision, Massacre of the Innocents, Flight into Egypt, Jesus amidst the Pharisees.

Third pillar: Judas's kiss, Crucifixion.

Fourth pillar: Jesus's entry into Jerusalem, Descent into Limbo, Beheading of St. John the Baptist.

The capitals in the ambulatory are decorated with animals and leaf motifs.

L'ILE-BOUCHARD

St-Maurice. – The church's octagonal tower, dating from 1480, is crowned by a many sided spire. The main vessel in the transitional Flamboyant-Renaissance style has vaulting supported by pilasters decorated with Renaissance medallions. The early 16C **bishop's throne★** in the chancel has sculptured panels portraying the Annunciation, Nativity and Flight into Egypt. The craftsmen are represented on the cheekpieces.

Standing near the church is a charming early 17C manor with pedimented dormer windows.

St-Gilles. – On the north bank of the Vienne and formerly part of an 11C priory (nave), this church was enlarged in the 12C and altered again in the 15C (chancel). Two attractive Romanesque doorways, without tympana, have remarkable geometrical and foliage decoration. The dome on squinches over the transept crossing is surmounted by a squat Romanesque tower.

The old mill behind the church ceased to operate in 1970.

EXCURSIONS

Tavant Church. – *3 km - 2 miles west by the D 760.*

The interest of Tavant Church is not due to the building itself, in spite of its charming round arched doorway and the fine capitals in the chancel, but to the **frescoes★** which adorn it and the crypt.

The caretaker, Mme Ferrand, lives on the right, in the street leading to the church; if absent apply to the Mairie.

The ribbed vaulting of the crypt and the roof and oven vaulting of the chancel were decorated in the 12C with figures which show a degree of realism, extremely rare in the Romanesque period, with their lively movement and power of expression, more marked in the crypt than in the church. The themes are varied.

Parçay-sur-Vienne. – *4.5 km - 3 miles to the east by the D 18 which follows the south bank.*

This 12C church, with oven vaulted apsidal chapels, has a square belfry, rebuilt in 1747, crowning the transept crossing. The fine Romanesque doorway has intricately carved archivolts representing bearded faces, foliated scrolls and palmettes. The interior was much altered in the 19C and only the chancel capitals, portraying fantastic animals, are original.

Avon-les-Roches; Roches-Tranchelion; Crissay-sur-Manse. – *Round trip of 20 km - 12 miles by the D 757 to the north, then the local road to the right in the direction of Avon. See also Michelin map* **64***, south of 14.*

Avon-les-Roches. – Pop 750. This is a small village in the Manse tributary valley. The Romanesque **church** is famous for its covered entrance vestibule with carved archivolts and historiated capitals. Angevin vaulting covers the nave.

Follow the Crissay road and after 1 km - ½ mile turn left into a narrow road.

Roches-Tranchelion Collegiate Church. – Founded in 1527 it was run by five canons. The main façade is an example of the transitional Flamboyant-Renaissance style. Of a certain elegance the individual elements include a triumphal arch, niches, buttresses ending in pierced pinnacles and Italian medallions.

Crissay-sur-Manse. – Pop 137. This small village has plenty of charm with several remaining 15C houses and the imposing ruined château of the same period.

Return to l'Ile-Bouchard by the D 21 in the direction of Avon and shortly after leaving Crissay take the local road to the left.

If you are looking for a pleasant hotel or camp site
in peaceful surroundings
you couldn't do better than look in the current Michelin Guides
FRANCE and CAMPING CARAVANING FRANCE.

INDRE Valley ★

Michelin maps **64** 14 to 16 and **68** 6

The calm, sinuous Indre, so lovingly praised by Balzac, aptly symbolises Touraine across which it flows. Châteaux crowd its banks, the most famous of them all being Azay-le-Rideau.

GEOGRAPHICAL NOTES

Upstream of Châtillon, when crossing the Berry, the Indre has cut its course across the Brenne and Écueillé clays. Once in Touraine the river flows in a confined valley between steep banks of tufa chalk, known as *tuffeau* in Touraine.

The river becomes languid in the basin of river deposits, beyond Loches, formed by the confluence of the Indre with the Indrois. Then come the lacustrine limestones and "Little Switzerland of Touraine", at Courçay. Finally from Montbazon to Azay the river meanders gently before skirting the soft tufa chalk which borders the flat alluvial plains or *varennes (see p 10)* of Bréhémont and Rigny-Ussé, the last stage before joining the Loire.

Sinuous and deeply incised, the Indre Valley is not an important line of communication. Compartmented, it is an area of mixed farming with vineyards and orchards on the well exposed slopes near Saché and Azay-le-Rideau. There are numerous mills to grind the grain from the neighbouring plateaux.

The floor of the valley, covered with osier beds and meadows, favours stock rearing and dairy farming. Sheep graze on the plateau's edge. Between the Indre and the Loire, an unusual crop, hemp, is grown on the *varennes*, which also produce fruit, flowers and early vegetables, replacing the vanished mulberries.

The tree species flourishing on these wet soils are walnut on the slopes, aspens and Italian poplars, willows, alders and osiers at river level. The river abounds in fish, enough to justify a factory manufacturing small fishing boats at Saché.

From Châtillon-sur-Indre to Loches – *28 km - 17 miles – about ½ hour*

On leaving Châtillon *(p 66)* take the N 143 which follows the south bank.
Having traversed a countryside of vines and cereals, the road crosses into Touraine near Fléré. The typical roofing material in the area is now slate, especially in the built up areas. Leave the N 143 briefly to reach Bridoré.

Bridoré. – Pop 363. The late 15C church, dedicated to St. Roch, contains a monumental 16C statue of the Saint, to the right in the nave. The legend of St. Hubert is evoked on a bas-relief.

The castle built in the 14C by Marshal Boucicaut and altered in the 15C by Imbert de Bastarnay, Louis XI's Secretary, forms an imposing ensemble bordered on three sides by deep, dry moats. The most interesting parts are the gatehouse flanked by a round tower with machicolations and the rectangular keep with a Louis XII style dormer window and lateral bartizans with pepperpot roofs. The main apartments adjoin the keep *(Guided tours 15 June to 31 August from 2 to 6pm; time: 50 mins; 7F.)* Legend has it that Gilles de Rais (the Bluebeard of Perrault's story), the castle's Governor, had his wives imprisoned here.

Return to the N 143. The valley narrows. Take the D 89 to the left and then the D 41.

Verneuil-sur-Indre. – Pop 576. The château, now used by a horticultural centre *(not open to the public)*, comprises a keep, rebuilt in 1820 in the style of the 15C, and an 18C building, surmounted by a dome with gores. The waters of the moat, fed by a spring, flow among water lilies and tall grasses and are bordered by washing houses. Good view of the château from the bridge.

Follow the fork to the left of the D 41 to reach once again the N 143.
Between Perrusson and Loches *(p 93)* the road is overlooked by a cliff face pierced with troglodyte dwellings. The ruined tower of Mauvière stands sentinel over the valley.

From Loches to Azay-le-Rideau – *54 km - 34 miles – about 5½ hours – Local map below*

Leave Loches *(p 93)* by ①, the N 143. After 6 km - 4 miles branch off to take the D 17 which beyond Chambourg-sur-Indre is a scenic stretch following the valley floor. Shortly before Azay-sur-Indre the road, close to the river, skirts fine parkland before passing pines and cultivated fields on the gentler slopes.

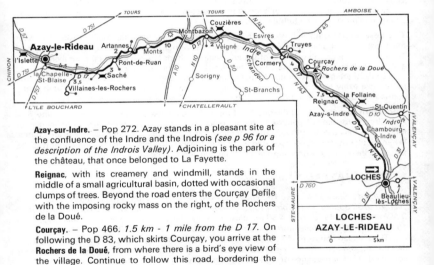

Azay-sur-Indre. – Pop 272. Azay stands in a pleasant site at the confluence of the Indre and the Indrois *(see p 96 for a description of the Indrois Valley)*. Adjoining is the park of the château, that once belonged to La Fayette.

Reignac, with its creamery and windmill, stands in the middle of a small agricultural basin, dotted with occasional clumps of trees. Beyond the road enters the Courçay Defile with the imposing rocky mass on the right, of the Rochers de la Doué.

Courçay. – Pop 466. *1.5 km - 1 mile from the D 17.* On following the D 83, which skirts Courçay, you arrive at the **Rochers de la Doué**, from where there is a bird's eye view of the village. Continue to follow this road, bordering the plateau which affords a good view of the valley.

Between Courçay and Cormery, the Indre flows, amidst great meadows and wooded slopes.

Cormery. – Pop 1 106. This once fortified town is renowned for its macaroons, ruined abbey and Romanesque church.

The **former abbey** *(access by the Rue de l'Abbaye; visit the exterior only)* was founded in the 8C by Ithier, the Abbot of St-Martin in Tours, who was succeeded by Alcuin of York *(p 151)*. The only remaining vestige of the early abbey is the massive belfry porch, **Tour St-Paul**, dating from the 11C, which was restored in the 15C. Note the decorative motifs and Romanesque bas-reliefs on the west façade. Also visible are the Abbot's lodging and, on the north side, remains of the conventual buildings.

Notre-Dame-du-Fougeray has elements which are typical of the Poitou region: a large apse with three apsidal chapels and a dome on pendentives over the transept crossing. There is a 13C fresco on the north wall of the nave.

On leaving Cormery follow briefly the N 143, which climbs up to the plateau.

Truyes. – Pop 1 210. *1 km - ½ mile from Cormery.* 12C church with tall Romanesque tower.

Take the D 17 which descends to the river flowing amidst fields of cereals, fruit trees and groups of beehives. Beyond Esvres the banks are lined with poplars. The road skirts the park of the Château de Couzières.

Château de Couzières. – *Not open to the public.* This 15C château – altered in the 17C – standing in a vast park, was the home of the ducal family of Rohan-Montbazon. One of the reconciliations between Louis XIII, the former Regent, and his mother Marie de' Medici took place here, on the 5 September 1619.

Montbazon. – Pop 2 447. *Facilities p 38*. This is one of the twenty strongholds built by Foulques Nerra *(p 43)*. The dismantled **keep** *(open from 1 May to 30 September 9.30am to 12.30pm and 2 to 7.30pm; out of season 10am to 12.30pm and 2 to 6pm; 2F)* provides a good vantage point. Take the road to the left of the Mairie, the Rue des Moulins, go through a former town gate, then take a path to the right.

Shortly after Montbazon the road closely follows the river before passing the industrial zone near Monts. The river subdivides into several arms at this point.

Artannes-sur-Indre. – Pop 1 217. This calm village is tightly crowded between its 16C château (restored) and its 12-15C church on the bank of the winding Indre. The next stretch of the river is overlooked by a series of châteaux.

Pont-de-Ruan. – Pop 425. Attractive village.

Château de Saché. – *Description p 50*.

Continue by the D 17 which overlooks the river; plantations of walnut trees on the slopes, meadows and osier beds on the valley floor.

Villaines-les-Rochers. – *3.5 km - 2 miles from the D 17. Description p 50.*

At La Chapelle St-Blaise take the D 751 to reach Azay-le-Rideau (p 49).

LANGEAIS ★★

Michelin map 🔠 14 – *Local map p 103* – Pop 3 902 – *Facilities p 38*

The Château de Langeais, though smaller than those of Blois and Chambord, is one of the most interesting in the Val. It was built all in one piece, in four or five years, which is rare; it has undergone no alterations or additions, which is rarer still. Moreover, it has been admirably furnished by the patient efforts of the last owner, M. Siegfried, who presented it to the Institut de France in 1904. The house facing the château is Renaissance.

HISTORICAL NOTES

A disputed fortress (Middle Ages). – Langeais was first a Roman *castrum*, then a fortress. At the end of the 10C, Foulques Nerra *(p 43)* built the keep, the ruins of which still stand in the gardens. It is considered to be the oldest in France. The Houses of Anjou and Touraine vied for the keep. The struggle continued between the kings of England, who had become counts of Anjou, and the kings of France. Richard Lionheart won the keep. Philippe-Auguste recaptured it. Langeais emerged in ruins from the turbulent period.

The new castle (15C). – It was Louis XI who had the present edifice built (1465-69) under the supervision of Jean Bourré who became its Governor. Bourré was the King's Notary and Treasurer of France. He was one of the counsellors whom Louis used to take familiarly by the arm, calling him "my colleague". He entrusted him with the education of the Dauphin.

Louis XI intended, no doubt, to make Langeais a strongpoint on the road from Nantes, the route most likely to be taken by an invading Breton army. This possibility vanished after the marriage of Charles VIII and Anne of Brittany was celebrated at Langeais itself in 1491.

Uncertain tenure. – Until the middle of the 17C the château remained Crown property. The kings lent it for limited periods to highly placed persons whom they wished to reward or indemnify. Because of this uncertain tenure, the occupants hesitated to make alterations. When regular owners succeeded one another in the 18C the lack of gaiety and comfort in the place led them to make only short visits. They, too, left the old building intact.

■ THE CHÂTEAU ★★ *time: ¾ hour*

Guided tours: 15 March to 15 September from 9am to noon and 2 to 6.30pm; the rest of the year: 16 to 30 September to 5.30pm; 1 to 15 October to 5.30pm; 16 October to 2 November to 5pm; 3 November to 14 March to 4.30pm; closed on non holiday Mondays: in the mornings from 15 March to 30 September and all day from 1 October to 14 March; 8F.

The château stands in the centre of the town, on a little promontory. Seen from outside it has the appearance of a powerful mediaeval fortress *(illustration p 23)*. Seen from the inner courtyard, it is the residence of a great lord of the 15C.

The fortress. – The principal range, consisting of a keep and main building, is adjoined by two wings at right angles. The keep is a large tower with barracks for the garrison while the main building houses the seigneurial residence and is protected at each end by a tower.

The street giving access to the château is on a level with the bed of the former moat and leads to a staircase and finally the entrance drawbridge.

The seigneurial residence. – The courtyard façade has few windows or decorations and the grey building stone is unrelieved by brick or white tufa. The origins of the castle account for this military austerity.

The apartments★★★. – Well presented with contemporary period furnishings the atmosphere is more alive than in most other old castles and gives an accurate picture of aristocratic life in the 15C and early Renaissance. There are many fine tapestries mostly Flemish but with some *mille-fleurs*. Note the repetition of the monogram K and A for Charles VIII and Anne of Brittany.

The guardroom, now transformed into a dining room, has a monumental chimneypiece the hood of which represents a castle with battlements manned by small figures.

One of the first floor bedchambers has an early four poster bed, a credence table and Gothic chest. The room where Charles VIII and Anne of Brittany celebrated their marriage is hung with a series of tapestries portraying the Nine Heroes. Charles VIII's chamber has a fine Gothic chest and a curious 17C clock. The upper great hall, rising through two storeys, has a chestnut timber roof in the form of a ship's keel. The Creation is the theme of the hangings here.

Formal French gardens extend between the château proper and the keep, at the foot of which is the tomb of the Siegfrieds.

EXCURSIONS

Cinq-Mars-la-Pile. – Pop 2 141 – *5 km - 3 miles northeast by the N 152.*
The village gets its name from a curious monument in the form of a tower or pylon, dating from the Gallo-Roman period, which dominates the ridge. The structure with sides of 5 m - 16½ ft and 30 m - 98 ft high, ends in four small pyramids. Its origin and purpose are wrapped in mystery.

The **château** *(open 1 March to 2 November from 9am to noon and 2 to 7pm; time: ½ hour; closed on non holiday Mondays; 4F)*, a little away from the village, recalls the celebrated favourite of Louis XIII, Henri d'Effiat, marquis de Cinq-Mars. With his friend De Thou he was convicted of having conspired against Richelieu, and was beheaded at Lyon at the age of twenty-two. The feudal castle was partly razed. Two towers dating from the 11 and 12C and some fine moats remain.

In the towers are several rooms with beautiful Gothic vaulting, and other rooms have sets of armour and various old pieces. From the summit there is an extensive view of the Loire Valley.

Les Essards. – Pop 109. *10 km - 6 miles west by the N 152 then the D 125 to the right.* The **church** *(to visit apply to the Café Couineau)* on the hillside, was built in the 11 and 12C. The flat east end is 13C and is adorned by statues and polychrome capitals. The seigneurial chapel to the south dates from the 16C.

LAVAL ★

Michelin map **53** 10 – *Local map p 115* – Pop 54 537

This attractive town in the Bas-Maine is pleasantly situated on the banks of the Mayenne. The old town, clustered round the 11C castle, stands on the west bank with modern urban development confined to the outskirts. The town centre, Place du 11-Novembre, is overlooked by the town hall (**H**) and the statue of one of Laval's famous sons, the physician Ambroise Paré.

Formerly a linen manufacturing centre, industry is playing an ever important role in the town's economy. The livestock market is one of the most important in the region.

HISTORICAL NOTES

The "Chouannerie". – During the Vendéen War *(p 114)*, the name **Chouan** was applied to the Royalist supporters (Whites) from the Laval area led by the Cottereau brothers, who had adopted the hooting of the tawny owl as their rallying cry *(chat-huant)*. As part of the campaign north of the Loire, Laval occupied by the Royalists saw the defeat of the Republican (Blues) Army under its very walls. During a general retreat towards the Loire, the Royalist commander La Rochejaquelein withdrew his forces from Laval. During this operation, a certain La Trémoille, prince de Talmont and leader of the Vendéen cavalry was captured and guillotined at the gateway to his own castle.

Famous citizens of Laval. – Many of the sons of Laval have gained fame. The notable Renaissance surgeon **Ambroise Paré** (1517-90) served several French monarchs and is regarded as the father of modern surgery. His innovations included the treatment of wounds, the ligature of arteries during amputations and the invention of new surgical instruments. **Henri Rousseau** (1844-1910), nicknamed "Le Douanier", was the forerunner of the naïve school of painters. His works were vividly colourful and full of meticulous detail. Rousseau was friendly with another Laval notable, the eccentric and writer **Alfred Jarry** (1873-1907). Known as the creator of the drama *Ubu roi* the production of which caused riots, and which is generally acknowledged as the first work of the Theatre of the Absurd. The navigator, **Alain Gerbault** (1893-1941) was known also as the tennis partner of the French champion Jean Borotra.

■ MAIN SIGHTS *time: 2 hours*

Pont A.-Briand. – The bridge offers a typical view of the Mayenne and its quays with the barges. Also visible are the old riverside washing houses. Upstream the view is blocked by the tall viaduct which carries the Paris-Brest railway line. Downstream one sees the Pont Vieux, the belfry of the basilica and the tiered arrangement of the old town dominated by the dark mass of the Old Castle and the lighter tones of the New Castle.

Old town★ (Vieille ville). – *Follow on foot the itinerary marked on the plan p 90.* Start from Place de la Trémoille then take the Rue des Orfèvres, lined by fine 16C houses with overhanging upper storeys and 18C hôtels. At the junction with the Grande-Rue stands the Renaissance mansion of the Master of the Royal Hunt *(Grand Veneur)*.

The main street of the mediaeval town, **Grande-Rue**, goes down to the Mayenne lined alternately by half timber dwellings with overhangs or stone built houses with Renaissance decoration. The 13C Pont Vieux, a hump back bridge once fortified, offers a view of the Old Castle with its formidable keep crowned with hoardings *(p 23)*. The Rue du Pont-de-Mayenne on the opposite bank is still lined by some old houses with overhangs which once bordered the main road to Paris: the house at no 96 has carved beams.

Return to the Grande-Rue to take on your left the Rue de Chapelle which climbs between mediaeval and Renaissance houses: at the top note in a niche to the right the statue of St. René.

The 14C gateway, **Porte Beucheresse** (**B**), flanked by two round machicolated towers was formerly part of Laval's perimeter wall. Henri Rousseau was born in the right hand tower, where his father exercised the trade of tinsmith.

One of the houses in the Rue de la Trinité is decorated with statues of the Virgin and other saints, including St. Christopher. The Rue du Pin-Doré leads back to the Place de la Trémoille.

Château. – The property of the counts of Laval till the Revolution, the castle comprises two parts, the Old and New Castles.

On the far side of Place de la Trémoille is the Renaissance façade of the New Castle or **Nouveau Château**, also known as the Gallery of the Counts of Laval. The building was restored and enlarged in the 19C to serve as Law Courts (Palais de Justice). The courtyard of the Old Castle or **Vieux Château★** is reached through a rusticated, 17C gatehouse with pilasters, which adjoins an early 16C half timber house. In contrast to the austere military aspect of the river front, the courtyard façade surprises by its delicate Renaissance decoration. Access to the ramparts (to the right on entering the courtyard): attractive views of the rooftops of the old town. The terrace to the left of the château affords other views of the town and the Mayenne.

The Old Castle houses a **museum**. *Open from 9am (10am out of season) to noon and 2 to 6pm; closed on Tuesdays; 3F.*

The 12C crypt and keep are the oldest parts of the castle. The two 13-15C wings at right angles, were modified in the 16C: the white tufa chalk dormer windows are pilaster flanked and ornamented with sculptured Italian motifs.

A staircase leads down to the lower chapel or Romanesque crypt terminated at the east end by three apsidal chapels. The groined vaulting springs from finely carved capitals.

On the first floor, the Great Hall, 32 m - 105 ft long, with its wooden roof, contains several frescoes and sculpture including the 15C tombs of Guy XII of Laval, his wife and his mother.

The ground floor houses a collection of naïve paintings. Three rooms and the lower floor of the keep present, round one of Le Douanier's works, canvases by other French, Yugoslav, Brazilian and German naïve painters. The remaining two floors of the keep have sections on the tools of the various craftsmen of the mediaeval guilds and local history.

The round **keep**, 36 m - 118 ft high with three storeys, has walls which attain a thickness of 5 m -

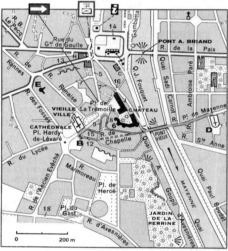

Déportés (R. des)	5	Serruriers (R. des)	12
Gaulle (R. Gén. de)		Souchu-Servinière (R.)	13
Grande-Rue	6	Strasbourg (R. de)	14
Jeu-de-Paume (R.)	7	Trinité (R.)	15
Orfèvres (R. des)	8	Val-de-Mayenne (R.)	16
Pin-Doré (R. du)	9	Vaufleury (R.)	18

16 ft. The **timber roof★★** is quite exceptional *(see notes on timberwork p 148)*. A central pivot supported by great oak beams which extend outside to form the hoardings, in turn upholds the conical roof. The hall on the second floor has elegant 16C star vaulting.

Gardens★ (Jardin de la Perrine). — These terraced gardens offer very good views of the Mayenne, the lower town and the keep. Lakes, a rose garden and waterfalls alternate with lawns, flowerbeds and many fine trees: palms, limes, chestnuts, Lebanese cedars and larches.

■ ADDITIONAL SIGHTS

Basilica of Notre-Dame d'Avénières. — The **chevet★** with its ring of five apsidal chapels is crowned by a pretty spire which was reconstructed in 1871 in the original transitional Gothic-Renaissance style.

Inside, on either side of the entrance, are two enormous wooden statues representing Christ and St. Christopher carrying the Infant Jesus (16C).

In the fine Romanesque chancel with a three storey elevation are a 15C wooden statue of Christ and at the triforium level the miraculous statue of Our Lady.

The modern stained glass is by Max Ingrand.

The sacristy *(to visit apply to the presbytery, 52 Allée du Ronceray)* has a *Pietà* and a 15C triptych donated by Jeanne de Laval, wife of the Good King René of Anjou.

Cathedral. — Dating from the Romanesque period the edifice has been greatly altered. The exterior facing the Palais de Justice is adorned with 17C terracotta statues. Enter by the doorway looking on to the Place Hardy-de-Lévaré. Angevin vaulting covers the nave and transept. Early 17C Aubusson tapestries portray the story of Judith and Holofernes in six hangings.

Several **works of art** are worthy of note: the monumental 17C chancel reredos with a painting of the Glorification of the Virgin; in front of the chancel against the left pillar a remarkable triptych by the 16C Antwerp Mannerist school, portraying St. John the Baptist; near the sacristy to the right of the chancel a white marble Baroque Virgin.

St-Vénérand (D). — *Restoration in progress.* This church with one principal and four collateral naves is entered through a Flamboyant doorway with a 17C terracotta Virgin and pedimented canopy with Renaissance motifs. The nave is separated from the chancel by a Louis XVI screen. The stained glass is typical of the Renaissance: that in the north transept evokes the Passion while the Story of Moses is related in the south transept. In the north transept are the 17C terracotta statues of St. Vénérand carrying his head, St. Sebastian and the Virgin Mary.

Tower (Tour Renaise – E). – This 15C round tower with machicolations was formerly part of the city wall.

Pritz Church★. – *2 km - 1 mile to the north. Leave Laval by the Quai Gambetta and the D 104.* This church stands in a garden on the right. Dating from approximately the year 1000, the modest edifice was altered and enlarged during the Romanesque period. To the left of the nave is a stone statue of St. Christopher and a 17C terracotta of Christ bearing the Cross. Above the wooden chancel railing the roodbeam carries a 15C Crucifixion. The retable is adorned with terracotta statues of local origin. Two niches to the right of the nave have 13C recumbent figures.

The church's main feature is the series of **mural paintings**. On the east wall fine 11C frescoes represent scenes from the life of the Virgin: Visitation, Nativity, Nursing Virgin (the only known example of the Romanesque period); at the triumphal arch a 13C Calendar of the Months; in the chancel the Old Men of the Apocalypse; at the double arch three Signs of the Zodiac; in the nave and transept the 13C martyrdom of St. Catherine, a Virgin and Child; the Bringing of the Good News to the Shepherds (14C), St. Christopher partly effaced by a later one, St. Margaret and a 16C St. Agatha in the south chapel.

EXCURSIONS

St-Pierre-le-Potier. – *6 km - 4 miles to the south. Leave Laval by ④ and turn right at Thévalles.* The road descends abruptly into the Mayenne Valley.

This charming hamlet hemmed in by the river and the valley side is a popular Sunday outing for the people of Laval. The Romanesque chapel in ironstone has an unusual bell gable.

Château de Montjean. – *16 km - 10 miles to the southwest. Leave Laval by ⑤, the N 178 bis and take the D 564 to the right.*

Overgrown with vegetation, this ruined but impressive fortress stands at the edge of a stretch of water. One can still discern its moat, remains of the perimeter wall and two vaulted chambers in the basement of the keep and round tower, which stand in stagnant waters.

Clermont Abbey. – *15 km - 9 miles to the northwest. Leave Laval by ⑥, the N 157, and at La Chapelle-du-Chêne turn right into the D 115. Michelin map 59 south of 19.*

Open 1 May to 30 September 9am to noon and 2 to 7pm; the rest of the year 10am to noon and 1 to 4pm; closed on Sunday mornings; 5F.

This former Cistercian abbey belonging to the Cluniac Order was founded in 1152 by St Bernard with the support of Guy V, Count of Laval. The west front of the church, embellished with buttresses and a Romanesque porch, is starkly harmonious. The interior shows a similar austerity: the nave has a simple timber roof. The flat east end is lit by three registers of windows and the rectangular chapels off the transept are typical of the Cistercian plan. The storeroom with fine groined vaulting has four central pillars and the refectory three.

Rochefort Bridge. – *16 km - 10 miles to the north. Michelin map 59 20. Leave Laval by the D 104 via Pritz and Changé.*

The road following the Mayenne Valley in an upstream direction is particularly scenic between St-Jean and the bridge at Rochefort. Further north the attractive site of Montgiroux is well known to local fishermen.

LAVARDIN ★

Michelin map 64 5 – *Local maps pp 99 and 118* – Pop 222

The romantic ruins of this feudal fortress present a jagged silhouette towering high above the village on a rocky promontory. Stronghold of the counts of Vendôme in the Middle Ages, its strategic importance greatly increased when the area became borderland country between the kingdoms of the Capetians and Angevins. The fortress was dismantled on the orders of Henri IV during the Wars of Religion.

■ **SIGHTS** *time: ½ hour*

Château★. – *Ruins open daily in July, August and September from 8.30am to 8pm; at other times apply to the town hall. The lower chamber of the keep is open to visitors.*

The track running along the south side of the fortress offers good views of the gatehouse and keep.

Of the three sets of ramparts originally surrounding this fortress, the outer one was defended by a small 14C gatehouse. An underground passage led below the second wall, passing the storerooms dug out of the living rock. Incorporated into the second rampart was a 15C building with a fine staircase and prismatic vaulting. Below the stairs is an interesting vaulted room. The third rampart or revetment wall defended the 11C rectangular **keep** 26 m - 85 ft high, to which towers were added in the 12C. A doorway adorned with the Bourbon-Vendôme blazon gives access to the staircase turret now in a ruinous state.

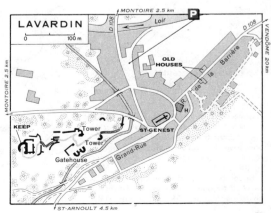

St-Genest. – The church, preceded by a square belfry porch, was built in an archaic Romanesque style by the monks of a nearby priory, a dependant of the Abbey of St-Georges-des-Bois *(p 119)*. The bas-reliefs of the apse represent the Signs of the Zodiac.

Interior. – The vessel is divided into three by primitive piers with delicately carved 12C imposts. A triumphal arch gives access to the chancel, terminated by an oven vaulted apse, where curious Romanesque pillars support roughly hewn capitals. Framing the windows of the north aisle are delightful twisted Romanesque colonnettes *(see illustration)*.

The splendid **mural paintings**★ date from the 12 to 16C. The oldest, most stylised and majestic ones are on the pillar at the entrance to the left apsidal chapel: Baptism of Christ and a Tree of Jesse.

The well conserved group in the chancel and apse shows scenes from the Passion: to the right the Feet Washing, to the left Christ in Majesty surrounded by the symbols of the Evangelists.

In the right apsidal chapel note a St. Christopher and Last Judgement (15C) where Paradise and Hell are colourfully portrayed. On the pillars in the nave are 16C figures of saints venerated locally. Note the Martyrdom of St. Margaret, on the wall of the south aisle and the Crucifixion of St. Peter on a pillar on the north side of the nave.

Old houses. – *Rue de la Barrière*. One is half timbered of the 15C while the other is Renaissance with an overhanging oratory, pilastered, mullioned dormer windows and a loggia overlooking the courtyard.

*(After photo:
Éd. du Zodiaque)*

St-Genest Church
Romanesque colonnette

LAYON Valley

Michelin map 🔢 – 6, 7

The Layon Valley abounds with picturesque sites and views. In addition it is a region of rich soils which produce the delicious white wines of the Layon vineyards.

The Layon, canalised under Louis XVI, follows the junction between the Mauges schists and the Saumur limestone escarpments, except between Beaulieu and St-Aubin where the river has traversed the ancient massif. In the clear air, the deeply incised meanders sometimes create an impression of a hilly terrain. The region has a certain attraction with its vineyards, its crops sometimes interspersed with fruit trees (walnut, peach, plum, etc), its hillsides crowned with windmills, its wine growers' villages with their cemeteries planted with cypresses. The *chenin* often known as *pineau* variety of vine produces fruity, liqueur like wines. They are harvested in late September when the grapes begin to be covered with a mould known as *pourriture noble*.

From Passavant to Chalonnes-sur-Loire – *69 km - 43 miles – about 3 hours – see local map below*

Passavant-sur-Layon. – Pop 185. Attractive village on the edge of a lake formed by the Layon. The very romantic château comprises a late 16C main building and a ruined feudal wall covered with ivy and Virginia creeper: majestic entrance gateway. The church has a Romanesque chancel.

The landscape at this point is still typical of the Poitou with its hedgerows, sunken paths and farmsteads with Roman tiles. It is at Nueil that slate roofing reappears. The vineyards are grouped on the well exposed slopes.

The D 69 passes in front of the Château d'Echuilly.

Château d'Echuilly. – *Not open to the public.*

Leading off from the road junction marked by a Calvary is the surfaced private road to the château. Finished in 1740 the château

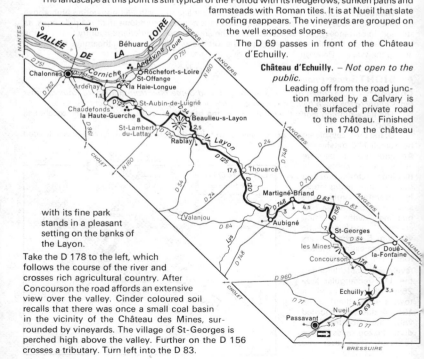

with its fine park stands in a pleasant setting on the banks of the Layon.

Take the D 178 to the left, which follows the course of the river and crosses rich agricultural country. After Concourson the road affords an extensive view over the valley. Cinder coloured soil recalls that there was once a small coal basin in the vicinity of the Château des Mines, surrounded by vineyards. The village of St-Georges is perched high above the valley. Further on the D 156 crosses a tributary. Turn left into the D 83.

Martigné-Briand. – Pop 1 790. This wine growers' village clusters round its ruined château, burnt during the struggles between the Blues and the Whites *(p 114)*.

Beyond Martigné-Briand and its vineyards the road crosses the Layon with its masses of floating water lilies.

Aubigné. – Pop 271. A once fortified village.

The road climbs up to an undulating plateau, affording *en route* views of Martigné-Briand, before descending amidst oaks where the Lys joins the Layon. On the approach to Thouarcé there are fine glimpses of the vine clad slopes.

The D 125 gives views of a countryside of rounded ridges and crosses a region of vineyards and arable plots climbing in terraces up the steep valley sides. A roadside Calvary, before Rablay, affords remarkable views of the vine covered slopes.

Rablay-sur-Layon. – Pop 507. This attractive wine growers' village in a well sheltered position has gardens sporting magnolias, fig and palm trees. The brick and half timber houses have overhanging upper storeys.

Take the D 54 to the right, which crosses the Layon, then skirts a vine covered cirque. From the plateau dotted with windmills there is an extensive view of the valley.

Beaulieu-sur-Layon. – Pop 944. This wine growers' village in the midst of the Layon vineyards has attractive mansard roofed houses including the 18C town hall. The **Hôtel Desmazières** is an elegant 18C building.

As you leave Beaulieu to the west by the D 55, to the right in a low building is a **Caveau du Vin** with a collection of old Angevin wine bottles and glasses and to the left a viewing table with extensive **views**★: of the Layon valley, its vineyards and châteaux, and to the south as far as Vihiers in the Mauges.

Take the N 160 to the left which descends into the valley with its steep sides riddled with caves and quarries (lime kilns). The bridge over the Layon offers an attractive view of the river and a ruined mediaeval bridge. Between St-Lambert and St-Aubin, this scenic road, winding and hilly, runs amidst the vineyards which produce the *Quart de Chaume* wine.

Before St-Aubin turn left into the D 106 and after 1.5 km - 1 mile turn right.

Château de la Haute-Guerche. – *Open 1 July to 31 August from 10am to 1pm and 4 to 8pm; apply to M. Lelong.* This romantic ruin was built during the reign of Charles VII and burnt down at the time of the Vendéen War *(p 114)*.

Take the D 125 in the direction of Chaudefonds. The D 121 leads to Ardenay on the Angevin corniche road.

Angevin Corniche Road★. – *Description p 105.*

Chalonnes-sur-Loire. – *Description p 105.*

LOCHES ★★★

Michelin map 🖸🖸 16 – *Local map p 87* – Pop 6 816 – *Facilities p 38*

This charming town lies in a pleasant setting on the banks of the Indre. Dominated by its mediaeval city, heavily fortified on a rocky spur, it is a gem of great historical and architectural interest.

HISTORICAL NOTES

A former prison. – The naturally strong position of Loches was used from the earliest times. A great feudal family, the counts of Anjou *(p 43)* established a large entrenched camp on it. When the counts of Anjou succeeded to the throne of England with Henry II Plantagenet, the defences of the castle were further developed.

After the death of Henry II, while Richard Lionheart was in captivity in Durnstein following his return from the Third Crusade, Philippe-Auguste intrigued with John Lackland (England's Bad King John), Richard's brother, and obtained possession of Loches. The impetuous Richard, soon after he was ransomed hastened to the spot and recaptured the castle by a surprise attack. Ten years later, in 1205, Philippe-Auguste had his revenge, but less brilliantly: his siege lasted a year. Loches then became the great French State prison and the kings of France tried to make it impregnable.

Agnès Sorel. – In the 15C a women's smile irradiates the dark history of the castle. Agnès Sorel, the "Lady of Beauty" *(1)* and favourite of Charles VII came to live at Loches. She deserted the court of Chinon, where the Dauphin – the future Louis XI – had made things difficult for her and had even taken "sudden" action, as a slap in the face was politely called.

The King picked her out from among the Queen's maids of honour. He remained always in love with her. They were an ill assorted couple: Agnès enchanting and the King ill favoured. The favourite had a great influence on Charles VII. Her advice was often good, but her taste for luxury, accompanied by her great generosity, was a heavy burden on the finances of the kingdom. In order to be buried in the collegiate church, Agnès loaded the chapter with gifts. After her death the canons were of the opinion that the presence of a notorious sinner in the sacred precincts was unedifying. They asked Louis XI to remove her remains to the castle. The old fox agreed, but on condition that the gifts took the same road. At this the scruples of the chapter promptly evaporated.

Louis XI's cages (end of 15C). – When inspecting the castle the visitor will see dungeons and barred cells, but he will not find the cages in which Louis XI liked to confine his prisoners.

The cages were made of wooden trelliswork, covered with iron. The most comfortable measured 2 m - 6½ ft on all sides. But there was a smaller model, of more refined cruelty, in which the prisoner could only lie or sit. The cages were often suspended from the roof of the cells. These "monuments to tyranny" were destroyed by the inhabitants of Loches in 1790.

---

(1) "Beauty" here had a double meaning. Agnès was very pretty and also owned a château at Beauté (now Nogent-sur-Marne, near Paris).

■ **THE MEDIAEVAL CITY★★** (**La cité médiévale**) *time: 1½ hours – excluding a tour of the fortifications*

For the purposes of this guide the term mediaeval city covers the area within the mediaeval town walls. Leave the car on the Mail de la Poterie.

Porte Royale★ and the museums (M). – The 13C gateway, Porte Royale, massive and powerfully fortified, now stands flanked by two towers which were built in the 15C. The slots through which the drawbridge chains ran and the machicolations can still be seen.

Go past the Porte Royale to the Rue Lansyer on the left. A few yards further on are the entrances to the Lansyer and Folklore Museums. Open from 9 to 11.45am and 2 to 6pm (5pm in March and October, 4pm from 1 November to 28 February); closed on Fridays and public holidays; 5F.

Guided tours at 9.30pm with illuminations from 1 July to 31 August; 6F.

The **Lansyer Museum** contains works by the local landscape painter Lansyer and curios from the Far East.

A visit to the **Folklore Museum** (Musée du Terroir) enables you to see inside the gatehouse in which it is installed. From the upper platform there is a fine view of Loches.

St-Ours★★. – This former collegiate church is distinguished by two octagonal pyramids which rise between its towers; these are formed by the vaulting over the nave. The porch with vaulting in the Angevin style *(see p 21)* shelters a richly decorated Romanesque doorway. A Gallo-Roman altar is used as a stoup.

In the nave you will see the famous pyramid vaulting, known as *dubes*, which was erected in the 12C by the Prior, Thomas Pactius.

Château★★. – *Guided tours from 9am to noon and 2 to 7pm (5.30pm from 1 October to 14 March); closed on Tuesdays in winter and in December and January; 5F.*

(After photo: Éd. du Zodiaque)

St-Ours — From the château courtyard

Tour Agnès Sorel. – This tower, known since the 16C as the "Beautiful Agnès Tower" contained between 1809 and 1970 the tomb of Agnès Sorel, which originally came from St-Ours.

Logis Royaux (Royal Residence). – From the castle terrace, overlooking a fine view of Loches and the Indre Valley, one sees that the building is in two parts which were erected at different periods. The Vieux Logis, the older, taller building is heavily fortified with four turrets linked by a watchpath at the base of the roof. It was enlarged under Charles VIII and Louis XII by the addition of the more recent Nouveau Logis, in the manner and style of the Renaissance.

On the first floor of the **Nouveau Logis** you will see Anne of Brittany's small oratory, finely worked and decorated with the ermine of Brittany and the girdle of St Francis *(p 18)*. The canopy opposite the altar originally surmounted the royal pew and the only door was the one to the right of the altar.

The third room contains an interesting **triptych★** from the school of Jean Fouquet (15C) which originally came from St-Antoine Church, with panels evoking the Crucifixion, Carrying of the Cross and Deposition.

The **recumbent figure of Agnès Sorel★**, placed in the Charles VIII Room, attracts the attention of the visitor. During the Revolution, soldiers of the Indre battalions, whose historical knowledge was not equal to their Revolutionary zeal, took the favourite of Charles VII for a saint, chopped up her statue, desecrated her grave and scattered her remains. The alabaster monument was restored in Paris under the Empire and again on the occasion of its transfer to the Nouveau Logis. Agnès is shown recumbent, with two angels supporting her lovely head and two lambs lying at her feet. In the same room you will see the portrait of the beautiful Agnès and a copy of the famous Madonna and Child, a panel of the *Melun Diptych* (in Antwerp) by Fouquet, which also portrays Agnès.

It was in the great hall of the **Vieux Logis** that Joan of Arc came on 3 and 5 June 1429 to urge Charles VII to go to Reims. She was accompanied at the time by Robert Le Masson *(p 104)*, Dunois *(p 62)* and Gilles de Rais.

Note in the last room, known as Charles VII's ante-chamber, a copy of the manuscript of the proceedings at Joan of Arc's trial (1431). There is a 16C tapestry narrating an allegorical depiction of Music.

Return to the Church of St-Ours and by way of the Rue Thomas-Pactius, make for the Mail du Donjon. Turn round, after a bend to the right, to get a view of the church.

Keep★★ (Donjon). – *Open 9am to noon and 2 to 7pm (5.30pm from 1 October to 14 March); closed on Thursdays in winter in January and December; 5F.*

Together with the towers, Ronde and Martelet, the keep forms an imposing fortified group.

The mediaeval town of Loches was vulnerable only on its south side. To defend this weak point a powerful keep supported by semi cylindrical buttresses was built in the late 11C.

On the outside can still be seen the pulog holes in which the timbers supporting the hoardings rested. To the left of the entrance in Philippe de Commines's dungeon, is an iron collar weighing 16 kg - 35 lb.

The floors of the three storeys have vanished but three sets of fireplaces and windows can still be seen on the walls. A staircase of 157 steps enables you to climb to the top of the keep from which there is a fine view.

Tour Ronde (F). – This round tower, which like the Martelet was built in the 15C to complete the fortifications where they formed part of the main wall of the castle, the keep and of the town, was, in fact, another keep.

Known as the Louis XI Tower, the round tower contains four rooms, one above the other. Over the torture chamber is a vaulted cell in which **Cardinal La Balue** is said to have been imprisoned. The son of a Poitiers tailor, this ecclesiastic became a counsellor to Louis XI. He betrayed his master to Charles the Bold, the Duke of Burgundy, but was unmasked and is said to have spent the following eleven years in a "cage" at Loches, appreciating, no doubt, the pleasures of an invention attributed to himself.

The other dungeons and cells are not open to the public.

Martelet (L). – The most impressive dungeons, occupying several floors below ground, are to be found in this building. The first was that of **Ludovico Sforza** the Moor, Duke of Milan, who was taken prisoner by Louis XII. For eight years (1500-08) at Loches, he paid for his trickeries and treacheries. On the day of his release the sunlight was so

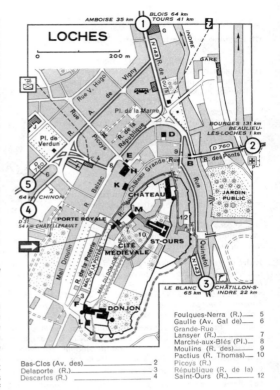

LOCHES

Bas-Clos (Av. des)	2
Delaporte (R.)	3
Descartes (R.)	4

Foulques-Nerra (R.)	5
Gaulle (Av. Gal de)	6
Grande-Rue	
Lansyer (R.)	7
Marché-aux-Blés (Pl.)	8
Moulins (R. des)	9
Pactius (R. Thomas)	10
Picoys (R.)	
République (R. de la)	
Saint-Ours (R.)	12

bright and the excitement of freedom so great that he fell dead. Ludovico, who was Leonardo da Vinci's patron, covered the walls of his prison with paintings and inscriptions. Next to the stars, cannons and helmets, may be seen a phrase, hardly surprising in the circumstances: *celui qui n'est pas contan* (he who is not content).

Below, lit by a solitary ray of light, is the dungeon where the Bishops of Autun and Le Puy, both implicated in the Connétable de France or Charles, Duke of Bourbon's change of allegiance to the Emperor Charles V, found leisure to hollow out of the wall a small altar and a symbolic Stations of the Cross. In another cell was interned the comte de St-Vallier, father of Diane de Poitiers. He was sentenced to death and informed of his reprieve – on the intervention of his daughter – only when on the scaffold.

On the same underground level as the dungeons, galleries open off to quarries, which in the 13C, provided stone for the small fortified covered passageways flanking the ramparts.

Tourists who are pressed for time should turn right on leaving the Martelet to reach the Mai de la Poterie and their cars. For those with another ½ hour to spare, we would warmly recommend a walk round the outside of the ramparts.

Walk round the outside of the ramparts★★. – *Turn left on coming out of the Martelet.*

This walk *(½ hour on foot)* shows one that this mediaeval town was in fact an entrenched camp, complete with all its own defences. The perimeter wall is 1 km - ¾ mile long and is pierced by only two gateways. During the walk you will see the three spur towers built in the 13C before the keep. The mass and height of the fortifications are impressive.

■ ADDITIONAL SIGHTS

Porte des Cordeliers (B). – Late 15C gateway which with the Porte Picoys, are the only two remaining of the town's four original gates. It was the main gate of the city.

Tour St-Antoine (D). – 16C. This is one of the rare belfries in central France. There is a balustrade curiously decorated with letters and monograms.

Porte Picoys (E) and **Hôtel de Ville★ (H).** – These two buildings are adjacent. The 15C Picoys Gate is ornamented on the side facing the town with a fine Flamboyant bay and a charming Renaissance recess. The town hall is a dignified Renaissance building.

Maison de la Chancellerie (K). – The Chancellery is a fine Renaissance building.

Jardin Public. – From this garden there is a good view of the castle.

EXCURSIONS

Beaulieu-lès-Loches. – Pop 1 769. *1 km - ¾ mile by ② on the plan.*

This old village contains the ruins of a famous abbey founded in 1004 by Foulques Nerra *(p 43)*, who was buried there by his wish. The **abbey church** *(apply for the key to Mme Allibrand, 2 Rue Foulques Nerra)* is dominated by a majestic, square Romanesque tower which is surmounted by an octagonal spire. The arms of the transept also date from the Romanesque period but the nave and the chancel were rebuilt in the 15C following their destruction by the English in 1412. At the back of the choir can still be seen traces of the original Romanesque apse.

A curious outdoor pulpit stands in the adjoining abbot's lodging on the site of the old cloisters, to the right of the church.

The former **Church of St-Laurent** still has three fine aisles with domical form Angevin vaulting and a beautiful Romanesque tower.

LOCHES★★★

Chartreuse du Liget. – *10 km - 6 miles east of Loches.*

The last remains of a charterhouse, (Carthusian monastery), founded by Henry II of England in expiation, it is said, for the murder of Thomas Becket, stand in a lonely valley on the verges of the Forest of Chinon.

Permission to visit the abbey may be obtained on the spot. Having entered by the monumental 18C gateway, you will see the ruins of the 12C chapel and the great 18C cloisters. In the round **Chapel of St-Jean-de-Liget** which stands alone in an open field 800 m - 875 yd from the monastery, are well known frescoes *(ask for the key at the monastery).*

At **La Corroirie**, a former annexe of the monastery 1 km - ¾ mile from it on the Montrésor road, you will see, in a pretty setting, a 12C chapel, a 15C fortified gateway and some interesting vaulted chambers *(apply for permission at the monastery).*

(After photo: Éd. du Zodiaque)

Chapel of St-Jean-de-Liget

Indrois Valley. – *Round trip of 51.5 km - 32 miles via Montrésor and Azay-sur-Indre leave Loches by ② and the D760 passing Liget on the way to Montrésor. For the upper reaches of the Indrois see p 119.*

This tributary of the Indre crosses the clays and chalks of the Montrésor gâtine. The river course is lined by willows, alders and poplars with lush meadowlands beyond. Fruit trees and vineyards cling to the well exposed slopes.

Genillé. – Pop 1 433. The houses climb up from the river to the late 15C château with its angle towers and dovecotes. Dominated outside by its Romanesque belfry, the interior of the church is striking for its elegant chancel in the transitional Flamoyant-Renaissance style. Note the lierne and tierceron vaulting. The white baptismal font in the nave dates from 1494.

St-Quentin-sur-Indrois. – Pop 373. A pleasantly situated village.

La Follaine. – This manor house stands high on the north bank just before the confluence with the Indre. This 15C residence with its adjoining round tower and its gabled dormer windows was in pre-Revolution days Lafayette's hunting lodge.

Return to Loches by the D 17 and the N 143.

LOIR Valley ★★

Michelin maps 囲 17 and 囮 2 to 7

Placid and slow the Loir from L'Ile-de-France to Anjou flows through a countryside more deeply rural than its mother river the Loire. Green meadow landscapes, attractive towns and charming villages all go to epitomise the saying *La Douce France* (Gentle France).

GEOGRAPHICAL NOTES

Over 350 km - 218 miles from its source to its confluence with the Sarthe, the meanders of this slow flowing river have steep banks on the outside of its bends. Riddled with caves or troglodyte dwellings, many have been inhabited since Neolithic times.

The generally chalky terrain is covered in areas of the upper reaches, on the south bank, with the sands and clays of the Beauce and Gâtine of Touraine. The hills of Perche and Gâtine of Maine peter out on the northern banks, nearer its confluence with the Sarthe.

Lines of trembling poplars, alders and silver willows follow the river's course, lush green meadows, orchards and gardens alternate along the banks, while vineyards cling to the hill slopes.

Originally navigable up to Château-du-Loir, few boats pass except for the flat bottomed ones of the fishermen in search of a good catch of trout, gudgeon, perch, pike and eel.

Always a much used line of communication even in the days of the pilgrimages to St. James's shrine in Santiago de Compostela – with its heritage of priories, commanderies, churches and chapels often decorated with frescoes on characteristic light backgrounds – it is followed in most parts by both road and rail. The valley has retained its charm and offers a pleasant drive at a more leisurely pace.

From Bonneval to Vendôme – *77 km - 48 miles – about 3 hours – Local map p 97*

Bonneval. – Pop 4 892. *Facilities p 38.* This former walled town surrounded by water filled moats, retains two of its original towers and gateways. On the southern outskirts is the Abbey of St-Florentin, now a psychiatric hospital *(interior not open to the public).* Founded in the 9C this former Benedictine abbey has an elegant entrance building with attractive chequered stonework, which once served as a bailiff's court.

Leave Bonneval by the D 144 at St-Maur and take the D 360 which passes on the left the **Baignon Dolmen.** Cross the Loir to reach the N 10 at Flacey and turn left again almost immediately, taking the D 110 which affords some far reaching views. At St-Christophe follow the D 361 and the river to reach Marboué and the N 10.

Marboué. – Pop 929. Site of a Gallo-Roman settlement this village has a good spot for river bathing, and a crocketed spire towering above its 15C belfry porch.

Châteaudun★★. – *Description p 62.*

Leave Châteaudun by ⑤ and 2 km - 1 mile after St-Denis-les-Ponts, take the D 23¹ to the left. At **Douy** there is a view of a late 15C manor house, mill and church clinging to the hillside. Turn right to take the D 23 which crosses the Yerre at St-Hilaire.

Montigny-le-Gannelon. – Pop 349. Between the cliff face with its troglodyte dwellings and the Loir, this once fortified stronghold retains a 12C gateway on the plateau side. The 15C brick and stone château, restored in the 19C, overlooks the Loir. The park *(open 9am to noon and 1 to 6pm; 2F)* with its fine trees is open to the public. From the terraces there are fine views of the valley and Cloyes.

Cloyes-sur-le-Loir. – Pop 2 552. *Facilities p 38.* This formerly fortified town on the edge of the Beauce was on the pilgrimage route to Santiago de Compostela. A welcoming small town with some old houses and a church surmounted by a 15C belfry, it was here that **Emile Zola**, the novelist lived while collecting material for his novel *Earth* in which action is centred on Cloyes and nearby Romilly-sur-Aigre.

Aigre Valley. – *Description p 163.*

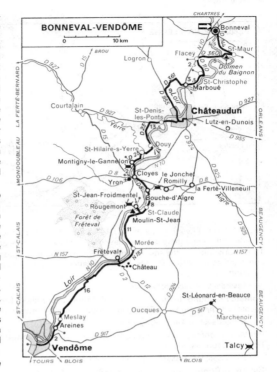

From Cloyes follow the Avenue du 11-Novembre which becomes the D 8 then branch to the right to follow the D 8¹ and branch right again in Bouche-d'Aigre to follow the D 145⁷, a picturesque road following the Loir.

St-Jean-Froidmentel. – Pop 439. The village on the far bank has a church with an attractive Renaissance doorway. The bridge affords good views of the Loir.

The road at this point runs very close to the river, passing on the way various quarries and mills. Note in particular the mill, Moulin St-Jean, which is still operated with water power.

Château de Rougemont. – *1 km - ½ mile beyond St-Jean-Froidmentel. Closed, work in progress.* The château was built in the 17C for a Florentine who was brought from Italy by Marie de' Medici.

Fréteval. – Pop 909. *Facilities p 38.* Known for its fishing, Fréteval on the far bank is dominated by a ruined **feudal fortress** *(access: ¼ hour on foot Rtn)* perched on a rocky spur on the near bank. The forest on the west bank is known as the Forêt de Fréteval.

Beyond Fréteval the houses cling to the slopes to avoid the river in spate.

Areines. – Interesting frescoes. *Description p 161.*

Arrive in Vendôme (p 159) by ②.

From Vendôme to La Flèche – *138 km - 86 miles – about 8 hours – Local map pp 98 and 99*

Leave Vendôme *(p 159)* by ⑤, the D 917, and after going under the railway line turn right in the direction of **Naveil** (Pop 1 358) with its country church. Cross the Loir and just after Montrieux there is a view of the valley. These vineyards produce the *rosé de Vendôme.*

Villiers. – Pop 831. Clinging to the hillside above the vineyards this village looks across to the Château de Rochambeau. There are 16C **mural paintings** in the church: portrayed on the north wall are St. Christopher carrying the Infant Jesus and the Legend of the Three Living and the Three Dead. 15C choir stalls.

Château de Rochambeau. – *2.5 km - 2 miles from Villiers.* This 16-18C building was the birthplace of General Rochambeau (1725-1807) the commander of the French forces in the American War of Independence. He is buried at nearby Thoré.

Le Gué-du-Loir. – Standing at the confluence of the Boulon with the Loir, this hamlet is surrounded by lush prairies. The nearby Renaissance **La Bonaventure Manor** *(not open to the public)*, now in ruins, belonged to Antoine de Bourbon-Vendôme, father of the future Henri IV and later to the poet **Alfred Musset's** family.

Fortan. – Pop 163. *6 km - 4 miles to the northwest by the D 148. For the key to the church apply to the épicerie.* The Renaissance **baptismal font** is highly original: Samson supports the bowl while the cover is crowned with a group showing the Baptism of Christ.

The cliff becomes lower and its face is punctuated with troglodyte dwellings inhabited by local farmers who specialise in cattle rearing.

Lunay. – Pop 1 007. *3.5 km - 2 miles by the D 53, having left the D 24.* The main square is bordered by several old houses. The Church of St-Martin, Flamboyant in style, has an attractive doorway with finely sculptured splayings. The sacristy has 14-16C murals.

Les Roches-l'Évêque. – Pop 284. This once fortified village is well known for its troglodyte dwellings which are often decorated with lilac and wistaria. A little upstream is the troglodyte Chapel of St-Gervais *(to visit apply to M. Hénault).*

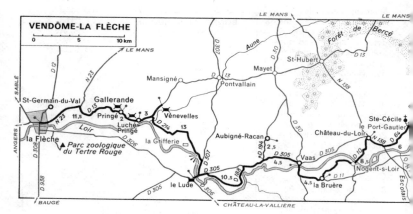

In Les Roches-l'Évêque take the D 917 to the left across the Loir and climb to the top of the hillside from where there is a fine view of the valley, Montoire and Lavardin.

Turn about and take the small road to St-Rimay and having passed under the railway turn right and right again to the D 168. In the distance is the silhouette of the ruined stronghold at Lavardin.

Lavardin★. – *Description p 91.*

Continuing round there are views of Montoire's ruined fortress and, in the foreground, Lavardin's imposing keep. The shaded road wanders between the cliff face and river.

Montoire-sur-le-Loir. – *Description p 117.*

Between Montoire and La Possonnière Manor follow the route described under the heading Ronsard countryside p 118.

La Possonnière Manor★. – *Description p 128.*

Return to Couture and continue to follow the D 57 crossing the Loir. Up ahead high on a wooded slope is the Château de la Flotte.

Château de la Flotte. – The ochre coloured mass of this château, rebuilt in the 19C, overlooks the valley. Marie de Hautefort, Lady in Waiting to Anne of Austria, and platonic friend of Louis XIII, was exiled here on the orders of Richelieu.

Take the D 305.

Poncé-sur-le-Loir. – *Description p 128.*

Villedieu-le-Château. – Pop 605. 5 km - 3 miles beyond Ruillé on the other bank by the D 80.

This attractive village in a pleasant **setting** is surrounded by slopes covered with vineyards and fruit trees and interspersed by troglodyte houses. The houses standing in colourful gardens, the ruined ramparts and belfry of the former priory of St-Jean compose a charming picture.

Private estates and vineyards alternate with arable land.

La Chartre-sur-le-Loir. – Pop 1 901. *Facilities p 38.* The nearby Jasnières estate produces a sweet white wine which ages well but is little known.

Continue from La Chartre to Marçon, known for its wines, and turn into the D 61. The road now crosses the Loir plain and high on the north slope is the Ste-Cécile Chapel.

Ste-Cécile Chapel. – *At Le Port-Gautier take the D 64 in the direction of Château-du-Loir. Shortly after the hamlet leave the car to follow a signposted path to the right which climbs up to the plateau surface (½ hour on foot Rtn).* The chapel is surrounded by a parish close.

The D 64 follows the foot of the valley side which is pierced here and there with troglodyte dwellings.

Château-du-Loir. – Pop 6 155. *Facilities p 38.* Spread out in the small Valley of the Yre there is no trace of the former château. The old part of the town clusters round the Church of St-Guingalois, which was once part of a priory headed by Ronsard. The monumental terracotta *Pietà* standing at the far end of the chancel, is by Barthélemy de Mello (17C) who also did the St-Martin on Horseback in the chapel to the right. Note in the north transept two wooden panels representing a Nativity (15C) and late 15C Resurrection by the Flemish Mannerist school. In the Romanesque crypt is a fine 16C wooden Outraged Christ.

Beyond Château-du-Loir and the bridge at Nogent, which affords fine views, the valley widens to form a basin of sandy soils supporting heaths, and open woodland country *(bocage)* where horses are reared.

La Bruère. – Pop 249. The church has coffered vaults over the chancel and 16C stained glass windows. Note the statues of saints in the nave.

Beyond La Bruère, rustling poplars and oaks are often replaced by conifer trees (pines). On recrossing the river admire **Vaas** *(facilities p 39)* with its church, houses, gardens and riverside washing houses, attractively situated on the north bank.

Aubigné-Racan. – Pop 1 942. *2.5 km - 2 miles from the D 305 via the D 194.* This peaceful market town built with the local white tufa stone climbs in tiers up the hillside. The church shelters two 17C terracotta statues and an altarpiece depicting the Nativity.

Between Vaas and Le Lude, meadows, nursery gardens and conifer forests succeed one another. The river is strewn with large islands.

Le Lude. – *Description p 107.*

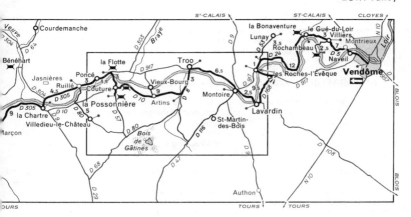

A sandy soil permits the growing of nut trees, asparagus, potatoes and maize. View of the valley before passing the Château de la Grifferie. Before reaching Luché-Pringé turn right on to the D 13 to have a glimpse of Vénevelles Manor.

Vénevelles Manor. – This 15-17C building in a pleasant setting is surrounded by moats.

Luché-Pringé. – Pop 1 384. *Facilities p 38.* Although the church was partly destroyed by fire in 1921, the magnificent Plantagenet chancel *(p 21)* remains. Note to the right on entering the remarkable *Pietà* carved in walnut wood.

On leaving Luché remark to the right a 17C manor house with mansard roofs.

Pringé. – Standing near a gracious priory the small Romanesque church, altered in the 15C, is pierced by a doorway with splaying. Inside *(restoration work in progress)* are statues and 16C mural paintings.

Château de Gallerande★. – Set in a park where peacocks strut on vast lawns bordered by fine cedars, limes and oaks. A stretch of water borders the D 13. The château itself *(not open to the public)*, once the seat of a marquisate, stands amidst a mass of greenery. From the railing of the courtyard one sees the northeast front, flanked by round machicolated towers. It includes a curious octagonal keep.

Here the valley is wide. Reach La Flèche *(p 80)* by the N 23 and ①.

From La Flèche to Angers – *50 km - 31 miles – about 2 hours*

Leave La Flèche by ④, the N 23, and after 7 km - 4 miles reach Bazouges.

Bazouges-sur-le-Loir. – Pop 1 368. From the bridge there is a charming **view★** of Bazouges in its riverside setting.

The 15-16C **château** *(open from Easter to 15 September, Tuesdays and Thursdays 10am to noon and Saturdays 2 to 5pm; 5F; on coming east out of Bazouges take the tree planted avenue)* still has a watermill intact. Two massive machicolated towers with pepperpot roofs flank the entrance. One of the towers contains the 15C chapel with elegant Angevin vaulting and several old statues. Above a guards' chamber is connected to the watchpath. Also included in the visit are the Guards' Room with its imposing stone fireplace, the 18C saloons and the French style park.

The 12C **church** has early 16C decorative paintings on the wooden vaulting of the nave. *(Open weekdays from 8.30 to 9.30am, Saturday afternoons at 6pm and Sundays from 10.30am to noon.)*

Continue along the N 23 to St-Leonard where you cross the river to reach Durtal.

Durtal. – Pop 3 255. *Facilities p 38.* Attractively situated Durtal offers a choice of recreations: bathing, fishing, walking in the nearby **Forest of Chambiers** and a racecourse. The **château** *(courtyard open to the public; views from the watchpath)*, now an old people's home, has 15 and 16C machicolated towers with pepperpot roofs and a six storey keep while the main wing and other buildings are typical of the Louis XIII style.

Continue to follow the N 23 on the south bank of the Loir and 2 km - 1 mile beyond Bourgneuf take the local road to the right to reach the Château du Verger.

(After photo: René Jacques)

Durtal

Château du Verger. – An imposing gatehouse, outbuildings, wide moat and flint towers with white tufa ornamentations and machicolations recall the once stately dwelling which belonged to the Rohan family. Started in 1482 by **Pierre de Rohan**, Marshal of France, the château was to suffer an ignominious fate when in 1776 Cardinal Rohan, of the Diamond Necklace Affair ordered its destruction. Priceless works of art were dispersed.

Return to the N 23 which leaves the Loir to reach Angers (p 43).

Michelin maps 63, 64 and 65

The Loire, so often sung by the poets since Ronsard and Du Bellay, for long brought life to the countryside, but today no river traffic plies the great waterway. None the less, the river still gives its character to the region and the finest landscapes are those it adorns with its long vistas and graceful curves.

GEOGRAPHICAL AND HISTORICAL NOTES

The Loire, a former tributary of the Seine. – The longest river in France – 1 020 km - 634 miles – rises at the foot of the peak, Gerbier-de-Jonc on the southern edge of the Massif Central, but only its middle course is treated in this guide.

Originally a tributary of the Seine, the Upper Loire was captured when an earth movement tilted the southwestern part of the Paris Basin causing the swing westward to a newly created arm of the Atlantic extending up to Blois.

A fickle river. – The Loire with its irregular and capricious régime is sometimes furious and sometimes indolent. In summer, only a few rivulets *(luisettes)* trickle between the sand or gravel banks *(grèves)*. In these conditions it has the appearance of a "sandy river", but in autumn, during the rains, or at the end of winter, when the snow melts, it is in spate and its swirling waters then run high. It sometimes bursts the dikes, known as *levées* or *turcies*, built to protect the countryside from floods. Many village walls bear the tragic dates of great floods: 1846, 1856, 1866 and 1910.

Shipping on the Loire. – Up to the mid 19C the Loire in spite of its whims – sandbanks, whirlpools, floods and tolls – was a much used means of communication. As early as the 14C navigation was organised by a guild of mariners centred on Orléans. In addition to merchandise – wood and coal from the Forez, pottery from Nevers, grain from the Beauce, wines from Touraine and Anjou – there was a great flow of passengers who preferred the river to the road. The journey from Orléans to Nantes by river took six days, and from ten to twenty for the return journey with a good wind. Coaches were transported on rafts. The river traffic comprised flat bottomed barges (scows or lighters) with large square sails. **Toues**, barges without

(After engraving: photo Éd. Larousse, Paris)

The Loire at Saumur. — Gabarres and N.-D.-des-Ardilliers

rigging, still used today, transported hay and livestock; **sapines** with a greater capacity and rudely made of fir planks, were destroyed at the end of the voyage; **gabarres** were much larger vessels with sails up to 20 m - 66 ft high. The boats travelled in groups with a mother ship pulling two decreasingly smaller boats, one of which carried the bargee's cabin. The convoy was preceded by a wherry or punt to sound the river bed. The bargees had to be skilled on the upstream voyage to negotiate the bridges, especially the Ponts-de-Cé and at Beaugency where ropes from the bridge were used to guide the boats.

The "Unexplodables". – In 1832 the first steamboat service was started between Orléans and Nantes. It caused a sensation. Two days were enough for the journey, but there were accidents, for boilers exploded. Enthusiasm died down. The appearance of new steamboats nicknamed "Unexplodables" restored confidence so much so that in 1843 more than 100 000 passengers were carried on the Loire and the Allier by the various steamboat companies which ran the services between Moulins and Nantes.

With the development of the railway, navigation on the Loire declined. In 1862 the last shipping company closed down.

THE ITINERARY

Divided into various sections the itineraries described follow closely the banks of the Loire with the detours being reserved for sights of prime importance only. However, the wealth of things to see in the valley means that the tourist may with the help of the Michelin maps 63, 64 and 65, the local maps and the map of principal sights *(pp 4–6)* compose his own itinerary, wandering from the river to include such sights as attract his attention.

From Gien to Orléans★ *– 66 km - 41 mile – about 3½ hours – Local map opposite*

Leave Gien *(p 84)* by ⑤, the D 951, and from the west bank glance back at the town rising in tiers above the river. Beyond Poilly-lez-Gien the fertile countryside is dotted with large estates.

Sully-sur-Loire★. *– Description p 147.*

On looking back at Sully admire the fortress, the keep of which would seem to rise straight out of the river.

St-Père-sur-Loire. *– Description p 148.*

The road momentarily follows the *levée* or embankment.

St-Benoît-sur-Loire★★. *– Description p 133.*

Germigny-des-Prés★. *– Description p 83.*

Châteauneuf-sur-Loire. *– Description p 66.*

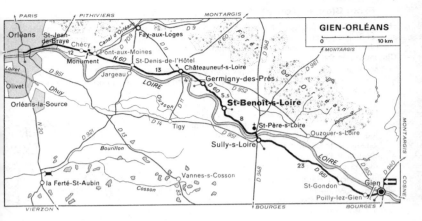

The street leading out of Châteauneuf-sur-Loire is lined by a series of picturesque houses.

The road soon enters the forests of pines and acacias so typical of the sandy soils of the Orléanais. Through the clearings, glimpses can be had, to the left, of the Loire and beyond, of the woods of the Sologne.

Two kilometres - 1 mile beyond Pont-aux-Moines where the road crosses the Orléans Canal stands a monument to commemorate the crossing of the Loire by Joan of Arc on 28 April 1429 *(p 16)*. Shortly after Chécy one gets a glimpse of Orléans Cathedral and soon the countryside gives way to suburbs.

> **St-Jean-de-Braye.** – Pop 12 974. The public may assist at services with Gregorian Chant in the Priory Church of Notre-Dame-du-Calvaire, Avenue de Verdun (Benedictine monks). *Mass: 8am weekdays, 10.30am Sundays and certain holidays; 5pm daily.*

Enter Orléans by ③ on the plan.

From Orléans to Blois★★★ *– 86 km - 53 miles – about 6 hours – Local map p 102*

Take Avenue Dauphine to leave Orléans *(p 121)*. Nursery gardens line both sides of the road until the bridge over the Loiret, flowing between wooded banks.

> **Olivet.** – *Description p 126.*

In Olivet take the D14 to the left which leads to Orléans-la-Source.

> **Orléans-la-Source★.** – *Description p 126.*

The D 14 leads to St-Hilaire-St-Mesmin amidst vineyard and orchard country. To the left is the Sologne and to the right a *varenne* or alluvial deposit reaching to Meung, and the limits of the Beauce limestone.

> **Cléry-St-André★.** – *Description p 77.*

> **Meung-sur-Loire★.** – *Description p 116.*

Soon to be seen on the horizon are the massive keep and bell tower of Beaugency.

> **Beaugency★★.** – *Description p 52.*

Leave by ③ or D 925 and after 6 km - 4 miles take the D 951 to the right. Turn right again just before St-Laurent-Nouan.

> **St-Laurent-des-Eaux Nuclear Power Station.** – *Tour: ½ hour.* Built on an artificial island in the Loire the St-Laurent A Nuclear Power Station is heralded by the gigantic masses of the two main production units St-Laurent 1 and 2. Entirely automatic the station has an annual production of 6 000 million kW (compare Dungeness A with an annual production of 2 303 million kW). With the completion of St Laurent B which was started in 1975, it is hoped to triple production by 1981. There is an exhibition room open to visitors where the construction and working of the plant is explained. A belvedere gives an overall view of the various installations.

> **Talcy★.** – *13 km - 8 miles from Muides via the D 112 and D 15. Description p 148.*

After Muides the road enters the walled Chambord Estate, where motorists are advised to drive slowly. The sudden apparition of the stately white mass of the Château de Chambord becoming ever bigger makes for an unforgettable experience.

> **Château de Chambord★★★.** – *Description p 60.*

Continue to St-Dyé on the banks of the Loire, in a verdant setting: magnificent plantations of poplars, fields of asparagus, tulips and gladioli. On the north bank stand the silhouettes of Ménars Château, then Blois with its basilica, cathedral and castle. On arriving in Blois *(p 54)* by ②, cross the Loire to reach the town centre.

> **Alternative route by the north bank.** – *13 km - 8 miles shorter.* Visitors who have already visited the Château de Chambord, should go straight on from Mer to Blois.

> **Suèvres.** – *Description p 147.*

> **Cour-sur-Loire.** – Pop 279. The church *(apply at the presbytery at Suèvres)* mainly in the Flamboyant style has, however, preserved its majestic Romanesque bell tower. The finest examples of Renaissance stained glass, in the south aisle, were presented by the Hurault de Cheverny family, the overlords of Cour. They portray the Jesse Tree, Death of the Virgin, Nativity of the Virgin and were all inspired by the school of Fontainebleau. In the north aisle small panels relate the history of the pilgrims on their way to St. James's shrine in Santiago de Compostela.

LOIRE Valley★★★

From Blois to Tours★★★ – 84 km - 52 miles – about 4 hours – Local map below

Having left Blois *(p 54)* by ⑤, the N 152, there is an attractive view of the town, dominated by the spire of St-Nicolas and the château, and the river. The Loire here is strewn with sandbanks which are a lush green in summer. An elegant metal bridge, built in 1969, leads to the Château de Chaumont, on the far bank.

Mesland. – Pop 540. *5 km - 3 miles from Veuves via the N152.* The 11C church has a fine Romanesque doorway and inside a fine Angevsm font of the same period. Note the 13C Virgin and the 16C Christ in wood. The 18C Virgin and Child above the high altar is the work of the school of Tours.

Limeray. – Pop 886. *1.5 km - 1 mile from the N152.* *Time: ¼ hour.* The church with fine Angevin vaulting has several works of art and old statues, see especially the group in the chapel to the Virgin to the north of the aisle: Mary Magdelene is by the 16C school of Tours.

Shortly after Le Haut-Chantier the Château d'Amboise is visible from the road. Cross the Loire to reach Amboise.

Amboise★★. – Description p 41.

A short detour via the Amboise Forest allows the tourist to visit one of the jewels of the Loire region, the Château de Chenonceau, standing on the Cher.

Chenonceau★★★. – Description p 68.

Return to Amboise and leave by ⑥.

Négron. – Standing below the N 152 this village has a charming square overlooked by the church, a Gothic house with a Renaissance front and a 12C barn with fine timberwork roof.

Further on the road passes charming villages nestling at the foot of the cliffs. Gardens and orchards rise above in terrace formation or go down to the riverbanks.

From La Frillière there is a view of Montlouis on the opposite bank.

Vouvray. – Pop 2 746. *Facilities p 39.* Situated at the heart of the famous Vouvray vineyard, the town retains numerous troglodyte houses *(illustration p 11)*. Local wine growers and merchants welcome visitors to their cellars. **Cave de la Bonne Dame**, a vast cellar dug out of the rock, holds in early January and on 15 August a wine exhibition. Tour of **the vineyard** *(round tour of 35 km - 22 miles – about 1 hour)*. Follow the signposts "route du Vouvray", leave to the east by the D 46, at Vernou-sur-Brenne take the D 1. After Bardouillère turn left on to the D 79 towards Reugny. Follow the Brenne Valley going south on the D 46. Turn right to Vaugondy and then via La Fuye make for La Vallée Coquette (Cooperative cellar) and finally return to Vouvray by Les Pâtis.

Rochecorbon. – Description p 156.

On the outskirts of Tours, heralded by the twin towers of its cathedral, one catches a glimpse of the entrance gateway to Marmoutier Abbey.

Marmoutier Abbey. – Description p 156.

Enter Tours (p 150) by ④.

From Tours to Saumur★★★ – 100 km - 62 miles – about 9 hours – Map opposite

Leave Tours *(p 150)* to the west by the D 88 passing on the way the Priory of St-Cosme, continue along the embankment *(levée)* between gardens and vegetable patches. Downstream after St-Genouph a fine view can be had, across the river, of the massive form of Luynes Castle.

At L'Aireau-des-Bourgeons turn left on to the D 288 to reach Villandry in the Cher Valley.

Savonnières. – Pop 1 461. The church has a pleasing Romanesque doorway, decorated with affronting animals and doves. Leaving in the direction of Villandry there are two limestone caves with calcite formations *(Guided tours 1 April to 15 September from 9am to 7pm; 16 September to 15 December from 9am to noon and 2 to 6pm; closed 16 December to 9 February, and Wednesdays from 9 February to 30 March; time: 1 hour; 8F; cave temperature: 14°C - 57°F).* This particular cave system extends for over 1 km - ¾ mile and shows typical limestone cave features – stalagmites, stalactites and flowstone in the process of formation and rushing waterfalls.

Ballan-Miré. – Pop 3 739. *7 km - 4 miles from Savonnières via the D 7 and D 127 to the right.* The church contains 16C **stained glass** showing a Crucifixion in the central window.

Villandry★★. – Description p 162.

Once beyond Villandry you are out of the region of troglodyte dwellings; continue by the D 39 to reach the Indre Valley and Azay-le-Rideau.

Azay-le-Rideau★★. – Description p 49.

102

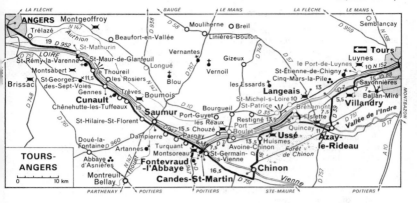

The D 17 running between the river and the Forest of Chinon, is overlooked to the right by the Château de l'Islette.

At Quincay, take the D 7 to the right then the D 119 towards Bréhémont, before branching left again on to the D 16, a narrow but pleasant road winding between hedges and spinneys and offering at various intervals glimpses of the river. From the bridge over the Indre one gets one of the best views of the Château d'Ussé.

Ussé★★. – *Description p 157.*

After the picturesque village of Huismes cross the fertile Véron, the setting for Rabelais's Abbey of Thélème, to reach Chinon dominated by the ruins of its massive fortress.

Chinon★★. – *Description p 73.*

Leave by ③ then take the D 751 in the direction of Candes-St-Martin and Montsoreau.

Alternative route along the north bank via Langeais: Tours to Candes-St-Martin – *16 km - 10 miles shorter.* Leave Tours by ⑬ following the N 152. Screens of poplars hide the countryside, however, from Le Port-de-Luynes there is a fine view of Luynes.

Château de Luynes★. – *Not open to the public.* The tourist must be content with the view from the bank of the Loire of this feudal mass which dominates the village *(facilities p 38)*. A Gallo-Roman *castrum* served by an aqueduct, still partly standing, and later a constantly disputed fortress which under the name of Maillé was to become the first barony of Touraine. Most of the present building dates from the 13C. In 1619 the Constable of Luynes bought Maillé, which was elevated to a duchy, and took the name of its new overlord. From that time on the castle has been in the hands of that same family.

The opposite bank is forested countryside.

St-Étienne-de-Chigny. – Pop 607. Standing back from the river this old village is sited in the Bresme Valley. The **church**, built by a former Mayor of Tours, **Jean Binet**, has a mourning band *(litre)* both inside and out, figuring his coat of arms. This lordly privilege was common in the Middle Ages and the height of the black band corresponded to the degree of nobility. The nave has a quite remarkable hammerbeam roof with tie beams sculptured in the form of large grotesque masks and in the choir Jonah inside the Whale. In the chevet a 16C stained glass window, depicting the Crucifixion, figures the donors, Jean Binet and his wife, Jeanne de la Lande. In the north transept is a Virgin and Child by the 16C French school.

Cinq-Mars-la-Pile. – *Description p 89.*

Beyond, the road, bordered by fruit trees and other intensive crops, moves away from the Loire returning again at Langeais.

Langeais★★. – *Description p 88.*

After Langeais make a slight detour from the N 152, to take the road to the right via St-Michel-sur-Loire and St-Patrice. This corniche road offers fine views. Continue along the D 35 to reach the N 152 and at Port-Boulet cross the Loire by the N 749 which leads to Avoine Chinon.

Avoine-Chinon. – *Description p 76.*

Take the D 7 to cross the Vienne near its confluence with the Loire.

Candes-St-Martin★★. – *Description p 59.*

Montsoreau★. – *Description p 121.*

Fontevraud Abbey★★. – *Description p 81.*

From the bridge at Montsoreau there is a fine view upstream of Candes and Montsoreau and down stream in the direction of Saumur, where the castle is just distinguishable. Between Montsoreau and Parnay note the troglodyte dwellings and white Renaissance houses in the roadside villages.

Turquant. – Pop 423. This attractive wine growers' village with its large tree planted square has a 15C church *(to visit apply at the presbytery)* containing a few relics from Fontevraud Abbey. 17C painted wooden high reliefs depicting the Crucifixion and Descent from the Cross. The baptistery and central altar are of the Louis XV period.

Parnay. – Pop 365. In the Saumur vineyard country, Parnay clings to the slopes of the chalky limestone. The Romanesque church, dominated by its elegant spire, is preceded by a Renaissance porch and terminated at its east end by a Gothic chevet.
From beside this church there are pleasant views of the valley.

Dampierre-sur-Loire. – *Description p 78.*

Arrive in Saumur (p 140) via ③.

From Saumur to Angers★ – *47 km - 29 miles – about 2½ hours – Local map p 103*

Leave Saumur *(p 140)* by ⑤ passing St-Hilaire-St-Florent lying between the River Thouet and the vine clad slope interspersed with caves, where wine is made by the champagne method. To the right vast meadows, protected by dikes, are bordered with trees. The more affluent suburbs start at La Mimerolle. Villages succeed one another almost without interruption. Note in passing the attractive doorway of the church belonging to the village of Chênehutte-les-Tuffeaux.

Chênehutte-les-Tuffeaux. – *Description p 142.*

Trèves. – Pop 416. The church and tower *(not open to the public)* – all that remains of a former 15C castle – form a picturesque group on the banks of the Loire.

The Romanesque **church** contains a 12C porphyry stoup, in the south transept the recumbent figure of a former Chancellor of France, Robert Le Masson (d 1443) and an elegant 15C reliquary in the north transept.

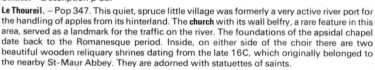

(After photo: Éd. du Lys, Clermont-Ferrand)

Trèves — Church and tower

Cunault★★. – *Description p 78.*

The area abounds in fruit trees, one of the principal riches of Anjou.

Gennes. – *Description p 83.*

Le Thoureil. – Pop 347. This quiet, spruce little village was formerly a very active river port for the handling of apples from its hinterland. The **church** with its wall belfry, a rare feature in this area, served as a landmark for the traffic on the river. The foundations of the apsidal chapel date back to the Romanesque period. Inside, on either side of the choir there are two beautiful wooden reliquary shrines dating from the late 16C, which originally belonged to the nearby St-Maur Abbey. They are adorned with statuettes of saints.

St-Maur-de-Glanfeuil Abbey. – *Description p 83.*

St-Rémy-la-Varenne. – Pop 600. *Facilities p 39.* An attractive village half hidden by foliage St-Rémy has a church which dates in part from the 10C. Unfortunately the interior is coated with roughcast. It is terminated by a Romanesque east end with oven vaulting and adorned by a frieze with sculptured brackets. A chapel to the right of the choir has 13C Angevin vaulting with liernes and tiercerons *(illustration p 21).*

Cross the Loire between St-Rémy-la-Varenne and St-Mathurin: the arable countryside is dotted with attractive houses. The road leaves the Loire just before reaching Angers *(p 43)* via ③.

From Angers to Champtoceaux★ – *83 km - 50 miles – about 3 hours – Map below*

Leave Angers *(p 43)* by the Boulevard du Bon-Pasteur and take the D 111 to the left, a winding and sometimes narrow road. Having crossed the more affluent suburbs of Angers, the road passes Bouchemaine just before the confluence of the Loire and the Maine. Beyond La Pointe, the road leaves the river to cross vineyard country. At Savennières cross to the other bank.

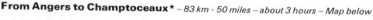

Béhuard★. – Pop 100. Attractively situated on an island of the same name this very old village with its 15 and 16C houses, in some cases raised to save them from river flooding, makes a peaceful setting for a 15C **church**. Built by Louis XI, following a vow he made when he was once in danger of drowning, one of the side walls is formed by living rock. The nave is covered by keel vaulting. Note the bell which was given to the church by Louis XI, the 15C statue of the Virgin and the 17C statue of St. John the Baptist. *Ex-voto* chains hang from the gallery while the 16C stalls have delightfully malicious carved misericords. The highly venerated statue, in plum tree wood, of Our Lady of Béhuard, stands in the choir. A 15C window of the Crucifixion in the aisle, shows the donor, Louis XI on the left, and there is a rare and ancient almsbox made from a hollowed oak.

Rochefort-sur-Loire. – Pop 1 622. Rochefort lies in a rural setting beside the Louet, a sidestream of the Loire. The nearby vineyards, produce the famous *Quart de Chaume*, a distinctive and heady wine. Several old houses, with turrets or watch towers line the square below the D 751. The only parts still standing of the Château de **St-Offange** are a few walls perched on a granite crest which was the origin of the island that now lies between the Louet and the Loire. In the late 16C it was a robbers' hideout.

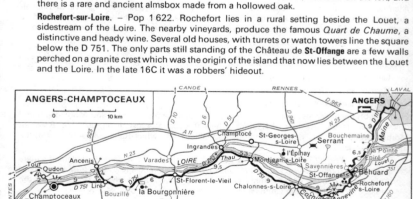

The Angevin Corniche Road★ (La Corniche Angevine). – Beginning at this point, with a winding and hilly section it climbs the hillsides and descends the valleys between Rochefort and Chalonnes. The road cut into the cliff face, affords magnificent bird's eye views across the full width of the valley and also of the small towns bordering the Loire between Angers and Ingrandes.

La Haie-Longue. – As you approach La Haie-Longue from Rochefort you will see from a bend a chapel dedicated to Our Lady of Loreto, the patron saint of aviators. Opposite is a viewing table *(telescope)* from which there is a remarkable **view★** of the Loire with its sidestreams, glinting silver in the light, and of meadows, turreted manor houses and hillside vineyards. The wine from these vineyards is known as *Coteaux du Layon*.

Chalonnes-sur-Loire. – Pop 4 708. *Facilities p 38.* Chalonnes has a pleasant setting and was the birthplace of St. Maurille, a 5C Bishop of Angers. There are attractive views of the river to be had from the quay-

(After photo: Knecht)

Salmon fishing

side which is lined with plane trees. Flax, once used by the sailcloth makers of Angers and grown on the midstream islands, has been superseded by tobacco, and the old port now harbours more pleasure craft than fishing boats. The nearby hillsides, at the confluence of the Louet and Layon, are covered with vines.

After Chalonnes the D 751 follows the edge of the plateau, cut at intervals by small tributary streams, till reaching Montjean.

Montjean-sur-Loire. – Pop 2 277. Montjean, with its tightly packed streets, stands on a rocky spur overlooking the Loire. The terrace beside the church affords a wide view of the valley, the suspension bridge and the numerous villages with their grey slate roofs.

The D 210 **from Montjean to St-Florent-le-Vieil★**, a narrow road following the embankment *(levée)* affords views to the south of the vineyard clad slopes rising above the Thau, a former sidestream of the Loire, and to the north over the river, the silhouette of Ingrandes.

Ingrandes. – Pop 1 517. *Facilities p 38.* The deserted quays and berths and imposing 17 and 18C houses are evidence of the former prosperity of this once bustling port. A majestic bridge bestrides the river recalling how in the past the town served as a link between Brittany and Anjou in the days of the salt tax *(la Gabelle)*. Since salt was stored here

and Anjou was not exempt from the tax, contraband dealing by smugglers flourished in the region. The **church** rebuilt in 1956 in the local style has an unusual bell tower and remarkable modern stained glass in brilliant colours by master glaziers from Chartres (Les Ateliers Loire) following cartoons by the artist Bertrand.

St-Florent-le-Vieil. – Pop 2 416. *Facilities p 39.* A good view of the **site** of this village perched on a rocky spur, dominated by its church, can be had from the bridge over the Loire. St-Florent was one of the first centres of Royalist insurrection in what was to be known as the Vendéen War

(After lithograph: photo Éd. Horizons de France)

St-Florent in the 19C

(see Les Mauges) following the execution of Louis XVI in March 1793. On 18 October, after a defeat at Cholet the Royalists with their mortally wounded leader, **Bonchamps**, a man of noble birth, withdrew to St-Florent. In revenge it was proposed to massacre the Republican prisoners gathered in the church. Only by the clemency of Bonchamps were the lives of the Republican captives spared – including among their number the father of the sculptor, David d'Angers.

The **church** contains in a chapel to the left Bonchamps's **tomb★** of white marble, a moving work executed by David himself. From the tree planted esplanade extending round the church there is an extensive **view★** of the Loire Valley.

Beyond St-Florent-le-Vieil the D 751 winds through gently rolling countryside.

La Bourgonnière Chapel★. – *Description p 58.*

Continue along the D 751 to Liré.

Liré. – Pop 2 161. This small village keeps alive the memory of its most famous son **Joachim Du Bellay**, who is commemorated by a statue and museum. Poet, friend of Ronsard, and member of the Pléiade, Du Bellay was born in 1522 of a noble family in the nearby Manor of La Turmelière, now replaced by a modern château. Author of *The Defence and Illustration of the French Language* (1549) – the manifesto of the Pléiade – his finest work is *The Regrets*.

The D 763 leads to Ancenis.

Ancenis. – Pop 7 304. *Facilities p 38. See town plan in the current Michelin Guide France.*
The old houses of Ancenis – Rue des Tonneliers, Rue du Château, Basse Grand-Rue, Place des Halles – rise in tiers above the Loire and the suspension bridge. An important strategic point Ancenis was formerly known as the "Key to Brittany" and was once a busy port with an active sailcloth making industry. Today it is renowned for its important pig market and its wines – Muscadet (white) and Gamay *(rosé).* The **château** *(now a school: tours of part of the interior during the school summer holidays afternoons only; 3F)* with its mixture of styles has an entrance flanked by round towers, a 15C gallery, a Renaissance wing with overhanging turret and elegant dormer windows and 17C pavilions.

Return to the south bank and continue to Champtoceaux.

Champtoceaux★. – Pop 1 252. – *Facilities p 38.* This town on the borders of Anjou has a good **site★** on the ridge of an outcrop dominating the valley. The reputation of the local white wines is fully justified. The **Promenade de Champalud★★**, a balcony behind the church *(viewing table),* affords a good view of the Loire as it divides into various branches to encircle the large islands.

Oudon. – Pop 1 599. *2 km - 1 mile from Champtoceaux by the D 751.* The village is dominated by a mediaeval keep. The use of limestone – in layers to mark each storey and alternating stones to emphasise the corners, encircle the openings and crown the crenellations – overcomes the severity of the main building stone, schist. From the top *(open 1 July to 31 August from 10am to noon and 3 to 5pm; 1F)* there is a fine view of the Loire Valley.

LORRIS

Michelin map 📖 1 – Pop 2 315

Lorris is famous for its customary law or *coutumes,* which is said to be the oldest in the kingdom. These varied from one region to the next and were in force prior to the Revolution throughout France. Hunting seat of the Capetian kings the town was often the place of residence of Blanche of Castile and her son St. Louis, Louis IX of France. Two spacious squares, namely Le Martroi and Les Halles, stand side by side. The latter is overlooked by the markets covered with an oak timber roof which were rebuilt in 1542 after being destroyed by the English in 1395. Several of the half timber houses use cob, a mixture of clay and straw, as wall material. Guillaume de Lorris, born in the early 13C, was the author of the first part of the *Roman de la Rose* or *Romance of the Rose,* a poem of courtly love which so influenced Chaucer in his writings.

The wine of the region, the *Gris-Meunier,* is light and fruity.

Church. – Preceded by a Romanesque belfry porch the church with its nave and two aisles is terminated by a 13C square east end. Among the statues in the ambulatory note in particular that of St. Sebastian. High up in the nave the Renaissance organ loft is carved with pilasters and medallions. The 15-16C **choir stalls★** are historiated portraying angels, Prophets and Sibyls on the cheekpieces and scenes from *The Golden Legend,* New Testament and everyday life on the misericords. The reverse side of the backs are carved with decorative motifs in the transitional Flamboyant-Renaissance style. The alabaster Virgin is late 15C.

Hôtel de Ville. – This restored 16C building has tall French style roofs with heavily ornamented dormer windows and other mullioned windows.

EXCURSION

Grignon. – *Round tour of 14 km - 9 miles. Leave Lorris by the V 5 to the west and then turn right.*

Grignon. – The hamlet occupies a calm setting overlooking the Orléans Canal with its three locks.

Étang des Bois. – *Bathing place.* This lake, very busy in summer, is set amidst woodland.

LOUDUN ★

Michelin map 📖 9 – Pop 8 245 – *Facilities p 38*

Situated on a mound encircled by shady boulevards taking the place of its former ramparts, Loudun's activities are based on a few new industries and its fairs.

Prosperous in the Middle Ages, the town had some 20 000 inhabitants in the 17C. The heritage of this former prosperity is a great diversity of dwellings – ancient houses, noble 17-18C stone built mansions, and modest squat houses with red tiled roofs – lining the old winding streets.

The Golden Age (17C). – In the early 17C Loudun was known as a meeting place for great minds where the ideas of the Reformation found ready acceptance. Among the more notable local intellectuals were the doctor **Théophraste Renaudot** (1586-1653) who was to found the first printed newspaper *La Gazette de France* and **Urbain Grandier,** a cultured and brilliant priest whose scathing comments about the religious Orders and lax moral standards earned him many enemies, numbering among them Richelieu. In 1634 the young priest was accused of bewitching the Ursulines of a Loudun convent. Found guilty, he was condemned and burned at the stake.

■ MAIN SIGHTS *time: ¾ hour*

Tour Carrée. – *Open from 10am to noon and 2 to 6pm; between 1 October and 1 May apply to the Tourist Information Office; 4F.*
Rising above the rooftops of Loudun this buttressed tower was built in 1040 by Foulques Nerra *(p 43).* The crown was dismantled in 1631 on Richelieu's orders at the same time as the razing of the adjoining castle. From the top *(143 steps)* there is a remarkable **panorama★** of the surrounding countryside.

Promenade du Château. – This forms an esplanade overlooking the countryside with the typical features of lime lined mall, sandy alleys and bandstand.

Couvent des Carmes (B). – Certain remains still stand of this Carmelite convent burnt during the Wars of Religion in the 16C. The 18C **chapter house** with its slender piers supporting elegant vaulting was the site on 18 August 1634 of the condemnation of Urbain Grandier to be burned at the stake. The chapel is now the Church of St-Hilaire.

St-Hilaire-du-Martray (D). – *For the key apply to the caretaker of the museum next door.* Begun in the 14C the entrance on the south side has a fine 16C doorway with covings adorned by canopied niches containing incense burning angels. Inside the primitive doorway is ornamented with vine branches. Above the 17C altar in the south aisle is a remarkable 15C **painting on wood** attributed to Gerard David of the school of Bruges representing the Virgin and Child. The great Flamboyant window behind the high altar has 19C stained glass. Downhill from the church is one of the town's former gateways, the **Porte du Martray** (E).

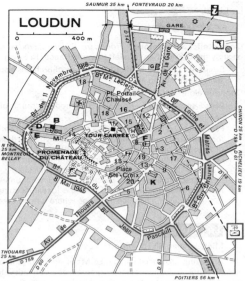

Abreuvoir (R. de l')	2	Marchands (R. des)	13
Carnot (R.)	3	Martray (R. du)	14
Chevreau (R.)	5	Palais (R. du)	15
Collège (R. du)	6	Portail-Chaussé (R. du)	16
Croix-Bruneau (R. de la)	7	Porte-de-Chinon (R. de la)	17
Gambetta (R.)	8	Porte-St-Nicolas (R. de la)	18
Grand-Cour (R. de la)	9	Renaudot (R. Th.)	19
Leuze (Av. de)	12	Vieille-Charité (R. de la)	20

St-Pierre-du-Marché (F). – Identified from afar by its 15C stone spire the church has an imposing Renaissance doorway. Angels and medallions adorn the recessed arches.

Ste-Croix (K). – This former church was greatly altered when it was transformed into a covered market. The Romanesque chancel with its historiated capitals, is still visible.

EXCURSION

The scenic route "La Côte Loudunaise". – *Round tour of 26 km - 16 miles. Leave Loudun by the D 759 and after 6.5 km - 4 miles turn right into the D 19.* The scenic route from Glénouze via Ranton and Curçay to Ternay follows the crest of the hills which dominate the Dive Valley and crosses a countryside of vineyards and orchards.

Glénouze. – Pop 129. Small Romanesque church with a bell gable.

Curçay-sur-Dive. – Pop 216. This small village with narrow streets is pleasantly situated overlooking the valley. The 12C keep was provided with machicolations and bartizans.

Return to Loudun by Ternay and the D 14.

Le LUDE

Michelin map 🟦 3 – Pop 4 120 – *Facilities p 38*

This small town with narrow streets and low houses is an ideal place for a holiday because of its proximity to the Loir. An important dairy, furniture factory, stud farm and the famous fairs are the town's principal activities.

Strategically important, Le Lude has seen a succession of fortified strongholds – the 10C "castellum Lusdi", the 13C fortress and the present structure – and owners. Held by the English from 1419 to 1427 the property passed twenty years later to the Daillon family.

Château*. – *Open 1 March to 31 October from 10am to noon and 3 to 6pm; guided tours on afternoons only; 7F. Son et Lumière*** performance see p 33.*

This massive but imposing building, surrounded by its now dry moat arranged as gardens stands in its own grounds on the banks of the Loir. The transformation of this feudal fortress into a stately home was started in the 15C by the Daillon family. Three main wings, each architecturally very different, are disposed round a central courtyard which is closed on the fourth or entrance side by an arcaded gallery. To the left the Louis XII Wing, the earliest, is adorned by an equestrian statue of the first Daillon owner, Jean de Daillon. To the right the François I Wing overlooking the park dotted with 18C marble vases is typical of the French Renaissance period: Gothic in structure with two massive machicolated towers linked by a curtain wall, the decoration is pure Renaissance: pilasters, pedimented dormer windows and medallions. The central, pedimented Louis XVI Wing in white tufa stone, overlooks the Loir.

The apartments have all the charm and interest of a lived in stately home. On the ground floor of the Louis XII Wing is the Ballroom, restored in the 15 and 16C style, where winter rehearsals are held for the *son et lumière* performance. The 18C range contains a fine suite of rooms: bureau, splendid oval saloon in a very pure Louis XVI style and portrait gallery.

In the François I Wing the library has a 17C Gobelins tapestry, the dining room where the window recesses reveal the thickness of the mediaeval walls has three Flemish tapestries including a *verdure* (showing a red parrot). The vast sculptured chimneypiece carries a salamander, Franciscan girdle and ermine tufts *(p 18)*.

Maison des Architectes. – Known as the Architects' House this elegant Renaissance building *(now the Post Office)* was built by Gendrot, the master mason who worked on the château's François I Wing.

Le LUDE

EXCURSION

Genneteil; La Boissière. – *Round trip 36 km - 22 miles – about 1½ hours.* Leave Le Lude to the west by the D 306, then turn left towards Baugé. In Savigné-sous-le-Lude turn left again.

Genneteil. – Pop 424. The Romanesque church has a splendid 11C **doorway** with sculptured splaying depicting animals.

Continue along the D 198.

Dénezé-sous-le-Lude. – Pop 326. The modest church of the 12 and 15C has finely worked capitals and mural paintings.

Former Abbey of La Boissière. – *The chapels are open from 10am to noon and 2 to 4pm, apply to the caretaker; time: ½ hour; 3F.* This is renowned as the one time sanctuary of the True Cross of Anjou *(p 50)*. In the 18C the abbatial buildings were transformed into a château. The chancel with two recumbent figures and an altarpiece are all that remain of the 12C abbey church. In the 13C the Cistercian monks built a chapel, **Chapelle de la Vraie-Croix** *(on the road to Dénezé)*, to shelter the precious relic. Several times during the Hundred Years War the relic was taken to the Château d'Angers for safekeeping and then in 1790 it was transferred to the chapel of a hospice in Baugé where it now remains.

Le MANS ★★

Michelin map **60** 13 – Pop 155 245

A thriving provincial capital, Le Mans stands on the banks of the Sarthe at its confluence with the Huisne. An important programme of urban redevelopment is changing the town centre, where the old houses with steeply pitched roofs crowd round the majestic cathedral. The modern quarters are traversed by wide avenues while, in the suburbs, industrial zones mingle with housing estates and university complexes.

A business centre, the main activity is insurance with over 3 000 employed by the various firms making it one of the more important centres in France. Numerous fairs or exhibitions add to the everyday bustle – to name only a few: the Spring Fair *(late March)*, the Quatre Jours or Four Day exhibition *(mid-September)* and the Onion Fair *(last Friday in August or first Friday in September)*.

A meal in the town should include some of the local specialities such as *rillettes*, potted pork; *poulardes dodues*, plump pullets; *chapons,* capons in sparkling cider and the famous *reinette* apple.

HISTORICAL NOTES

The Plantagenet Dynasty. – The Plantagenet connections with this town are many and various. When **Geoffroy Plantagenet**, Count of Anjou, married Matilda, the granddaughter of William the Conqueror he added Normandy and Maine to his domains. Geoffroy often resided at Le Mans and on his death in 1151 he was buried in the cathedral. His son Henri Plantagenet who was to become **Henry II** of England, was the founder of the Coëffort Hospital and it was to Le Mans, his birthplace, that he retired in his old age only to be expelled by one of his rebellious sons **Richard Lionheart**, then in alliance with the French King.

While on the Third Crusade Richard married Queen Berengaria of Navarre and it was to her in her widowhood that Philippe-Auguste gave the county of Maine which he had reconquered from Richard's younger brother, John Lackland. Berengaria founded Epau Abbey *(p 113)* where she was buried.

A famous writer. – The 17C poet and satirical writer, **Paul Scarron** was a member of the Le Mans Chapter. He was provided with a prebend and a canonical house in the cathedral precincts. This rhymer and gay fellow – married to Françoise d'Aubigné later Mme de Maintenon, Louis XIV's mistress – was rendered impotent by paralysis before the age of thirty. The work for which he is best known is *Le Roman Comique (The Comic Novel)* based on people and scenes from 17C Le Mans.

In the vanguard of progress. – Already under the *Ancien Régime*, Le Mans had several flourishing industries; including the production of a coarse, black woollen material used for clerics' and lawyers' gowns, candle making, tanneries and the making of sailcloth from locally grown hemp.

The Bollée family, father and two sons were innovators in the early development of the motor car. **Amédée Bollée** senior's (1844-1917) first steam propelled car *L'Obéissante* (1873) was a twelve seater vehicle with two motors and a maximum speed of over 40 km per hour. His later model, *La Mancelle*, was the first to have its single motor placed in front, under the bonnet. His son, **Amédée** (1867-1926) dealt mainly with racing cars some of which approached the then incredible speed of 100 km per hour. It was the second brother Léon who in 1908 invited the American, Wilbur Wright, to attempt one of his first flights in an aeroplane at nearby Les Hunaudières. The family firm is still active in the production of piston rings.

Association with the car industry continued when in 1936 Louis Renault built the first of his decentralised factories to the south of Le Mans. Employing around 9 500 people this important factory *(open but apply at least two months in advance)* in the Renault group comprises a works producing drive units, differentials and gear transmission systems for all Renault models and another works producing tractors and vehicle body paint.

Le Mans Twenty-four Hour Race. – This event, attracting thousands of spectators, takes place in a carnival-like atmosphere. Started in 1923 the race has become a sporting event of universal interest and a testing ground for car manufacturers. The difficulties of the circuit and duration of the race are a severe test for both the quality of the machines and the endurance of the two drivers who take it in turn to drive. The circuit has been considerably improved since the tragic accident of 1955 when several spectators died.

The scene is unforgettable with the revving and roaring of the engines, the whining and whizzing of vehicles hurtling past at more than 300 km per hour on the straight sections, the constant smell of petrol, the chasing searching headlights at night, all mingled in an atmosphere of great excitement and suspense.

ST JULIAN'S CATHEDRAL** (Cathédrale St-Julien) *time: 1 hour*

Organ music and special lighting on Saturday evenings 15 June to 15 September from 9.30 to 11pm.

This magnificent edifice, dedicated to St. Julian, the first Bishop of Le·Mans, rises proudly above the impressive tiered arrangement of the Gothic **chevet*****, amazing for its system of Y shaped two tiered flying buttresses. The present building comprises a Romanesque nave, Gothic chancel and Radiant or Middle Gothic transept flanked by a tower.

Exterior. – Overlooking the charming Place St-Michel the south porch has a superb 12C **doorway**** contemporary with the Royal Doorway of Chartres. A comparison of the two doorways shows that they portray the same themes: Christ in Majesty, the Apostles and a series of statue columns. The doorway is flanked by statue columns: on the jambs are the Sts. Peter and Paul while the figures on the splay embrasures represent Solomon and the Queen of Sheba, a Prophet, a Sibyl and the ancestors of Christ. The Apostles in serried ranks occupy the niches of the tympanum with Christ the King above, surrounded by the symbols of the Evangelists, being sprinkled with incense by the angels of the first recessed arch. The other scenes on the arches are the Annunciation, Visitation, Nativity, Presentation in the Temple, Massacre of the Innocents, Baptism of Christ, Wedding Feast at Cana.

Looking to the right of the porch note the transept pierced by immense windows and the 12-14C tower (64 m - 210 ft high).

The west front, overlooking the Place du Cardinal Grente, bordered by Renaissance dwellings, is in an archaic Romanesque style. One can clearly distinguish the original 11C gable embedded in the gable added the following century when the new vaulting was being built.

At the right hand corner of the west front is a pink veined sandstone menhir. Tradition has it that to have really visited Le Mans, visitors should insert a thumb into the hole in the stone.

Nave. – The Romanesque main building rests on great 11C round arches which were reinforced in the following century by pointed arches. The domical vaults or Plantagenet style vaulting *(p 21)* springs from majestic capitals which show great finesse of detail. Eight of the Romanesque windows in the side aisles together with the great window of the west front, heavily restored in the 19C, evoke the Legend of St. Julian. The most famous is the one in the south aisle representing the Ascension (1).

Transept. – The transept, pierced by a small columned gallery and immense windows, is striking for its ethereal quality and the audacity of its elevation.

The south arm is dominated by the 16C organ loft (2), while the north arm is suffused with light transmitted by the beautiful 15C stained glass. Three tapestry hangings represent the Legend of St Julian.

At the entrance to the baptismal chapel (Chapelle des Fonts), which opens on to the north arm, facing one another are two remarkable Renaissance **tombs****. The one on the left (3), that of Charles I of Anjou, the brother of King René *(p 44)*, is the work of Francesco Laurana. The recumbent figure lies, in the Italian style, on an antique sarcophagus and the delicacy of the facial features recall Laurana's talents as a portraitist. On the right the magnificent monument (4) to the memory of Guillaume Du Bellay, cousin of the poet, shows the figure reclining on one elbow in the antique manner, holding a sword and a book, on a sarcophagus which is adorned with an attractive frieze of Tritons and Naiads.

The tomb of Cardinal Grente was placed here in 1965.

Chancel. – This lofty and soaring Gothic chancel (13C) is one of the finest in France – 34 m - 112 ft high (compare Notre-Dame in Paris 35 m - 115 ft) it is encircled by a double ambulatory with a crown of apsidal chapels.

The serried ranks of the tall upward sweeping columns support lancet arches showing a definite Norman influence. Above the triforium level adorned with intricate stylised foliage, the 13C **stained glass**** is a blaze of colour dominated by vivid blues and reds. Binoculars are needed to identify the rather rigid and wild figures of the Apostles, bishops, saints and donors.

Hanging above the choir stalls is the famous series of 16C **tapestries** depicting the lives of Sts. Gervase and Protase.

(After photo: Archives Photographiques)

Cathedral : Stained glass window of Yolanda of Aragon

Map labels (ST-JULIEN plan):

ST-JULIEN
0   50 m
N
Place des Jacobins
N.D. du Chevet
Roman wall
Canon's Doorway
Chapelle des Fonts
CHANCEL
Sacristy
MAISON DE SCARRON
4
5
3
TRANSEPT
2
Tower
Place St-Michel
NAVE
South porch
Rue de la Reine Bérengère
Menhir
Place du Cardinal Grente
HÔTEL DU GRABATOIRE
Rue des Chanoines

Chancel precincts. – In the first chapel on the right (5) is a 17C terracotta Entombment. The sacristy door beyond was formerly part of the 17C rood screen. The beautiful 16C woodwork, in the sacristy, originally formed the high backs of the choir stalls. The 14C Canon's Doorway which follows has a tympanum with an effigy of St. Julian.

The 13C chapel Notre-Dame-du-Chevet, with its harmonious proportions, is closed by a delicate 17C wrought iron grille. The 13C stained glass windows depict the Tree of Jesse and the story of Adam and Eve.

The vaulting is covered with paintings dating from 1380. The scene illustrating an Angels' Concert, displays great delicacy of draughtsmanship.

■ THE MEDIAEVAL TOWN★★ (Vieux Mans) *time: 1 hour*

Closely packed inside the Gallo-Roman ramparts, the mediaeval town is built on a hill dominating the Sarthe, on the former site of a Gaulish *oppidum*.

Starting from the Place des Jacobins follow on foot the itinerary indicated on the plan below.

Place St-Michel. – Standing in the cathedral precincts is the Renaissance house (**W**) where Paul Scarron lived during his period as a member of the Chapter. The presbytery, no 1, has retained a 15C staircase turret.

Take to the left the **Rue de la Reine-Bérengère** which is bordered by a variety of old houses. Nos 7 and 9 are both Renaissance – the latter is adorned with charming statues of St. Catherine and St. Barbara.

Maison de la Reine-Bérengère★ (**BX M²**). – *Nos 11-13.* Built for a rich Le Mans Alderman between 1490 and 1515 this elegant residence known by the name the House of Queen Berengaria, was never actually lived in by Richard the Lionheart's Queen. The decoration consists of an ogee arch above the door and historiated brackets supporting the beams. The Museum of History and Ethnography is installed here *(p 112).*

Maison des Deux-Amis (**Y**). – *Nos 18-20.* The two friends are shown supporting a coat of arms. Built in the 15C, a century later it was the home of Nicolas Denizot, the poet and painter and friend of Ronsard and Du Bellay.

Take the bridge over the railway and at the beginning of Grande-Rue, on the right is the Maison du Pilier-Vert (**E**) and beyond standing back the 17C Hôtel d'Arcy (**F**) now the Conservatory of Music.

Turn about and go right into Rue du Pilier-Rouge, the house on the corner has a carving of a skull on the corner post.

Hôtel de Ville (**BXY H**). – This 18C building was formerly the palace of the counts of Maine and now houses the town hall. A staircase to the right affords a view of a 14C tower (**K**), part of the Gallo-Roman rampart and the former Collegiate Church of St-Pierre de la Cour (**L**).

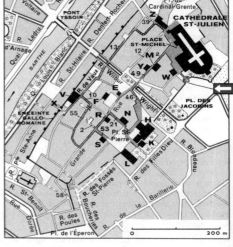

Assé (Cour d')	2	Pans-de-Gorron (R. des)	39
Blondeau (R. C.)		Pilier-Rouge (R. du)	46
Bouquet (R.)	10	Reine-Bérengère (R. de la)	49
Chanoines (R. des)	12	St-Honoré (R.)	53
Chapelains (R. des)	13	St-Pavin-de-la-Cité (R.)	55
Écrevisse (R. de l')	21	Truie-qui-file (R. de la)	58

Hôtel de Vignoles (**N**). – This late 16C mansion with tall French style roofs stands at the beginning of Rue de l'Écrevisse on the right.

Maison d'Adam et Ève (**R**). – *No 71 La Grande-Rue.* This superb Renaissance mansion was the home of Jean de l'Épine, an astrologer and physician.

At the corner of the **Rue-St-Honoré** a column shaft is decorated with three keys, the former coat of arms of Le Mans. The street is lined with half timber houses. In the courtyard of no 5 is the 16C Hôtel Perot (**S**). The picturesque Cour d'Assé opens opposite the Rue St-Honoré. From here onwards the Grande-Rue descends between noble Classical hôtels until the street on the right which is the more popular Rue St-Pavin-de-la-Cité.

Following the Rue St-Pavin-de-la-Cité round after a vaulted passageway turn left into the Rue Bouquet. At the corner of Rue de Vaux a 15C niche shelters a Mary Magdalene; at no 12 the Hôtel de Vaux (**V**), is late 16C. Further on to the left there is a view of the Great Postern staircase (**X**), part of the Gallo-Roman ramparts.

Gallo-Roman Ramparts (Enceinte Gallo-Romaine). – Built in the 3 and 4C these are the best preserved in France. Attaining in parts a thickness of 4 m - 13 ft, visible only in places, the best section overlooking the Sarthe still retains nine of its original twelve towers: Rues Ste-Anne, St-Hilaire and Denfert-Rochereau. Other sections of the ramparts are visible from Place des Jacobins and Rue des Filles-Dieu.

Hôtel du Grabatoire (**Z**). – *No 1 Place du Cardinal-Grente.* This much restored 16C mansion was originally the infirmary for sick canons. Today it is the episcopal palace.

A Renaissance house with an overhanging turret marks the junction with the Rue des Chanoines.

LE MANS

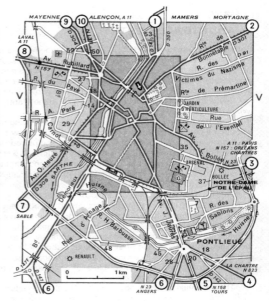

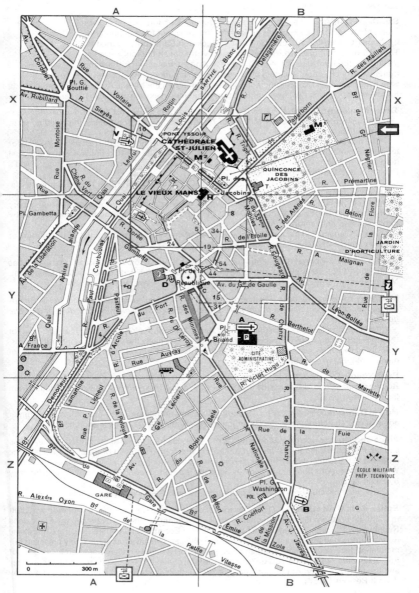

■ ADDITIONAL SIGHTS

Église de la Couture* (BY A). – This was formerly the abbatial church of a monastery. The twin towered west front is 13C. The doorway is intricately sculptured; the column statues on the jambs represent the Apostles; the Last Judgement on the tympanum shows Christ between the Virgin and St John; the recessed arches carry the heavenly court of angels, patriarchs and prophets (first arch), martyrs (second arch), and virgins (third arch).

The wide single nave, built in the late 12C in the Plantagenet style *(p 21)*, is lit by elegant twinned windows surmounted by oculi.

Note the forms of the Romanesque arches of the original nave, on the blind walls of the great pointed arches which support a narrow ledge below the windows. To the left on entering is a curious 11C pilaster sculptured with a Christ in Benediction. The enchanting white marble **Virgin**** (1571), on the pillar directly opposite the pulpit, is by Germain Pilon and originally came from the now vanished retable of the high altar. The blind arcades are hung with 17C **tapestries** and 16C painted panels.

The massive round 11C columns of the chancel with squat capitals showing Eastern influence in the decoration, support very narrow round arches. Above, the vaulting ribs spring from fine Plantagenet style statues.

The 11C crypt, altered in 1838, has pre-Romanesque or Gallo-Roman columns and capitals. An inverted Antique capital serves as a base for one of the pillars. The 6-7C shroud of St. Bertrand, Bishop of Le Mans and founder in 616 of the monastery, is exposed at the entrance *(automatic time switch for lighting)*. The presumed burial place of St. Bertrand is marked by a reclining plaster figure in a wall alcove.

The **conventual buildings**, now occupied by the Préfecture, were rebuilt in 1770. Glance at the cloisters with the original vaulting pattern. Superb staircase with straight flights of steps.

(After photo: Robert Château)

The Virgin

Ste-Jeanne-d'Arc* (BZ B). – This, the former Coëffort Hospital, was founded about 1180 by Henry II of England in atonement for the murder of his former Chancellor, Archbishop Thomas Becket in Canterbury Cathedral. The 12C great hall or ward for the sick is now the parish church. A similar institution, the former Hospital of St. John in Angers was built by the same monarch. The elevation is supremely elegant with slender columns, some of which are monolithic, supporting Plantagenet vaulting. In the Middle Ages wide canopied beds for several patients at a time, were aligned down the side aisles with an altar in the central passage.

Tessé Museum* (BX M¹). – *Open from 9am to noon and 2 to 6pm. Closed on public holidays.*

Originally the mansion of the Marshal of Tessé, then the episcopal palace, this building set in a fine park, houses the museum.

The rich collection of paintings occupies only part of the museum, the rest being reserved for temporary exhibitions. Italian painting is represented by a series of 14C primitives with the typical gold background, including works by Pietro Lorenzetti and Pesellino representing David's Penitence and the Death of Absalom.

There are several good portraits from the 16C French school: Henri III and Catherine de' Medici and some 17 to 19C canvases. Classical painting includes the works of Vouet and Poussin; Le Sueur, Philippe de Champaigne and Georges de la Tour are also represented. A very stately family portrait is attributed to David. The Dutch and Flemish schools are represented by Van Balen and Kalf, among others.

The 12C enamelled plaque was originally part of the tomb, in the cathedral, of the founder of the Plantagenet dynasty, Geoffroy Plantagenet.

Jardin d'horticulture (BY). – This fine garden with artificial rocks and cascading streams was designed in 1851 by Alphand, the landscape gardener of the Paris parks, Buttes-Chaumont, Montsouris and Boulogne. The terraced mall affords a fine view over the cathedral.

Museum of History and Ethnography (M²). – *Installed in the Maison de la Reine-Bérengère. Open from 9am to noon and 2 to 6pm; closed on Mondays, Tuesdays and public holidays.*

The varnished pottery from the Sarthe (Ligron, Malicorne, Prévelles, etc.) is astonishing for the vigour of the design and freshness of the colours, especially the yellows, greens and browns. The objects include statuettes, retables, jars and finials. There are paintings and sketches of mediaeval Le Mans and other local scenes.

Pont Yssoir (AX). – The bridge affords a view of the cathedral, the mediaeval town, the Gallo-Roman ramparts and, down beside the river, a walk passing remains of fortifications dating from the Middle Ages.

Notre-Dame-du-Pré (AX V). – Standing in a square planted with magnolias, this former abbatial church belonging to the Benedictines has Romanesque capitals and chancel.

Place and Quinconce des Jacobins (BX). – Famous for its view of the cathedral chevet, the square, Place des Jacobins, is laid out on the site of a former convent of the same name. At the entrance to the tunnel which crosses the old town is a monument to the American aviator Wilbur Wright and a curious floral clock. Directly opposite is a modern concert hall with inside a tapestry by Picart Le Doux.

The gardens, Quinconce des Jacobins, are a series of terraced avenues of lime trees.

Église de la Visitation (AY D). – This former chapel of the Convent of the Visitation was built in 1730. Its northern façade with chain courses and flame ornaments overlooks the Place de la République. The ornate façade has a portico with four Corinthian columns sheltering a fine stone door sculptured with shell shapes and liturgical objects. The nave has some finely chiselled but mannered decoration. The Corinthian pilasters support a narrow gallery bordered by a wrought iron balustrade. Admire the 18C grilles enclosing the chancel, the transept arms, the organ lofts, and the narrow gallery. At the high altar is a 1751 retable in stone and marble with a canvas by Jean II Restout (1754).

EXCURSIONS

Notre-Dame-de-l'Epau*; Connerré. – *25 km - 14 miles to the east following the Huisne Valley. Leave Le Mans by Avenue Léon Bollée and the road to the right which crosses the railway (follow the signs) and then turn left into the D 152. After the bridge over the Huisne turn left.*

Notre-Dame-de-L'Epau Abbey*. – *4 km - 2½ miles from Le Mans. Guided tours every hour from 9.30 to 11.30am and 2 to 6pm; closed 25 December, 1 January and on Thursdays from 15 September to 15 April; 3F; evening tours on weekends and on public holidays at 10.30pm in June and July; 10pm in August; 9.30pm in September; 3F.*

In 1229 **Queen Berengaria**, Richard Lionheart's widow, founded on the secluded banks of the Huisne, the Monastery of La Piété-Dieu, which she committed to the charge of the Cistercian Order. It was here in 1230 that she found her resting place, a replica recumbent figure still exists. Standing in a large park, the abbey buildings are grouped round a courtyard that was once the cloisters which were destroyed by fire in the 14C. To the right is the frater range with the wall arcades of the former laver or washbasin and the refectory, facing one is the restored dorter range, a continuation of the south transept, with the chapter house and dormitory above. On the left the south aisle façade with its buttresses is pierced by a doorway with a 14C sculptured tympanum showing the Mystic Lamb.

Enter by the **scriptorium**, where manuscripts were copied, with its primitive vaulting indicating an early phase in the construction. At the first floor level stone now replaces wood for the cradle vaulting of the dormitory. A staircase leads to the abbey church.

The restored Gothic **church** portrays the well established Cistercian plan and the square east end is pierced by the delicate tracery of a rose window. The transept, as long as the unfinished nave is bordered by chapels to the east. The roof is supported by a fine 15C **woodwork** structure *(access by a spiral staircase in the north arm of the transept)*. The sacristy (1250) in the south transept is divided into two chambers by columns with square capitals decorated with water lily leaves. Traces of distemper paintings done in the 14C can be distinguished round the walls. The **chapter house** ogive vaulting springs from the octagonal capitals of four cylindrical columns.

Cross the Huisne to reach the N 23 turning right on to it in the direction of Connerre.

Approximately 5.5 km - 3 miles before Connerre make a detour to the left to Pont-de-Gennes.

Pont-de-Gennes. – Pop 1 218. Attractively situated, this village is popular with the people of Le Mans. Already a bridging point in Roman times there is a quaint 15C narrow, hump backed bridge.

Return to the N 23.

Connerré. – Pop 2 523. This small town on the banks of the Dué is famous for its *rillettes* or potted pork. The **Dolmen de la Pierre Couverte** is 2.5 km - 1½ miles from Connerre. Follow the local road to Le Luart then branch off to the right, and 1.5 km - 1 mile beyond this fork, the imposing dolmen stands to the right hand side of the road.

Motor racing circuits. – To the south of Le Mans between the N 158 and the D 139 are the racing circuits which are the venue for both motor and motorcycle Grand Prix races which have made Le Mans famous to the world.

Circuit des 24 heures. – *13.64 km - 8½ miles.* This road circuit is the scene of the Twenty-four Hour Race, a sporting event of universal interest. See the historical notes on p 108. Set amid pinewoods this 10 m – 33 ft wide circuit follows public roads for part of its layout. Coming from Le Mans pick up the track at the Tertre Rouge corner, then follow the N 158 along the Hunaudières straight where some cars exceed 320 kph – 200 mph. The Mulsanne hairpin bend is followed by a stretch on the D 140 which leads through woods to the double or S-bend at Arnage. The D 139 then leads back past Maison Blanche to the tribunes and pits before veering right to rejoin the N 158 at the Tertre Rouge corner. The course was realigned in 1972 to give the public a better view of the race. The unique Le Mans running start has now been abandoned.

Inside this track is the Les Hunaudierès Racecourse where Wilbur Wright attempted one of his early flights. A signposted path leads to the racecourse. The main entrance, a tunnel from the D 139, gives access to both the Bugatti racing circuit and the interesting Automobile Museum.

Circuit Bugatti. – *4.24 km - 2½ miles. For further information apply to the Automobile-Club de l'Ouest-Circuit Bugatti, CEDEX no 19, 72040 – Le Mans, Tel 84–05–80.* This track, with a school for racing drivers, can be used by motorists and manufacturers for trials *(excepting Mondays and race days)*.

Automobile Museum*. – *Open from 9am to noon and 2 to 7pm (6pm from 1 November to Palm Sunday); closed on Tuesdays out of season; 9F.*

With more than sixty bicycles and motorcycles and 150 vintage cars, the history of the automobile is vividly evoked from its earliest beginnings to 1949: steam driven cars, De Dion Bouton 1884, Serpollet; oil and petrol driven Bollée cars, Delahaye 1896, Panhard et Levarsord 1898, Renault 1901; Moto-Rêve 1907, Douglas 1914–18, and various racing models.

Château de la Buzardière. – *18 km - 11 miles. Leave Le Mans by ④ taking the N 823, D 304, D 145ᴱ and finally the D 145 to the left.*

This 12C manor house, belonging to the Clinchamps family, stands in Loudon Forest, surrounded by a moat and defended by a turreted doorway.

Some race records

Year	Constructor	Total distance run	Fastest lap
1923	Chenard et Walker	2209 km	107 kph
1971	Porsche	5335 km	222 kph
1972	Matra	4691 km	195 kph
1978	Renault-Alpine	5044 km	229 kph

Michelin maps 🖪 18, 19, and 🖪 5, 6

This green mysterious countryside is delimited by the valleys of the Divatte in the west, the Loire to the north, the Layon to the east and the Moine and town of Cholet in the south. The basic relief, a ridge of schist rocks, is dissected by small valleys and ravines and covered by *bocage*, the open woodland landscape so typical of the Armorican Massif. This silent hedge compartmented countryside, so suitable for ambushing, was the theatre of some of the most tragic events in the Vendéen War.

GEOGRAPHICAL AND HISTORICAL NOTES

A continuation of the Armorican Massif, the region of Les Mauges culminates in the Puy de la Garde (210 m - 689 ft). Livestock rearing is the principal activity with the Durham-Mancelle breed being fattened on the rich pastures and sold in their thousands at the markets of Chemillé and Cholet. Flax, the original source of Cholet's prosperity, has been superseded by corn, rye and buckwheat.

On the heights stand lone sentinels, ruined windmills once used during the civil war to transmit signals while a network of sunken paths, resembling a labyrinth, leads to long, squat houses often roofed with Roman tiles. The straight main roads, often deserted, were built for strategic reasons during the Revolution and the Empire. There is little industry, except at Cholet and Chemillé. Both the former coal mines of the Layon Valley and gold workings of St-Pierre-Montlimart have long since been silent.

The Vendéen War (1793). – Long live God and the King. This civil war between Royalists (**Whites**) and Republicans (**Blues**) takes its name from the province, Vendée, to the southwest of Les Mauges.

The execution of Louis XVI, the persecution of priests and military conscription were some of the causes of the first insurrections in March 1793 at Cholet and St-Florent. The counter revolt spread quickly and the peasants eagerly followed their leaders whether of noble birth like d'Elbée, Bonchamps and La Rochejaquelein or of their own background like the gamekeeper Stofflet and the pedlar Cathelineau, known as the "Saint of Anjou".

Cholet fell immediately into Royalist hands (after the Battle of Golleau Wood) followed by Chemillé, Vihiers, etc, and by May, Les Mauges was held by the Whites. The Convention, worried by the turn of events, sent the Mayence Army commanded by Westermann, Kléber and Marceau to deal with the Royal, Catholic army of Vendéens. After an initial victory at Torfou the Royalists suffered a massive defeat at Cholet on 17 October 1793. The Royalist campaign continued to the north of the Loire but in December 1793 following a defeat at Savenay all was lost. Royalists were executed by their thousands on the Place du Ralliement in Angers. Reprisals continued and the "infernal columns" commanded by Turreau were to sack Les Mauges and quell any sporadic resistance that was to arise from then on.

TOUR OF LES MAUGES

Great sights are rare and many of the churches and châteaux were destroyed during the period of civil strife but those interested in the Vendéen War will find many poignant and "glorious" reminders.

Beaupréau. – Pop 5 729. *Facilities p 38*. Sited in the heart of Les Mauges this small town with narrow winding streets was the Royalist headquarters in 1793. It was here that the leader d'Elbée was born. The 15C **château** overlooking the Evre has been much altered since its construction. Set fire to by the Blues in 1793, it was restored in the early 19C. Two small round towers with slate covered cupolas flank a 17C pavilion.

The bridge affords a pleasant perspective of the river and château. The late 15C mansion, **Maison du Sénéchal** is adorned with a turret and mullioned windows.

Chemillé. – Pop 5 128. An important livestock market the town is known for its crops of medicinal plants *(exhibition in the gardens of the Mairie)*. Ruins of the citadel overlook the river and the Romanesque church was altered in the 16C.

Cholet. – Pop 52 698. *Facilities p 38. Town plan in the current Michelin Red Guide France*. Since the 11C Cholet has been associated with the cultivation and weaving of hemp and flax and even today its production of cloth, handkerchiefs, table and household linen is world famous. Other industries include dyeworks, footwear factories, wireless and electronic components, toys, prams and tyres. There are vast livestock markets and an associated meat canning industry.

The **Vendéen War Museum** in the former Hôtel de Ville, Place Travot *(10am to noon and 2 to 5pm; closed on Tuesdays and public holidays)* recounts this violent period of local history, evokes local leaders and other Royalist memories.

A small fine arts museum *(open 10am to noon and 2 to 5pm; closed on Tuesdays and public holidays)* has been installed in new premises in the Pérotaux Park. Among the works displayed is a canvas by Carle Van Loo, who was principal painter to Louis XV.

Maulévrier. – A pyramidal monument commemorates the local Royalist leader Stofflet and in the nearby Forest of Maulevin is the Martyrs' Cemetery.

Nuaillé. – On the Cholet road this village has La Rochejaquelein, another Royalist leader's funeral monument.

Le Puy de la Garde★. – Rising to a height of 210 m - 689 ft, Le Puy de la Garde forms a ridge running parallel to the D 265 linking the villages of Gardes (pilgrimage) and St-Georges-du-Puy-de-la-Garde. Acting as a watershed Le Puy offers a vast **panorama★** of Les Mauges countryside with its schist hills, occasional villages and abundant hedges and groves. To the north in the direction of Chemillé the view extends as far as the slopes of the Loire and the Layon valleys.

St-Florent-le-Vieil. – *Description p 105.*

La Sorinière Chapel. – Belonging to a château, this modest chapel *(closed temporarily)* was built about 1500. Inside there are interesting early 16C **mural paintings★** rich in picturesque detail portraying the Nativity, Adoration of the Magi and St. Christopher.

Torfou. – A column evokes the Vendéen victory of 18/19 September 1793 against the Mayence Army sent by the Convention.

Winding and deeply embanked, wending from north to south, the Mayenne follows a majestic course.

Crossing the schists, a prolongation of the Armorican Massif, the river flows between steep slopes where broom and chestnut grow in abundance. The deep, narrow form of the valley has prevented the siting of villages on the valley floor.

Only the occasional château with its landscaped park has been erected on the riverbanks, often in the 19C, by the notables of the region. Often occupying picturesque sites at the confluence of tributaries they are generally reached by sunken paths.

Canalised in the 19C the Mayenne has thirty-nine locks between Laval and Angers, making it navigable but slowing down considerably the river traffic. Some barges laden with construction materials still ply the canal.

From Laval to Angers – *116 km - 72 miles – about 1 day – Local map below*

Leave Laval *(p 89)* to the south by the D 1 which parallels the west bank of the Mayenne until level with St-Pierre-le-Potier *(p 91)*, then offering pleasant perspectives of the valley, climbs towards L'Huisserie. 1 km - ½ mile after L'Huisserie on the D 112, take to the left a surfaced route which goes down to the Mayenne: very pretty **viewpoint*** of the river, mill and château.

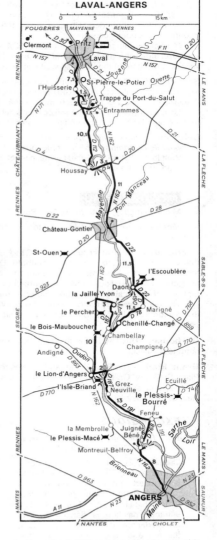

Return to the D 112, then take the D 103 to the left and carry on to La Trappe du Port-du-Salut.

Trappe du Port-du-Salut. – The Trappist monks produced the famous Port-Salut cheese up until 1959, when they surrendered their licence. A cheese factory now independent of the abbey, is situated beside the latter, at Entrammes.

Return to the D 112, which crosses tributary valleys; cows graze in the meadows planted with apple trees; views to the left over the valley. At Houssay cross to the east bank; from the bridge there are views of the Mayenne. Take to the right the N 162 which leads to Château-Gontier.

Château-Gontier. – *Description p 65.*

Leave Château-Gontier by ③ and the D 22: views to the right over the valley.

Daon. – Pop 461. *Facilities p 38.* Well placed on the hillside, overlooking the Mayenne, Daon, the birthplace of the Abbot Bernier who negotiated the peace between the Chouans and Republicans, still has a 16C manor.

Manoir de l'Escoublère. – *Excursion of 2 km - 1 mile after leaving Daon.*

16C manor, encircled by a moat, lost in the heart of the countryside: follow the D 213 for 1.5 km - 1 mile and then to the left a tarmac road and a fine avenue of plane trees. One can walk round the moat *(ask the owner in advance for permission)*.

After Daon turn right on to the D 190.

Chenillé-Changé. – Pop 155. Well situated on the banks of the Mayenne.

La Jaille-Yvon. – Pop 267. Village perched on the cliff dominating the river and offering a fine view of the wide, winding valley, with many meadows.

From there, make for the N 162, which offers to the left fine views of the Château du Percher and further on the Château du Bois-Mauboucher.

Château du Percher. – *Not open to the public, but one can get a glimpse of the façade.* From the N 162 an avenue leads up to this charming small château in the transitional Gothic-Renaissance style. Surmounted by high dormer windows with decorated gables, it has a delightful staircase tower.

Château du Bois-Mauboucher. – Encircled by water these imposing but much restored 15-17C buildings stand in a majestic site on the edge of a vast lake. Great woods and lawns planted with fine trees (cedars, chestnuts and oaks) surround it.

Le Lion d'Angers. – Pop 2 328. *Facilities p 38.* This small town is set in a picturesque site on the banks of the Oudon at the centre of a stock rearing region, specialising in half bred horses.

St-Martin Church has a doorway, the upper part of which presents a pre-Romanesque delicate tracery pattern formed by the red cement; the nave is Romanesque. Above the entrance doorway and on the left wall of the nave are 16C mural paintings representing the demon vomiting the Deadly Sins, Purgatory, and Christ amid the Saints. In a recess one can see a diptych of Christ with the Crown of Thorns.

Lying to the east between the Oudon and Mayenne is a vast green wooded park *(open from 9am to 7pm)* belonging to the **Isle-Briand** Estate. This is the home of the National Stud (Haras National). *Guided tours from 9am to noon and 2 to 5pm; time ½ hour; the full complement of stallions is present between 15 July and 15 February.*

After Le Lion d'Angers, return to the east bank bordered with poplars. The D 187 (view to the right of the Château de l'Isle-Briand) then the D 191 dominate the river, sometimes overhanging the river; vines and orchards appear on the hillside.

At Feneu, take the D 768 which crosses the Mayenne, wide at this point, and climbs towards Montreuil-Belfroy before continuing to Angers *(p 43).*

MEUNG-SUR-LOIRE ★

Michelin map **64** 8 – *Local maps pp 102 and 145* – Pop 4 630 – *Facilities p 38*

The town commemorates its most famous son, **Jean de Meung**, with a statue on the Mail. It was he who, at the beginning of the 14C, added 18 000 lines to the original 4 000 lines of the *Roman de la Rose* or *Romance of the Rose*, written about fifty years earlier by Guillaume de Lorris *(p 106).* This allegorical narrative was the greatest literary achievement of a period in which patient readers abounded. Chaucer translated it in part and was much influenced by it throughout his poetic career.

Most of the village lies between the N 152 and the Loire and makes an attractive place to visit and stroll along the shady Mail and avenue of limes which follows the winding course of the **Mauves**, a tributary of the Loire, so well known to anglers.

St-Liphard★. – This is a fine building, erected from the 11 to 13C, including a plain and massive tower, a semicircular chevet and an original transept with rounded ends. From behind the chevet there is a good view of the church and the château.

On the left side of the belfry will be seen a military structure of the 12C – a sort of ruined keep. In it the poet François Villon underwent one of his numerous terms of imprisonment.

Château. – *Guided tours 1 May to 30 October from 10.30am to 12.30pm and 2.30 to 5.30pm; château: 5F; an additional 5F for dungeons and the oubliettes.*

Built in the 13C the château has been much modified. This was the residence of the bishops of Orléans until the end of the 18C.

MONDOUBLEAU

Michelin map **60** south of 15, 16 – Pop 1 814 – *Facilities p 38*

Mondoubleau, on a hillside, clusters round two main squares bordered by 17 and 18C houses.

Castle ruins. – Built at the end of the 10C by Hugues Doubleau who gave his name to the town that was to grow up around the stronghold. On an elevated site the fortress has some fine remains: entrance gatehouse, outer ramparts, outer bailey, inner ramparts and curtain wall protecting the keep. Nicknamed the "butter pot", the keep – a round 11C tower 35 m - 115 ft high – is of the local red sandstone known as *roussard*.

The keep leans very noticeably to one side. When inside try the following experiment. Stand in the middle and look up to the top of the walls and you may well feel that you are losing your balance.

Old house. – This 15C house stands at the corner of the Rue de la Basse-Ville and the entrance ramp to the castle.

Grand Mail. – The Rue Gheerbrandt passes the post office (PTT) on the way to the square, Place St-Denis. Go behind the post office and cross the public gardens to reach the Grand Mail, a long shaded alley affording a fine view of the valley.

EXCURSIONS

Arville. – *Round tour of 26 km - 16 miles to the north by the D 921 – about 1 hour.*

    Château de St-Agil. – *Only the exterior can be visited.* This interesting château is encircled with moats. The part of the building dating from the 13C was remodelled in 1720. The early 16C entrance pavilion is flanked by two towers decorated with patterns made by the red and black bricks. The white masonry of the machicolations follows the watchpath which is dominated by pepperpot towers. The main building has a medallioned dormer window figuring the local lord, Antoine de la Vove. The park was landscaped by Jules Hardouin-Mansart and transformed

in 1872 into the English style. There are still some splendid lime trees dating from 1720.

Arville. – Pop 178. This small village is known for the Templars' commandery situated slightly to the north, at the side of the D 921. This was one of the commanderies erected by the military and religious Order of the Templars (founded 1119) to protect the main pilgrimage routes. Fortified in the 13C they also served as banks and consequently the Order amassed considerable wealth, independence and influence which were to be its undoing in 1307 when the Order was disbanded by Philippe the Fair.

The commandery has a 12C chapel preceded by a bell gable which is linked to a flint tower, formerly part of the ramparts. The late 15C gateway through the wall has two brick turrets with curious roofs.

Take the road to the left towards Oigny and Souday.

Souday. – Pop 688. The pre-Romanesque nave of the church is extended by a curious 16C two storeyed chancel. Two staircases with wrought iron railings (1838) climb to the upper chancel glazed with Renaissance stained glass (1540) representing the Passion and the Resurrection.

In the crypt the elegant ogive vaulting springs from columns without capitals. The south transept has 16C mural paintings of various saints.

Return to Mondoubleau by the D 117.

(After photo: C. Breteau, Éd. Delmas)

Arville — Commandery

Sargé. – *Round tour of 24 km - 15 miles* – Map 🔢 north of 5, 6 – *Leave Mondoubleau to the southeast by the D 151.*

Le Temple. – Pop 180. The Templars' commandery has now disappeared but a 12–16C church still remains.

Turn right on to the D 56.

Sargé-sur-Braye. – Pop 911. In the 11 and 15C Church of St-Martin *(key from Mme Botineau at the baker's)* with painted wainscoting dating from 1549, 16C wall paintings have been uncovered in the nave evoking the *Pietà* and St. Martin and some from the 14C in the chancel showing Christ in Majesty and the Work of the Months: note in particular Janus with three faces symbolising January.

Baillou. – Pop 276. The houses of Baillou are pleasantly grouped at the foot of a restored 16-17C château. Isolated on a mound the **church** (rebuilt at the beginning of the 16C) has a Renaissance doorway with pilasters adorned by foliated scrolls, the whole surmounted by the figures of Adam and Eve. Inside, notice the ogive vaulting springing from columns without capitals. To

(After photo: Arlette de la Moussaye)

Sargé Church — Janus' Feast

the left in the nave, with its monster decorated beams, is a unique and rather curious painting by Correa of the 17C school of Toledo, portraying St. Francis Borgia refusing the mitre. The north transept has a sculptured altarpiece (1618) evoking the Death of the Virgin with the Apostles and the donor.

The D 86 takes you back to Mondoubleau.

MONTGEOFFROY, Château de ★

Michelin map 🔢 11, 12 – 24 km - 15 miles east of Angers – *Local map p 103*

This fine building on a regular plan – an imposing main building joined to two large wings at right angles to it by terrace pavilions – was erected in the 18C for Marshal de Contades.

Guided tours from Palm Sunday to All Saints' Day 9.30am to noon and 2.30 to 6.30pm; time: ¾ hour; 10F.

It remained the property of this one family and it is to this fact that it owes the preservation of its original furniture, signed by Gourdin, Garnier and Durand, and fine pictures by Rigaud, Drouais, Pourbus the Younger, Van Loo, Desportes, etc. The whole is a model of proportion and harmony. Every piece of furniture stands in the place for which it was designed. The hangings and tapestries, with their magnificent designs and colours, seem to date from yesterday. The tour ends in the chapel, which has a fine 16C stained glass window, and in the harness room, which is well arranged.

MONTOIRE-SUR-LE-LOIR

Michelin map 🔢 5 – *Local maps pp 99 and 118* – Pop 3 966 – *Facilities p 39*

Former capital of Bas-Vendômois, Montoire attracts many anglers because of the good fishing provided by this stretch of the Loir.

Pilgrimage routes. – The 7C Priory of St-Gilles was followed by a fort in the 9C as defence against the Norman incursions. In the Middle Ages several pilgrimage routes passed by Montoire, the first to the tomb of St. Martin in Tours and the second to St. James's shrine in Santiago de Compostela. Hospices and leper hospitals were built in both Montoire and Troo.

A momentous meeting. – Following an initial meeting with one of his Ministers of State it was here, at the station in Montoire, on the 24 October 1940 that Marshal Pétain, head of the Vichy Government, met Hitler in a specially built train. On this occasion Hitler tried in vain to convince the Marshal to take up arms against Britain.

- **SIGHTS** *time: 1½ hours*

Bridge. – Affords attractive views of the Loir flowing between banks lined with weeping willows and wistaria covered old houses. The numerous small rowing boats moored along the banks belong to the anglers and clubs of the region.

Chapel of St-Gilles*. – An attractive Renaissance house (D) with small columns and a very curious chimneystack marks the entrance to the narrow lane leading to the chapel *(ask for the key at the ironmonger's shop, droguerie, opposite).*

On entering the gateway there is a view of the apse, a gracious Romanesque chapel, which once belonged to a Benedictine priory, of which Ronsard held the charge. It was from there that he left in October 1585 for his other priories of Ste-Madeleine de Croixval and St-Cosme near Tours, where he was to die two months later. A cypress, yew trees, a garden sloping down to the Loir and the Prior's lodging make a pleasant setting for the chapel.

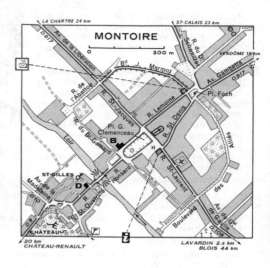

Mural paintings**. – These cover the apses and transept. Compare the two Christs of different periods on the oven vaults. The oldest on the main apse, dating from the first quarter of the 12C, shows a very majestic Christ of the Apocalypse, surrounded by angels. At the end of the south transept a 12C mural of Christ proffering the keys to St. Peter (faint) shows a marked Byzantine influence with the tightly symmetrical folds. The mural in the north transept showing Christ and the Apostles recounts the story of Pentecost. The unnatural attitudes and colours are typical of the early works of the local school *(p 26).* The arches of the transept crossing are also adorned with paintings: see the Battle of the Virtues and Vices on the western arch.

Château. – *Apply for the key at the Hotel de Ville* (H).
Ruined but imposing this fortress, standing on a rocky spur comprises an 11C square keep preceded by a stone and flint wall. There is a fine view over the Loir Valley and the keep at Lavardin.

There is a model of the Château as it was in the entrance hall of the Hôtel de Ville *(open on weekdays from 8.15am to 12.30pm and 1.45 to 5.30pm and on Saturdays from 10am to noon).*

Renaissance houses. – Two stand side by side on Place Clemenceau (B). The biggest with its mullioned and very high dormer windows is also the oldest. In Rue St-Oustrille note the house (D) with the curious chimney.

EXCURSIONS

Fargot. – *4.5 km - 3 miles. Leave by the road to St-Calais and after a level crossing turn right in the direction of Fosse, then left towards the Château de Fargot. This former abbey for girls known as de la Virginité, a dependent of Cîteaux was founded in the 13C: ruins of surrounding wall and outbuildings. Not open to the public.*

Ronsard Countryside*. – *Round tour of 43 km - 27 miles – about 2 hours.*
Ronsard held ecclesiastical livings in Montoire, Château-du-Loir and Tours but it was the surrounding countryside that he praised so ably in his verses. Smiling and rich, a patchwork of vineyards, grain fields and orchards stitched with poplars and willows.

Leave Montoire by the D 917 passing below the Château de Chalay.

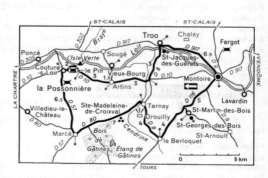

Troo*. – *Description p 157.*
Cross the Loir.

St-Jacques-des-Guérets. – *Description p 157.*

Follow the D 8 before turning right on to the D 10.

Vieux-Bourg d'Artins. – *1.5 km - 1 mile from Artins.* Situated on the banks of the Loir, the village church has retained its Romanesque walls pierced with Flamboyant windows and a pointed arched doorway.

3 km - 2 miles beyond Artins turn right into the road signposted L'Isle Verte and after 100 m - 109 yd turn left to pass in front of the Château du Pin. From the bridge opposite the castle there is a view upstream of the **L'Isle Verte** at the confluence of the Braye and the Loir. It was Ronsard's wish to be buried here.

Couture-sur-Loir. – Pop 535. The church has a Gothic chancel with Angevin vaulting. The chapel to the right of the chancel has 17C woodwork. The recumbent figures in the nave are those of Ronsard's parents.

The D 57 takes you to La Possonnière Manor.

La Possonnière Manor*. – Ronsard's birthplace. *Description p 128.*

Take the D 57 to Marcé then left along the D 80.

Gâtines Wood (Bois de Gâtines). – This is the last outpost of the natural forest which in the Middle Ages covered the entire plain between the Loir and Loire. A fine stand of oaks surrounds a solitary lake, Etang de Gâtines.

Ste-Madeleine-de-Croixval. – The priory ruins stand on a rocky ridge. It was here that Ronsard spent the latter years of his life, racked by gout, before moving to St-Cosme.

At Ternay take the D 8 to the right, passing the Château de Drouilly, from where there is a fine view of Troo and the Loir Valley. At Le Berloquet turn left on to the D 116.

St-Martin-des-Bois. – Pop 686. The church *(if closed apply to the post office opposite)* has a Romanesque nave and an Angevin chancel.

To the south of St-Martin, the former Benedictine Abbey of **St-Georges-des-Bois** has conserved an attractive Angevin style church with a Classical façade. This was formerly one of the stopping places on the pilgrimage route to Santiago de Compostela.

Return to the D 116 and turn right towards Montoire.

MONTPOUPON, Château de

Michelin map 64 16 – 20 km - 12 miles to the northeast of Loches – *Local map p 70*

The Château de Montpoupon, a 12C fortress, was reconstructed in the 15C and refurbished in 1920. The still intact and most unusual entrance gatehouse dates from the early 16C. The imposing mass of this fortress dominates a small wooded valley. The outbuildings house two museums: a Touraine folklore collection and a hunting exhibition.
Guided tours of the gatehouse and museums 15 June to 30 September, from 10am to noon and 2 to 7pm; during the Spring and Easter holidays, at weekends and on public holidays in May, June and October from 2 to 6pm only; 6F.

On the D 764, coming from Le Liège, there is a good **view*** of the château.

EXCURSION

Céré-la-Ronde. – Pop 571. *4 km - 2½ miles to the east.* The Renaissance church has retained a Romanesque tower.

MONTRÉSOR *

Michelin map 64 south of 16, 17 – *Local map p 70* – Pop 465.

Montrésor rises high above the right bank of the Indrois.

Church*. – This was formerly a canons' collegiate church consecrated in 1532. Gothic in style with Renaissance decoration it has a fine doorway. Inside, you will notice at the end of the nave, on the left, the tomb of the Basternays, who were overlords of Montrésor, a remarkable 16C work. The stalls and stained glass windows are Renaissance. The most beautiful window is in the chevet and depicts Jesus carrying the Cross (it is after a German engraving). There are also some good 16 and 17C paintings in the church.

Château*. – *Guided tours 1 April to 31 October from 9am to noon and 2 to 6.30pm; time: 25 mins; 10F.*
Built in the 11C by Foulques Nerra *(p 43)* and remodelled in later centuries, it was restored by Count Branicki in 1849. His descendants still live in the château.
Walk round the fortified promontory to get a good idea of the position and size of the building. The furnishings are as they were from the Restoration to the beginning of the Second Empire (1814-1850s). Also worthy of note are pictures by French and Polish painters, bas-reliefs representing the battles of John III Sobieski of Poland (late 17C), a solid mahogany staircase, a boudoir containing Italian primitives, and Polish mementos and art objects.
Near the esplanade are the old timbered market and a 16C building, Le Logis, which now serves as the *gendarmerie.*

EXCURSION

Nouans-les-Fontaines. – *8 km - 5 miles to the east by the D 760. The lower reaches of the Indrois Valley are described on p 96.*
The Indrois is a deeply rural valley winding across the clay and limestone of the Montresor Gâtine. Willows, alders and poplars line the river course while the better exposed slopes are covered with fruit trees and occasional patches of vines.

Villeloin. – Pop 694. In a pleasant setting on the banks of the Indrois, stand several buildings of the former Benedictine Abbey of St-Sauveur. From 1626 to 1674 the Abbot was **Michel de Marolles**, a great collector of prints and engravings. Originally bequeathed to the King his collection was later to form the nucleus of the Prints and Engravings Department of the Bibliothèque Nationale. The remains of former fortifications are a round tower and curtain wall linked to a fine 15C entrance gatehouse. The riverside building has a 16C overhanging turret. On entering the courtyard note to the left a basket handled doorway, originally from the church at nearby Coulangé, the conventual buildings straight ahead and the abbey church on the right.

Nouans-les-Fontaines. – Pop 872. The 13C church harbours a masterpiece of primitive art: the large altarpiece known as the **Deposition**** or *Pietà of Nouans* by Jean Fouquet and his school. This painting on wood, of monumental dimensions for the period, is one of the finest late 15C French works. The deliberately neutral colours employed, the resigned expressions of the figures and their majestic attitudes make this a moving composition.

MONTREUIL-BELLAY ★

Michelin map **64** south of 12 – *Local map p 103* – Pop 4 237 – *Facilities p 39*

The little terraced town of Montreuil-Bellay, behind 15C town walls, rises pleasantly above the Thouet.

Recalcitrant vassals. – Montreuil's earliest feudal lords were the warlike Du Bellays who from the security of their stronghold, one of the surest in Anjou, did not hesitate to plot and intrigue even against the great Foulques Nerra. It was only after three years of siege and the ensuing famine, that another Du Bellay finally capitulated to Geoffroy Plantagenet. The latter razed the castle's fortifications in 1150 and through the following centuries the castle was transformed into a delightful residence.

■ SIGHTS *time: 1½ hours*

Château★. – *Guided tours 1 July to 31 August from 10am to noon and 3 to 7pm; 1 April to 30 June and 1 September to 31 October from 10am to noon and 2 to 6pm; closed all day on Tuesdays in winter and the mornings only during the high season; 10F.*

Two bridges span the moat: that on the right leads to the church, that on the left to the castle.

The castle, which is enclosed within walls, is protected on the town side by an outwork or barbican *(p 23)*. It consists of three buildings.

The **Châtelet** or Gatehouse (13-15C) forms the entrance. You pass through it to reach the terrace overlooking the Thouet (pretty view).

The **Petit Château** or Little Castle (15C) contains, in one wing, a **kitchen** with a central chimney inspired by that at Fontevraud, and in the other wing, four private dwellings each with its own entrance and turret staircase. This is an unusual arrangement.

Ardiller (Bd de l')	2	D'-Gaudrez (R. du)	5
Ardiller (R. de l')	3	Douves (R. des)	6
Château (R. du)	4	Ormeaux (Pl. des)	7

The **Château Neuf** or New Castle, also 15C, is a splendid building. The left tower (on the courtyard), with six tiers of richly decorated windows, contains the grand staircase up which the Duchess of Longueville once rode on horseback. The New Castle has fine rooms and an oratory adorned with 15C frescoes.

Notre-Dame (B). – This the former seigneurial chapel is in the Flamboyant style. It has a single nave with a painted litre *(p 77)* and a small oratory on the north side.

Bridge. – This affords a picturesque **view★** of the château and the church.

Boulevard de l'Ardenne. – Extensive view of the Thouet Valley.

Porte St-Jean (D). – The arch of this fortified gateway opens between two large rusticated towers with sixteen rows of canon balls.

EXCURSION

Asnières Abbey. – *7.5 km - 5 miles to the northwest by the D 761; after 5.5 km - 3 miles turn right. Guided tours from 1 July to 31 August from 10am to noon and 2 to 6pm; closed on Tuesdays; time: 20 mins; 3F.*

The romantic ruins, lying north of the Cizay Forest, were once an important monastery. It was founded in the 12C. The **chancel★**, with that of St-Serge at Angers, is the most perfect specimen extant of the Angevin style *(p 21)*.

The south transept is the oldest part of the building. The north transept, like the chancel, dates from the early 13C. The Abbot's chapel was added in the 16C. This charming little oratory is decorated with trefoils and festoons, and contains a 14C Crucifix.

MONTRICHARD ★

Michelin map **64** 16, 17 – *Local map p 70* – Pop 3 857 – *Facilities p 39*

For the passing tourist it will suffice to take a look from the old bridge over the Cher at the ruined keep dominating the town and to see the old 15 and 16C houses in the Rue Nationale. The cliff upstream from the town is pitted with quarries which have now been transformed into wine cellars *(Guided tours from 9am to noon and 2 to 5.30pm; 6.30pm in July and August; time: 30 mins)*, troglodyte houses or converted into caves for growing mushrooms.

■ SIGHTS *time: ¾ hour*

Keep. – *Open 14 June to 1 September from 9.30 to 11.30am and 2.30 to 6.30pm; Palm Sunday to 8 June and in September, on Sundays and public holidays only at the above times; 4F.*

The keep was built by Foulques Nerra *(p 43)*, with two further sets of ramparts being added in the 12 and 13C and dismantled by Henri IV in 1589. From the top of the keep there is a good view of the town and the Cher Valley.

Ste-Croix. – This former seigneurial chapel has a fine Romanesque doorway. The marriage of the future Louis XII with Jeanne de France, the daughter of Louis XI, was celebrated here in 1476.

Maison du Prêche. – This dates from the 11C.

Maison de l'Ave Maria. – The carving on the corner post of this 16C house represents the Annunciation.

Hôtel Jacques de Beaune. – Now a hospice, this 16C building was bequeathed to the town in 1719 by the marquis d'Effiat.

Nanteuil Church. – *305 m - 330 yd west of Montrichard by the Rue du Faubourg-de-Nanteuil.* This 12, 13 and 15C church has a statue of the Virgin which is the object of a very ancient pilgrimage on Whit Monday. The generosity of Louis XI and his court made it possible to build a chapel situated at the corner of the north transept and the nave. It has a ground floor which serves as a porch and an upper storey from which the church can be entered.

MONTSOREAU ★

Michelin map 🔢 13 – *Local maps pp 76 and 103* – Pop 503 – *Facilities p 39*

The village, prettily situated a little downstream from the confluence of the Loire and the Vienne, is known for its château.

Château★. – *Guided tours from 10am to noon and 2 to 7pm; closed on Tuesdays and 12 to 25 February; time: 1 hour; 5F.*
It was built in the 15C by a Chambes. This family produced bold warriors and enterprising women. A lady of Montsoreau attracted the Duc de Berry, brother of Louis XI, and through him formed the *Ligue du Bien Public* (League for Public Good) which the king defeated only by the assassination of the pretender and his mistress. A century later another Chambes was one of the most ferocious executioners in the massacre of the Huguenots on St. Bartholomew's Day, 1572.

The château owes its renown to Alexandre Dumas's novel *La Dame de Montsoreau*. The heroine, the Countess of Montsoreau was compelled by her outraged husband to make a rendezvous with her lover, Bussy d'Amboise, on which occasion the unsuspecting lover was assassinated. In spite of this affair the couple were seemingly reconciled and continued to live on excellent terms for many years to follow. The novel was, however, not always historically accurate, notably as regards the place of the crime, which was at the Château de la Coutancière across the river.

The château best seen from the river rises, imposing and severe, through two floors before being topped by a decorative watchpath and two storey dormer windows themselves crowned by pediments and pinnacles. The courtyard façade has a more smiling aspect, with an attractively decorated staircase tower.

The château has a Goums Museum, illustrating the history of the *goums* or cavalry units recruited in Morocco. There are also souvenirs of the conquest of Morocco and of Marshal Lyautey and his campaign.

Panorama★. – *1 km - ½ mile by car.* A cliff top belvedere in the heart of the vineyard affords a view downstream of the village, château and the Val and upstream of the confluence of the Loire and Vienne.

ORLÉANS ★

Michelin map 🔢 9 – *Local maps pp 101 and 102* – Pop 109 956

Orléans has always been an active business centre. The wheat of the Beauce, the honey, poultry and potatoes of the Gâtinais, the game of the Sologne, the vegetables and wine of the Val, together with local products – vinegar, canned vegetables, trees, shrubs and flowers – keep trade going.

Though the town suffered considerably during the Second World War, the reconstruction has been extremely well planned. At the Chapelle-St-Mesmin, to the west of the industrial zone, Michelin has erected a tyre factory. Orléans is now the seat of a new university campus, which is located at Orléans-la-Source. Several industrial estates have been created on the outskirts of the town. One to the north of Fleury-les-Aubrais, two to the west at St Jean de la-Ruelle and Ingré and a fourth at St-Jean-de-Braye.

THE SIEGE OF 1428-29

The Adversaries. – On 12 October 1428, Lord Salisbury, with an English and Burgundian army, arrived before Orléans on the south bank of the Loire. The people of Orléans had razed the suburbs to a distance of 185 m - 200 yd beyond the walls to make the attack more difficult for the enemy. The English captured the fort, Les Tourelles, at the head of the bridge, but could not debouch from it. The defenders had blown up an arch and hastily erected a small wooden outwork in front of the Bastille St-Antoine. For their own protection the attackers destroyed another arch in front of Les Tourelles.

Divided into thirty-four companies, the 5 000 citizens who were fit to bear arms, manned the thirty-four towers on the walls. Altogether about 10 000 men defended Orléans. The English effectives were about the same, at least at the beginning.

Salisbury, being obliged to lay siege to the place, surrounded it with trenches overlooked by strongpoints. These were works made of earth and wood and protected by ditches. Each sheltered a garrison of 400 to 500 men and a few bombards. These works commanded only the Loire and the western part of the town, for the English had not enough men to close the circle and resist any sorties by the besieged garrison. The people of Orléans could communicate with the country to the northeast without too much risk.

The artillery. – Artillery already played an important role at this time. The bombards, made of a wooden tube bound with iron or of an iron tube, could throw a stone ball weighing 10 to 100 kg (22 to 220 lb) for a distance of up to 1 000 m - 1 093 yd. The adversaries could, therefore, reach one another across the Loire. There were seventy-two bombards in Orléans, but the damage done by their missiles was limited, for they were not explosive. Their firing was also inaccurate in range, because the firing powders were unreliable.

Daily life. – After a few months, besiegers and besieged found time lay heavy on their hands. They would shout at one another, arrange small exchanges and watch single combats to relieve the tedium.

Salisbury was struck by a shot and died of his wounds. An astonishing version, which delighted the people of Orléans, made the rounds: a loaded bombard had been left for a moment by its gunner in the Tour Notre-Dame. A small boy, imitating what he had seen the gunner do, touched the gun with the red hot rod that served as a match. The gun fired, and the shot, guided by the Virgin who wished to punish Salisbury for having burnt the Basilica Notre-Dame de Cléry, decapitated the English nobleman just as one of his officers, pointing out Orléans to him, exclaimed: "My Lord, there is your town!"

Another subject of endless talk was the prowess and cunning of Master-Gunner Jean. With his two bombards, *Rifflart* and *Montargis*, he gave the English a hard time. Sometimes he pretended to be killed. He was carried away with every sign of grief and the enemy shouted for joy. But the next day Master Jean, hale and hearty, opened fire once more.

Five months passed. The morale of the defenders was getting low. The English became no more aggressive; some of their troops had been withdrawn and there were only two or three thousand rather tired men left.

Arrival of Joan of Arc. – Joan came from Blois via Olivet. The Domrémy shepherdess, unfamiliar with local topo-

THE SIEGE OF ORLÉANS

graphy and no doubt purposely deceived by her military advisers, was surprised, on reaching the Loire, to find Orléans on the far side of the river. To transfer her troops to the north bank she had to send them back to Blois, since the English held the bridge at Beaugency. Having crossed the bridge at Blois the troops avoided the English defences to the north and arrived at Orléans five days after Joan. The Maid, with a few companions, had gone 10 km - 6 miles upstream, and on 28 April 1429, she crossed the Loire in a boat at **Chécy**. She spent the night at the Château de Reuilly, which she left on 29 April to enter Orléans by the Porte de Bourgogne.

Joan of Arc was welcomed with enthusiasm by the people of Orléans. She also had a great effect on the troops. For love of the Maid they gave up their debaucheries, went to church and bit their lips to keep from swearing. They followed her with the good people who dogged her footsteps to kiss her sword or touch her horse.

Among the military leaders, however, with the exception of Dunois, Joan found only envy, deceit and ill will. The most hostile was **Gaucourt**, the Governor of the fortress.

The animator. – After four days of discussion and argument Joan obtained consent to an attack on the Bastille St-Loup. Gaucourt attacked without warning her and was repulsed with losses. The heroine, hearing the noise of battle, hurried to the spot. Raising her banner, she charged the ditch of the fort, followed by soldiers shouting: "Hurrah for the Maid!" The English gave away, leaving 200 killed.

St-Loup having fallen, the warlike Joan proposed to attack the Bastille de St-Jean-Le-Blanc, on the opposite side of the river, the next day (5 May). The Captains' Council refused. It was not until 6 May that the Maid, with 4 000 men, crossed to the Ile St-Aignan and from there to the south bank over a bridge of boats.

As a tactical ruse, the English had evacuated St-Jean and retired to the Augustinian monastery, the ruins of which they had fortified. The French gave chase, but a counter attack threw them back to their boats in disorder. Joan was at first swept back with the retreating troops, but she rallied her men and faced the enemy. The English were impressed, withdrew in their turn, failed to hold the Augustinian monastery and took cover in the Boulevard des Tourelles. The heroine pitched her camp on the spot and returned to Orléans to arrange for the next day's attack. She proposed a feint towards Les Tourelles, starting from the Bastille St-Antoine. Gaucourt opposed this. When Joan tried to go out by the Porte de Bourgogne he barred her way, but the people swept the man aside and Joan hurried to rejoin her troops.

Deliverance. – In her constant desire to spare the lives of her men and with her usual intuition Joan quickly understood the importance of artillery. Before attacking the Boulevard des Tourelles she had it pounded by the bombards in Orléans and those she had brought with her.

But the resistance of the English was desperate. To inspire her soldiers Joan jumped into the ditch and tried to set a ladder against the wall. She was struck by an arrow which pierced her flesh above her shoulder and projected six inches behind her neck, and she fell backwards. The English, thinking they had killed her, shouted for joy: "The witch is dead!"

Carried away by her companions, Joan pulled out the arrow herself, crying with pain. But the saints appeared to her and she overcame her weakness. A compress of fat and olive oil relieved her. She returned to the attack and the English, seized with panic at the approach of her standard, abandoned the ramparts and retreated to the fort. Meanwhile, on the bridge, the people of Orléans had thrown gangways over the broken arches and the feint began. The English, caught between the crossfire, capitulated. Two hundred were taken prisoner and 300 were killed or drowned in the river.

The next day, 8 May, the besiegers withdrew from the last forts, leaving behind their equipment, stores and sick. Joan of Arc re-entered Orléans in a storm of enthusiasm.

This deliverance is celebrated solemnly every year in May, when the Saint of France accomplishes the final miracle of uniting citizens of all opinions in a common fervour.

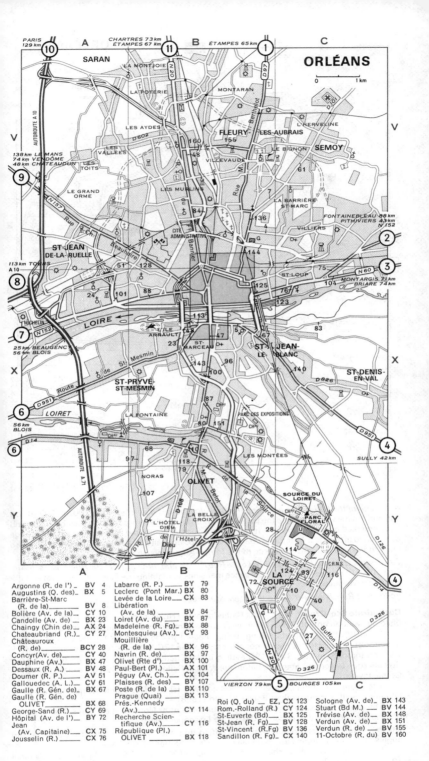

ORLÉANS

■ MAIN SIGHTS *time: 1 hour*

Place du Martroi (DZ). – Martroi is derived from the Latin *martyretum*, as the sites of Christian cemeteries were called in the 6C. In the centre stands the statue of Joan of Arc (1855), by Foyatier. The bas-reliefs on the pedestal, by Vital-Dubray, depict the life of the Saint. The artist wished to imitate certain Italian Renaissance sculptures.

Take the car to the southwest corner of the Place du Martroi – down streets Rue de la Hallebarde and Rue Cheval Rouge to the Quay Cypierre, where you turn left before crossing the bridge, Pont George-V.

Pont George-V (DZ). – This bridge took the place, in 1760, of the one that existed at the time of Joan of Arc. It was built about 100 m - 109 yd farther downstream. When Mme de Pompadour crossed it, the people of Orléans, who were known as the *Guépins* (Waspies) for their caustic wit, commenting on the crushing burdens imposed on the people by Louis XV's mistress said: "Our bridge is strong. It has borne the heaviest burden of France."

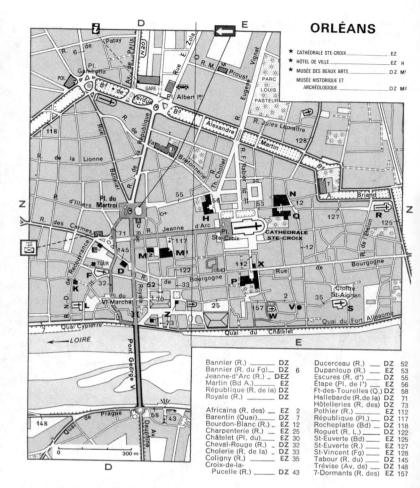

ORLÉANS

★ CATHÉDRALE STE-CROIX	EZ
★ HÔTEL DE VILLE	EZ **H**
★ MUSÉE DES BEAUX ARTS	DZ **M¹**
MUSÉE HISTORIQUE ET ARCHÉOLOGIQUE	DZ **M²**

At the end of the bridge turn left along the Quai du Fort-des-Tourelles. After 100 m - 109 yd you will find, on the wall alongside the Loire, inscriptions recording the position of Les Tourelles, and its site marked out on the ground. It was here (a good general view of the town) that the bridge debouched in the 15C. A statue of Joan of Arc stands opposite. In the Rue Croix-de-la-Pucelle a cross indicates the approximate site of the former Augustinian monastery.

Turn round, cross the bridge again, take the Rue Royale and turn right into the Rue Jeanne-d'Arc. On your right you will see the Renaissance mansions containing the Fine Arts Museum and the Historical Museum.

Follow the Rue Jeanne-d'Arc to the Place Ste-Croix.

Cathédrale Ste-Croix* (EZ). – The Cathedral of the Holy Cross was begun in the 13C and its building went on until the 16C, but it was partly destroyed by the Protestants in 1568.

Henri IV, the first Bourbon King, being grateful to the town for having supported him, undertook to rebuild the cathedral, not in the style of the 17C, but in the Gothic manner. The work went on throughout the 18 and 19C ending under Charles X, the last Bourbon King. The old Romanesque towers still standing before the Wars of Religion (1562-98), gave place to pseudo Gothic towers.

The chancel vaulting collapsed in 1904 and was rebuilt. The Gothic steeple has had to be rebuilt twice. It was the work of Boeswildwald (1858).

The church is of really imposing size, about the same as Notre-Dame in Paris. The best view of it can be had from the garden of the former Episcopal Palace.

Interior. – Note the great organ with parts dating from the 17, 18 and 19C. The caryatids and angels on the great organ case, originally came from St-Benoît-sur-Loire.

On the north side of the chancel, in the Chapel of St. Joan of Arc, is the statue of Cardinal Touchet (1894-1926), who made incessant efforts to propagate the cult of the Maid. In the central chapel of the apse is a fine marble Virgin by Michel Bourdin (early 17C), a sculptor born in Orléans. In the side aisle of the central nave are late 19C stained glass windows, representing the life of Joan of Arc.

Splendid early 18C **woodwork**** adorns the chancel. It was made to the designs of Mansart, Gabriel and Lebrun by Jules Degoullons, one of the decorators of Versailles and designer of the stalls in Notre-Dame, Paris. Superbly carved the main theme, the life of Christ, is portrayed in the various oval medallions. these are surrounded by other panels adorned with trophies and other symbolic groups of church objects.

Guided tours of the chancel to see the woodwork, of the crypt and the treasury (timetable in the ambulatory to the right of the choir); 3F.

In the crypt may be seen traces of the three buildings which preceded the present cathedral. The **treasury** contains Byzantine enamels of the 11C, goldsmiths' work of the 13C, the Tree of Jesse (late 15C Flemish work) and interesting 17C paintings. Note in particular Zurbarán's Christ's bearing of the Cross.

■ ADDITIONAL SIGHTS

Fine Arts Museum★ (Musée des Beaux-Arts – DZ M¹). – *Open from 10am to noon and 2 to 6pm (5pm 1 October to 31 March); closed on Tuesdays, 1 January, 1 May, 1 November, 25 December; 2F; free on Sunday mornings and Wednesday afternoons.*

The museum is installed in the 15-16C Hôtel des Créneaux, the town hall from 1428 to 1790. In the courtyard is a 15C belfry.

In the gallery containing the primitives there are two outstanding pictures from the 15C Sienese school. One of these by Matteo di Giovanni shows the Virgin and Child guarded by two angels. Among the works shown in the next gallery is a bust of Cardinal de Morvillier by Germain Pilon and several works from Richelieu's château: particularly noteworthy are Deruet's *Les Quatre Éléments* (The Four Elements) and *Louis XIV as a Child* and *Anne of Austria* by Pourbus the Younger. From the 17C there is *St. Sebastian Carrying a Lantern* by the school of Georges de la Tour and *Bacchus and Ariadne* by Louis le Nain.

In the pastel gallery there are precious 18C portraits and a family group of Mme Perronneau and M. and Mme Chevotet by Peronneau. In the same gallery are several good portrait busts in terracotta by Pigalle and Houdon. There is a remarkable collection of portraits in the 18C gallery: those especially worthy of note are *Mme de Pompadour* by Drouais, *Moyreau* (the engraver) by Nonotte and the *Marquis de Lucker* by Tocqué. In the cabinets are beautiful medallions.

The 19 and 20C galleries are represented by such well known artists as Gauguin, Soutine and Max Jacob. Pictures from the foreign schools are shown in rotation – *(St. Thomas* by Velazquez).

Hôtel de Ville★ (EZ H). – *Guided tours from 10am to 6pm; closed 1, 7 and 8 May.*

This is a Renaissance mansion which has been extensively remodelled. François II died there after opening, in 1560, the States-General, which met in a tent set up in the square. It was there also that Charles IX met the beautiful **Marie Touchet**, to whom he remained attached for the rest of his life.

In the centre of the porch is a statue of Joan of Arc at prayer executed by the Princess, Marie d'Orléans, daughter of Louis-Philippe.

The façade of the former Chapel of St-Jacques (15C) has been set up in the garden.

Local Historical Museum (Musée Historique et Archéologique – DZ M²). – *Same opening times as the Fine Arts Museum.*

The museum is in the small but elegant 16C Hôtel Cabu, burnt in 1940 and since restored. Two rooms are devoted to the art of the Gallo-Roman period and the Middle Ages. On the ground floor is the interesting **Gallo-Roman treasure★** from Neuvy-en-Sullias, 31 km - 19 miles east of Orléans. The treasure comprises a series of expressive statues, horses and wild boar in bronze and statuettes from a pagan temple. Local folklore from the 17C to the 19C is portrayed in a third room. Examples of Orléans ceramics complete the exhibition.

Centre Charles Péguy (DZ D). – *Open from 1.30 to 6pm; closed on Sundays and public holidays.*

This museum traces the life and career of Charles Péguy (1873-1914), a poet and philosopher, from Orléans. He combined Christianity, Socialism and patriotism into a deeply personal faith that he carried into action. In 1900 he published a journal, *Cahiers de la Quinzaine* (Fortnightly Notebooks), which exercised a profound cultural influence. He also wrote two important works on Joan of Arc; a Socialist play (1897) and a philosophic poem, *Mystère de la charité de Jeanne d'Arc* (1910). His last work *Eve* (1913), was a poem of 4 000 alexandrines.

Maison de Jeanne d'Arc (DZ E). – *Open from 10am to noon and 2 to 6pm (afternoons only from 1 November to 31 April); closed Mondays; 2F.*

Known as Joan of Arc's House, this building contains old documents and interesting maquettes, in particular of the fort, Les Tourelles and on siege warfare during the Hundred Years War (1337-1453).

St-Paul (DZ F). – This was burnt out in June 1940. Only the 15C façade and the Chapel of Notre-Dame-des-Miracles remain. In the chapel is displayed a Black Virgin whose cult goes back to the end of the 5C, when a Syrian colony settled a short distance west of Orléans. The present statue took the place of the original one in the 16C, which was burnt by the Protestants. Joan of Arc prayed before it during the week which saw the delivery of Orléans (1429).

Maison de François I (DZ K). – *Inner courtyard open from 9am to noon and 2 to 6pm; closed Sundays and holidays.* Built in 1540, it was lived in by François I's mistress, the duchesse d'Étampes.

Notre-Dame-de-Recouvrance (DZ L). – *To visit apply to the priest, 8 Ruelle St-Paul.* There is a fine window above the high altar of this 16C building.

Lycée Jeanne-d'Arc (EZ N). – *To visit apply in advance to the Directrice. Visiting times to be arranged with the caretaker.* The crypt is 11C.

Former Episcopal Palace (Ancien évêché – EZ Q). – This 17C building now houses the municipal library. It has an attractive stone staircase with a wrought iron balustrade. There is some fine woodwork on the ground floor. At the bottom of the garden behind the cathedral, on the right, are remains of the former Gallo-Roman walls.

St-Euverte (EZ R). – 12, 15 and 17C. Former convent chapel dedicated to one of the first bishops of Orléans. The neighbouring convent buildings are now a college.

St-Aignan (EZ S). – *Open on Mondays, Wednesdays and Fridays from 6 to 7pm, on Tuesdays and Thursdays from 9 to 10am and Saturdays from 5 to 6pm; otherwise apply to the Tourist Information Centre, SI).* Consecrated in 1509, there remains only the chancel and the transept. The nave was burnt down during the Wars of Religion (1562-98). The early 11C crypt *(to visit: apply to the Tourist Information Centre, SI)*, which was part of the church founded by Robert the Pious, son of Hugues Capet, has decorated capitals.

Recent excavations have uncovered the foundation of the crypt and several more capitals, one of which is a rather curious, coloured one.

ORLÉANS★

Tour Neuve (EZ V). – This is part of the 15C city walls as they were in the time of Joan of Arc. The base is Gallo-Roman.

St-Pierre-le-Puellier (EZ W). – Romanesque. It probably owes its name to the fact that a convent for young girls (*puellae* in Latin) stood nearby.

Préfecture (EZ P). – A former Benedictine monastery of the 17C.

Salle des Thèses (EZ X). – 15C. This "bookshop" is all that remains of the famous university, which had 4 000 to 5 000 students in the Middle Ages. Calvin, the great Reformer, studied law there in 1528.

Maison de la Coquille and Maison d'Alibert (DZ Z). – Renaissance mansions.

Rue Ducerceau (DZ). – A Renaissance mansion at no. 6.

OLIVET and ORLÉANS-LA-SOURCE

9 km - 6 miles to the south by the George-V Bridge and Avenue Dauphine through the suburb of St-Marceau.

Olivet. – Pop 12 382. *Facilities p 39.* On the banks of the Loiret, in a charming setting, Olivet is popular for fishing and boating. Most of Olivet is given over to market gardens, fields of flowers and nurseries. The floral clock, near the bridge, is composed of 5 000 flowers.

The Loiret is lined by old watermills and fine houses. The tourist can stroll alongside or take a rowing boat. *Landing stage near the bridge over the Loiret.*
Turn left on to the D 14, making eastwards.

Orléans-la-Source. – This new town has been built to the south of the floral park and the new campus of Orléans University.

Floral Park★ (Parc Floral – CY). – *Open from April to 15 November 9am to 6pm; the rest of the year from 2 to 5pm; 6F.*

One can visit the park on a miniature train which is in service from May to September, on Wednesdays, Saturdays and Sundays from 2.30 to 5pm; 4F.

The floral park, 35 ha - 86 acres, is a constantly changing pleasure. From April to October flowers – tulips, irises, roses, dahlias and chrysanthemums – form colourful masses surrounded by centuries old trees.

The flower shows are popular events. The rose garden has approximately 200 000 rose bushes; there are fountains, modern sculpture, animals and other attractions.

The **Source du Loiret★** (CY) (Spring of the Loiret) is the resurgence of a branch of the Loire which is formed near St. Benoît and reappears in the park. It is manifested by an intense bubbling; the flow is from 35 to 40 m³ - 1 200 to 1 400 cu. ft a minute.

ORLÉANS FOREST (LA FORÊT D'ORLÉANS)

Round tour of 93 km - 58 miles – about 3 hours.
Michelin maps 🖽 19, 20; 🖽 11; 🖽 9, 10 and 🖽 1,2

The forest spreading out on the north bank of the Loire between Orléans and Gien is bordered to the north by the Beauce and the east by the Gâtinais. Consisting mainly of pines and oaks it covers 50 000 ha - 124 000 acres of which 34 565 ha - 85 000 acres are State property and is interspersed with large clearings, cut and brought into cultivation by the monks in the Middle Ages. Formerly known as the Forêt des Loges (*loge:* clearing cultivated by the monks), this is France's largest State Forest.

As in the Sologne the soils are sands and clays of the Tertiary era. The isolated pools, refuges for migrating birds, the heather moors, the oak, hornbeam and pine woods make this good hunting (deer) and shooting (game) territory.

The scattered villages are encircled by areas growing subsistence crops. The Orléans Canal, finished in 1692, crosses the forest to join the Loing downstream from Montargis. Now disused the reaches provide good fishing.

Leave Orléans (p 121) by ③, the N 152. At Mardié take the D 709 which follows the Orléans Canal.

Fay-aux-Loges. – Pop 1 982. *Facilities p 38.* Standing in a forest clearing the town is heralded from afar by its curious **church** spire. The vaulting of the nave is 13C while the chancel is Gothic. Note the fine 17C lectern and the 17C paintings hanging in the side aisles.

Follow the D 9 as far as Combreux and from there continue to the pool, Étang de la Vallée, on the left.

Étang de la Vallée★. – This reservoir of the Orléans Canal is situated in a wild setting amidst dense woodland and tall grasses where water hen and ducks take refuge. Facilities are provided for the fisherman and tourist: bathing place, boats and pedal boats for hire, yachting permitted.

Take the road leading to Seichebrières.

Les Caillettes. – *4 km - 2½ miles to the north of Seichebrières, by the D 137 and a road to the right.* An **observation tower** is situated at a good vantage point (182 m - 597 ft).

Taking the D 137 and the D 143 to the right in Vitry-aux-Loges, reach the picturesque D 921 which one follows for 11 km - 7 miles.

Turn left into the D 109 which crosses Courcy and passes in front of the 15-17C **Château de Chamerolles.**

Return to Orléans by the N 51.

Gastronomy. Here are a few regional specialities:

Rillons and rillettes – potted pork.

Matelote d'anguilles – eels simmered in red wine with mushrooms and small onions. In Anjou they sometimes add prunes.

Fricassée de poulet – casserole of chicken in a white wine and cream sauce with onions and mushrooms.

PLESSIS-BOURRÉ, Château du ★

Michelin map **63** east of 20 – 20 km - 12 miles to the north of Angers – *Local map p 115*

Le Plessis-Bourré stands far away at the end of a vista of meadowland, a white building beneath blue grey slate roofs, bringing to the mind's eye the seigneurial life of the 15C.

Jean Bourré (1424-1506). – Born in Chateau-Gontier Jean Bourré first entered royal service under the dauphin Louis, the son of Charles VII, whom he served faithfully. When Louis XI assumed the Crown in 1461, Bourré was appointed Financial Secretary and Treasurer of France.

In addition to building several châteaux – Jarzé *(p 51)* and Vaux *(p 164)* among others – he bought the estate of Plessis-le-Vent and in 1468 ordered work to begin on the new château. The design was inspired by the château at Langeais. The building of Le Plessis continued without interruption and thus has a magnificent unity of style.

Among the many illustrious guests that Bourré welcomed to his new residence were Pierre de Rohan *(p 99)*, Louis XI and Charles VIII.

■ THE CHÂTEAU ★ *time: ¾ hour*

Guided tours from 1 April to 30 September 10am to noon and 2 to 7pm (5pm the rest of the year); closed 15 November to 15 December and on Wednesdays except in July and August; 10F.

Le Plessis, isolated by a wide moat spanned by a many arched bridge 43 m - 47 yd long looks, from outside, like a fortress protected by a gatehouse with a double drawbridge and four flanking towers. The largest of these is battlemented and served as a keep. A platform 3 m - 10 ft wide at the base of the perimeter wall provided for artillery crossfire.

The chapel's slender spire rises above the roof to the left of the gatehouse.

Beyond the entrance archway, Le Plessis is transformed into a country mansion with a spacious courtyard, low wings, an arcaded

Château du Plessis-Bourré

gallery, turret staircases and high dormer windows of the Seigneurial Wing.

On the ground floor the visitor will see the Chapel Ste-Anne and the Hall of Justice before visiting the richly furnished and decorated state apartments.

The first floor has among other rooms a great vaulted chamber with a monumental fireplace. The guardroom has a coffered wooden **ceiling** ★★ painted at the end of the 15C with such allegorical figures as Fortune, Truth, Chastity (a unicorn) and Lust, the Musician Ass, etc. Humorous and moral scenes depict the unskilled barber at work on a patient, the overweening man trying to wring the neck of an eel, a woman sewing up a chicken's crop, etc. There is a large collection of fans in the library.

The towns and sights described in this guide are shown in black on the maps.

PLESSIS-MACÉ, Château du

Michelin map **63** 20 – 13 km - 8 miles to the northwest of Angers – *Local map p 115*

Hidden amidst greenery this château is surrounded by a wide moat.

Started in the 11C by a certain Macé, the château became the property in the mid 15C of Louis de Beaumont, the Chamberlain and favourite of Louis XI, who transformed it into a residence fit to accommodate his royal master. The year 1510 saw the beginning of a 168 year old ownership by the Du Bellay family.

From the exterior Le Plessis still has the appearance of a fortress with its tower studded wall and rectangular keep defended by moats, dismantled but still battlemented.

Guided tours from 10am to noon and 2 to 6.30pm in July, August and September; out of season from 1.30 to 5.30pm; closed on Tuesdays and from 1 December to 28 February; time: 1 hour; 5F.

Once inside the great courtyard the country residence becomes apparent: the decorative elements in white tufa stone enhance the grey of the schists, while windows testify to the search for light.

To the right are the outbuildings hous-

(After photo: Chrétien, Angers)

Château du Plessis-Macé — Balcony

ing the stables and guardroom. To the left are the chapel, an unusual staircase turret, and the main dwelling surmounted by pointed gables.

At the corner of the main dwelling is a charming **balcony** which served as a vantage point for the ladies during jousting tournaments and other entertainments. The balcony opposite, in the outbuildings, was reserved for the servants.

The **chapel**, an attractive Flamboyant building was erected by the Du Bellays and is graced by an intricately sculptured, ogee arched, doorway. The original 15C altar still exists as does a unique wooden seigneurial pew with openwork design.

PONCÉ-SUR-LE-LOIR

Michelin map **64** 5 – *Local map 99* – Pop 433

Poncé, on the north bank of the Loir, has a delightful Renaissance château.

Château. – *Open from 10am to noon and 2 to 6pm; Sundays and holidays from 2 to 6pm; time: 1 hour; 5F.*

The château originally consisted of two pavilions, flanking the central staircase tower, one of which was destroyed in the 18C and replaced by a characterless wing. Mullioned, pedimented windows and pronounced horizontal cornices give a balanced but geometrically severe aspect to the façade. The north front, formerly the main one, has at ground level an elegant Italian style arcade which forms a terrace at the first floor level.

The stone **Renaissance staircase★★** is one of the most remarkable in France. The coffered ceilings of the six flights are sumptuously sculptured, with a delicacy, fantasy and art of perspective rarely attained. Over 130 motifs portray realistic, allegorical and mythological subjects.

The dovecote remains with its 1 800 holes and revolving ladders for gathering the eggs.

The outbuildings house a museum of Sarthe folklore and nearby a crafts centre gives a glimpse of certain craftsmen at work: wood and iron working, weaving and pottery making *(workshops open on weekdays from 9am to noon and 2 to 6pm; exhibition open on Sunday and holiday afternoons).*

PONTLEVOY

Michelin map **64** 17 – Pop 1 607

This pleasant, small town is situated between the Loire and the Cher.

Former abbey. – *Guided tours from Easter to All Saints' Day 10.30am to noon and 2.30 to 6.30pm; the rest of the year 2.30 to 6pm; on Sundays and holidays from 10.30am to noon and 2.30 to 6.30pm; 7F.*

Gelduin de Chaumont, in recognition and thankfulness to the Virgin for being saved from shipwreck, established here in the 11C a community of Benedictine monks, originally from the abbey at St-Florent near Saumur. The monks organised a college.

The abbey was originally enclosed by a fortified wall, of which one 15C tower remains.

Built from the 13 to 15C the former **abbey church** is composed uniquely of an ambitious chancel with ambulatory and radiating chapels. The 17C monks' stalls at the back can be distinguished from those of the Abbot and Prior. The 1651 retable of the high altar was the result of the combined efforts of the Tours sculptor, Antoine Charpentier and the Blois painter, Jean Mosnier. Charpentier was also responsible for the retable in the apsidal chapel. The founder, Gelduin, and some of his descendants are buried here.

The 17C **conventual buildings** stand to the right of the church. Note the cloisters and refectory which contains a great 18C porcelain stove, one of four commissioned by the Marshal, Maurice de Saxe, for Chambord. A remarkable staircase leads to a great gallery off which were the monks' cells, now transformed into conference rooms. The particularly majestic garden front is adorned at regular intervals with emblazoned pediments.

A magnificent cedar tree dating from 1774 stands in the courtyard.

La POSSONNIÈRE Manor ★

Michelin map **64** 5 – 1 km - ½ mile to the south of Couture – *Local maps pp 99 and 118*

To visit apply in writing to the owner.

When Louis de Ronsard, soldier and man of letters returned from Italy in the early 16C he undertook the building of a country seat in the new Italian style. Here at La Possonnière the decoration is undisguisedly Renaissance.

It was here in 1524 that **Pierre de Ronsard**, the famous poet and leader of the Pléiade group of poets, was born. He held a court appointment – accompanying Princess Madeleine, James V's future wife to Scotland – and undertook diplomatic missions but it was to the Church that he finally turned, holding several benefices. He then began his prolific poetry writing achieving, in his lifetime, fame and recognition as the poet of the Renaissance. He died in the Priory of St-Cosme *(p 156).*

The white stone of the house against the green of the wooded hillside makes it visible from afar despite a surrounding wall.

Inscribed with Latin sayings, the walls of the garden façade are pierced at ground level by mullioned windows in the Louis XII style. Those higher up are flanked by medallioned pilasters which are undisguisedly Renaissance.

Projecting from the courtyard façade is a gracious staircase turret, pierced by a doorway, surmounted by a bust adorned pediment. Note the Ronsard arms on the pediment at the top of the tower, accompanied by the family motto – "the future belongs to the capable".

POUANCÉ

Michelin map **63** 8 – Pop 3 202 – *Facilities p 39*

Pouancé surrounded by a ring of pools stands on the borders of Brittany and Anjou. Already a flourishing town in the Middle Ages it was of both strategic and economic importance, due to its iron foundries using the ore from the Segré Basin. The surrounding woods served as refuges for the Chouans *(p 89)* during the Vendéen War.

Fortress. – *Open from 10am to noon and 2 to 7pm; 5pm out of season; 3F.*

The 12-14C Vieux Château with its sombre schist mass overlooks the pools, Étangs de St-Aubin and de Pouancé, both formed by the Verzée. Nearby is the manor's mill. Encircled by a moat it is preceded on the roadside by a barbican or outwork and postern linking it to the keep. The entrance gatehouse, towers and watchpath form an imposing ensemble.

Three underground chambers and several towers are visible only during guided tours, which generally take place on Saturday afternoons and Sundays.

EXCURSIONS

Menhir de Pierre Frite. – *Round tour of 12 km - 8 miles. Leave Pouancé to the south by the D 878.* In the village of **Prévière** there are a number of Chouan tombs.

Take the D 6 to the left then follow the signposted path. This menhir is 6 m - 20 ft high.

Return by Armaillé and the D 181. Shortly after Armaillé to the left of the road on the banks of the Verzée is an attractive manor, **Manoir du Bois-Geslin** (14-16C) now a farmhouse.

La Primaudière; Château de la Motte-Glain. – *17 km - 11 miles to the south by the D 878.*

La Primaudière. – In a small green valley, to the left of the road, stands this former priory which belonged to the Grandmont Order. There is a Gothic church and 17C Prior's lodging.

Château de la Motte-Glain. – The most interesting features are the gatehouse flanked by towers with pepperpot roofs and the seigneurial dwelling adorned with pointed gable dormer windows on both the courtyard and vegetable garden fronts.

Le PUY-NOTRE-DAME

Michelin map 🔢 southwest of 12 – 7 km - 4 miles west of Montreuil-Bellay – Pop 1 516

Church*. – Built in the 13C, this is a remarkable specimen of Angevin architecture. Its bell tower is adorned with a moulded bay forming a niche in which is a Virgin and Child.

The church owns a **girdle** worn by the Virgin and brought back from Jerusalem in the 12C. *To see it, apply to the nuns.*

The interior, though its plan and elevation are typical of the Poitiers region, definitely shows the Angevin style in its vaulting, especially in the chancel, which has a square east end. Behind the high altar are 16C carved stalls, and in the south transept *The Assumption* by Jean Boucher (17C).

RICHELIEU ★

Michelin map 🔢 southeast of 10 – Pop 2 529 – *Facilities p 39*

Lying on the southern limits of Touraine, bordering on Poitou, Richelieu is what La Fontaine called "the finest village in the universe". A peaceful town it comes to life on market days. This rare example of Classical town planning was the project of one man, the statesman and churchman, **Richelieu**, who was eager to lodge his court near his château which was then under construction. The building of the town itself started in 1631 at a time when Versailles was still only an idea.

Cardinal de Richelieu. – In 1621 when **Armand du Plessis** (1585-1642) bought the property of Richelieu it consisted of a village and manor on the banks of the Mable. Ten years later the estate was raised to the status of a duchy. On becoming Cardinal and First Minister of France he commissioned Jacques Le Mercier, the architect of the Sorbonne and Cardinal's Palace, now Palais-Royal in Paris, to prepare plans for a château and a wall enclosed town. Built under the supervision of the architect's brother, Pierre Le Mercier, the project was considered at the time to be a marvel of urban planning which Louis XIV was to visit at the age of twelve.

Determined not to have his creation outstripped in grandeur, Richelieu created a small principality around his masterpiece and jealously razed entirely or partially many other châteaux in the vicinity. He already owned Bois-le-Vicomte and was to add to his estates Champigny-sur-Veude, L'Ile-Bouchard, Cravant, Crissay, Mirebeau, Faye-la-Vineuse and even the royal residence of Chinon, which he was to allow to fall into disrepair. The great fortress of Loudon also suffered destruction but only after its owner, Urbain Grandier, an arch enemy of the Cardinal, had perished at the stake.

■ **SIGHTS** *time: 1 hour*

The town. – Built to a rectangular plan 700 m - 766 yd long and 500 m - 547 yd wide, the site was to be surrounded by walls and a water filled moat. The entrance gatehouses still stand rusticated, pedimented and crowned with tall typically French style roofs.

Grande-Rue. – This the main artery crosses Richelieu from end to end. In addition to the gateways note the Louis XIII style hôtels with the decorative elements in white tufa stone, especially no 17, Hôtel du Sénéchal, which has retained its elegant courtyard with busts of Roman emperors.

The Place des Religieuses is overlooked by the Académie, a college founded in 1640. On the Place du Marché opposite the Classical church is the fine 17C covered market roofed with slates. The nearby Palais de Justice now serves as town hall.

Richelieu museum. – *Installed in the town hall* (**H**). *Guided tours 1 July to 31 August from 10am to noon and 1 to 6pm; out of season from 10am to noon and 2 to 4pm; closed all Tuesdays and weekends out of season; apply at the secrétariat in the town hall; 2.50F.*

Documents and works of art pertaining to both the Richelieu family and the château are kept here.

RICHELIEU
Collège (R. du) — 2
Marché (Pl. du) — 3
Religieuses (Pl. des) — 4

Notre-Dame. – Built in the Classical or Jesuit style, this edifice in white masonry has a certain harmony and nobleness. The main façade has a series of niches containing statues of the Evangelists and the chancel is flanked by two towers surmounted with obelisks.

RICHELIEU★

The park. – *Open 10am to noon and 2 to 7pm; 6F in July, August and September; free the rest of the year.* At the southern end of the town the park, preceded by a majestic statue of Richelieu by Ramey, covers 475 ha - 1 174 acres and is crossed by a number of straight, chestnut or plane tree-lined avenues. At one time the centrepiece was a marvellous palace filled with great works of art.

Two vast courtyards surrounded by outbuildings preceded the château proper, which was protected by moats, bastions and watch towers. The entrance porch was adorned with a statue of Louis XIII and surmounted by an allegorical figure of Fame, both the works of Guillaume Berthelot. The pavilion at the far end of the château's main courtyard was originally graced by obelisks, rostral columns (in the form of ships' prows) and Michelangelo's famous group, *The Slaves*, once intended for the tomb of Pope Julius II.

(After engraving: photo Combier, Mâcon)

Château de Richelieu in the 17C

The apartments, gallery and chapel were hung with works by Poussin, Claude, Champaigne, Mantegna, Perugino, Bassano, Caravaggio, Titian, Giulio Romano, Dürer, Rubens and Van Dyck. The gardens were dotted with copies of antique statues and artificial grottoes which concealed the, then popular, water farces. It was in these gardens that the first poplar trees from Italy were planted.

The dispersal of the riches gathered here began in 1727 when the then Marshal de Richelieu, the Cardinal's great nephew, transported some back to his Parisian town house and sold others. Confiscated in 1792 the château was visited by Tallien a collector of silverware, and the Dufourni and Visconti who took all that was suitable for the Museum of French Monuments. The Revolution over, the descendants of Richelieu ceded the château to a certain Boutron who demolished it for the sale of the building materials.

Of the many splendid buildings there still exists a domed pavilion, canals and at the far end of the formal gardens two pavilions, the orangery and wine cellar. The entrance is on the D 749.

The works of art were dispersed: the Louvre has *The Slaves* by Michelangelo, Perugino's paintings and a marble table encrusted with precious stones; the series of twelve paintings depicting the victories of Louis XIII are in Versailles; the local museums in Tours and Azay-le-Ferron have several paintings and sculptures; the museum in Poitiers has Berthelot's statue of Louis XIII. The Orléans Fine Arts Museum in its Richelieu Gallery has the works of Fréminet and Deruet. The obelisks are now at Malmaison and the rostral columns in the Maritime Museum, Paris.

EXCURSIONS

Faye-la-Vineuse. – Pop 490. *7 km - 4 miles to the south by the D 749 and the D 757 to the left.*
Situated on a formerly vine covered mound overlooking a tributary of the Veude Faye, fortified in the 11C, has retained several of its 15-17C dwellings.

The **Church of St-Georges** in the Romanesque style, but unfortunately a little over restored, shows both Berry and Poitou influences. The lofty transept is roofed by a dome on pendentives and has Romanesque capitals. The transept is connected to the nave by two narrow passages known as Berrichon passages. In the nave is a curious 15C stone pulpit. The crypt *(to visit apply to the presbytery)* is of interest with its historiated capitals showing horsemen and an Adoration of the Three Kings.

Château de la Roche du Maine. – *11 km - 7 miles to the southwest by the D 749 then the D 22 to the right. Open, except on Tuesdays, from 2 to 6pm; 5F.*
The château stands on a slight eminence to the left of the road. Rebuilt during the reign of François I the château was abandoned and fell into a serious state of disrepair. This is one of the earliest examples of the Renaissance style in Poitou and it exhibits the greater concern for comfort and elegance which followed the troubled times of the Hundred Years War. Note the fine Renaissance windows with tall sculptured dormer windows and its vaulted cellar.

Bois-Aubry. – *16 km - 10 miles to the east of Richelieu.*
Isolated in the very heart of the countryside are the buildings of a Benedictine abbey founded in the 12C. *A community of Orthodox monks now occupy the premises; open daily except during services.*

The **abbey church** with its square belfry quartered by pinnacled buttresses terminates in a many sided spire. Also standing *(restoration in progress)* are the 12C chapter house with the dormitory above and the 15C guest house for important visitors and their travelling households.

Richelieu to Chinon by steam train. – *Every weekend between 14 May and 17 September with 3 departures in all; single: 18F; return 25F; children: 11F; return: 13F; time 1 hour 30 minutes. Further information from the station at Richelieu on the days of trips only Tel (47) 58 12 97.*
Stops are made at Champigny-sur-Veude, Coutureau and Ligré-Rivière.

La ROCHE-RACAN, Château de

Michelin map 🔢 4 – 2 km - 1 mile to the southeast of St-Paterne-Racan

The Château de la Roche-Racan stands perched on a rock (*roche* in French) overlooking the Escotais Valley which together with the nearby Loir, were a constant source of inspiration to the first owner and poet, **Racan** (1589-1670). Born at Champmarin near Aubigné, Honorat de Bueil, marquis de Racan, was a member of the well known local family, the Beuils *(p 163)*. Little inclined to the life of a soldier and unlucky in love, Racan retired to his country seat for the last forty years of his life, a period described in his work, *Stances sur la retraite*.

Château. – *Guided tours 5 August to 15 September from 10am to noon and 3 to 5pm; 4F.*
In 1634 Racan commissioned a local master mason, Jacques Gabriel, a member of a long established family of architects to build this château. The main building was originally flanked by two pavilions only one of which remains standing today, pedimented and adorned with a corner turret and caryatids.

Long balustraded terraces, above mask decorated arcades, overlook the park and Escotais Valley, the perfect bucolic setting for a pastoral poet.

ROMORANTIN-LANTHENAY ★

Michelin map 🔢 18 – *Local maps pp 71 and 145* – Pop 17 041 – *Facilities p 39*

This attractive town with several ancient houses, formerly the capital of the Sologne, grew up at a point where the Sauldre subdivided into several arms. Always an important Sologne market centre, various industries (electronics, refrigeration and ciné cameras) and other activities such as flour milling, sheet iron and steel plate rolling have given the town a new impetus. New suburbs have sprung up to the south of the town, while in the east a Matra plant has been producing plastic car bodies and assembling a medium range of touring cars since 1968.

The bridge affords an attractive **view** of the Sauldre itself, some mills or moulins du chapitre and the château.

Royal associations. – In the 15C Romorantin was the fief of the Valois-Angoulême *(p 17)* branch of the French royal family and it was here that François d'Angoulême, later **François I**, spent his turbulent childhood. Always a favourite place of residence with the cavalier king, in 1517 he was to prove his attachment by commissioning Leonardo da Vinci, then at Amboise *(p 41)*, to draw up plans for a palace destined for his mother Louise de Savoie. Leonardo envisaged a palace astride the Sauldre, to be built with prefabricated units, but the death of Louise put an end to the project. The genius also studied the possibility of creating a canal to link Romorantin to the Loire.

(After photo: Sologne Museum)

Romorantin
La Chancellerie, corner post

In France, the Epiphany *(la Fête des Rois)* is celebrated by eating the Twelfth cake *(la Galette des Rois)* which contains a bean. The finder of the bean is the bean king of Twelfth Night. On 6 January, Epiphany, 1521, François I led a mock attack on the Hôtel St-Pol, where a bean king reigned. The occupants of the hôtel were defending themselves by hurling snowballs, apples and eggs, when some ill advised person threw a glowing log out of a window which landed on the royal cranium. To dress the wound the doctors shaved his head; the King then grew a beard. His courtiers followed suit.

■ MAIN SIGHTS *time: ¾ hour*

Old Houses★ (Maisons anciennes - B). – The finest examples are to be found in the Rue de la Résistance. At the corner of the latter with Rue du Milieu, is La Chancellerie, a corbelled Renaissance house, of brick and half timber construction, where the royal seals were kept when the King sojourned in the town. The carved corner post portrays a coat of arms and a musician playing an instrument similar to the bagpipes. Opposite, the Hôtel St-Pol, built of stone and glazed bricks is pierced by charming windows with mouldings.

Standing where the Rue Milieu and the Rue de la Pierre meet is the charming Maison du Carroir d'Orée (archaeological museum) with its remarkable carved corner posts showing, to the left, the Annunciation and to the right St. George killing the Dragon.

Further on towards the east, along the D 724 is the Chapel St-Roch (D), a gracious building. The west front is flanked by small turrets. The semicircular windows are typical of the neo-Renaissance.

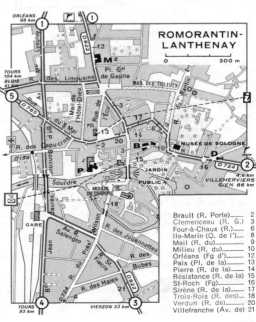

ROMORANTIN-LANTHENAY

Brault (R. Porte)	2
Clemenceau (R. G.)	3
Four-à-Chaux (R.)	6
Ile-Marin (Q. de l')	8
Mail (R. du)	9
Milieu (R. du)	10
Orléans (Fg d')	12
Paix (Pl. de la)	13
Pierre (R. de la)	14
Résistance (R. de la)	15
St-Roch (Fg)	16
Sirène (R. de la)	17
Trois-Rois (R. des)	18
Verdun (R. de)	20
Villefranche (Av. de)	21

131

Sologne Museum★ (Musée de Sologne). – *Open from 9.30 to 11.30am and from 2 to 5.30pm; closed on Tuesdays and 1 January, 1 May and 25 December; 5F.*

Installed in the town hall (**H**) the collections are well presented in a modern setting. The natural geographical region of the Sologne *(p 145)* was for a long time a closed economy with its own particular way of life. The museum presents the Sologne in all its diversity: geology, soils, vegetation, fauna, people, occupations, crafts, tools, traditions and costumes.

The Sologne has retained crafts and cottage industries such as cartwrights and coopers, itinerant woodcutters and charcoal burners and the making of sabots, fire lighters and broom handles, which are fast disappearing elsewhere. Note also the salient features of the local architecture – low timber framed buildings with brick or cob infillings sometimes thatched but more often tiled. Two interiors have been recreated: the main room of a peasants cottage and a sabot maker's workshop.

■ **ADDITIONAL SIGHTS**

Racing car museum (Musée de la course automobile – M²). – *29-31 faubourg d'Orléans. Open from 8am to noon and 2 to 6pm; Sundays from 9am to noon and 2 to 7pm; 5F.*

Various Matra cars are on display including the Formula One model which won the 1969 World Championship. A series of showcases illustrate the numerous innovations, especially technical, made in the world of Grand Prix racing. A specialist library *(free access)* covers all aspects of this sport.

Public gardens (Jardin public). – Well situated on the banks of the Sauldre.

Château royal (P). – This 15-16C building now serves as the sous-préfecture *(not open to the public).* Of this once splendid palace there remains the main residential building and a round tower flanked by a turret staircase with tall Renaissance dormer windows.

SABLÉ-SUR-SARTHE

Michelin map **64** 1 – *Local map p 139* – *Pop 11 761* – *Facilities p 39*

Situated at a point where two tributaries, the Vaige and Erve, flow into the Sarthe, Sablé is dominated by the austere façade of its château *(not open to the public),* which once belonged to the Colbert family.

Yesteryear to the present. – Originally the fief belonged to Laval-Boisdauphin, marquis de Sablé in the 17C. In 1711 Colbert de Torcy, the nephew of the great Jean Baptiste Colbert, Louis XIV's Minister, rebuilt the château and radically changed the aspect of the town: many houses and the hospital date from this period.

The town was once renowned for a black marble veined with white, which was extracted from the quarries on the north bank of the Sarthe, upstream from the town. It was much used at Versailles.

The small port on the canalized part of the Sarthe used to receive sand laden barges from the Loire.

Secondary metallurgical industries such as wire drawing, screw cutting, smelting, bolt and nut

SABLÉ SUR-SARTHE

0   300 m

Briand (R. Aristide)	2
Carnot (R.)	3

Elisé (Pl. Raphaël)	4
Grande-Rue	5
Legludic (R. Léon)	6
Mans (R. du)	7
National (Quai)	8
Primaudière (Bd de la)	9
St-Nicolas (R.)	10

works and the production of foodstuffs (milk, cheese and biscuits) are the main sources of employment today.

Public Gardens (Jardin Public). – Well situated on a hillside overlooking the Sarthe, it has many fine trees – notably cedars, umbrella pines and acacias. An elm shaded mall leads to a terrace from which there is a pleasant **view** over the valley, railway viaduct and Solesmes Abbey.

EXCURSIONS

Solesmes Abbey. – *3 km - 2 miles to the northeast by the D 138. Description p 144.*

Auvers-le-Hamon. – *Pop 935. 8.5 km - 5 miles to the north by ①, the D 24.* The church's nave is ornamented with 15-16C mural paintings depicting a series of local saints: to the right St. Mémès holding his intestines, St. Céneré as a Cardinal, St. Eutropius, St. Andrew with his cross, St. Luke riding a bull, the Nativity and the Flight into Egypt. To the left a macabre dance, St. Avertin, St. Apollonia whose teeth were pulled out by her torturers, St. James and the Sacrifice of Isaac.

These paintings have the same curious iconography as those in the church of the neighbouring town of Asnières-sur-Vègre.

La Chapelle-du-Chêne. – *6 km - 4 miles to the southeast by ④, the D 306. At Les Nœuds turn left.* The basilica is the object of pilgrimages to Notre-Dame-du-Chêne (Our Lady of the Oak), represented by a 15C terracotta statue. In the park there is a small scale model of the Holy Sepulchre and the Stations of the Cross.

Michelin map **64** 17 – *Local maps pp 70 and 71* – Pop 3 680 – *Facilities p 39*

There is a picturesque view to be seen from the bridge of this small town which rises in tiers above the Cher. The church and the château are interesting as is also the Rue Constant-Ragot which includes two old houses and affords the best glimpses of the church's chevet.

Son et Lumière *performance see p 33.*

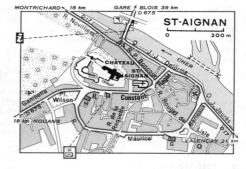

St-Aignan★. – *Time: ½ hour.* The building dates from the 11 and 12C. In the nave, which is very high, fine Romanesque capitals with interlacing adorn the pillars supporting the early Gothic style vaulting. The transept crossing is roofed with an attractive square cupola on squinches. In the chancel, which is enclosed with beautiful grilles, and in the ambulatory the capitals freely and fancifully represent human and animal subjects. This is a well known series of sculptures.

The Romanesque **crypt★** *(enter from the north transept)* has a similar plan to the chancel and is adorned with frescoes. The painting in the apsidal chapel which depicts Christ in Majesty goes back to the 12C, the others date from the 12 to the 15C.

Château. – *The interior is not open to visitors.* A monumental staircase leads to the château. You may go into the courtyard to enjoy the view from the terrace.

EXCURSION

Chémery. – *13 km - 8 miles to the northeast by the D 675 to St-Romain and then turn right.*

Manoir de Beauregard. – This 15C manor has a turret staircase and bartizans.

Chémery. – Pop 1 021. On the western limits of the Sologne in a rather desolate pool covered landscape, this village has an interesting 15-16C manor. Fortified and protected by a moat, the Renaissance doorways are surmounted by shell decorated pediments.

> *Castles, châteaux and churches will be more interesting*
> *if you read the chapter on Art and Architecture on pp 20 to 27.*

ST-BENOÎT-SUR-LOIRE ★★

Michelin map **64** 10 – 10 km - 6 miles southeast of Châteauneuf – *Local map p 101* – Pop 1 790.

The Basilica *(1)* of St-Benoit is one of the finest and most famous Romanesque buildings in France.

HISTORICAL NOTES *(2)*

Origins of the abbey (7C). – The religious role of this corner of the Loire country appeared early. In Gaulish times the Druids held a sort of council there every year. In the 7C a Benedictine abbey with the name of Fleury was built.

The founder of the Benedictine Order, St Benedict (St. Benoît), who died in the 6C, was buried in the Monastery of Monte Cassino in Italy, which he had founded. About 672 the Abbot of Fleury learned that the monastery had been destroyed by the Barbarians; St. Benedict's body and that of his sister, St. Scolastica, lay under the ruins. Distressed by this neglect he sent a few monks beyond the Alps. The bodies were exhumed and the precious relics were brought back to France. It was then that the Abbaye de Fleury took the name of St-Benoît.

The Middle Ages (beginning of 9C). – Under Charlemagne, the abbey had an exceptionally distinguished abbot in Theodulf, Bishop of Orléans *(p 83)* who founded the celebrated monastic schools of Fleury. The fame of these schools spread through all the Christian world – here was taught theology and the seven liberal arts: grammar, rhetoric, logic, arithmetic, geometry, music and astronomy. An army of copyists and illuminators piled up manuscripts. Pious writers collected histories of the saints; chroniclers told the story of their time. The abbey employed masters of agriculture, industry, art and medicine. It was a great centre of culture and civilisation.

9th and 10th centuries. – The day of the Norman invasions dawned. When the Barbarians were reported approaching, the monks and their pupils took flight, carefully carrying the relics of their sainted patron. Orléans received them within its walls. When the pirates were gone they returned to their devastated home and repaired the damage as they waited for the next attack.

Monastic discipline suffered under this régime. But in the 10C strict and pious abbots restored the Rule in all its rigour: rising at 2am, work between the services, total abstention from meat, corporal chastisement, etc. St-Benoît once more became prosperous. Pupils flocked to it again. The kings of France and great personages came to it often and loaded it with gifts. The opening of the 11C was marked by the building of a tower (the belfry porch) designed by Abbot Gauzlin, a future Archbishop of Bourges. The present church (crypt, chancel and transept) was built from 1067 to 1108. The nave was completed only at the end of the 12C.

---

(1) A basilica is not a cathedral: the bishop does not preside there. The name is an honorary title given to a church for its importance or its relics.

(2) For further information, in English, read St. Benoît-sur-Loire *by J. M. Berland (Collection Art et Tourisme).*

ST-BENOÎT-SUR-LOIRE★★

Modern times. – St-Benoît passed *in commendam* in the 15C, when the revenues of the abbey were granted by the kings to "commendatory abbots", often laymen, who were simply beneficiaries and took no active part in the religious life of the community.

The monks did not always make them welcome. Under François I they refused to receive Cardinal Duprat and shut themselves up in the tower of the porch. The King had to come in person, at the head of an armed force, to make them submit.

During the Wars of Religion (1562-1598) one of these abbots, Odet de Châtillon-Coligny, the brother of the Protestant leader Admiral Coligny, was himself converted to Protestantism. He had St-Benoît looted by Condé's Huguenot troops. The treasure was melted down – the gold casket containing the relics of the Saint alone weighed 17.5 kg - 39 lb – the marvellous library was sold and its precious manuscripts, about 2000 in number, were scattered to the four corners of Europe. Some are now to be found in Berne, Rome, Leyden, Oxford and Moscow.

The celebrated Congregation of St-Maur, introduced to St-Benoît in 1627 by Cardinal Richelieu, restored its spiritual and intellectual life. The abbey was closed at the Revolution, its archives transferred to Orléans and its property dispersed. At the beginning of the First Empire the monastic buildings were destroyed *(1)* and the church fell into disrepair. In 1835 it was registered as an historical monument, and it was restored on various occasions between 1836 and 1923. Monastic life was revived there in 1944.

The poet and artist Max Jacob (1876-1944) retired to the abbey in St-Benoît-sur-Loire, before he was arrested in 1944.

■ THE BASILICA★★ *time: ¾ hour*

Individuals may hire audio guides, apply at the Benedictine bookstall, to the right of the porch from Easter to 1 November 9 to 11am and 3 to 5pm; for groups of more than 10 people guides are provided, apply in writing to the Frère chargé des visites, abbaye de St-Benoît-sur-Loire, 45110 Châteauneuf. The public is allowed to follow services (Gregorian Chant): Conventual Mass at noon (11am on Sundays and holidays), Vespers at 6.15pm.

This imposing edifice was built between 1067 and 1218. The towers were originally much taller.

Belfry Porch★★★. – The belfry originally stood by itself, and is one of the finest examples of Romanesque art. The richly carved capitals are particularly worthy of attention. The tourist can pick out for himself in the beautiful golden stone brought from Nivernais the delicately carved abaci and corbels. Stylised plants and, particularly, flowing acanthus leaves alternate with fantastic animals, scenes from the Apocalypse, and events in the life of Christ and the Virgin Mary. On the porch (second column from the left), one of the capitals is signed *Umbertus me fecit.*

(After photo: Éd. du Zodiaque)

The Basilica

North Doorway. – *Groups only.* This was executed at the beginning of the 13C and mutilated during the Reformation. It is one of the last examples of doorways with statue columns in the manner of Chartres.

Nave. – This was begun in the mid 12C. The central quadripartite vaulting was finished in 1218.

Transept. – Like the chancel, this was finished in 1108. The dome, built on superimposed squinches, carries the central bell tower. Under the dome are the stalls dated 1413, and the remains of a choir screen in carved wood presented in 1635 by Richelieu, when he was Commendatory Abbot of St-Benoît.

In the north transept is the precious 14C alabaster statue of Notre-Dame-de-Fleury. A plaque on the right recalls that the poet Max Jacob lies in the village cemetery.

Chancel★★. – This was built from 1065 to 1108 and is one of the most graceful specimens of Romanesque art. Note the apse and its small transept, the colonnade, the blind arcade with fifty-eight colonnettes and the fifteen clerestory windows.

The floor is paved with a Roman mosaic brought from Italy in 1531. The recumbent figure is that of Philippe I, the fourth Capet King, who died in 1108.

Crypt★. – An impressive masterpiece of the second half of the 11C, it was restored in the 19C, but has kept its original appearance. Its centre is formed by a large pillar containing the tomb of St. Benedict, whose relics have been venerated here since the 8C.

---

(1) Only a small façade, belonging to the former students' chapel, remains. It is in the village on the Place de l'Université, opposite the war memorial.

*The **Michelin Map series** at a scale of 1:200000*
(1cm:2km) covers the whole of France. For the
maps to use with this guide see page three.
You may pick out at a glance
> *the motorways and major roads for a quick journey*
> *the secondary or alternative roads for a traffic free run*
> *the country lanes for a leisurely drive*
These maps are a must for your holidays.

ST-CALAIS

Michelin map 64 5 – Pop 4 577 – *Facilities p 39*

St-Calais, an agricultural market town on the northwestern limits of the Vendômois, is dominated by the ruins of a feudal fortress. The narrow streets are occasionally bordered by old gabled dwellings.

Situated astride the Anille, five bridges connect the main thoroughfares on either bank. The western part of the town grew up under the St-Calais Benedictine Abbey founded by Calais, a cœnobite monk from Auvergne, during the reign of Childebert in the 6C. The monastery was destroyed during the Revolution, and those buildings that survived now serve as town hall, theatre and museum.

ST-CALAIS

Coursimault (R.)	2
Dauphin (R. du)	3
Dr-Olivier (R. du)	4
Gare (Av. de la)	5
Gautray (R. du)	6
Guichet (R. du)	7
Image (R. de l')	8
Mans (R. du)	9
Maubert (R. Henri)	10
Sadi-Carnot (R.)	12

Every year since 1581 the town has celebrated its patron saint's day, to commemorate the end of the Plague *(first Saturday and Sunday in September)*.

■ **SIGHTS** time: ½ hour

Notre-Dame. – *To visit apply to the priest.* The building of this church was begun in 1425 with the chancel, and it is partly Flamboyant and partly Renaissance. The bell tower is surmounted by a stone steeple.

Finished in 1549 the Italian **façade★**, typical of the second Renaissance, is particularly remarkable for its rhythm and sculptured decoration. The carved panels of the twin doors portray scenes from the life of the Virgin with above two cornucopias framed in the semi-circular arch. The whole is framed by Ionic pilasters. The charming side doorways are surmounted by curvilinear pediments and niches. A window with a pediment and occuli open on to the upper part of the gable.

The first three Renaissance bays have vaulting resting on pendentives and conical capitals in turn, the whole supported by majestic columns. The 17C organ loft originally came from the abbey and has an organ case of the same period. A Baroque style retable adorns the high altar; a stout cupboard to the right of the chancel contains the shroud of St. Calais made of Sassanian or 6C Persian material.

Quais de l'Anille. – This tree lined way offers attractive views of the riverside wash houses now disused and moss covered, and colourful gardens backed by a picturesque jumble of roof tops.

Château. – Founded on a mound in the 11C, only parts of the ramparts and a ruined tower remain standing. There is a **view** of the Anille Valley, the church tower, and rooftops of St-Calais.

(After photo: Artaud, Nantes)

Notre-Dame Church — Main doorway

EXCURSION

St-Gervais-de-Vic. – *Pop 478. 4 km - 2½ miles to the south by the D 303.* Lying in the Anille Valley this hamlet has a 15-16C church with a painting of Louis XIII by Vœu. *The church key is obtainable from M. Daumas at the café, Place de l'église.*

ST-GEORGES-SUR-LOIRE

Michelin map 63 19, 20 – *Local map p 104* – Pop 2 330

St Georges on the north bank of the Loire is situated not far from a famous vineyard, *La Coulée de Serrant*, where some of Anjou's finest white wines are produced.

Former priory. – The village developed round a priory founded in 1158 under the auspices of the Augustinian Order. Only a few buildings remain to remind us of this former establishment. One dating from 1684 houses both the town hall and the presbytery. Note the monumental staircase with its remarkable wrought iron railings, and the wainscoted chapter house.

EXCURSIONS

Château de Serrant★. – *2 km - 1 mile by N 23 in the direction of Angers. Description p 144.*

Épinay Priory (Prieuré de l'Épinay). – *3.5 km - 2 miles to the southwest by the road leading to La Villette, then turn right after passing under the railway.*

Isolated in pleasant countryside the 15-17C priory still retains the Prior's lodging, the chapel, a dovecote and numerous outbuildings. *Not open to the public.*

The monks were involved in a litigious case against the monks of St-Georges-sur-Loire and it was this that inspired Racine to write *Les Plaideurs.*

ST-PATERNE-RACAN

Michelin map 👤 4 – Pop 1 718 – *Facilities p 39*

St- Paterne stretches out along the Escotais, which is bordered by riverside wash houses and weeping willows.

Church. – The church contains interesting works of art, some of which came from the nearby Abbey of La Clarté-Dieu. The 16C terracotta group to the left of the high altar portrays the Adoration of the Magi and in the centre is a charming **Virgin and Child***.

In the nave, 18C polychrome statues represent the four great Latin Doctors of the Church – Ambrose, Augustine, Jerome and Gregory the Great – while in the south chapel a large retable (the Virgin of the Rosary) of the same period is accompanied by a 16C terracotta group of St. Anne and the Virgin.

EXCURSIONS

Valley of La Clarté-Dieu*. – *3.5 km - 2 miles to the west by the D 6 going towards St-Christophe-sur-le-Nais, before turning left on to the D 54. After 1 km - ½ mile turn right.* Follow the winding, lonely Valley of La Clarté-Dieu with its rocky slopes pitted with caves.

Dark patches of oak and fir forests mark the valley slopes while on the valley floor numerous pools are choked with reeds, rushes and water lilys. Appearing at various intervals are sawmills and 16-17C manor houses.

The remains of the Cistercian **Clarté-Dieu Abbey** stand in an attractive site. At the roadside are a chapel and, on the far bank of the river, the lay members' building with an external staircase leading to the dormitory and the pedimented abbatial palace (1713).

Château de la Roche-Racan. – *2 km - 1 mile to the south by the D 28. Description p 131.*

St-Christophe-sur-le-Nais. – Pop 932. *2.5 km - 1½ miles to the north by the D 6.*

Also in the Escotais Valley this village is the scene of a car rally pilgrimage to St. Christopher, the patron saint of wayfarers and motorists today *(second last Sunday in July).* The **church** is in reality composed of two separate buildings, a former 11-14C priory chapel and the parish church with its 16C nave and belfry.

At the threshold to the nave a gigantic St. Christopher welcomes the visitor. To the right in a recess is a reliquary bust of the Saint.

To the left of the chancel, the door leading to the Prior's oratory is surmounted by a fine 14C statue of the Virgin and Child. Two curious terracottd medallions decorate the church's wooden roof.

Neuvy-le-Roi. – Pop 1 084. *9 km - 6 miles to the east by the D 54.* The church *(closed on Saturdays and Sunday afternoons)* dating from the 12 and 16C has a Romanesque chancel with an elegant seigneurial chapel to the right, and a nave covered with Angevin vaulting. A bas-relief in alabaster depicts the Holy Trinity.

Neuillé-Pont-Pierre. – Pop 1 365. *10 km - 6 miles to the south by the D 28.* The church *(closed on Sunday afternoons)* with its Renaissance façade has a fine white marble 14C statue of the Virgin and Child and a 16C lectern.

STE-CATHERINE-DE-FIERBOIS

Michelin map 👤 southwest 15 – Pop 529 – *Facilities p 39*

This village has many associations with Joan of Arc. Grouped round its church with its tapering steeple, the latter acts as a landmark from afar.

Church. – Following directions given by Joan of Arc on 23 April 1428, a sword marked with five crosses was found here. It was said to have been placed there by Charles Martel after his victory against the Saracens at Poitiers (732).

Rebuilt in 1479 and finished during Charles VIII's reign, the building is emblazoned with the coats of arms of Charles and Anne of Brittany. Restored in 1859 this Flamboyant edifice dominated by its 41 m - 135 ft tall spire, has an interestingly sculptured doorway with pierced tympanum.

Inside the barrel vaulting springs directly from the piers. The north aisle has a small but very realistic 15C Entombment. The south transept contains a 15C altar surmounted by a statue of St. Catherine, whose image is also portrayed on the front of the altar. Opposite is an unusual Flamboyant style confession box, very delicately carved.

Maison du Dauphin (1415). – This, the so called Dauphin's House, has a gracious doorway and sculptured well wall in the courtyard.

STE-MAURE-DE-TOURAINE

Michelin map 👤 north of 4, 5 – Pop 4 016 – *Facilities p 39*

This pleasant small town occupies a sunny site on a knoll commanding the Manse Valley and the Paris to Bordeaux road. Roman in origin, the settlement developed in the 6C round the tombs of St. Bridget and St. Maure, then round Foulques Nerra's keep. The Rohan-Montbazon family were the overlords from 1492 to the Revolution. The town is known for its busy poultry markets and its local goats' milk cheeses.

Church. – *When closed apply at the presbytery.* Dating back to the 11C, the original appearance was altered by a restoration in 1866. A chapel to the right of the chancel has an attractive 16C white marble Virgin by the Italian school while in the north aisle the small late 16C painted panel representing the Last Supper is by the Dutch school. The crypt has a curious series of archaic Romanesque arcades and a small lapidary museum.

Covered market. – Standing well above the town, the 17C covered market was built by the Rohan family. The aisles are still used for the weekly markets while the central or main aisle has been restored and serves as the village hall. The inscriptions and armorial bearings were destroyed during the Revolution.

THE STE-MAURE PLATEAU

Round tour of 61 km – 38 miles – about 1 hour – Local map below

Dissected by the green valleys of the the Manse and Esves, bounded by the Indre, Creuse and Vienne this plateau is composed of lacustrine limestones, easily eroded by running water. The plateau ends in the south with marl pits, bands of sand and shells, deposited during the

Tertiary era by the Falun Sea. This rich mixture was formerly much used in the improvement of the soil. Wheat is the primary crop with maize or fodder crops as the main alternatives, all interspersed with occasional fruit trees. Stock raising is increasing in popularity and cattle are to be found alongside the traditional goats, pigs, geese and famous small hen, the *géline noire de Touraine*. The folklore traditions of Touraine have been fiercely preserved by the local people.

Leave Ste-Maure to the southeast by the D 59 taking the itinerary shown on the above map. The itinerary follows the deep, winding small valleys often marked out by poplars with the limestone evident along the sides. There are numerous good viewpoints.

Bournan. – Pop 249. The Romanesque church has a fine apse with a tower rising above the side chapel, terminated by a many sided spire.

Château de Bagneux. – Built in the 15C the château commands the confluence of two valleys. The building comprises four round towers two of which are superbly battlemented.

Ligueil. – Pop 2 436. This small white stone town with several old houses has an important creamery and its markets are lively affairs attracting large crowds.

Esves-le-Moutier. – Pop 176. In a pleasantly green site on the banks of the Esves, this village takes its name from a wall encircled priory. The 10-12C church's square tower is flanked by bartizans.

Château de Grillemont. – This great white château stands midway up the slope of a small **valley**★ whose crests are crowned with pines and oaks. During the reign of Charles VII it was equipped with large round towers with pepperpot roofs. In 1765 the 15C curtain walls were replaced by majestic Classical buildings.

SANCERRE ★

Michelin map 🖽 12 – Pop 2 542

Sancerre is perched on a hillock on the west bank of the Loire, overlooking the villages of St-Satur and St-Thibault. From this **elevation**★ there is a wide panorama over the river and the Nivernais region to the east, and Berry to the west. The little town, with its narrow winding streets has considerable character.

As the chief town of a region famous for its vineyards and goats, Sancerre is well known for its delicious white wine with a gunflint flavour *(pierre à fusil)* and its little round cheeses made from goats' milk, bearing the unexpected name of *crottins* (goat droppings) and made at Chavignol.

Sancerre, the stronghold. – Sancerre, because of its strategic position, and as the key to the Berry region, played an important part in the Hundred Years War, opposing both the Burgundians and the English. It was here that Charles VII, King of Bourges amassed an army of 20 000 soldiers which he commanded in person for some time.

In 1534 Sancerre adopted Protestantism and became a Protestant citadel and the butt for the unavailing attacks of the Royal forces. The Treaty of St-Germain in 1570 and the Massacre of St. Bartholomew in 1572 in no way affected those adhering to the "so called Reformed religion" who continued their unrest, with the result that on 3 January 1573, Marshal de la Châtre with 7 000 men laid siege to the town. After an intense period of preparatory artillery fire, the assault was launched by means of three gaps in the walls, but the people of Sancerre maintained their ground. Then La Châtre decided to starve them out by imposing a rigorous blockade. The besieged reduced to the most dire famine, were forced to eat powdered slates and all the leather and skins that the town could provide. Only after seven months of resistance did the town give in. They were awarded military honours along with the freedom to practise their chosen religion.

The wine of Sancerre. – "Wine", wrote Balzac in 1844 in the *Muse du Département*, "is the principal activity and provides the chief source of business for a countryside that has several generous vintages, with full bouquets; it is like enough to the wines of Burgundy to deceive the vulgar palates in Paris. Thus the wine of Sancerre is much drunk in the Parisian cabarets, which after all is only right with wines that cannot be kept for more than seven or eight years." Vineyards are found on all slopes exposed to the sun. The "regional" name Sancerre is reserved for white wines from the *Sauvignon* vine as well as the red and rosé wines of the *Pineau* variety.

■ **SIGHTS** *time: 1 hour*

Old town. – Stroll through the old quarter with its narrow streets and note the gables, doorways, turrets and sculptured decoration. Plaques indicate the interesting houses and other points of interest.

Tour des Fiefs. – This late 14C round keep is all that remains of the castle of the counts of Sancerre, a Huguenot fortress which was fiercely defended during the siege of 1573. *The tower is open 1 March to 31 October on Sundays and holidays from 2 to 6pm.*

From the top there is a vast **panorama**★ over the Loire Valley and the Sancerre Hills.

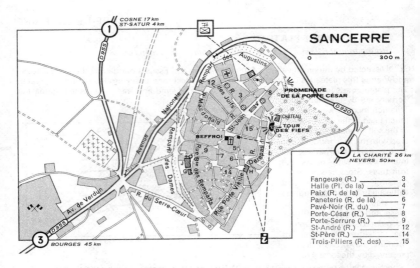

Promenade de la porte César. – This affords a good view of the vineyards, St-Satur with its viaduct, St-Thibault and the Loire Valley and the Morvan foothills on the horizon.

Belfry (Beffroi). – Dating from 1509 this former alarm tower now serves as the belfry to Notre-Dame de Sancerre.

EXCURSIONS

St-Satur. – Pop 1 777. *4 km - 2½ miles by* ①, *the D 955*. Only the chancel and apse were completed of the abbey church begun by the Augustinian Canons in 1362. The vaulting was rebuilt in the 17C.

Château de la Grange. – *10 km - 6 miles by* ②, *the D 920*. This two storeyed building with its series of tall windows was built in the reign of Henri IV. The central part is topped by a curious many sided dome. The pedimented façade overlooking the main courtyard is decorated with an attractive pattern created by alternating stone and brick.

Léré. – Pop 880. *Facilities p 38. 20 km - 12 miles by* ①, *and the D 955 and D 751*. The Collegiate Church of St-Martin with its Romanesque nave and 15C chancel has a lectern and 16C statues. The crypt is 9C.

Chavignol. – *3 km - 2 miles by* ①, *the D 955. At Fontenay turn left into the D 183*. This picturesque wine growers' village has given its name to one of the best known wines of the Sancerre vineyards and also to a goats' milk cheese.

The Sancerrois. – *Round tour of 79 km - 49 miles – about 2 hours – Local map below*. Leave Sancerre by ③, *the D 955*. The road affords far reaching views to the south of a hedge compartment, undulating countryside dotted with elms and chestnuts. Flocks of sheep and goats pasture round isolated farmsteads.

After 16 km - 10 miles take the D 44 to the right in the direction of La Borne. Following the crest this road passes the **Motte d'Humbligny** (altitude 431 m - 1414 ft), the highest point in the Sancerre Hills. Further on to the right can be seen the mast of the Bourges-Neuvy-deux-Clochers television relay station. La Borne is the next village.

La Borne. – Pop 200. In this small village, lost amidst the woods, are pottery workshops which have gradually been replaced by other craft industries. The local clays have been exploited for over 300 years. *An exhibition in the school presents the locally produced pottery, during school holidays from 3 to 7pm; the rest of the year on Sundays and public holidays only at the aforementioned times.*

Henrichemont. – Pop 1 894. In the early 17C Sully, Minister to Henri IV, was eager to create a small principality in Berry where he and his fellow Huguenots could take refuge. Although he already owned the Château de Béthune at nearby La Chapelle d'Angillon *(p 62)* he decided to build in a deserted sandy spot. Although never completed it was Sully himself who supervised the construction. The plan provided for eight streets all converging on a vast central square. A well and some of the 17C houses still exist.

On reaching Villegenon take the D 926 which offers attractive views of the Sauldre Basin. At **Vailly-sur-Sauldre** (pop 749), in its riverside site, take the D 923 towards the south and then the D 74 which overlooks the Sauldre Valley.

Jars. – Pop 552. This charming village is dominated by a round tower flanked manor house. The 15-16C red sandstone and white limestone church is preceded by a belfry porch. The nave has lierne and tierceron vaulting. From behind the church there is a fine view of the Sancerre countryside.

Château de Boucard. – *Open 1 February to 31 October from 10am to noon and from 2 to 7pm; 6pm the rest of the year; 7F.* This 15-16C château has been restored and contains 17C furniture.

At Sens-Beaujeu take the D 7. Just before the junction with the D 923 there is a remarkable **view*** to the right of the village of Bué and the Sancerre Hills. At the road junction itself the admirable **view**** is of Sancerre, the vineyards, St-Satur and the Loire Valley beyond.

SARTHE Valley

Michelin map **64** 1 to 3

A northern tributary of the Loire, the Sarthe flows slowly across the rich smiling countryside of the Angevin Maine, meandering on the floor of the spacious valley carved out of the soft Upper Cretaceous rocks. In the vicinity of Sablé the river has forced a way across a granite outcrop.

Navigable up to Le Mans, the Sarthe is paralleled in places by canals. Woodlands and prairies alternate with light agricultural soils, on which are cultivated cereals, potatoes and cabbages.

From Le Mans to Sablé – *70 km - 44 miles – about 2½ hours – Local map below*

Leave Le Mans (p 108) by ⑦, then the D 147ᴱ and finally the D 51 to the left.

Fillé. – Pop 617. The village church, rebuilt since 1944, has a late 16C, varnished terracotta statue of the Virgin.

Continuing on the north bank with the D 51, pass through Roëze-sur-Sarthe to reach La Suze.

La Suze-sur-Sarthe. – Pop 3 606. *Facilities p 39.* The bridge affords a fine glimpse of the Sarthe, the remains of the 15C château and the church.

Once on the south bank follow the D 79 across woodland towards Fercé. Just before reaching the river turn left into a local road, the V 5 towards St-Jean-du-Bois. Turn right on to the D 229, passing a Troubadour style castle and offering good views of the Sarthe, before reaching Noyen.

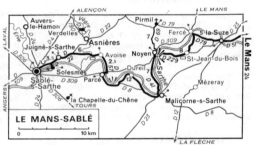

LE MANS-SABLÉ
0   10 km

Noyen-sur-Sarthe. – Pop 2 023. Noyen rises in tiers above the north bank of the wide Sarthe, which is doubled at this point by a canal. From the bridge there is an attractive **view** of a barrage, mill, midstream island and the jumble of gardens and rooftops.

Pirmil. – Pop 474. *7 km - 4 miles from Noyen by the D 69.* The buttressed Romanesque church dates from 1165. The finely sculptured capitals represent floral motifs. The springers of the **Angevin vaulting** portray a series of statues, namely St. Stephen, St. Michael, a bishop, a priest and a grotesque head.

Malicorne-sur-Sarthe. – Pop 1 733. *Facilities p 38.* Set in a pleasant riverside site, Malicorne's bridge offers attractive views of the mill and poplar planted banks. **Potters** still produce rustic faience ware and specialise, in particular, in reproductions of period pieces. *Guided tours of the workshops: Easter to 15 September, on weekdays from 8am to noon and from 2 to 6pm; Sundays and holidays from 2.30 to 6pm; 1 October to Easter on weekdays only from 8am to noon and from 1.30 to 5.30pm; closed on Mondays, 1 January, 1 and 11 November and 25 December; time: ¾ hour; 5F; free on Sundays.*

The 11C **church** contains some interesting works of art: recumbent figure, *Pietà* and 16C piscina.

Downstream and standing a little way back from the river in a fine park is a restored 17C **château** with small turrets and mansard roofs, encircled by moats, crossed by a charming 17C hump backed bridge. The famous 17C woman of letters, Mme de Sévigné often came here to see her friend, the marquise de Lavardin.

Between Malicorne and Parcé the itinerary follows the wooded south bank giving occasional glimpses of the Sarthe.

Parcé-sur-Sarthe. – Pop 1 190. The village is grouped round its Romanesque belfry. At one end of the settlement the cypress shaded cemetery is the setting for a chapel surmounted by that unusual architectural feature, a bell gable.

Cross to the north bank and after the canal turn left into the D 57.

Beyond Avoise take a road to the left passing in front of a manor house with its farm buildings before crossing the Vègre, and coming to the D 22 which leads to Juigné.

Juigné-sur-Sarthe. – Pop 837. This pleasant village, situated on a promontory jutting across the valley, has several 16 and 17C houses and an 18C château, the seat of the marquis de Juigné. From the church square there are plunging views of the Sarthe and the great mass of the Abbey of Solesmes.

Solesmes. – *Description p 144.*

Continue along the D 22, which follows the canal and passes former marble quarries, to reach Sablé-sur-Sarthe *(p 132).*

SAULGES

Michelin map 60 south of 11 – Pop 420

This peaceful village overlooks the Erve Valley.

Caves. – *To visit apply to the restaurant near the Grotte à Margot (8am to sunset); time: allow ½ hour per cave or 1¼ hours for both; 6F.*

The Saulges caves are in an attractive site to the north of the village of the same name. They have interesting geological formations and have provided varied evidence of early human habitation such as bones and flint tools.

Grotte de Rochefort. – On the north bank, this cave is cut out of dark coloured rocks. A passageway and steep ladder lead to a small underground lake situated at river level.

Grotte à Margot. – This cave is interesting for its narrowness, fissures and erosional phenomena.

St-Céneré-Oratory. – *1 km - ½ mile.* On leaving Saulges in the direction of Vaiges, after the bridge, follow to the left a gently rising road which leads to a car park. Take the footbridge across the river to reach the hermitage, pleasantly surrounded by trees, at the foot of rocks.

SAUMUR ★★

Michelin map 64 12 – *Local map p 103* – Pop 23 601 – *Facilities p 39*

Saumur is famous for its cavalry school, its wines, especially *mousseux* or sparkling wines and its mushrooms. The region's production of the latter represents 70 per cent of the national figure. The traditional local industry, the making of religious medals and chapelets dates from the 17C. Recent additions to the industrial sector include toymaking, hosiery, and mechanical and electrical firms. Saumur also has Europe's most important carnival mask factory.

HISTORICAL NOTES

Saumur was a bone of contention between the counts of Anjou and the counts of Blois and was sacked by the Normans. It became Crown property under Philippe-Auguste.

The town enjoyed its zenith at the end of the 16C and in the 17C. It was one of the great centres of Protestantism. Henri III gave it to the King of Navarre as a stronghold. The future Henri IV installed there as Governor one Duplessis-Mornay, a great soldier, a great scholar and a fervent Reformer. The Catholics called him "the Pope of the Huguenots"; in the town he founded a Protestant academy, which acquired great fame. The Revocation of the Edict of Nantes (1685), depriving French Protestants of their religious and civil liberties, was a great blow to Saumur. Many of the inhabitants emigrated.

In 1940 the town was badly damaged, when the cavalry school made an heroic three day stand against superior German forces.

■ MAIN SIGHTS *time: 2½ hours*

Pont Cessart. – Good **view**★ of the town and the Loire.

Notre-Dame-de-Nantilly★. – A fine Romanesque building. Louis XI, who was greatly devoted to Our Lady, added the south aisle. His oratory is now the baptismal chapel.

In the same aisle, on a pillar on the left, is an epitaph composed by King René of Anjou for his nurse, Tiphaine. Opposite is the enamelled copper crosier of Gilles, Archbishop of Tyre, Keeper of the Seals to St. Louis.

The wooden statue of Notre-Dame de Nantilly (12C) stands in the small apse to the right of the chancel.

Fine **tapestries**★★ adorn the church. These date from the 15 and 16C, except for eight pieces, made at Aubusson in the 17C, representing the life of Christ. Note the *Tree of Jesse* (left arm of the transept).

The collection of eighteen capitals is extremely interesting.

Château★★. – *Open 1 July to 31 August from 9am to 7pm and 8.30 to 10.30pm till 15 September; 1 April to 30 June and 1 September to 31 October from 9 to 11.45am and from 2 to 6pm; 2 November to 31 March, from 10 to 11.45am and from 2 to 5pm (closed on Tuesdays). Closed on 1 January, 1 November and 25 December; 7F; (museums and the historical presentation are included).*

(After photo: Yvon)

Château de Saumur

Several fortresses succeeded one another on this sheer promontory. The present building was erected at the end of the 14C by Louis I, Duke of Anjou, and finished by Louis II. The interior was re-modelled in the 15C by René of Anjou and fortified at the end of the 16C by Duplessis-Mornay *(see above)*. It was the residence of the Governor of Saumur under Louis XIV and Louis XV, became a prison and then a barracks, and today houses two museums.

From the Guet Tower, there is a beautiful **panorama**★ of the town and the valleys of the Thouet and the Loire.

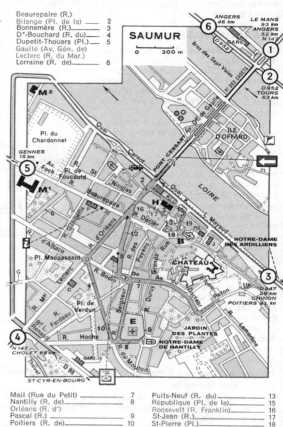

Museum of Decorative Arts★★ (Musée d'Arts décoratifs). − *Open during the normal visiting hours for the castle and evenings from 8.30 to 10.30, from 1 July to 15 September; also on Whitsun and Easter weekends and Mondays.*

Formed partly from the Lair Collection, this museum shows fine specimens of mediaeval and Renaissance work: Limoges enamels, sculptures in wood and alabaster, tapestries, furniture, paintings, church ornaments and a large collection of pottery and French porcelain of the 17 and 18C, together with furniture and tapestries of the same period.

Among the 15 and 16C tapestries note the series entitled *The History of Titus* and in particular the *Coronation of the Emperor Vespasianus* and the *Capture of Jerusalem.*

Equine Museum★ (Musée du Cheval). − The museum depicts the history of the horse throughout the ages and in all countries. Note especially the collection of saddles, bridle bits, stirrups and spurs and the series of fine engravings by George Stubbs.

Return to the town, following the itinerary shown on the plan; go to the Hôtel de Ville.

Hôtel de Ville★. − Only the left part is old (16C). The building used to be washed by the Loire and was part of the town wall, forming a bridgehead; this explains its military appearance. Seen from the courtyard the building is not at all warlike. Its architecture is Renaissance.

From Place de la République the Rue de la Tonnelle leads you to the Church of St-Pierre.

St-Pierre. − A partly 12C Romanesque building. The west front collapsed but was rebuilt in the 17C. Enter by the fine Romanesque door *(illustration*

Beaurepaire (R.)
Bilange (Pl. de la) ──── 2
Bonnemère (R.) ──────── 3
Dᵣ-Bouchard (R. du) ──── 4
Dupetit-Thouars (Pl.) ── 5
Gaulle (Av. Gén. de)
Leclerc (R. du Mar.)
Lorraine (R. de) ──────── 6

Mail (Rue du Petit) ─────── 7
Nantilly (R. de) ─────────── 8
Orléans (R. d')
Pascal (R.) ───────────────── 9
Poitiers (R. de) ──────────── 10
Portail-Louis (R. du) ────── 12

Puits-Neuf (R. du) ──────── 13
République (Pl. de la) ──── 15
Roosevelt (R. Franklin) ── 16
St-Jean (R.) ─────────────── 17
St-Pierre (Pl.) ──────────── 18
Tonnelle (R. de la) ──────── 19

p 20) in the south transept. You will see 15C stalls and two sets of **tapestries**★ of the 16C, one representing the life of St. Peter, the other the life of St. Florentius.

■ ADDITIONAL SIGHTS

Cavalry and Armoured Corps Academy (École d'application de l'Arme blindée de la Cavalerie). − It was in 1763 that the Carabiniers Regiment, a crack corps recruited from the best horsemen in the army, was stationed in Saumur and to garrison the regiment the central range was built from 1767 to 1770. It now serves as headquarters for the Cavalry Academy which trains the élite of the French cavalry, both mounted and armoured.

In 1972 the **National Riding School** was created with the aim of training civilian riding instructors. The famous **Cadre Noir** belongs to this school. The school has modern premises at St-Hilaire-St-Florent outside Saumur and in addition occupies some of the buildings overlooking the Place du Chardonnet.

The Place du Chardonnet is the venue for the very popular annual displays *(p 32)* by the Cadre Noir and both the mounted and armoured corps.

Cavalry Museum★ (M¹). − *Enter from Avenue Foch. Guided tours from 2 to 5pm; closed on Mondays, Fridays, Saturday mornings, holidays and during August.*

There is a large collection of souvenirs, which tells the history of the Cavalry Academy and the armoured corps since the 18C. Among the objects shown are elegant swords encrusted with mother of pearl, ebony or shell; sabres belonging to Egyptian mamelukes; military equipment belonging to famous field marshals and generals of the Empire. The uniforms of Napoleon's Army and the Garde Impériale are evoked by a collection of porcelain figures from Sèvres and Meissen. There are also Dragoon and Hussar helmets and breastplates.

Finally the history of the French cavalry is portrayed from 1870 through the two world wars and the Indo-Chinese and Algerian campaigns.

Museum of Armoured Cavalry (Musée des Blindés − M²). − *At the north end of Place du Chardonnet. Open from 9 to 11.30am and from 2 to 5.30pm; 5F.*

There are some 150 armoured vehicles showing the evolution of the armoured corps since 1918. The hall to the left is devoted to French equipment including the Renault tank of 1918. The hall to the right contains foreign equipment: Soviet T34s, several German "Panthers" and the imposing British "Conqueror".

SAUMUR★★

Notre-Dame-des-Ardilliers. – *Access by the Quai L-Mayaud.* This 17C building was finished by Mme de Montespan, who often stayed at Saumur on her way to see her sister the Abbess of Fontevraud.

Hospices "Jeanne Delanoue" (E). – *Apply to the Director of the Hospices.* It dates from the 18C. There are fine 17C Aubusson tapestries in the board room of the governing committee. Admirers of Philippe de Champaigne will find a picture by this 17C painter in the chapel.

Jardin des Plantes. – This garden is laid out in terraces. From the upper terrace there is a pretty view of the town.

EXCURSIONS

Château de Boumois★. – *7 km - 4 miles to the northwest by ⑥, the D 952 and then the first road on the right.*

Boumois Château lies hidden in the trees, 300 m - 328 yd from the D 952. Built at the beginning of the 16C it has a double aspect: the feudal exterior hides an inner dwelling house of graceful Flamboyant and Renaissance styles.

Guided tours from 10am to noon and 2 to 6pm; closed on Tuesdays except in July and August and from 15 November to 15 March; time: 30 mins; 9F.

The drive leads to the main entrance, on the left of which stands a dovecote. A moat and fortified perimeter wall protect the seigneurial courtyard which is reached by a massive doorway.

The main building, which was built at the end of the 15C, is flanked on the left by two great machicolated towers. A turret staircase leads to the living quarters, and this is closed by a door embellished with an extraordinary wrought iron lock and detailed Renaissance motifs. The visitor may go through the guard-room and along the parapet walk. There is a beautiful Flamboyant chapel with a pointed roof. The dovecote still has its revolving ladder for collecting the eggs.

(After photo: Karquel)

Château de Boumois

Aristide Dupetit-Thouars was born at Boumois in 1760. He died gloriously on the quarterdeck of his ship, the *Tonnant*, in the Battle of Aboukir in 1798 rather than haul down his flag.

Dolmen de Bagneux; Artannes-sur-Thouet. – *Round tour of 18 km - 11 miles – about 1 hour. Leave Saumur by ④, the N 147.*

> **Bagneux Dolmen.** – The great dolmen, or prehistoric tomb, is to be found in the town of Bagneux, near the café restaurant du Dolmen *(apply at the café).* This is Anjou's most important megalithic monument: 20 m long by 7 m wide it is really a covered gallery grave or long rectangular burial chamber with thirteen upright stones supporting a roof of four horizontal stone slabs 3 m off the ground (66 ft × 23 ft × 10 ft).

Continue along the N 147 before forking right in the direction of Doué-la-Fontaine.

> **Pocé.** – This château, now a farmstead, has retained its square keep, formidable 15C entrance gatehouse, and parapet walk above the battlements.

> **Distré.** – Pop 983. Romanesque church, formerly part of a priory.

> **Artannes-sur-Thouet.** – Pop 162. A 12C **chapel** with wall belfry stands in the cemetery.

Return to Saumur by the D 160 and the N 147.

Launay Manor. – *2 km - 1 mile to the east by ②, the D 952.*

This was one of King René's retreats where he used to give fêtes. With the outbuildings now serving as a farm the remains of the actual manor include elegant turrets, a clock tower adjoining the chapel and parts of battlemented walls.

Chênehutte-les-Tuffeaux. – *Round tour of 26 km - 16 miles. Leave Saumur by ⑤, the D 751.*

> **St-Hilaire-St-Florent.** – Pop 3 329. In St-Hilaire visit the small 12-15C church and the wine cellars, where the famous Saumur mousseux are produced by the champagne method. High up in St-Florent note the 13, 15 and 19C church.

> **Chênehutte-les-Tuffeaux.** – Pop 583. These settlements are strung out between the river and steep cliffs. Chênehutte produces mushrooms grown in former quarries dug out of the tufa stone. The Romanesque church with its double doorway stands near the Loire. The château – a former priory transformed into a hotel – terraces provide good views over the Loire *(access is limited to hotel clients only).*

Take the D 214 to return to Saumur turning right on to the D 305 at Beaucheron and pass via Pompierre and Verrie.

> **Verrie.** – Pop 236. The church with its primitive stonework is crowned with an elegant 13C bell tower.

St-Cyr-en-Bourg. – Pop 983. *8 km - 5 miles to the south by the Boulevard Louis-Renault and the D 93.* The wine making enterprise, Les vignerons de Saumur, allows the visitor to follow the entire production process from grape to wine, while descending 25 m - 82 ft in all, within its plant at various underground levels. The underground galleries can be visited in a motorised vehicle. *Guided tours including wine tasting from May to the end of September.*

Michelin map 🅖🅖 9 – Pop 7 167 – *Facilities p 39*

The schist houses of Segré rise in tiers above the river with its quays and picturesque bridges.
Segré is the capital of the Segréen, an area of *bocage* or wooded farmland, where mixed
farming – both crops and livestock
rearing (pigs, cattle and horses) is
common. The town has also given its
name to a high grade (55 per cent) iron
ore deposit, lying to the northwest near
Pouancé and Renazé.

Old bridge. – This hump backed bridge
of schist crosses the Oudon and offers
attractive views of the older parts of the
town.

St-Joseph. – From this chapel there
are views of the old town and the Oudon
Valley.

EXCURSION

Le Bourg-d'Iré; Nyoiseau. *– 21 km -
13 miles – about 1 hour. Leave Segré by
the D 923 in the direction of Candé to the
south and after a level crossing turn right
into the D 181.*

    Le Bourg-d'Iré. – Pop 911. Situated in
    the Verzée Valley the bridge affords
    a charming **view** of the river.

(After photo: R. Jacques)

Segré — The old bridge

Follow the D 219 to reach the mining
town of Noyant-la-Gravoyère. Turn right on to the D 775 and after 1 km - ½ mile turn left to
Nyoiseau. This narrow road follows a gorge cut through schist rocks.

    Nyoiseau. – Pop 1 562. This village is perched on the slopes of the Oudon Valley. Note, in a
    riverside site, the remains of a Benedictine abbey for nuns.

Return to Segré by the D 71 and D 775.

Michelin map 🅖🅖 18 – *Local map p 71* – Pop 4 656 – *Facilities p 39*

Selles-sur-Cher is prettily situated in a bend of the Cher, the waters of which reflect the
towers of its château. It owes its origins to St. Eusice, who lived there as a hermit and founded an
abbey on the spot. Only the abbey church remains of the former building.

■ SIGHTS *time: ¾ hour*

St-Eusice*. – Built in the 12 and 15C and burnt out by Coligny in 1562, it was restored partly in
the 17C and much more completely last century. The west front is almost entirely Romanesque.

Apse. – Although in a sad state of disrepair this is the most interesting part of the church. It is
carefully built and adorned with two friezes of figures which are rough, naïve and heavy below
the windows but better proportioned and more delicate above. The lower frieze depicts scenes
from the New Testament; the upper, scenes from the life of St. Eusice.

    To the right of the apse there is a bas-relief of the Work of the Months and higher up on the
right, a beautiful Visitation sheltered and protected by the transept chapel.

    The north wall, which was built at the end of the 13C, has a delightful doorway with carved
capitals supporting tori divided by a rope of flowers and wild rose leaves.

    Inside the building is very high and built on a plan common to the region, with seven bays
flanked by side aisles. The chancel has been greatly restored. Note the Romanesque capitals in
the south aisle.

    The 6C tomb of St. Eusice is in the crypt.

Château. *– Open from 9am to noon and from 2 to 7pm daily during the Easter holidays and
1 July to 15 September; on Saturdays and Sunday afternoons after Easter to 30 June and
16 September to 11 November; 8F.*

    Hidden on the bank of the Cher are the remains of a grim 13C fortress with its rectangular
wall lined with wide ditches crossed by four bridges. In contrast to this are the two smiling and
graceful Renaissance buildings which overlook the present access bridge, on the east side. These
are joined by a broad wall, pierced by arcades and oculi (round windows), with a parapet walk on
top.

    Cross the small park, graced by mulberry trees and a splendid cedar, to visit the older part of
the castle on the west side: the Intendant's room (a small collection of halberds and coats of mail)
and the "pavillons dorés" (gilded or golden pavilions), the apartment towers of Pierre-Philippe
de Béthune, the brother of Sully.

    In the Renaissance building to the northeast is the bedroom of Marysieńka, the French wife
of John III Sobieski of Poland. Often separated his letters to his wife are famous. The former
guardroom, later to become the dining room, contains a magnificent example of a low
asymmetrical arch serving as a lintel to a very large and fine fireplace. The freshness of the
residence's internal walls of white tufa with decorative brick quoins, has a curiously modern
aspect, in spite of the 16 and 17C furniture.

Local history and folklore museum. *– Open 1 July to 31 August on Tuesdays and
Thursdays from 3 to 6pm; weekends and public holidays from 10am to noon and from 2.30 to
6.30pm; 3F.*

    This museum is installed in the cloisters of the former abbey.

SEMBLANÇAY

Michelin map 📓 northeast of 14 – *Local map p 103* – Pop 922

The owner at the beginning of the 16C was **Jacques de Beaune-Semblançay**, François I's Intendant of the Royal Finances. Falsely accused of embezzlement he was hanged in Montfaucon on 12 August 1527.

Château. – Originally founded by Foulques Nerra only ruins now remain. The square keep and its revetment wall *(p 23)* are intact. To the east near the approach road is a small Renaissance chapel built by Jacques de Beaune.

Church. – The 16C stained glass windows present a Crucifixion, St. John the Baptist, and the donors Jacques de Beaune and his wife Jeanne Ruzé being presented by their patron saints. A 15C Crucifix and a 16C stone statue of the Virgin are also worthy of notice.

SERRANT, Château de ★

Michelin map 📓 20 – 2 km - 1 mile to the northeast of St-Georges-sur-Loire – *Local map p 104*

This sumptuous mansion although built over a period of three centuries, 16-18C, has great unity of style. Massive round towers topped by cupolas, the dark schist and contrasting white tufa all go to give it considerable character. The architect of the Tuileries in Paris and Fontaineblau, Philibert Delorme, worked on the plans for this château. The building is surrounded by a moat which becomes a lake on the park side.

Jacobite Connections. – Begun in 1546 by Charles de Brie, the château was bought in 1596 by Hercule de Rohan, duc de Montbazon, then in 1636 by Guillaume Bautru, whose granddaughter married the marquis de Vaubraun, Lieutenant General of the King's armies. On the death of her husband after the Battle of Altenheim in Alsace, the Marquise continued to supervise the work on the house till 1705. It was she who commisioned the architect Jules Hardouin-Mansart (The Invalides, Paris) to build the chapel in commemoration of her husband, and the sculptor Coysevox to create the white marble mausoleum.

Bought in 1749 by Walsh, Serrant was raised to the status of county by Louis XV as a reward to the Irishman Anthony Walsh for the support he had given to the Stuart cause in transporting Bonnie Prince Charlie to Moidart in 1745. Two generations earlier it had been another Walsh that carried the fleeing James II to exile in France.

The château is now owned by Jean-Charles de Ligne.

Château. – *Guided tours Palm Sunday to 31 October from 9am to noon and from 2 to 6pm; closed on Tuesdays except in July and August; time: ¾ hour; 10F.*

The **apartments**★★ are magnificently furnished. Rich Flemish tapestries hang in the main dining room. Admire the main panelled staircase, the first floor apartments with their coffered ceilings and the library with its 10 000 volumes. Note in the latter the portrait of the Young Pretender and Anthony Walsh. The state rooms were used by both Louis XIV and Napoleon. The art objects are many and various: Flemish and Brussels tapestries, a fine Italian cabinet, a bust of the Empress Marie-Louise by Canova and many portraits.

SOLESMES

Michelin map 📓 1, 2 – *Local map p 139* – Pop 1 003 – *Facilities p 39*

This village to the north of Sablé owes its fame to the presence of a Benedictine abbey. The north bank and the bridge both offer good **viewpoints**★ of the impressive, towering mass of abbey buildings, built at the end of the 19C in a Romanesque-Gothic style. The massive ensemble, built close to the riverside, is extended by a more ordered 18C building, the original priory.

Under the Benedictine Order. – Founded in 1010 by a local lord the Benedictine Priory of Solesmes was served by monks from the Abbey of St-Pierre-de-la-Couture in Le Mans. It expanded rapidly and was extremely wealthy in the early 16C and decadent by the 17C – it was rescued by the Maurists who exploited the local mines and quarries.

Ruined by the Revolution, it was restored to its grandeur by a certain Dom Guéranger, a Sablé priest, and in 1837 became the mother house for the Benedictine Order in France. Dispersed again in 1901 it was more than twenty years before monastic life was to be resumed.

The name of Solesmes Abbey is closely associated with liturgical changes and in particular the revival of the Gregorian Chant.

The public is admitted to Mass, a unique opportunity to appreciate Latin liturgy as celebrated in a Benedictine abbey. *From 24 June to 14 September, Mass at 10am, Vespers at 5.30pm (4pm on Thursdays from May to September); the rest of the year Mass at 9.45am, Vespers at 5pm.*

St-Peter's Abbey (Abbaye St-Pierre). – *Time: ¼ hour. Only the abbey church at the far end of the main courtyard is open to the public.*

The church is composed of an original nave and transept (11-15C) which were added to in 1865 with the construction of a domical vaulted chancel.

The famous groups of carvings known as the **Saints of Solesmes**★★ are to be found in the transepts. These are highly intricate monumental or even architectural pieces. The works in the south transept were commissioned by the Prior Guillaume Cheminert. They include an Entombment figuring an admirable Mary Magdalene dating from 1496 and to the left an earlier terracotta *Pietà*.

The group in the north transept dating from 1530 to 1556 is consecrated to the Virgin Mary and was commissioned by the Prior Jean Bougler. The composition is crowded but it is well worth trying to make out the different subjects. The main scene shows the Death of the Virgin Mary. Jean Bougler is portrayed holding one end of the shroud. Above are the Four Fathers of the Church and the Assumption. On the wall to the left Jesus is shown with the Four Doctors while opposite are scenes from the life of the Virgin.

The conventual buildings include the 18C priory and the great granite buildings dating from 1896 to 1901 which were added to in 1956.

Michelin map **64** 8, 9, 18, 19

The Sologne, immense and flat, stretching into infinity with its heaths, forests – occupying 40 per cent of the total surface – and solitary pools, is a paradise for shooters and anglers. Occupying the Orléans loop of the Loire, the Sologne is bordered to the south by the Loir and to the east by the Sançerre Hills.

History and development. – Formerly a desolate waste due to the fever ridden stagnant waters, the aspect of the region changed radically under Napoleon III. Having acquired the property of Lamotte-Beuvron he instigated

improvements: the planting of pines and birch trees, the digging of canals, the building of roads, the clearing, dredging and draining of pools and improvement of the soils. The fevers vanquished, the population grew and living conditions became tolerable. In recent years with the selling and subsequent subdividing of the estates and the increasing number of residences, the ecological and economic balance of the Sologne has been put in jeopardy. In 1976 a plan was launched to safeguard the Sologne with, among other measures, the creation of an ecological reserve and research centre in addition to other facilities for the tourist (information centres, open air museums, etc).

The Sologne today. – Of the 200 000 ha - 494 260 acres cultivated, those given over to cereals are diminishing in favour of fodder crops, while many farms are converting to pheasant rearing or the growing of fodder for the game. Vegetables and fruit are grown in the richer region of Contres and where man has mastered the waterlogged soil, as at the onetime Ex-

(After photo: Revue géographique et industrielle de France)

A Sologne landscape

perimental Fruit Farm at Vernon-en-Sologne where the first experiments with irrigation were conducted. This area, with part of the Loire Valley, is France's main asparagus producing region.

The traditional local industries (sawmills, packaging materials) have witnessed the establishment of other factories: porcelain at Lamotte-Beuvron; armaments at La Ferté-St-Aubin and Salbris; sports cars at Romorantin; bee rearing at Theillay and an extensive enterprise for the cultivation of dahlias at Villeherviers. The increase in shooting – with abundant cover for the game – means an added source of revenue for the landowners and a stimulus to the hotel and gunsmith trades. The shooting season provides the added attraction of great spectacles in the courtyards of often hidden châteaux. The region is well described by Maurice Genevoix in his novel *Raboliot* the story of a poacher.

TOUR

Attractive in spring and summer, the Sologne is at its best in autumn when the russets and greens vie with the purple carpet of heather to colour the melancholy landscape of pools.

The salvoes of shots, the ever present fences and no entry notices – aimed at the protection of the forest and wildlife – do little to destroy the charm of the region.

The Sologne Tourist Road, the D 922 from La Ferté-St-Aubin to Romorantin, passes through some of the most typical Sologne countryside.

Argent-sur-Sauldre. – Pop 2 737. *Facilities p 38*. This small town has numerous industrial enterprises specialising in lingerie, furniture, hoisting machinery and printing. The 15C **château**, with its two large round towers, has terraced gardens overlooking the Sauldre. **St-André**, the former chapel to the château preceded by a great belfry porch, contains a 16C group of the Trinity in the baptismal chapel.

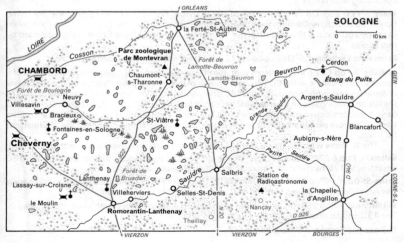

The SOLOGNE

Aubigny-sur-Nère. – *Description p 48.*

Blancafort. – Pop 943. The church of this Sologne village has an unusually shaped belfry porch. The 15C brick **château** *(guided tours 1 April to 2 November 10am to noon and 2 to 6pm; the rest of the year gardens only 2 to 5pm; closed on Tuesdays except in July and August; time: 30 mins; 10F.)* has a square keep. The courtyard is flanked by two 17C pavilions and the gardens are in the French style.

Bracieux. – Pop 1 019. *Facilities p 38.* Lying in the Beuvron Valley on the borderland of the Sologne and the Blésois, Bracieux has a 16C covered market.

Cerdon. – Pop 1 078. This village has a 15C church which is reputed to have a painting by the school of Raphael.

Château de Chambord★★★. – *Description p 60.*

La Chapelle d'Angillon. – *Description p 62.*

Chaumont-sur-Tharonne. – Pop 932. *Facilities p 38.* The line of the former ramparts can still be traced in the layout of this village. Occupying an attractive site, perched on a mound, Chaumont is dominated by its 15-16C church.

Château de Cheverny★★. – *Description p 72.*

Étang du Puits★. – *8 km - 5 miles to northwest of Argent-sur-Sauldre.* This vast stretch of water stands in a woodland setting. The road following the retaining causeway offers a good view of the lake. A venue for regattas, other facilities include beaches, pedal, rowing and sailing boats and children's amusements. The reservoir abounds with carp, bream and pike.

La Ferté-St-Aubin. – Pop 4 284. *Facilities p 38.* Strung out along the N 20 La Ferté-St-Aubin is contained to the west by the railway line. In the vicinity of the castle, the old quarter has some houses typical of the Sologne – squat brick and half timber constructions they are covered with great flat tiled roofs.

The 17C **château** *(not open to the public)* of brick with stone string courses is a majestic building surrounded by moats with domed pavilions flanking the main entrance. The 12-16C church with its belfy porch overlooks the Cosson.

Fontaines-en-Sologne. – Pop 706. The church dating mainly from the 12C shows features typical of the Angevin style *(p 21)*: square east end, a single nave with remarkable domical vaulting. It was fortified in the 17C. Nearby is a fine half timbered house.

Lanthenay Church. – Dating from the 12 to the 19C this church contains a painting (c. 1523) of the Virgin attributed to Timoteo Viti from Urbino who greatly influenced Raphael in his early days, in addition to various statues, etc.

Lassay-sur-Croisne. – Pop 127. A typical Sologne village, the **church** *(to visit apply to the Mairie)* formerly belonged to a priory and contains an early 16C **fresco** showing St. Christopher and to the right Lassay Church with the Château du Moulin in the background. The tomb below belongs to the one time Lord of the Manor: Philippe du Moulin *(see château below)*, who once saved the life of Charles VIII.

Montevran Zoo★. – *Open weekdays from 9am to noon and from 1.30 to 7pm; on Sundays and public holidays from 9am to 6pm; 12.50F; children: 8F.* In the heart of the Sologne this zoo with its spacious park and varied collection of animals makes a good day's excursion.

Château du Moulin. – *Guided tours from 1 March to 15 November from 9 to 11.30am and from 2 to 6.30pm; time ½ hour; 8F.* This red brick building, moat encircled, is reflected in the waters of the Croisne. Built for Philippe du Moulin, the first part consists of the gatehouse, with its original nail studded doors and unusual system of locks and bolts, and the former kitchen known as the Guardroom. The latter has a roof supported by a central pillar, a fine fireplace dating from 1492 and some handsome pieces of furniture. The main building has been well restored and is tastefully furnished with 15 and 16C furniture and hung with tapestries. The salon's painted ceiling dates from the 16C.

Nançay. – Pop 717. *Facilities p 39.* To the north of this village on the right hand side of the D 29 is the experimental research station in radio astronomy. *A terrace at the entrance is open to the public and has explanatory noticeboards; the station is open to visitors at 2.30pm on the second Saturday of each month, apply in advance in writing to the station.* One of the most powerful of its kind, the radio telescope has a large metal dish 40 m wide by 200 m long (131 ft by 656 ft) which captures the Hertzian waves and then reflects them to fixed points at a distance of 460 m - 503 yd. Further afield is a series of forty-eight parabolic metal mirrors for capturing the sun's electromagnetic waves.

Neuvy. – Pop 288. On the north bank of the Beuvron, Neuvy is on the edge of the Boulogne Forest. Its church, isolated on the opposite bank, was partially rebuilt in 1525. The rood beam supports 15C statues. In the south arm a 17C canvas shows the Dead Christ being supported by two angels.

Romorantin-Lanthenay★. – *Description p 131.* Home of the Sologne Museum *(p 132).*

St-Viâtre. – Pop 1 223. In an isolated spot, the village was the site of a pilgrimage to the relics of a hermit who lived here in the 6C. The belfry porch of this Gothic **church** *(closed on the afternoons of Sundays and public holidays)* has a 14C doorway and is built over an 11C crypt. The chapel to the left on entering has an unusual 16C baptismal font and a 17C gilt wood chandelier. The 18C carved wooden lectern at the entrance to the chancel is surprisingly large. In the south arm of the transept are four **painted panels★** dating from the 16C evoking with realism the lives of Christ and St. Viâtre.

The **St. Viâtre** wayside altar, a small 15C brick construction, stands to the north of the town.

Salbris. – Pop 6 204. *Facilities p 39.* On the left bank of the Sauldre, Salbris has a 15 and 16C church with 17C furnishings. The retable of the high altar has a *Pietà*.

Selles-St-Denis. – Pop 1 071. This church (12-15C) with Flamboyant apsidal and lateral chapels has mural paintings dating from the 14C, retracing the life of St. Genoulph.

Villeherviers. – Pop 359. Situated in the wide Sauldre Valley, planted with vines and asparagus. The 13C church possesses Angevin vaulting.

Château de Villesavin. – *Description p 162.*

SUÈVRES

Michelin map **64** southeast of 7 – *Local map p 102* – Pop 1 147 – *Facilities p 39*

This small old town has two churches of archaeological interest and some old houses.

St-Lubin. – The church stands south of the N 152 *(to visit apply in summer to the château next door or to the presbytery)*. All that remains from the 10C are the transept crossing and the belfry. The nave has gone. The chancel is 12C, the south aisle was rebuilt in the 16C and the apse is modern. The building's chief interest lies in its very fine Romanesque tower which is perfectly proportioned with a double tier of paired bays topped by a low pyramid roof of stone. A beautiful 16C doorway, opening off the south aisle, is surmounted by the arms of the lords of the Château des Forges.

St-Christophe. – *To visit apply to the presbytery 4 Rue du 8 mai.* The west front is adorned with characterisically Merovingian fishbone and chevron patterns. A wooden gallery adjoins the building.

To the pre-Romanesque nave were added, in the 12C, another nave, and in the 15C a chancel and side aisles, finally producing a somewhat eccentric whole. The windows in the apse contain some beautiful fragments of stained glass dating from 1547. The church furnishings are interesting and include a carved wood 17C pulpit.

SULLY-SUR-LOIRE ★

Michelin map **65** 1 – *Local map p 101* – Pop 5 184 – *Facilities p 39*

The Château de Sully, so interesting for its history, its picturesque site on the bank of the Loire and its splendid timber roof, was damaged in 1940. It has since been restored. The best view of the château is from the D 119, which skirts the Loire between Ouzouer and Sully

HISTORICAL NOTES

The early stronghold commanded a crossing of the Loire. Four great names stand out in its history: Maurice de Sully, Bishop of Paris when he commissioned the building of Notre-Dame, Joan of Arc, Sully and Voltaire.

The Ardent Life of Joan of Arc. – In 1429 Sully belonged to Georges de la Trémoille, a favourite of Charles VII. The King was living in the castle when Joan defeated the English at Patay and captured their leader, the famous Talbot, Earl of Shrewsbury. The Maid hurried to Sully and at last persuaded the indolent monarch to be crowned at Reims. She returned to the castle in 1430 after her check before Paris, and there felt the jealousy and hostility of La Trémoille gaining influence over the King. She was kept almost a prisoner but escaped to continue the struggle.

Sully's capacity for work. – In 1602 Maximilien de Béthune, the Lord of Rosny, bought the château and the barony for 330 000 *livres*. Henri IV made Maximilien the duc de Sully, and it was under this name that the great Minister passed into history.

Sully began to serve his King at the age of twelve. He was a great soldier, the best artilleryman of his time and a consummate administrator. He was active in all the departments of State: Finance, Agriculture, Industry and Public Works.

SULLY-SUR-LOIRE

0 — 300 m

Gd-Sully (R. du)	6
Porte-de-Sologne (R.)	12
Champ-de-Foire (Bd du)	2
Chemin de Fer (R. du)	3
Epinettes (R.)	5
Jeanne-d'Arc (Bd)	7
Marronniers (Rue des)	9
Porte-Berry (R.)	10
St-François (R. du Fg)	15
St-Germain (R. du Fg)	16

Sully made his fortune while he made that of France. He lived like a minor sovereign, with his own guard and court of retainers.

A glutton for work, Sully began his day at 3am and kept four secretaries busy writing his memoirs. He entitled them: *Wise and Royal Economies of State.* Fearing indiscretions, he had a printing press set up in one of the towers of the château and the work was printed on the spot, although it bore the address of a printer in Amsterdam. The old Duke had a mania for orderly accounts. Every tree to be planted, every table to be made, every ditch to be cleaned was the subject of a legal contract.

Sully had an awkward character, and he often went to law, especially with the Bishop of Orléans. Since the Middle Ages it had been the custom for the Lord of Sully to carry the Bishop's chair on the day of his entry into Orléans. The former Minister, very much the ducal peer and a Protestant into the bargain, refused to conform with this custom. Finally he obtained permission to be represented at the ceremony.

Sully embellished the feudal pile. The building originally stood on the Loire itself. He separated it from the river by an embankment, dug moats which he filled by deflecting a nearby river, laid out the park and enlarged the buildings.

The spirit of Voltaire (18C). – Exiled from Paris by the Regent for his too biting epigrams, Voltaire spent several seasons with the duc de Sully, who welcomed new ideas and surrounded himself with philosophers and "libertines". Voltaire was then only François-Marie-Arouet; he was twenty-two. His gaiety and wit made him the life and soul of the castle. A theatre was built for him in the château and there he had tragedies and comedies performed.

In the shade of the park among trees "carved upon", he said, "by urchins and lovers", young Arouet indulged in flirtations which he transferred to the stage, where the roles were played by his lady friends.

SULLY-SUR-LOIRE★

■ THE CHÂTEAU★ *time: ¾ hour*

Guided tours 1 April to 30 September from 9 to 11.45am and 2 to 6pm (5pm in October); 10 to 11.45am and 2 to 4.30pm in November; time 45 mins; 5F.

The château or castle is an imposing feudal fortress dating largely from before 1360. The keep faces the Loire. It is rectangular, with round towers at the four corners. The wing added by Sully to the living quarters dates from the early 17C.

One can visit several apartments in the 14C keep, notably the large guardroom on the ground floor, another immense hall on the first floor where Voltaire watched his plays being performed and the oratory in which there is an excellent copy of the funerary group showing Sully and his wife *(the original is at Nogent-le-Rotrou)*. Finally, on the second floor, there is the unique chamber with its famous timber roof. The apartment, unfortunately, is cut in two by the chimney-stack. The visit ends with a tour of the watchpath.

(After photo: Yvon)

Château de Sully

The timber roof★★. – The upper hall of the keep has the finest timber roof that has come down to us from the Middle Ages. Dating from 1363 and keel shaped it is still like new. There are no worms in the wood, no rot to attract flies and, therefore, no cobwebs. This is due to the type of wood, chestnut, and the great care taken by the carpenters of the day. Trees aged fifty to a hundred years were chosen, barked standing and squared off, leaving only the heart. The beams were then weathered under water for several years to wash the sap out of the wood, dried in the open air for several years more, coated with disinfectant and finally assembled in such a way that air could circulate freely.

Renaissance pavilion. – This contains Sully's study and, on the first floor, the great saloon which was the Minister's bedroom. Both rooms with wall hangings and painted ceilings have been refurnished.

■ ADDITIONAL SIGHTS

Collegiate Church of St-Ythier (Collégiale de St-Ythier – B). – Built in 1529, the Chapel of Notre-Dame de Pitié was enlarged in 1605; it then became the Collegiate Church of St-Ythier. There are two 16C **stained glass windows**: the one at the end of the south aisle shows pilgrims on their way to St. James's shrine in Santiago de Compostela; the second showing the Tree of Jesse with the Virgin and Baby Jesus is in the central apse. In the north aisle is a 16C *Pietà* above the high altar.

16C House (D). – Restored since the Second World War.

St-Germain (E). – Remarkable for its fine spire, 38 m - 125 ft high, which can be seen from all around. The church itself is in ruins.

St-Père-sur-Loire. – *1 km - ½ mile to the north by the suspension bridge and* ①.

This charming modern church (1959) is built of wood and brick. Inside there is some fine varnished timberwork from Gabon.

TALCY

Michelin map 🔢 7 – *Local maps pp 97 and 102* – Pop 223

The village standing isolated in the Beauce Plain, is linked to Mer by a road bordered at intervals with rose bushes.

Château de Talcy★. – *Open 1 April to 30 September from 9 to 11.45am and from 2 to 6.30pm; 1 October to 31 March from 10 to 11.45am and from 2 to 3.30pm; closed on Tuesdays, 1 January, 1 May, 1 November, 25 December; time: 45 mins; 6F; Sundays and public holidays: 3F.*

Sold to the State in 1932, the château is severe in appearance, but interesting for its literary history, its furniture, and, on more familiar ground, for two little masterpieces: the dovecote and the wine press.

This 13C manorial dwelling was sold at a public auction in Paris in 1466.

Talcy was bought in 1571 by a rich Florentine, Bernardo Salviati, a cousin of Catherine de' Medici. This Salviati family so famous in literary history retained the estate until 1667. Bernardo was the father of Cassandra, to whom **Ronsard** dedicated so many sonnets, and of Giovanni Salviati, whose daughter, Diana, similarly inspired the young Agrippa d'Aubigné. Cassandra's daughter married Guillaume de Musset and one of her direct descendants was the great poet Alfred de Musset (1810-57).

Fine furniture (16-18C) and Gothic tapestries grace the severe setting of the feudal halls under the French style roofs with fine Renaissance beams. The 15C keep with two doorways, postern and carriage gate, has two corner turrets and a battlemented watchpath mediaeval looking but dating in fact from 1520. The fenestration at the first floor level was modified in the 18C.

The first courtyard owes its charm to a gracious gallery and an attractive well. In the second courtyard is a large 16C **dovecote**, with its 1 500 pigeon holes which are admirably preserved.

An old **wine press** is still fit for use after 400 years of wear. A carefully balanced mechanism enables two men to obtain ten barrels of juice at a single pressing.

EXCURSION

St-Léonard-en-Bouce. – Pop 570. *10 km - 6 miles to the northwest by the D 15, D 15A and the D 917 to the left.* The Romanesque **church**, with its buttressed belfry, was finished in the 16C. Being the resting place of St. Leonard's relics, it is now a pilgrimage centre *(procession: the fourth Sunday after Easter)*.

THOUARS

Michelin map **67** 8 – Pop 12 631 – *Facilities p 39*

Approach Thouars from the south, crossing the River Thouet by the new bridge (le Pont Neuf), a perfect viewpoint from which to discover the town's **site***: a rocky promontory, encircled by the river. On the borders of Poitou and Anjou, the rooftops of Thouars are a mixture of Romanesque tiles and Angevin slates.

The lords of Thouars. – The viscounts of Thouars were for a long time faithful to the Plantagenets and afterwards to the kings of England, but Du Guesclin seized the city in 1372 after a memorable siege. Having bought Thouars from the Amboise family, Louis XI stayed here several times. His first wife Margaret of Scotland had even expressed the wish to be buried here.

Charles VIII gave Thouars to the La Trémoille family, who remained the owners until the Revolution. Thouars, like Saumur, was one of the centres of the Reformation, but after the Revocation of the Edict of Nantes (1685) the town lost half its population.

■ **MAIN SIGHTS** *time: ¾ hour*

St-Médard. – Alongside a square 15C tower with a watch tower, St-Médard is a Romanesque building despite the Gothic rose window adorning the beautiful **west front*** in the Poitou style.

St-Médard Church
West front (detail)

The very ornamented central doorway is surmounted by Christ in Majesty adored by the angels; the recessed arches, the latter of which is broken by a Resurrected Christ fall on to historiated capitals showing the Chastisement of the Vices. Above the lateral doorways there are fine statues of St. Peter and St. Paul, the Prophets and the Sibyls. The curious Romanesque naves were altered in the 15C to a single nave with flattened vaulting.

Old houses. – These are numerous in the Rues St-Médard and du Château, formerly Thouars' main street which ended at the old bridge. They include the brick and half timber house, beside the Church of St-Médard, now occupied by the Tourist Information Centre, and the Hostellerie St-Médard (**B**) of the same period. Standing close together along the Rue du Château are several corbelled façades with pointed gables. It was in no 11, the 15C Hôtel des Trois Rois (**D**), that the Dauphin, the future Louis XI, is said to have passed the night. Passing by the former postern go down to the Thouet which is crossed by a **Gothic bridge** (**E**), defended by a fortified gateway.

Sainte-Chapelle. – Gabrielle de Bourbon had the chapel built over a series of crypts, one of which still serves as the La Trémoille family vault. The charming Flamboyant façade is surmounted by a Renaissance gallery.

Château. – *The château is not open to the public but access is allowed to the porticoed gallery, apply to the caretaker for permission.* The present château replaced a mediaeval fortress and now serves as a school. This imposing group of buildings was started in 1635 by Marie de La Tour d'Auvergne, duchesse de La Trémoille and Turenne's eldest sister. The central wing has a projecting domed pavilion which houses the grand staircase.

Other pavilions flank the main wing.

The esplanade and small suspension bridge over the river, both afford good views of Thouars, in its exceptional site, and the Thouet Valley.

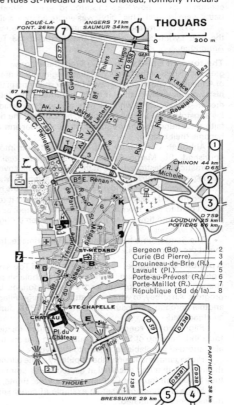

THOUARS

Bergeon (Bd)	2
Curie (Bd Pierre)	3
Drouineau-de-Brie (R.)	4
Lavault (Pl.)	5
Porte-au-Prévost (R.)	6
Porte-Maillot (R.)	7
République (Bd de la)	8

■ ADDITIONAL SIGHTS

Tour du prince de Galles (F). – The Prince of Wales or Grénetière (corn chandler) Tower as it is sometimes known, was once the grain store and part of the city ramparts. Reinforced by small barbicans this massive round tower also served as a prison.

Porte au Prévôt (K). – It was by this gateway that Du Guesclin entered the town following its capitulation in 1372. It is flanked by two fine crescent shaped towers with octagonal bases.

Former Abbey (Ancienne abbaye St-Laon – L). – Formerly Benedictine and Augustinian from 1117, the abbey has a 12-15C church, founded by Margaret of Scotland wife of Louis XI, and it now serves as her resting place. The 17C conventual buildings serve now as the town hall (H).

Chemin du Panorama. – Leave by ⑥ and take to the left of the D 759 a signposted steeply descending path which affords an attractive **view** of the town and Thouet Valley.

TOURS ★★

Michelin map **64** 15 – *Local maps pp 70, 102 and 103* – Pop 145 441

For many tourists Tours is the centre from which they will explore the whole châteaux country. The town itself offers visitors a fine cathedral, churches, monasteries, old houses, interesting museums and the luminous landscapes of the Loire.

Tours, now an urban agglomeration of 251 320 inhabitants, has greatly outgrown its original site between the Loire and Cher, and urban development has followed the canalisation of the Loire along 7 km - 5 miles of its course. An industrial zone has been created in the north round St-Symphorien.

The industrial sector includes light ancillary industries in metallurgy, chemicals, plastics, electronics and textiles; pharmaceutical laboratories, Michelin tyre factory and printing works.

A communications crossroads, Tours is the economic focal point for the Centre-West and a regional agricultural and wine centre. The fairs *(ten days from the first Saturday in May and 18-21 September)* include the rather folkloric Garlic and Basil Fair *(in July on St. Anne's Day)*.

A centre for higher education Tours has a University with 12 000 students continuing the traditions of its illustrious mediaeval predecessor. The various faculties and departments cover the arts, science, medicine, pharmacy, law, economics, town and country planning, insurance and technology. In addition there is a School for Renaissance Studies, a Regional Music, Dance and Drama Conservatory, a Regional Fine Arts and three Nursing Schools, a foreign language institute for the training of interpretors and an applied arts and crafts conservatory.

■ HISTORICAL NOTES

The Gallo-Roman metropolis. – During the *Pax Romana*, the area, Turons, consisting of more than 100 ha - 250 acres, became a prosperous city and was named Caesardonum or Caesar's Hill. However, constant pillaging forced the inhabitants to live in the administrative and economic centre, now the area surrounding the cathedral, which was also where the arenas and baths were located. This "city" was encircled by a wall which still remains in part.

In 375 the city took back its former name, Turones, and became the seat of government of the IIIrd Lyonnaise, a province that included the Touraine, the Maine, the Anjou and the Armorique.

The town of St. Martin (4C). – From the 4C onwards Tours was the town of St. Martin. The greatest bishop of the Gauls was first a legionary in the Roman army of occupation. At the gates of Amiens the young soldier saw a beggar shivering in the cold wind. He cut his cloak in two with his sword and gave half of it to the poor man. The following night the future St. Martin had a dream – he saw Christ with half his cloak, and this decided his future; he was baptised and began his apostolate. At Ligugé, in Poitou, he founded the first monastery on Gallic soil. His burning faith and boundless charity spread his renown far and wide. The people of Tours begged him to become their bishop.

Although Christianity had been introduced into Gaul a century before, paganism still flourished. St. Martin fought it with pitiless zeal: idols, statues and old shrines were systematically destroyed; but, at the same time, he covered Touraine with churches and chapels. At the gates of Tours he founded the Monastery of Marmoutier.

St. Martin died at Candes *(p 59)* in 397. Both the monks of Ligugé and those of Marmoutier claimed his body, but the men of Touraine carried it to a boat while those of Poitou slept, and rowed hard to their town. Then a miracle occurred: as the corpse passed, the trees grew green, plants burst into flower and the birds sang, even though it was November – so came about "St. Martin's summer".

The Saint's tomb became a place of pilgrimage. In 470, a magnificent basilica was erected round the sarcophagus.

A popular pilgrimage. – In 573, the people of Tours brought from Clermont-Ferrand the heir of a great Gallo-Roman family, known for his scholarship and his piety, to be their bishop. He was Gregory of Tours, the forerunner of French historians. Under his direction the town made further progress. An abbey, to which was attached a large village, grew up round the basilica; to the west another borough, Châteauneuf sprang up; in 1354, during the Hundred Years War, the two areas amalgamated.

Pilgrims of all conditions and all countries, including the sick who hoped to be cured by touching the tomb of St. Martin, succeeded one another in this medieval Lourdes. The basilica also afforded inviolable sanctuary to fugitives.

Propaganda maintained the popularity of the pilgrimage. A little history of the Saint's life and the miracles that had occurred at his tomb was composed. Copies of the text were distributed: they have been found at Carthage, Alexandria, Rome, the Thebaid (Upper Egypt) and Syria.

Kings and great men set an example of generosity in the cult of St. Martin and immense riches were accumulated.

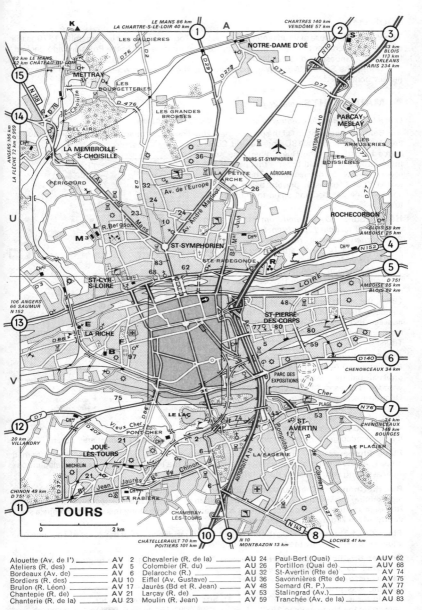

A great teacher: Alcuin (end of 8C). – In the Carolingian period (8C) Tours, while remaining a great religious centre, became a seat of art and learning under the direction of Alcuin. This monk of Anglo-Saxon origin, after fifty years in a cathedral school in Yorkshire, was brought from Italy by Charlemagne. The Emperor, wishing to raise his people from their ignorance, installed a model educational centre in his palace at Aachen and placed Alcuin in charge of it. When the organisation was complete Charlemagne sent the monk to Tours as Abbot of St. Martin.

Alcuin also formed a school for copyists. A new calligraphy, clear and elegant, was designed. Illuminators joined the calligraphers. Masterpieces issued from this school, include the famous Bible of Charles the Bald as well as Charlemagne's Gospel Book.

Ups and downs (from the 9 to 14C). – The Norman invasions reached Tours. Its basilica, its abbeys and its twenty-eight churches were burnt down. Then rivalry developed between the counts of Blois and the counts of Anjou, whose domains were contiguous in Touraine. It ended in victory for the Angevins, who were supplanted in their turn by Philippe-Auguste (1204).

Nevertheless the 13 and 14C were a happy period for Tours.

The silk industry at Tours (15 and 16C). – Louis XI introduced the manufacture of silk and cloth of gold to Tours. At first the King set up this industry at Lyon, but as the people of that town were not enthusiastic the workers and looms were transferred to Tours. The industry reached its peak in the 16C.

It was in this world of artisans, intellectuals and artists that the Reformation found its first supporters, and Tours, like Lyon or La Rochelle, became one of the most active centres of the new religion. The Calvanists created grave disorder which was pitilessly avenged by the Catholics. The town had its Massacre of St. Bartholomew ten years before Paris.

This was the beginning of a decline which was to continue until the opening of the 19C. By 1801 the 80 000 inhabitants were reduced to 20 000. But the railway revived the town by providing easy communications and by the installation of its vast railway workshops at St-Pierre-des-Corps.

TOURS★★

The Wars. – Because of its advantageous position, Tours was chosen in September 1870 as the seat of the government for national defence; but three months later as the Prussians approached, the government escaped to Bordeaux.

During the Second World War, the centre and the parts of town bordering the Loire were heavily bombarded.

■ MAIN SIGHTS *time: 2½ hours*

Leave from the Rue du Commerce and follow the itinerary below.

Before the opening up of the present main street going north-south and the construction of the Pont Wilson in the 18C, the Rue du Commerce formed, with the Rue Colbert, the main thoroughfare of the old town – this part of the town is now being restored. The **mediaeval quarter★★** of Tours is at present being restored and will one day become again the hub of the town.

Hôtel Gouin★ (D). – *Open from 9am to noon and from 2 to 6pm (5pm from 1 November to 28 February); closed on Tuesdays between 1 October and 14 March and during December and January; 4F.*

This mansion, a perfect example of living accommodation under the Renaissance, is one of the most interesting in Tours. Burnt out in 1940, the north and south façades with the staircase tower were, however, spared. The **museum** includes a Gallo-Roman collection, mediaeval art and Renaissance works of art from Tours.

Rue Paul-Louis Courier. – The late 15C Hôtel Binet at no 10 (enter into the courtyard) has an unusual balcony which is reached by two wooden staircases. At no 15, the Hôtel Robert-Quantin *(restoration in progress)*, an early 17C mansion stands on the site of the house where Joan of Arc was received in April 1429. The second courtyard (access by no 20 Rue Littré)

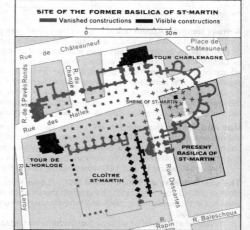

★★ LE VIEUX TOURS

★ CLOÎTRE ST-MARTIN _____ B   ★ MUSÉE DU GEMMAIL _____ M¹
★ HÔTEL GOUIN _____ D   ★ PLACE PLUMEREAU
★ MAISON DE TRISTAN _____ K   ★ RUE BRIÇONNET

has an arcaded gallery adorned with carved figures and an elegant pedimented porch.

Place Plumereau★. – This picturesque square is bordered by several 15C timber framed houses. At the far end of the passageway at no 4, to the left of the *crêperie*, is an elegant oak staircase hung with slates on the courtyard side.

Rue du Change. – The house at the junction with the Rue de la Monnaie, has a corner post representing the Virgin as a 15C bourgeois woman of Tours; at the intersection of the Rue de la Rôtisserie is a timber framed house hung with slates. Continue along this street to admire a small courtyard flanked by a crooked tower.

Place de Châteauneuf. – On the left is the 14-17C residence (N) of the dukes of Touraine. The square is overlooked by the tower, Tour Charlemagne (Q).

Former Basilica of St. Martin (Ancienne Basilique St-Martin). – The original 5C sanctuary, destroyed by the Normans, was rebuilt from the 11 to 13C. The new building was justly as famous as the old for its size and splendour. Sacked by the Huguenots in 1562 it fell into disrepair during the Revolution, when its vaulting collapsed. The nave was pulled down in 1802 to make way for the Rue des Halles.

The **Tour Charlemagne** (Q) originally dominated the north transept. Isolated since the destruction of the main building, it suffered partial collapse in 1928 but was ably restored to its noble aspect. During restoration 11C frescoes were uncovered.

The **Tour de l'horloge** (V), stood on the right of the façade. In the 19C it was crowned with a dome.

The **St. Martin Cloisters★** (B – cloître St-Martin) still have a fine 16C range.

New Basilica of St. Martin (Nouvelle Basilique St-Martin – W). – This was built between 1887 and

SITE OF THE FORMER BASILICA OF ST-MARTIN
■ Vanished constructions   ■ Visible constructions

(After R. Ranjard - La Touraine archéologique)

1924 by Laloux, in the Romano-Byzantine style. In the crypt the the shrine of St. Martin continues to occupy exactly the same spot that it did in the old basilica. The shrine is the object of a popular pilgrimage *(on 11 November and the following Sunday)*.

Return to Place Plumereau.

Rue Briçonnet*. – This charming street is bordered by houses showing a rich variety of typically Tours styles: from the Romanesque façade at the corner of Rue du Poirier to no 21, the 18C Hôtel de Choiseul, at the far end of the street.

No 31 has a late 13C Gothic façade, now restored, while no 32 opposite is a Renaissance house with wooden statues.

The elegant staircase tower to the right marks the entrance to a **former cloister of St-Pierre le Puellier**, where excavations have uncovered a Gallo-Roman and mediaeval cemetery.

Part of the church's nave is still visible on the right and from Rue Briçonnet. Further along on the right is a large, ogive vaulted porch which opens on to a charming little **square**, where four centuries of architecture are harmoniously represented together. Take the porch to reach Rue de la Paix from where you can see the façades of these houses.

Return to the cloister and take Rue du Mûrier, across the street.

Gemmail Museum* (Musée du Gemmail – M¹). – *7 Rue du Mûrier. Open Palm Sunday to 15 October from 10am to noon and from 2.30 to 6pm; closed on Mondays; 7F.*

The **Hôtel Raimbault**, built in 1825, contains the glaziers' workshops and some of their remarkable works.

The **gemmail** method *(p 27)* produces non leaded stained glass compositions. Fragments of coloured glass are assembled and illuminated from behind by an artificial light source – the system achieves a rare brilliance, unusual tones and a three-dimensional effect.

Maison de Tristan* (K). – *16 Rue Briçonnet. Open during school term time: to visit apply to the Secrétariat in the courtyard.*

This remarkable late 15C stone and brick building, with its pierced gable, now houses a school of foreign languages. This was once the home of a certain Pierre du Puiz whose motto, an anagram of his name, is carved on the lintel of one of the courtyard windows *(Prie Dieu pur)*. From the top of the turret there is an attractive **view** of the old town.

The Arts Faculty, on Place des Joulins has greatly added to the animation of the quarter. From the terraces of the Faculty building there is a fine view over the rooftops of the old town.

Place des Carmes. – This attractively provincial small square is overlooked on the east side by an 18C hôtel.

Take the Rue Paul-Louis-Courier and the Rue de Maillé to reach the Rue Constantine (15C houses with an overhang) and the Quai de la Loire.

St Gatien Cathedral** (Cathédrale St-Gatien – DX). – Begun in the early 13C and completed in the 16C the building demonstrates the complete evolution of the French Gothic style. The chevet is typical of the early phase, the transept and nave the development and the Flamboyant west front the last stage. The west front towers have Renaissance crowns.

Pass to the right of the church to reach the Place Grégoire-de-Tours, from where you will have a fine view of the remarkable **chevet**, in the pure style, typical of the St. Louis period *(p 14)*. Return to the Place de la Cathédrale.

This soaring **west front** is attractive in spite of the mixture of styles. Monotony is avoided by the delicate asymmetry of details. The foundations of the towers are set on the Gallo-Roman wall. The bases are Romanesque, as are the solid side buttresses so typical of this style. The rich Flamboyant decoration – pierced tympana, festooned recessed orders and leaf adorned gables over the doorway – was added in the 15C. The buttresses soaring up to the base of the steeples were adorned at the same time with niches and crocketed pinnacles. The upper part of the north tower, dating from the 15C, was crowned by an early Renaissance dome with lantern. The 16C south bell tower, built directly above the Romanesque tower, is also terminated by a dome and lantern but from the late Renaissance.

St-Gatien Cathedral — West front

The **interior** of the cathedral is striking for its purity of line.

The 14 and 15C nave complements harmoniously the 13C **chancel**. The balanced arrangement of its windows strongly resembles that of the Sainte-Chapelle in Paris.

The **stained glass windows**** are the pride of the cathedral. Those of the chancel with their warm colours are 13C; the rose windows of the transepts are 14C; while those of the third chapel off the south aisle and the great rose window of the nave are 15C. The chapel opening on to the south transept contains the tomb of Charles VIII's children, a fine work by the school of Michel Colombe (16C). The finely worked base is by Jerome de Fiesole.

The Psalette or St Gatien Cloisters* (Cloître St-Gatien – DX F). – *Temporarily closed to the public.*

The canons and choir masters of the cathedral lived in this elegant 15 and 16C building. Hence the name Psalette – the place where Psalms were sung. This was the setting for Balzac's novel *Le Curé de Tours* (The Vicar of Tours), a description of provincial life.

There is a fine view from the entrance on the north side of the cathedral. Note the prop that divides the rose window of the transept into two and also the later additions of two immense flying buttresses. An elegant Renaissance staircase leads to a gallery where the early 13 to late 14C frescoes from the church of Beaumont-Village are on display.

The Museum of Fine Arts *(p 155)* stands to the right of the cathedral.

TOURS

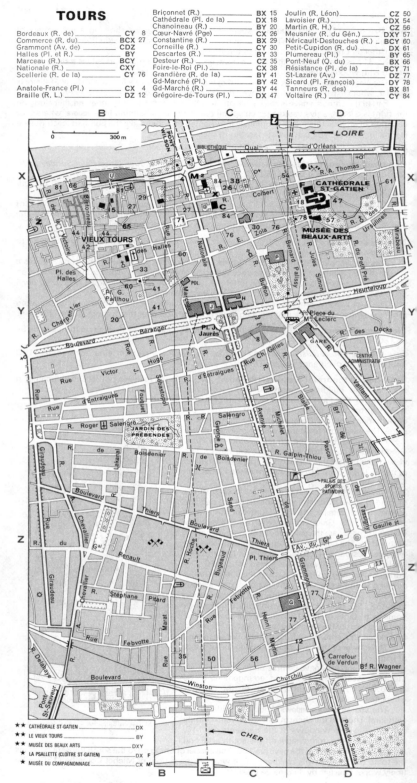

★★	CATHÉDRALE ST-GATIEN	DX
★★	LE VIEUX TOURS	BY
★★	MUSÉE DES BEAUX ARTS	DXY
★	LA PSALLETTE (CLOÎTRE ST-GATIEN)	DX F
★	MUSÉE DU COMPAGNONNAGE	CX M³

■ ADDITIONAL SIGHTS

Place-A.-France (CX). – The **Pont Wilson** commonly known as *pont de Pierre* or stone bridge is an attractive work (1765-78) which spans the 434 m - 475 yd of the Loire. Damaged in 1978, two provisional bridges have assured the crossing until the reconstruction which is scheduled for 1982. The municipal library *(bibliothèque)* stands nearby, overlooking the river.

St-Julien (CXX). – In the 13C this church belonged to the St-Julien Abbey. The belfry porch is all that remains of an earlier 11C church. The restrained Gothic interior has modern (1960) stained glass windows by Max Ingrand and Le Chevallier.

Craft Guilds Museum* (Musée du Compagnonnage – CXM²). – *8 Rue Nationale. Open from 9am to noon and from 2 to 6pm; closed on Tuesdays and 1 January, 1 May, 14 July, 11 November, 25 December; 3F.*

This museum in the 16C monks' **dormitory**, above the chapter house, traces the history, customs and skills of the various associations of craftsmen, or guilds. The trades of the past are shown alongside those of the present, with their respective tools and **masterpieces** that the **compagnons** (*cum+panis*=the one with whom we share our bread) had to submit before becoming master craftsmen.

Museum of Touraine Wines (CXM²). – *16 Rue Nationale. Same opening times as for the Craft Guilds Museum.* Lying to the north of the Church of St-Julien, the cloisters encircle a 16C wine press. The ranges directly opposite one another include the Gothic chapter house *(temporary exhibitions)* on the one hand and the 12C **wine cellar** with its great chamber on the other. The latter with quadripartite vaulting houses the museum. Various themes are treated: mythology, religions, social and family customs, wine brotherhoods, festivals, day to day work in the vineyards and cellars, etc.

Beaune-Semblançay Gardens and Palais du Commerce (CXC). – *Enter by the porch at no 28 Rue Nationale.*

The Hôtel de Beaune-Semblançay belonged to François I's unfortunate Intendant of the Royal Finances, Jacques de Beaune-Semblançay *(p 144)*. This Renaissance hôtel was destroyed in 1940 except for an arcaded gallery with a chapel above, a fine pilaster decorated façade and in the garden the beautiful, finely sculptured **Beaune fountain**.

On the opposite side of the Rue Jules-Favre is the sober but elegant façade of the **Palais du Commerce**, which was built in the 18C for the merchants of Tours. Go into the more elaborately decorated courtyard.

There are many antique dealers' shops on the Rue de la Scellerie.

From the Place François-Sicard there is a pleasant view of the cathedral. No 15 is a fine 18C hôtel.

Fine Arts Museum** (Musée des Beaux-Arts – DXY). – *Open from 9am to noon and from 2 to 6pm (5pm 1 November to 28 February; closed on Tuesdays 1 November to 28 February and 1 January, 1 May, 14 July, 11 November and 25 December; 5F.*

This very fine museum is housed in the 17 and 18C former Archiepiscopal Palace. The main courtyard is shaded by a gigantic cedar, planted in 1804. The round tower to the left, formerly a part of the Gallo-Roman wall, has alternating courses of stone and brick. From the formal French style gardens there is a good **view** of the cathedral and the front of the museum.

The rooms, decorated with Louis XVI panelling and Tours silks, make a perfect setting for furniture, works of art and paintings taken from the now demolished châteaux of Richelieu and Chanteloup and some of the great Tourangelle abbeys: the duc de Choiseul's bureau, a laquered commode, paintings by Boucher, portraits by Largillière, Tocqué, Perronneau and Vestier, as well as sculptures by, among others, Le Moyne and Houdon.

The 17 and 18C North European schools are well represented: Rembrandt's *Flight into Egypt* and Rubens's famous *ex-voto*.

The second floor displays works of the 19 and 20C: Delacroix, Degas and a portrait of Balzac by Boulanger. Note the faience by the local craftsman Avisseau.

On the ground floor are the Italian primitives and the museum's masterpieces: **Mantegna's** *Christ in the Garden of Olives* and the same artist's *Resurrection*, as well as a room with Greek and Etruscan pottery.

The cathedral quarter (DX). – No 17 Rue des Ursulines now occupies the buildings of the 17C Convent of the Ursulines.

At the corner of the Rue du Petit Cupidon, at the far end of a small public garden stands the best preserved part of the **Gallo-Roman wall**: the postern gate, with ruts from chariot wheels, and the southeast rampart tower. Stones from the earlier town buildings were used as foundations for the wall.

Behind the cathedral, the curious **Rue du Général-Meusnier** follows the circular layout of the arenas.

The **Place Grégoire-de-Tours** is overlooked by the remarkable chevet of the cathedral. To the left the much altered building was the archbishops' residence in the Middle Ages and now belongs to the Fine Arts Museum. The judgements of the ecclesiastical court were delivered from the Renaissance tribune.

Across the way, the Rue de la Psallette passes under a flying buttress between the cloisters and an attractive 18C canons' residence.

Château. – *Rue Lavoisier and Quai d'Orléans.* The 12C battlemented **Guise Tower** (Tour de Guise – DXY) is all that remains of a castle built by Henry II Plantagenet to serve as a bridgehead on the Loire. The tower is named after the young duc de Guise who, imprisoned here after the assassination of his father *(pp 54, and 56)*, managed to escape. Joan of Arc was received here by Charles VII on 14 May 1429, after raising the siege of Orléans *(p 121)*. The 13C round tower, the Louis XVI period Pavillon de Mars, and the late Renaissance Governor's Lodging are being restored.

Place Foire-le-Roi (CX). – The fairs, where tolls were not levied, established by François I, and mystery plays performed on the arrival of a sovereign in the city were held in this square. On the north side are 15C gable houses. No 8, an elegant Renaissance mansion once belonged to Philibert Babou de la Bourdaisière, near Montlouis-sur-Loire. This famous 16C family in addition to Philibert, François I's Treasurer, included several royal mistresses. On the right side coming from the quay, at the end of a small passageway, is the narrow and winding Passage du Cœur-Navré (Passage of the Broken-Hearted), a typical mediaeval thieves' alley.

At no 39 Rue Colbert, a sign, *à la Pucelle Armée* or to the Armed Maid, reminds us that Joan of Arc had her armour made here before the siege of Orléans.

Place Jean-Jaurès (CY). – Often called the Square of the Palace. Among the fountains, flowers and cafés the city's main thoroughfares intersect: the north-south one laid out in the 18C and the Boulevards Béranger and Heurteloup, where elm trees were planted in 1796 on the former ramparts.

TOURS★★

Gardens. – The **Botanical Gardens** (AV F) *see map p 151 – open in summer from 7.30am to sunset and in winter from 8am to 5pm)* has a park with some animals (bear pit) and a horticultural school *(exhibition greenhouses: open from 9.30 to 11.30am and from 2 to 5pm)*.

The **Jardin de Prébendes** (BZ) *(see plan p 154)* is a colourful landscaped garden.

Notre-Dame-La-Riche (BY Z). – *West of the town by the Rue Georges-Courteline.* The church has fine 16C stained glass in the chancel. It was on the site of this church that St. Gatien the first Bishop of Tours was interred in the 3C.

Le Lac (AV). – *To the south of the town see map p 151. Car park on the far side of the Avenue de Grammont.*

This complex with an Olympic standard swimming pool offers a pleasant walk round the lake bordered with undulating grassy slopes.

EXCURSIONS map p 151

Prieuré de St-Cosme★; Plessis-lès-Tours. – *3 km - 2 miles to the west by the Quai du Pont-Neuf and its continuation the Avenue Proudhon, before finally following the embankment to the priory.*

St-Cosme Priory★ (AV E). – *Open from 9am to noon and from 2 to 7pm (5.30pm 1 October to 14 March) closed in December and January; 5F.*

Ronsard was Prior here from 1565 until his death in 1585. His remains were found in 1933 in the ruins of the church and were reinterred on the same spot. A stone slab marks the grave.

The only parts of the church still standing are the 11 and 12C chancel and ambulatory and part of one of the 15C nave walls. The ruined cloisters now made into a garden, lead to the 12C monks' refectory with its restored timber roof. All that remains of the reader's pulpit, on the left, are two highly decorated arcades. The Prior's lodging was altered in the 17C and the great hall on the first floor, where Ronsard died, was divided into smaller rooms by his successor. In an adjoining room is a small lapidary museum and an exhibition of drawings, plans, photos and engravings evoking Ronsard's life.

Château de Plessis-lès-Tours (AV B). – *Open from 10am to noon and from 2 to 6pm (5pm 1 November to 28 February) closed on Tuesdays in January and certain public holidays; 3F.*

What remains of Louis XI's château – the main building contains the room in which he died – houses souvenirs of Louis XI and St. Francis of Paola, who was recalled to Plessis to succour him in his last illness.

Abbaye de Marmoutier; Rochecorbon. – *4 km - 2½ miles to the east taking the road along the north bank of the Loire, the N 152.*

Marmoutier Abbey (AU R). – *Not open to the public.* The abbey was founded by St. Martin in 372, fortified in the 13 and 14C and partially destroyed in 1818. The **Portail de la Crosse★**, the gatehouse to this once rich and powerful abbey dates from the 13C. It is flanked by a watch tower, the 12C Prior's lodging, the Tour des Cloches, the former abbey church's belfry, the **grottes des solitaires** and the **troglodyte chapels**.

Rochecorbon (AU). – Pop 2 349. The troglodyte dwellings of this small town are built right into the cliff face. The town is dominated by a watch tower known as the **lanterne**.

La Béchellerie; Grange de Meslay★. – *Round tour of 41 km - 26 miles to the northwest – about 2½ hours. Leave Tours by the N 138. 1 km - ½ mile beyond the fork with the N 10 turn left into the Rue Henri-Bergson. At the end of the street turn first left and then right following the signposts La Béchellerie.*

The avenue leading to it begins opposite **La Gaudinière** (AU L), where the French philosopher Henri Bergson once lived. *Temporarily closed to the public.*

It was at **La Béchellerie** (AU M³) that Anatole France lived from 1914 to 1924. It is located in St-Cyr-sur-Loire as is **La Grenadière** where both Balzac and Béranger lived. This charming retreat, which remains just as the great writer arranged it, shows the peaceful life he led there among his books and works of art brought back from his travels, in particular Italy. He wrote his reminiscences *Le petit Pierre* and *La Vie en fleur*, while living at La Béchellerie. From the garden there is a fine view of the Choisille Valley.

Continue along the N 138 and at La Membrolle-sur-Choisille take the D 76 to the right.

Mettray Dolmen (AU K). – The beautiful "fairy Grotto" dolmen stands about 2 km - 1 mile north of Mettray, on the right bank of the Choisille in a small wood *(access by a stony, signposted path)*. The dolmen is one of the most skilfully worked megalithic monuments to be found in France – 11 m - 36 ft long and 3.70 m - 12 ft high it is composed of twelve very evenly cut stone slabs.

Return to St-Symphorien, turn left on to the N 10 and right on to the D 77.

Parçay-Meslay (AU V). – Pop 1 317. The 12C Church of St-Pierre has **Romanesque frescoes** on the chancel's oven vault. They portray Christ surrounded by his Apostles.

Return to the N 10 for 2.5 km - 2 miles then turn right.

Grange de Meslay★ (AU S). – *To visit apply to M. Patrick Lefebvre, Tel 51 31 21, Grange de Meslay.*

This former fortified farm belonging to the monks of Marmoutier Abbey has a beautiful porch, the remains of a perimeter wall and a remarkable **tithe barn**. The latter is a very good example of a 13C agricultural building. The rounded main door is set in a pointed gable and the roof is 15C chestnut timberwork. Touraine music concerts *(p 32)* are held in this barn as well as art exhibitions.

Return to Tours by the N 10.

Montlouis-sur-Loire. – Pop 5 717. *Facilities p 38. 12 km - 8 miles to the east by ⑤, the D 751.* This small village clings to the tufa slopes, riddled with cellars. It is renowned for the vineyards between the Loire and the Cher which produce a white wine from the *Pineau de la Loire* grape. The Renaissance mansion (now the presbytery), next to the church, is enhanced by shell ornamented dormer windows. The Babou family from the nearby Château de la Bourdaisière, were the overlords of Montlouis in the 16C.

TROO *

Michelin map **64** 5 – *Local maps pp 99 and 118* – Pop 476

The rather strange little town of Troo, perched on a steeply rising slope and distinguished from afar by its belfry tower, still has numerous troglodyte dwellings. The houses rising in tiers, one above the other, are linked by narrow alleys, stairways and mysterious passageways. An inextricable labyrinth of galleries, called *caforts* (short for *caves fortes*), exists underground in the white tufa rock. In times of war these *caforts* served as hideouts.

■ UPPER TOWN

La "Butte". – This feudal motte or Gaulish burial mound, affords a splendid **view*** *(viewing table and telescope)* of the winding Loir and its valley and on the opposite bank the small Church of St-Jacques-des-Guérets.

Collegiate Church of St-Martin. – Founded in 1050 and altered a century later, the church is dominated by a remarkable square **tower*** pierced by openings. The splays are ornamented with small columns so typically Angevin.

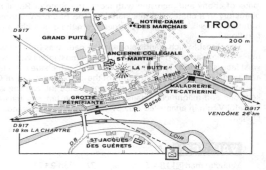

The Romanesque apse is lit by Gothic windows. The historiated capitals at the transept crossing are Romanesque. The choir stalls and communion table are 15C. The 16C wooden statue of St-Mamès is invoked for all stomach ailments.

Grand Puits. – Known as the talking well because of its excellent echo, this well is 45 m - 148 ft deep and is protected by a shingle board roof.

Chapel Notre-Dame-des-Marchais. – *Not open to the public.* Built in 1124 in an attractive site, there remain several arcades with historiated capitals. The 16C Prior's lodging adjoins the chapel.

■ LOWER TOWN

Maladrerie Ste-Catherine. – This 12C building standing on the D 917 at the eastern end of the town, has fine Romanesque blind arcades. It served as a lazar house (hospice) on the pilgrimage routes to St-Martin in Tours and St. James's shrine in Santiago de Compostela.

Limestone Cave (Grotte pétrifiante). – *Open 1 April to 30 September from 8am to 8pm; 2F.* Stalactites and lime encrusted objects.

■ ST-JACQUES-DES-GUÉRETS

Church. – *Time: ¼ hour.* It was ministered by the Augustinians from the Abbey of St-Georges-des-Bois. The **mural paintings*** dating from between 1130 and 1170, show a strong Byzantine influence. They are especially interesting for the draughtsmanship and the freshness of the colours, sky blue, jade, purple, etc. The finest paintings are in the apse: on the left the Crucifixion and the Resurrection of the Dead; Christ in Majesty and the Last Supper to the right. St. Augustine and St. George are portrayed on the embrasures of the central window. Further to the right are the Martyrdom of St. James and Paradise.

Continuing round to the south wall of the nave note above the Miracle of St. Nicholas with the Saint throwing gold pieces to three girls to save them from prostitution as proposed by a profiteering father; below is the Resurrection of Lazarus. Further on a vast composition represents Christ's descent into Limbo: a most majestic Jesus delivers Adam and Eve. The opposite wall has paintings of various periods from the 12 to the 15C: the Nativity and Massacre of the Innocents.

USSÉ, Château d' **

Michelin map **64** 13 – 14 km - 8 miles north of Chinon – *Local maps pp 76 and 103*

Overlooking the Indre and turning its back to the cliff where the Forest of Chinon ends, this castle stands above flowered terraces. Its massive shape and its fortified towers are rather grim, but the white stone and the number of its roofs, turrets, dormer windows and chimneys, bristling against the green background, is fascinating. Its poetic and slightly mysterious appearance has always appealed to the imagination. It is said that Perrault, the great writer of fairy tales, looking for a worthy setting for his *Sleeping Beauty*, took Ussé as his model.

To get the best view the tourist should stand either on the bridge, 200 m - 220yd ft from the castle, or on the Loire embankment.

From the Bueils to the Blacas. – Ussé is an ancient fortress. In the second half of the 15C it became the property of a great family of Touraine, the Bueils. They had distinguished themselves in the Hundred Years War (1337-1453) and they wished to create a new dwelling worthy of their rank.

In 1485 Antoine de Bueil, the husband of a daughter of Charles VII and Agnès Sorel, sold Ussé to the Espinays, a Breton family who had supplied chamberlains and cup bearers to the Duke of Brittany, to Louis XI and to Charles VIII. To them we owe the living quarters overlooking the courtyard, and the pretty chapel in the park.

The castle often changed hands. Among its owners was Vauban's son in law. The great military engineer made frequent visits to Ussé.

Today the estate belongs to the marquis de Blacas, grandson of the founder of the Egyptian Department of the Louvre.

USSÉ, Château d'★★

Château★★. – *Open Easter to 1 October from 9am to noon and from 2 to 7pm; 6pm the rest of the year; closed 5 November to 15 March; 11F.*

The 15C outside walls look as though they were built as fortifications while the courtyard buildings are open and inviting to look at and some even have a Renaissance air. Three ranges, which have been much restored, stand round the courtyard: the east block is Gothic, the west is Renaissance and the south is partly Gothic and partly Classical. The north block was removed in the 17C to open up the view from the terraces of the valleys of the Loire and the Indre. The west wing is prolonged by a 17C pavilion.

On entering note the fine 17C *trompe l'œil* ceiling. The former kitchens now have a collection of Saracen arms brought back from his travels by a member of the Blacas family. Also worthy of note is the grand staircase dating from the 17C, with its fine wrought iron balustrade. The ante chamber to the State Bedroom has a very beautiful 16C Italian cabinet made of ebony and incrusted with ivory. The State or Royal Bedroom (chambre du roi) was obligatory in a château of this standing. The Bedroom with its great State Bed has fine 18C furniture and silk hangings. Tapestries adorn the ground floor gallery and paintings that on the first floor.

The **chapel**, which stands alone in the park, was built between 1520 and 1538. It is in the purest Renaissance style and has remained almost intact with its sculptures and decorations. The west face is the best. The initials "C" and "L", which are to be found on this wall and elsewhere and are one of the decorative motifs of the chapel, are those of Charles d'Espinay, who built the chapel, and of his wife, Lucrèce de Pons. Inside the chancel is ornamented by a fine hanging keystone and magnificent stalls. An Aubusson tapestry traces the history of Joan of Arc. A graceful Virgin in enamelled clay by Luca della Robbia stands in the little ogive vaulted south chapel.

VALENÇAY ★★

Michelin map **64** 18 – *Local map p 71* – Pop 3 171

Valençay belongs geographically to the Berry district. The château dates from the 16C, the Golden Age of the Loire Valley. The great size of the château gives it a family resemblance to Chambord.

A financier's château. – Valençay was built about 1540 by Jacques d'Estampes, the owner of the feudal castle that already existed there. This lord, having married a financier's well dowried daughter, wished to have a seat worthy of his new fortune. The 12C castle was demolished and the present sumptuous building rose on its site.

Finance often mingled with the history of Valençay: among its successive owners were several Farmers-General and even the notorious John Law, whose dizzy financial adventure was an early and masterly example of inflation.

In 1803 Valençay was acquired by **Talleyrand**, that astonishing figure who began his career as Bishop of Autun under Louis XVI and ended it in 1838 after having occupied the highest posts in a whole series of régimes. He gave princely receptions at the château.

■ **THE CHÂTEAU★★** *time: 1 hour*

Guided tours from 15 March to 31 October 9am to noon and 2 to 6pm; the rest of the year 9am to noon and 2 to 5pm; closed 2 November to the eve of Palm Sunday; time: 1 hour; 10F. Son et lumière performance see p 33.

The entrance pavilion is a huge structure designed like a keep, but a "pleasure keep" with many windows, harmless turrets and false machicolations. The pointed roof is pierced with high dormer windows and surmounted by monumental chimneys. This architecture is also found in the Renaissance châteaux of the Loire Valley, but in this case the first signs of the Classical style may be detected in the shape of pilasters above the Doric (ground floor), Ionic (first floor) and Corinthian capitals (second floor).

The Classical style is even more evident in the roofs of the large corner towers. Here domes take the place of the pepperpot roofs which were the rule on the banks of the Loire in the 16C.

Museum. – Installed in the outbuildings it contains historical souvenirs of Prince Talleyrand. The Prince's bedroom has been restored to its original aspect.

West Wing. – This was added in the 17C and remodelled in the following century. At roof level dormer windows alternate with *œils-de-bœuf* (ox eyes or rounded openings). On the ground floor you can see the gallery and two rooms containing many art objects and sumptuous Louis XVI, Regency and especially Empire furniture; a room with fine Louis XVI wainscoting; and the vestibule, the walls of which are hung with prints concerning Prince Talleyrand and his contemporaries.

On the first floor is the room occupied by Ferdinand VII, King of Spain, when he was confined to Valençay from 1808 to 1814 on the orders of Napoleon. A glimpse of the gallery may be had from the antechamber.

Park. – This fine park is the home of llamas, deer and birds including cranes, peacocks, swans, flamingoes and parrots.

VALENÇAY

0 _____ 300 m

Blois (R. de)	2	
Pinard-Pinon (R.)	9	
République (R.)	10	
Châtaigniers (R.)	3
Château (R. du)	4
Hymans (R. M.)	6
Nationale (R.)	7
Résistance (Av.)	12
St-Maurice (R.)	13
Talleyrand (R.)	15
Tourne-Bride (R.)	16

At the foot of a steep, castle crowned hillside, the Loire subdivides into several narrow arms which pass under a series of multiple span bridges. Vendôme, centred on the islands thus created, is a huddled mass of belfries and gables with tall slated roofs, but urban development now reaches as far as the hillside.

The traditional glove trade dates from the Renaissance. Other activities include the manufacture of shoes, car components, machine and aircraft control instruments, plastics, and an important printing works.

HISTORICAL NOTES

A much disputed place. – Although its origins date from Neolithic, Gaulish and Gallo-Roman times (Vindocenum), the town only really began to acquire importance under the Bouchard family, faithful supporters of the Capetian dynasty and in particular in the 11C under Foulques Nerra's son, Geoffroi Martel who founded the Abbey of La Trinité.

This seat of the counts of Vendôme, vassals of the Plantagenets, was caught up in the Hundred Years War due mainly to its border position between lands held by the rival camps of the English and the French. It was the theatre of many a battle. In 1371 the royal house of Bourbon inherited Vendôme and in 1515 François I raised it to the status of a duchy.

The town sided with the Catholic League but, in 1589, it was recaptured by its rightful feudal lord, Henri IV, suffering in the process a cruel sacking – only the Abbey Church of La Trinité was to remain standing.

César, the son of Henri IV. – The town was passed to **César de Vendôme**, Henri IV's son by Gabrielle d'Estrées, who often resided here during his lifetime of continual conspiring: firstly during the minority of Louis XIII and then against Richelieu. He spent four years imprisoned in the Château de Vincennes before being exiled. In the end he renounced his principles and threw in his lot with Cardinal Mazarin but he was to die in 1655.

Balzac's schooldays. – The register of the Oratorians' College in Vendôme has an entry on the 22 June 1807 recording the admission of an eight year old boy, Honoré de Balzac. The future novelist of prodigious output, proved to be an inattentive and undisciplined pupil. Discipline was strict and many was the time that the young Balzac had himself sent to the punishment cell, so as to be able to read in peace. When his health showed signs of suffering, Balzac's parents were quick to recall him to Tours.

■ **FORMER TRINITÉ ABBEY★** (Ancienne Abbaye de la Trinité) *time: 1 hour*

One summer's night, Geoffroi Martel, the Count of Anjou having witnessed the spectacle of three swords of flame falling into a fountain, decided to found a monastery which was consecrated on 31 May 1040 to the Holy Trinity. Under the Benedictines the abbey experienced considerable growth to such an extent that the holder of the abbot's post was automatically nominated cardinal, as was the case of a 12C abbot who detained the famous Geoffroi de Vendôme, friend of Pope Urbain II, a native of Champagne.

Up to the time of the Revolution La Trinité was the centre of a pilgrimage to the Holy Tear which Christ wept on the sepulchre of Lazarus and which Geoffroi Martel brought back from Constantinople. The Vendôme knights used to rally to the cries of "Holy Tear of Vendôme" and "Lazarus' Friday". The faithful came to venerate this relic which was invoked for eye diseases.

Abbey Church★★. – This is a remarkable example of French Gothic architecture.

Exterior. – Enter the abbey precincts from the Rue de l'Abbaye which cuts through the visitor's hostel. To the right, standing on its own is the 12C **belfry**, 80 m - 262 ft high, which is said to have served as a model for the Clocher Vieux, one of the two spire towers of Chartres Cathedral. Note the increasing size of the arches, blind at the foot, which also become more recessed with an increase in height. The octagonal spire rises from the final storey of the belfry, which is also octagonal, being covered at the corners by pinnacled turrets. Marking off the base of the first floor are a series of grinning masks and animals.

(After photo: Arthaud, Grenoble)

La Trinité Abbey Church
Misericord

The present church comprises a chevet with a coronet of apsidal chapels and a transept which is the only part to date from the 11C. The eastern bays were built in the mid 14C but the nave itself was only finished after the Hundred Years War. The astonishing Flamboyant **west front** with its great openwork gable, was built in the early 16C by Jean de Beauce, architect of the Clocher Neuf or second of the Chartres Cathedral towers. Delicately pierced like lace, the gable contrasts with the simplicity of the Romanesque tower.

Interior. – The nave is remarkable for the width of its triforium and the height of its windows. Note how the progression from the 14C to the 15C phase of construction is achieved without altering the unity of conception. There are no longer capitals, the design of the frieze and the decoration of the triforium and ribs all change.

The transept crossing has conserved its primitive capitals surmounted by 13C polychrome statues portraying the Archangel Gabriel and Virgin of the Annunciation, and St. Peter with St. Eutropius, who was venerated in this abbey church.

The transept vaulting with its historiated keystones was transformed in the 14C to the Angevin style *(p 21)*. To the left of the high altar are statues of St. John the Baptist (14C) and the Virgin (16C).

The 14C chancel, with stained glass of the same period, is adorned by fine late 15C choir stalls ( ). Going round the ambulatory note the choir screen (2) which shows a decided Italian influence. On reaching the high altar note the base adorned with tears of the celebrated "monument of the Sainte-Larme", with an opening to allow the faithful to venerate the relic.

VENDÔME★★

The windows of the chancel are glazed with much restored 16C stained glass: the best, representing the Meal at Simon's House after a German engraving, is found in the first chapel to the left of the axial one. The latter has the famous **Virgin and Child window** (3) dating from the 12C.

Conventual buildings. – For some time these have been occupied by the Rochambeau or Twentieth Light Cavalry Regiment. Of the 14C cloisters only the gallery alongside the church remains intact. The chapter house has been uncovered and restored. The adjoining Classical buildings house a museum *(see opposite).*

From the cloisters take the passage leading under the monks' building, then turn round to admire the monumental façade built between 1732 and 1742. The pediment adorned with the royal fleur-de-lis, carries the motto *Pax* and the lamb emblem of the Benedictine Order.

■ ADDITIONAL SIGHTS

Old town* (Quartier ancien). – Behind the chevet are the chapel and early 16C lodging of the commendatory abbots *(p 134).*

Public gardens (Jardin Public). – Bordered by the waters of the Loir, these gardens offer a pleasant view of the town, La Trinité and the 15C Porte d'Eau, also known as the Arches des Grands Prés.

In ruins this battlemented structure, originally part of the town walls, was flanked by two round towers.

The gardens are extended to the north by the Place de la Liberté.

Former Oratorians' College (Ancien collège des Oratoriens – **D**). – Now occupied by a school, this is the college, with its harmonious Classical buildings in brick and stone, which Balzac attended in the early 19C.

The college has within its precincts the **St-Jacques Chapel**, with its small Renaissance bell tower. The chapel formerly belonged to a hospice built to give shelter to pilgrims going to Santiago de Compostela in Spain.

The north front of the chapel, overlooking Rue-St-Jacques, has retained several Romanesque elements: pillars, capitals and a half sunken doorway.

In Rue du Change to the left of the chapel's chevet, is the attractive Flamboyant façade which was the entrance to the hospice. The intricate decoration includes a grotesque sticking out its tongue.

La Madeleine (**E**). – This church of 1474 has an elegant bell tower surmounted by a crocketed spire.

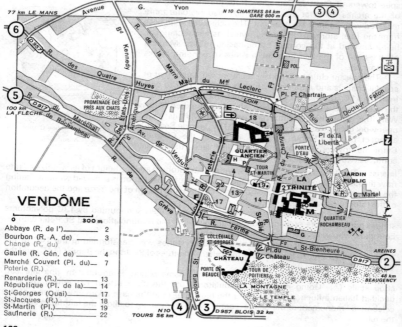

Rue Poterie. – On the left are the unusually tall roofs and turrets of the late 15C Hotel du Saillant. A branch of the Loir laps the foot of this edifice which once belonged to the Du Bellay family.

Porte St-Georges (F). – Flanked by great towers and crowned by pointed roofs, this massive gateway has stonework dating from the 14C. The battlements and sculptured decoration were added in the early 16C by Marie de Luxembourg, Duchess of Vendôme: Renaissance medallions and gargoyles.

Place St-Martin. – This square was the site of a Gallo Roman cemetery and it is now dominated by the lofty form of the St-Martin Tower. Dating from the 15-16C this bell tower is all that remains of an earlier parish church. With its corner buttresses and decreasing tiers it is crowned by a dome and lantern.

Château. – *Guided tours from 9am to noon and from 2 to 6pm; closed on Tuesdays; 3F for château; 2F for park; apply to the caretaker.*

Arrive by car via the Faubourg St-Lubin and the hamlet Le Temple which originally grew up round a Templars' commandery *(p 116)* and then on foot by the ramp which starts from the Place du Château.

Perched along the ridge known as La Montagne, which dominates the Loir, this ruined castle has an earth wall and ramparts marked out by round battlemented towers. On the eastern side the great tower, Tour de Poitiers, rebuilt in the 15C served as the keep.

Enter the castle precincts via the early 17C gateway, Porte de Beauce, now laid out with a vast garden. Here the foundations of the St-Georges Collegiate Church, founded by Geoffroi Martel, can still be discerned. This was the resting place of the lords of Vendôme, notably Antoine de Bourbon and Jeanne d'Albret, the parents of Henri IV.

On leaving the car park, follow the promenade de la Montagne: a series of terraces which afford picturesque **views✶** of Vendôme and the Loir Valley.

Museum (M). – *Open from 9am to noon and from 2 to 6pm; closed on Tuesdays, 1 January, 1 May, 11 November and 25 December; 6F.*

Installed in the La Trinité Abbey monks' building, with its majestic staircase, the collections are well displayed.

The rooms most worthy of attention on the ground floor deal with mural painting in the Loir Valley and religious art in the Vendôme region during the Middle Ages and the Renaissance: fragments of the 16C tomb of François de Bourbon-Vendôme and of Marie de Luxembourg, vaulting keystones from the cloisters, abbey church holy water basin, etc.

Upstairs are the prehistory and antiquity collections. Other rooms contain furniture and paintings of the French and Flemish schools of the 16-18Cs, including some good portraits and faiences. Note the harp by Naderman (1773-1835) Marie-Antoinette's instrument maker.

Another room shows the tools and instruments of once flourishing regional crafts and the reconstruction of a typical Vendômois rural interior.

EXCURSIONS

Areines. – Pop 779. *3 km - 2 miles to the east by ②, the D 917 and the first road to the left.*

An important market town in Roman times, Areines is now one of the many small villages in the Loir plain.

The 12C church whose sober façade is adorned with a 14C Virgin contains an ensemble of **frescoes** interesting for the draughtsmanship and freshness of the colours.

In the oven vault of the apse a majestic Christ is surrounded by the symbols of the Evangelists: note St. Mark's very stylised lion so typically Byzantine; below are the Apostles with their sky blue haloes, a colour typical of the Loir Valley frescoes; in the central openings are the warrior saints.

The chancel's vault shows the angels in adoration before the Lamb, with an elegant Annunciation and Visitation at the sides and a fairly faded Nativity. The frescoes on the chancel walls would appear to be more recent: on the right is the Marriage of the Virgin.

(After photo: Hurault)

Areines Church — Holy warrior

Nourray. – Pop 112. *11 km - 7 miles to the south by ④, the N 10 and the third road on the left.*

The Romanesque church has an **apse** decorated with sculptured arcadings and brackets.

Rhodon. – Pop 109. *19 km - 12 miles to the southeast by ②, the D 917. At Villetrun turn right towards Selommes and there left into the D 161.*

The charming 12-13C church has 14-15C mural paintings.

VILLANDRY, Château de ★★

Michelin map 🔢 14 – *Local map p 103*

Villandry is one of the most original châteaux in Touraine for the arrangement of its esplanade, terraces, moats and canals, and especially of its famous gardens.

■ THE GARDENS★★★

Open from 8am to sunset; time: 1 hour; 7F.

In the 19C, when the landscaped English garden was all the rage, the owners of the château redesigned the grounds. When Dr. Carvallo, founder of Demeure Historique, the French Historic Houses Association, bought Villandry he patiently reconstructed the formal French gardens of the 16C; there is no other example of such gardens.

(After photo: Burthe d'Annelet)

Château de Villandry — The Gardens

Three tiers of terraces are superimposed. On the highest is the water garden, with its fine sheet of water, below this is the ornamental garden, and then the kitchen garden. The geometrically shaped flower-beds are emphasised by yew trees and box borders. Each border represents a different arrangement of hearts, the symbol of love. Canals, fountains, and vine bearing pergolas add various effects. This architectural design is due to the influence of the first Italian gardeners brought to France by Charles VIII, but French influence appears in many details. In the 16C, flowers, shrubs and fruit trees were practically the same that we know today. Among vegetables, the potato was missing – Parmentier, who brought it to France, lived in the 18C. The gardener's art was already advanced: he pruned and grafted and knew how to use the greenhouse and raise early vegetables.

The best view is from the belvedere behind the château.

The small Romanesque Church of Villandry forms a charming feature to the castle esplanade. It contains a 16C stained glass window.

The orchard, laid out in accordance with plans made by Du Cerceau, lies on the southern slope of the hill, separated from the rest of the property by a path, and overlooking both the property and the valley.

■ THE CHÂTEAU

Guided tours Easter to end of October from 9am to 6pm; additional 2F.

Of the original fortress only the keep remains. It is a great tower embedded in the present edifice, which was built in the 16C by Jean Le Breton, Secretary of State to François I. Three blocks of living quarters enclose a court of honour opening north on to the valley through which flow the Loire and the Cher. The salons, the dining room with 18C panelling and the main staircase are open to the public.

You then go up to the terraces from which you overlook the valley on one side, and, on the other, the gardens, with the old village and Romanesque church in the background.

VILLESAVIN, Château de

Michelin map 🔢 18 – *Local map p 145*

This charming Renaissance building, erected in 1537 by Jean Le Breton, Lord of Villandry, who was in charge of the work on the Château de Chambord, shows certain tendencies of the Classical style.

Guided tours from 10am to noon and from 2 to 6.30pm; closed 20 December to 20 January; 8F.

It consists of a central block on the ground level, framed between symmetrical pavilions. The attics with their fine dormer windows and the inscriptions on the rear façade give the building beautiful proportions. A very beautiful 16C Italian **basin** in marble adorns the main courtyard.

A few furnished apartments are open to view. They contain old serving dishes, jugs and pitchers and plates. Old carriages stand in the coach house.

To the left of the château is a large 16C **dovecote** with a well preserved revolving ladder.

OTHER PLACES OR INTERESTING SIGHTS

AIGRE Valley 🔢 7.

This tributary of the Loir is a peaceful rural valley. The **Château du Jonchet** is a 16-17C building encircled by moats and flanked by pavilions, one of which acts as the chapel. The tall roofs are typically French. The peaceful village of **Romilly-sur-Aigre** (Pop 360) is the Rognes of Zola's novel *Earth*.

The D 8 running along the north bank affords good views of the valley and climbs to the Plateau of the Beauce.

ALLUYES 🔢 17 – Pop 692 – 7 km - 4 miles to the northwest of Bonneval.

In the late 15C the overlord was **Florimond Robertet**, Royal Treasurer to successive kings and owner of the Hôtel d'Alluye in Blois and the Château de Bury to the southwest of Blois *(pp 57 and 58)*. The 15-16C **church** has two Gothic mural paintings depicting St. Christopher and the Legend of the Three Living and the Three Dead.

BEAUFORT-EN-VALLÉE 🔢 12 – Pop 4 103 – 27 km - 17 miles east of Angers.

Lying in the rich alluvial plains to the north of the Loire, this town once had a thriving sail cloth industry. From the hilltop, with the ruins of a castle, there is a wide panorama of the surrounding countryside. The **church** *(open between June and September)* has a fine bell tower built by Jean de Lespine. Inside are two altars a 17C wood one and a second in marble.

BLOU 🔢 12 – Pop 868 – 16 km - 10 miles from Beaufort-en-Vallée *(see above)* via the N 147, Longué and the D 206.

The Romanesque **church** with its massive buttresses has curious 11C lozenge shaped patterns on its south front. A 13C bell tower rises above the transept crossing.

BREIL 🔢 13 – Pop 414 – 6 km - 4 miles to the southeast of Noyant.

The **church** dominated by a tall stone spire has fine Plantagenet vaulting in the chancel. The pleasant 17C park *(apply to visit)* of the **Château du Lathan** offers a remarkable vista terminated by an elegant 18C pavilion.

BROU 🔢 16 – Pop 3 638 – 22 km - 14 miles northwest of Châteaudun.

This market town, characteristic of the Beauce, is grouped round its market place, Place des Halles. Half timber houses and sculptured woodwork are common features.

BUEIL-EN-TOURAINE 🔢 4 – Pop 502 – 15 km - 9 miles northeast of St Paterne-Racan via Neuvy-le-Roi.

This was the home of the Bueil family, which included an Admiral, several Marshals and the poet Honorat de Bueil *(p 131)*. A curious agglomeration of buildings includes the **Church of St-Pierre-aux-Liens** adjoining an incomplete tower. Inside are early 16C frescoes and statues. Continue via the chapter house to the **Collegiate Church of Sts-Innocents-St-Michel** *(closed restoration in progress)*. This was built to serve as the Bueil family vault. The Renaissance **baptistery** contains the recumbent figures of various members of that famous family.

CHAMPTOCÉ-SUR-LOIRE 🔢 19 – Pop 1 320 – 6 km - 4 miles to the east of Ingrandes by the N 23.

The rural church has a charming simplicity. Nearby are the ruins of the château of Gilles de Rais, the sinister personality who inspired Charles Perrault to create his character, Bluebeard.

DANGEAU 🔢 17 – Pop 850 – 9 km - 6 miles west of Bonneval.

This small village has some fine 15C brick and half timber houses round its main square. The **church** *(time: ¼ hour)* in a very pure Romanesque style was built by monks from Marmoutier in the 12C. The south doorway has intricately sculptured carvings. The wooden ceiling of the nave is supported by archaic pillars. The aisles have statues typical of 15-17C local work, the baptismal chapel a triptych and an engraving in the sacristy by Rigaud.

GIZEUX 🔢 13 – Pop 655.

The **church** is the resting place of the elder branch of the Du Bellay family *(p 105)*. The white marble figures are interesting for the costumes portrayed. The majestic Renaissance château has immense 18C outbuildings.

ILLIERS-COMBRAY 🔢 17 – Pop 3 569 – 29 km - 18 miles north of Châteaudun via Dangeau.

This market town, on the headstream of the Loir, serves both the Beauce and Perche regions. It was here in his father's native town that the novelist **Marcel Proust** (1871-1922) spent his childhood holidays providing many of the memories for his famous novel *Remembrance of Things Past*, in which Illiers is portrayed under the name of Combray. His aunt's house at 4 Rue du Docteur-Proust contains mementoes of the writer *(afternoons only, except Tuesdays; 6F)*. Also evoked in the novel are the pleasant landscaped gardens, the Pré-Catalan, which border the D 149 to the south of the town. The **church** has a splendid painted timber roof, a feature typical of the once forested Beauce.

LINIÈRES-BOUTON 🔢 13 – Pop 107 – 5 km - 3 miles east of Mouliherne *(see p 164)*.

The village church has a fine **chancel** with Plantagenet vaulting.

L'ISLE (Château de) 🔢 12 – approximately 17 km - 11 miles northeast of Sablé-sur-Sarthe.

The ruins of this former fortress stand sentinel in a meander of the Vègre. *To visit apply to M. Rivron, 7 Rue Chanzy, 72 000 Le Mans.* The 12C layout is still discernible: ramparts, outer bailey, keep and flanking towers. The priory and chapel are also in a ruinous state. The rocky escarpment on the far bank of the river is known as the **Rochers de Pissegrèle**.

MIRÉ 64 1 – Pop 961 – 16 km - 10 miles southwest of Sablé-sur-Sarthe.

The **church** has wooden keel vaulting decorated with forty-three painted panels dating from the late 15C. The paintings are very similar in style to the ones in the guardroom at Plessis-Bourré whose owner Jean Bourré was Lord of Miré.

MOULIHERNE 64 12, 13 – Pop 1 192 – 13.5 km - 8 miles southeast of Baugé.

The **church** has a 13C bell tower crowned by a twisting spire typical of the Baugeois *(p 51)*. Inside the vaulting demonstrates the development of the Angevin style. Chancel with groined vaulting; south transept: an early example of quadripartite vaulting with a more elaborate version in the north arm; nave: 12-13C Gothic vaulting, wide and soaring.

PARIGNÉ-LE-PÔLIN 64 3 – Pop 632 – 8 km - 5 miles southeast of La Suze-sur-Sarthe.

It was near this small market town that **Charles VI** on his way to do battle with the Duke of Brittany first showed signs of the madness which was later to possess him. On 5 August 1392, a very hot day, when the King was out riding, a stranger leapt from a thicket shouting, "Stop Your Majesty You are betrayed." A few seconds later the sound of an arm striking armour made the King believe he was being attacked by traitors: he drew his sword and killed four of his followers. The Church contains a fine 16C Entombment.

ST-ÉPAIN 64 14 – Pop 1 338 – 9 km - 6 miles to the northwest of Ste-Maure-de-Touraine.

The **church** of this market town has features characteristic of the Romanesque Poitou style: dome on pendentives and the east end. The double nave dating from the 12 and 15C is covered with Angevin vaulting. The church was dedicated to St. Épain, a disciple of St. Martin.

ST-LAURENT-EN-GÂTINES 64 6 – Pop 471 – 11 km - 7 miles to the west of Château-Renault by the D 766.

The 15C manor house was built by the monks from Marmoutier and later transformed into a church.

ST-OUEN (Château de) 63 10 – 7 km - 4 miles southwest of Château-Gontier by the D 20.

Before reaching Chemazé notice on the right this 15-16C château with its pedimented dormer windows and large square staircase tower topped by a crown structure. *Not open to the public.*

VAUX (Château de) – 3.5 km - 2 miles northwest of Miré *(see above).*

Standing back from the road this château now partly in ruins was built in the late 15C by Jean Bourré *(p 127)*. It was this same lord who introduced the *Bon Chrétien* variety of pear into Anjou. Covered with Virginia creeper, the château has preserved part of its ramparts and the elegant main building with its turret staircase and mullioned windows.

VERNANTES 64 13 – Pop 1 758 – 12 km - 8 miles west of Gizeux *(see p 163).*

The former church, now the Mairie, is dominated by the slim 12C **bell tower** which terminates in a 15C hexagonal spire. The chapel has a funerary monument to the lords of Jalesnes.

VERNOIL 64 13 – Pop 1 332 – 10 km - 6 miles west of Gizeux *(see p 163).*

Of a former Benedictine priory there remains a **church** with Romanesque parts dating from the 12C. The massive bell tower is of the same style but 15C and the apse Gothic. The 15C **Prior's lodging** has mullioned windows and a polygonal turret.

YÈVRES 60 16, 17 – Pop 1 292 – 1.5 km - 1 mile east of Brou *(see p 163).*

The 15-16C **church** has an elegant Renaissance doorway. Inside there is some remarkable Classical **woodwork***: pulpit, altarpiece, lectern, church officer's pew and door to the baptismal chapel. Note the chest with fine church vestments.

YRON (Chapelle d') 64 7 – 1 km - ½ mile from Cloyes-sur-le-Loir. Take the N 10, then the D 8¹ to the right.

Formerly part of a priory this Romanesque chapel has a doorway adorned with diamond pointed rustication. The interior is decorated with 12-14C mural paintings.

INDEX

MANUFACTURE FRANÇAISE DES PNEUMATIQUES MICHELIN
© Michelin et Cie, propriétaires-éditeurs, 1980
Société en commandite par actions au capital de 700 millions de francs
R. C. Clermont-Fd B 855 200 507 - Siège social Clermont-Fd (France)
ISBN 2 06 013 211-8

Photocomposition Jarrold & Sons Ltd of Norwich - Impression ISTRA, Strasbourg
Printed in France - 11.80.40 - Dépôt légal, 1er trim. 1981.